MACROMEDIA®
FLASH™ ENABLED
FLASH DESIGN & DEVELOPMENT FOR DEVICES

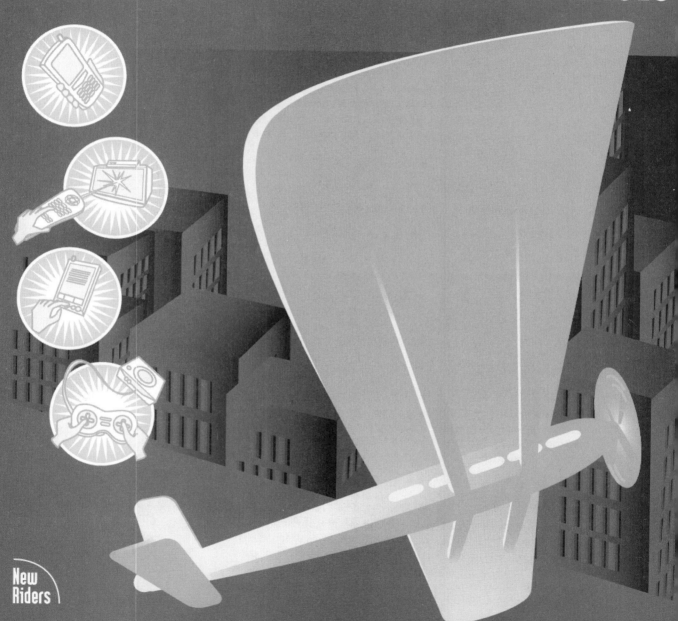

New Riders

CHRISTIAN CANTRELL | **MIKE CHAMBERS** | **BRANDEN HALL** | **ROBERT HALL**
ANDREAS HEIM | **CRAIG KROEGER** | **STEVE LEONE** | **MARKUS NIEDERMEIER**
BILL PERRY | **FRED SHARPLES** | **GLENN THOMAS** | **PHILLIP TORRONE**

Flash Enabled: Flash Design and Development for Devices

Copyright © 2002 by New Riders Publishing

International Standard Book Number: 0-7357-1177-1

Library of Congress Catalog Card Number: 2002104087

Printed in the United States of America

First Printing: May 2002

06   05   04   03   02   7   6   5   4   3   2

Interpretation of the printing code: The rightmost double-digit number is the year of the book's printing; the rightmost single-digit number is the number of the book's printing. For example, the printing code 02-1 shows that the first printing of the book occurred in 2002.

Trademarks

Warning and Disclaimer

Publisher
David Dwyer

Associate Publisher
Stephanie Wall

Executive Editor
Steve Weiss

Production Manager
Gina Kanouse

Managing Editor
Sarah Kearns

Acquisitions Editor
Theresa Gheen

Development Editor
Kathy Murray

Project Editor
Michael Thurston

Copy Editor
Linda Seifert

Product Marketing Manager
Kathy Malmloff

Publicity Manager
Susan Nixon

Manufacturing Coordinator
Jim Conway

Cover Designer
Steve Leone

Interior Designers
Steve Leone
Suzanne Pettypiece

Compositor
Wil Cruz

Proofreader
Teresa Hendey

Indexer
J. Naomi Linzer

Contents at a Glance

TABLE OF CONTENTS

OUR CONTRIBUTORS

Christian Cantrell is a software developer specializing in web-based and network applications. After studying writing at George Mason University in Northern Virginia, Christian began designing and building web-based data collection systems in ColdFusion. For the past two years, he has been integrating Java, Java Server Pages (JSP), Flash, and Generator into various large-scale commercial applications. He is the author of the white paper "Macromedia Generator and Java" posted on Macromedia's online Support Center and is listed as the lead inventor on two pending patents involving user interface design and real-time rich media generation. Most recently, he has turned his attention toward platform-independent development for mobile and embedded devices, concentrating on integrating Flash user interfaces with lightweight Java server software.

Mike Chambers has been creating applications primarily utilizing Flash, Generator, and Java for the past three years. He also has experience working with ASP, JSP, PHP, and ColdFusion. He has spoken about Flash and Generator at various conferences, including Macromedia UCON and FlashForward. He is co-author of *Generator and Flash Demystified*. Mike received his Masters degree in International Economics and European Studies from the John Hopkins School of Advanced International Studies (SAIS) in 1998. Mike currently works with Macromedia.

Branden Hall, a well-known member of the Flash community, can most often be found regulating on the highly popular Flashcoders (**http://chattyfig.figleaf.com**) mailing list that he founded over a year ago. He also can often be found speaking at various conferences, teaching, or geeking out one of his many bits of electronics. In his spare time (ha!) he loves playing with Linux, working on the arcade machine he is building, mountain biking, and playing with his lovely wife Patti. Both he and Patti work at Fig Leaf Software in Washington D.C.

Robert M. Hall is currently the Senior Developer for mCom LLC (**www.mcom8.com/**) located in Philadelphia, PA. Robert architects projects and develops ATM machine interfaces, award-winning Internet banking software, and wireless device applications. Robert uses a variety of technologies in his work but his favorite tools of choice are Flash, PHP, and MySQL. Prior to mCom, Robert was a consultant at Citicorp and a web developer for USABancShares.com. Recently, Robert contributed a chapter to *Flash MX Magic* for New Riders.

If Robert is not enjoying the outdoors with his girlfriend, he can be found listening to music, reading, or tinkering with electronics and trying out new technologies. Usually a piece or two of his experiments will wind up on his personal web site: Feasible Impossibilities (**www.impossibilities.com/**).

Andreas Heim is from the small town of Hattenhofen, close to Stuttgart, in Germany, a center of German car engineering. Originally intending to become a professional soccer player, his education took him into the area of media studies and programming. After creating an interactive CD-ROM, his focus shifted from film and video to interactive media. His school required him a six-month internship, which brought him to Smashing Ideas where being a soccer-playing-and-beer-drinking German intern was highly respected. He had so much fun in Seattle that he extended his stay to one year, before deciding to stay permanently. Andreas currently works on all kinds of cutting-edge digital media projects, including bringing Flash to devices. He enjoys his time outside of work snowboarding and playing soccer.

Craig Kroeger creates Flash-friendly, vector-based pixel fonts perfect for large or small screen applications available at **www.miniml.com**. The purpose behind miniml is to encourage functional and beautiful design by providing inspiration and resources.

After Craig received his BFA in Communication Design from the Milwaukee Institute of Art & Design, he co-founded Fourm Design Studio. Craig would like to thank his beautiful wife, Jen, for her belief, his friends and family, and those who believe in the true value of design.

Steve "Leo" Leone (**www.unplug.tv**) is currently a freelance illustrator/ designer, and former Art Director of NexusGroup. Prior to joining NexusGroup Leo was Director of New Technology for Braincraft. He holds multiple design awards and has been involved in some of the most innovative Flash projects to date. Leo was a key player on such award-winning projects as USABancShares.com, Mitsubishi Imaging, Space.com's Space Arcade, and Braincraft.com. Recently, Leo co-authored *Flash 5 Dynamic Content Studio* for Friends of Ed.

Markus Niedermeier is a producer, writer, and director in Munich, Germany, who frequently works on integrated concepts for TV and the Internet. Markus' production experience ranges from multimedia theater to a major network soap opera, from indie DV to high-end 3D animation. For the German Film Awards, he has supervised the production of videos and graphics for the live show, TV broadcast, and web site. With Munich design collective coma]2, he has provided content and consulting for leading web clients. Markus wrote and directed Germany's first commercial Flash web-cartoon, animated by Smashing Ideas, for hugely popular "Diddl-Maus". Another collaboration with Smashing Ideas resulted in a Flash-generated cartoon character for a German TV-show pilot by Schwanstein Entertainment.

Bill Perry is a senior consultant at Prosum where he focuses on web design and wireless application development for various clients. With a degree in industrial design, Bill brings with him a discipline in design that has helped him adapt to the changing environment of multimedia over the past seven years. Always wanting to be on the cutting edge of technology, and Flash in particular, Bill found an area in which he can excel—the combination of Flash, Pocket PCs, and wireless connectivity. He put together **www.pocketpcflash.net** as a Flash development resource for Pocket PCs and has received much recognition from this effort. He is a member of Team Macromedia, has spoken at several conferences, is on the advisory board for the Pocket PC Summit, and has been a technical editor for several books. Currently, Bill is exploring alternative uses of Flash applications in wireless Pocket PC environments.

Fred Sharples studied film with an animation emphasis at San Francisco State University. He went on to work at Macromedia as director of the Multimedia Creative Services Department. Fred is the founder of Orange Design, a digital creativity company that specializes in Flash application and game development. Under Fred's direction, Orange helped develop the first Flash user interface for a Sony PlayStation 2 game, the first Flash "dashboard" for a broadband portal with live weather and stock reports, and a Flash user interface for a television set-top box. Orange also created Old Navy's online game collection and, in collaboration with MarchFIRST, also helped develop Barbie Pix, a Flash-based painting program that lets users make online pictures, save them, and send them to friends. Fred has been a speaker at FlashForward New York and San Francisco. Additionally, Fred was a contributing author for the bestselling Flash book *Flash Web Design—The Art of Motion Graphics* by Hillman Curtis.

Glenn Thomas is one of the founders of Smashing Ideas, a leading digital media services company. Smashing Ideas' projects include the Madonna "Music" Shockwave Single, Email Chess, webcasting the Sydney 2001 Paraolympics, Pocket PC games, and web animation shows, such as *Zombie College*. He has been involved with Flash since its inception and has spoken at numerous industry conferences. He authored the book *Flash Studio Secrets* that details innovative ways of using Flash in the real world.

Phillip M. Torrone is director of product development of Fallon Worldwide. Co-author of many books on rich media and mobile devices, Phillip Torrone is a designer, developer, and inventor. From developing applications and hardware for the first PDA, the Apple Newton; to creating the first 100% Flash-based Generator-driven online bank; to creating rich data-driven content for cell phones, devices, and automobiles, Phillip applies his diverse skill set to push the boundaries of current technologies. Recently featured in *Wired* magazine, Phillip currently sits on the Macromedia Advisory Board and regularly keynotes industry conferences and events around the world. As this book was going to press, Phillip was awarded Microsoft's Most Valuable Professional award in the mobile devices category. This award recognizes a recipient's technical expertise, community spirit, and willingness to share information.

Fallon's clients include BMW of North America, And1, Citi, drugstore.com, EDS, Holiday Inn, International Truck and Engine Corp., Lee Company, Microsoft, Nikon, Nordstrom, Nuveen Investments, PBS, Ralston Purina, Starbucks Coffee Company, Timberland, Timex, and United Airlines.

In Phillip's spare time he runs flashenabled.com/mobile—a collection of reviews, news, applications, and inventions. The site, which has been featured in *Wired*, on TechTV and CNN, and hundreds of other places, currently has over three million visitors per month.

ABOUT THE TECHNICAL EDITORS

Greg Burch is a Software Engineer who specializes in Flash. He is a true advocate of seeing Flash being in everything from your car to your refrigerator. In Greg's most recent project he was a programmer for a company building out an extended Flash Player for a wireless device. He also has a lot of experience with its conventional uses, for things such as web applications and games. Although Greg dabbles in all sorts of programming, his true love is pushing Flash beyond its limits.

Troy Evans is currently the Macromedia Flash Player Product Manager and has served as Product Manager since 1999.

DEDICATION

In memory of those who died on September 11, 2001, and in honor of the heroes who gave their own lives to save so many others.

You are missed.

ACKNOWLEDGMENTS

Christian Cantrell: Michelle, thank you for your forbearance and support. I hope you understand how much it means to me. Mom and Pop, I also thank you for your support, and for spending all that money on our first PC. I'd like to acknowledge Ben Yaroch for remaining my friend during all my quirkiness, Mike Chambers for being as good a friend as he is a resource, everyone at Amazing Media for being like a second family to me, and finally my beautiful daughter, Hannah, for having become the inspiration for everything I do.

Mike Chambers: First and foremost, I would like to thank my wife, Cathy, for all of her love and support, without which my contribution would not have been possible. My work on this book is dedicated to her and my daughter, Isabel.

Thanks to Theresa Gheen at New Riders, whose persistence, perseverance, and vision made this book possible.

Thanks to everyone at Macromedia including (in no particular order) Eric Whittman, Jeremy Clark, Troy Evans, Brian Schmidt, Kevin Lynch, Jeremy Allaire, and Ed Krimen.

Finally, thanks to mom, dad, Debbie, Beth, Lois, Doug, T, V, Michelle, Harel, and Christian for all their help and support.

Branden Hall: I would like to thank Phil and Mike for making this book actually happen, Theresa (a.k.a. Our Lady of Perpetual Deadlines) for kicking me as needed and having way too much faith in me, and my wife Patti for letting me buy my iPaq (those things ain't cheap you know!) and putting up with me in general.

Robert Hall: Thanks to Mike Chambers, Anna Marie Pises, and Niamh O'Byrne of Macromedia, Phillip Torrone of Fallon and Flashenabled.com, Steve "Leo" Leone of NexusGroup, Daniel Taylor and my friends at mCom LLC, and all the folks who post to the Flashcoders list.

Special thanks to David Dwyer and Theresa Gheen and the rest of the New Riders family for this opportunity. Extra special thanks to my friends Scott, Bill, and Chuck, my brother Jimmy, my parents, and my girlfriend Melissa for all their support and inspiration.

Andreas Heim: I would like to thank all the people that helped me to get in this fortunate situation that allows me to do what I love to do and even write about it. Special thanks go to my parents for their continued support far away from home, to Glenn Thomas and all the other great folks at Smashing Ideas for the opportunity I was given and the great environment there, to Shannon Ecke for helping me with the design of my game, and to Anna Hall for all her support through my nights of writing.

Craig Kroeger: I would like to thank my wife, Jen, for her belief, and my partners at Fourm for their continual inspiration.

Steve Leone: My beautiful wife Jenn, for her patience, support, and her unbiased critiquing of my work. Team Braincraft and the Nexus Group. Mike, Phil, Theresa, and New Riders for the opportunity. Chris and Nicole for the support and feedback. Prof. O for his enthusiasm. The Atlanta crew for their sarcasm. The old schoolers from the '40s and '50s whose sense of style and class gave me inspiration. The design and Flash community for their openness and sharing. Lastly, Marlboro and Choc Full o' Nuts for the fuel to keep me going.

Markus Niedermeier: Thanks to my friends and partners for support and inspiration: Stephan Reichenberger and everyone at Schwanstein Entertainment; Marina, Collin, Mario, Sascha, and Rudi at coma]2; Luis and Danielle Aguilar, Rob Mitchell, and Shannon Callies; and of course Glenn Thomas and Smashing Ideas.

A special thanks to Tomas F. Lansky who taught a literature student a long time ago that it's good to know technology.

A very special thanks to Georgi Page.

Bill Perry: To my amazing girlfriend Rebekah for being so loving and understanding with the long hours I put in almost every night. My Mom for believing in me and never letting me quit, my brother Chris for being competitive and my best friend, my grandma and my relatives in Hawaii and Indiana. Phil and Mike for being such great friends and opening so many doors, Macromedia and Prosum for their constant support, to all my good friends scattered around the world and everyone else in the Flash community from whom I've learned a great deal. Finally thanks to Theresa, NRP, and the other co-authors for giving me this unique opportunity to share my knowledge with everyone else.

Fred Sharples: I'd like to thank my wife Pamela for helping to edit my chapter and for supporting me through writing and projects and life in general. I would also like to thank Karl Ackerman and Fearghal O'Dea for their ActionScript ideas and inspirations. I would like to thank Daron Stinnett and Reeve Thompson from LucasArts for choosing Orange and being the dream clients that they are. Brett Douville from LucasArts has my eternal gratitude for being so fast, smart, and patient with us while we connected all the code between Flash and the game. Thanks to Secret Level for porting the player. A very special thanks goes to Mark Del Lima and Keiko Chafee who quietly and perfectly "kicked 10 flavors of ass" creating the artwork on the user interface for *Starfighter*. You are the unsung heroes of the project. Thank you!

Glenn Thomas: I want to thank my family, friends, and the Flash community for all their support over the last five years of the Flash revolution. They've all helped make this possible.

Phillip Torrone: I'd like to thank the following folks: Beth (Hi Rabbit!), Chris Wiggins, Derek Brown, Christian Erickson, Tom Kunau, Jim Park, Jim Chesnutt, Eric Wittman, Troy Evans, Jeremy Clark, Margaret Carlson, Tom Hale, Suzanne Mattis, Natalie Zee, Mike Chambers, Glenn Thomas, Branden Hall, David Daniels, Brian Schmidt, Brooke Posard, Anna Mare Pises, Robert Hall, Jason Dunn, John Tidwell, Theresa Gheen, Dan Bjorkegren, Martin Fasani, and the entire Pocket PC and Flash community.

The folks at Fallon who truly inspire me on a daily basis: Pat Fallon, Rob White, David Lubars, Mark Goldstein, Anne Bologna, Joe Duffy, Rob Buchner, Paul Schield, Bob Moore, Bruce Bildsten, Kevin Flatt, John King, Beth Perro-Jarvis, Todd Allard, Nicole Nye, Tom Julian, Jane Delworth, John Blackburn, and the Swedes.

To my mother, thanks Mum. And to Mike and Florence.

A Message from New Riders

As the reader of this book, you are our most important critic and commentator. We value your opinion and want to know what we're doing right, what we could do better, in what areas you'd like to see us publish, and any other words of wisdom you're willing to pass our way.

As Executive Editor at New Riders, I welcome your comments. You can fax, email, or write me directly to let me know what you did or didn't like about this book—as well as what we can do to make our books better. When you write, please be sure to include this book's title, ISBN, and author, as well as your name and phone or fax number. I will carefully review your comments and share them with the authors and editors who worked on the book.

Please note that I cannot help you with technical problems related to the topic of this book, and that due to the high volume of email I receive, I might not be able to reply to every message. Thanks.

Fax:	317-581-4663
Email:	steve.weiss@newriders.com
Mail:	Steve Weiss
	Executive Editor
	New Riders Publishing
	201 West 103rd Street
	Indianapolis, IN 46290 USA

Visit Our Web Site: www.newriders.com

On our web site, you'll find information about our other books, the authors we partner with, book updates and file downloads, promotions, discussion boards for online interaction with other users and with technology experts, and a calendar of trade shows and other professional events with which we'll be involved. We hope to see you around.

Email Us from Our Web Site

Go to **www.newriders.com** and click on the Contact Us link if you

- Have comments or questions about this book.
- Want to report errors that you have found in this book.
- Have a book proposal or are interested in writing for New Riders.
- Would like us to send you one of our author kits.
- Are an expert in a computer topic or technology and are interested in being a reviewer or technical editor.
- Want to find a distributor for our titles in your area.
- Are an educator/instructor who wants to preview New Riders books for classroom use. In the body/comments area, include your name, school, department, address, phone number, office days/hours, text currently in use, and enrollment in your department, along with your request for either desk/examination copies or additional information.

1

INTRODUCTION TO MACROMEDIA FLASH FOR EMBEDDED DEVICES

by Phillip Torrone

Welcome to *Flash Enabled*, the first and best resource (we think) on creating content with Macromedia Flash for embedded devices and beyond. This book has many audiences: developers, designers, marketers, and the curious. How can one resource have so many audiences? Convergence is really (and finally) here—honest. In less than 10 years, Internet technologies have embedded themselves in almost everything we touch. Often, we don't even notice (which is a good thing). ATMs, TVs, DVDs—they're all reaching out using the Internet, and all have interfaces that humans interact with.

It's been a long road, but 2002 seems to be the year we're going to truly make contact—contact with the user. The biggest hurdle in the race to convergence of media, content, and technology has been the disparate tools that programmers and designers have been forced to use. It's not the user's fault that every interface looks different and every button behaves differently, but it often means the user spends more time learning an interface than actually using it.

We're finally able to look forward and develop connected mediums such as console gaming, PDAs, cell phones, interactive television, tablets, and more. Why? Those tools, which at one time kept the silos of interactivity from cross-pollinating, are now distilling to something more approachable, scalable, and usable. Which tool in particular? Flash.

A LITTLE FLASH HISTORY

Flash arrived on the scene as a product called SmartSketch, which was created to make it easier for people to draw and sketch with a computer. It is somewhat ironic the full circle which has formed since Flash's early incarnations, with this book dealing with pen input and Flash.

SmartSketch was a great tool, but the only real way to distribute animation was via CD-ROM or VHS. That was about to change, however. The Internet and the World Wide Web were gaining traction and it seemed that this new pipe could be used to transfer animations and graphics. Work began to make FutureWave's SmartSketch into the animation tool that would also play-back within Netscape's new plug-in architecture, which gave web browsers more functionality. SmartSketch was renamed Cel Animator to foster the animation theme, but it was quickly renamed FutureSplash Animator so it would gain more acceptance than simply being associated with cartoons. In 1996, FutureSplash began to ship as a boxed product, and companies such as Microsoft and Disney started to flock to FutureSplash for its television-like animation qualities over limited bandwidth (at the time 9.6kps was fast). In 1996, Macromedia bought FutureSplash and it became Flash 1.0.

We're now six versions of Flash later, and 417,415,830 users (as of January 1, 2002) can view Flash content. Flash is one of the most distributed pieces of software in history and is the most ubiquitous format on the web, along with GIF. Although that seems a fantastic feat, the best is yet to come. With millions of developers creating content with Flash, the next evolution has just begun—the new vessels of creativity.

Macromedia has created SDKs (Software Development Kits), which means that device manufacturers and developers of existing and emerging platforms and devices can easily include Flash playback for their devices. This opens up a community of Flash developers to create compelling content and intuitive applications for the next generation of Internet-connected devices (**www.macromedia.com/software/flashplayer/licensing/sourcecode/**).

THE EXPANDING POPULARITY OF FLASH

Where has Flash shown up? More places than we could ever list. This book is one of the first to demystify how to create content for interactive TV, gaming consoles (such as Sony's PlayStation and Microsoft's Xbox), broadcast TV, Pocket PCs, PDAs, tablet computers, and user interfaces for pretty much anything—and anywhere—humans touch machines.

Why is Flash so appealing to device manufacturers and developers? Its attraction goes beyond a clever interface and good marketing. Flash has been created over time *with* developers and *by* developers. By listening to the people using the tools the most in current and emerging markets, Macromedia has created a tool for both designers and developers. The convergence of the two is where we're heading as opposed to pre-Flash days, with designers and developers never interacting during the creation process.

Return on Investment (ROI)

Return on Investment (ROI) is something that we'll hear more and more about in the forthcoming years. Not just because the economy ebbs and flows, but ROI is something that works in everyone's benefit to get the best possible product for fair compensation. Flash offers the speed and ease of development of any world-class design tool (such as Illustrator or FreeHand) and the development environment of any traditional coding tool. Project budgets and timelines will continually decrease, while the learning curve of the development staff will need to keep pace. If you've developed content for other devices, you've suffered through variants of languages, processor specific code, compiling issues, short life spans, the development tools, and the dead-end formats. With Flash, content you create now, or have created in the past, will run now and forever. Many developers are speechless when the content they created for a project runs seamlessly and flawlessly on a new embedded device or a pocket PC—a platform they never even thought of during development.

Portability

As is the case in many innovations, the original purpose is often not fulfilled. It's when people take a creation and use it in new and amazing ways that the creation truly shines. Flash is a good example of this. Earthlink, for example, has recently created a series of television commercials using Flash and have reduced their production costs and time to market. Levis Strauss and Co. has also used Flash to reduce application development time. Their "Buddy Lee Staring Contest" application works on both the desktop and pocket PC. The application, which was Flash-based, did not need to be re-created for the specific device because Flash was used on the device to deliver the content and still fits on the device.

Embedded Devices

With embedded devices such as Set Top boxes and PDAs always having smaller amounts of storage space, and that space costing a premium as compared to their older desktop cousins, Flash is a valued option. The Flash Player fits nicely on most embedded systems, as well as with the content files. With most embedded systems living on existing wireless networks with maximum transfer speeds barely exceeding 9.6kbps, not only is a small file format such as Flash needed, it's required. Also, because all the Internet connectivity is built inside the Flash Player, a developer does not need to create connection libraries and new protocols just for a one-off application.

In fact, there are already companies building entire devices around the Flash format, such as the Pogo device (**www.pogo-tech.com/device.html**) (see Figure 1.1).

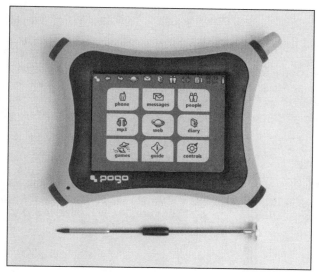

FIGURE 1.1

Devices, such as Pogo, are being developed specifically for the Flash format.

This is just one of many devices and companies that we're excited to see leading the charge with Flash being used as the glue between hardware, connectivity, and user interfaces.

Game Development

For game developers, most game titles are created for multiple game systems. The most important part of a game (besides the game play) is the menu and informational systems used to operate the game. Game developers should not spend large amounts of precious development time on the menu systems. By using Flash for user interface elements, interfaces can be created by UI experts and designers and the game developers can focus on the actual game. In early 2001, Orange Design, Inc. (in partnership with LucasArts Entertainment Company LLC, Secret Level Tools, and Macromedia) announced the first ever Flash application for the PlayStation 2, for "Star Wars Starfighter." The Flash approach can easily be extended to DVD menus and interactive TV interactive applications.

Built for Branding

A common theme across many Flash applications is branding. Brands increasingly are becoming more than just a logo, typeface, and the messaging to the consumer. Brand developers often choose Flash because of its support for vector graphics allowing logos to be preserved, full font support, and photographic images. Brands are becoming a part of the user interface itself; the only thing more memorable than a good user interface is a bad one. On every Windows XP CD there is a Flash presentation that showcases the latest operating system from Microsoft while still preserving the entire Microsoft brand and messaging.

Accessibility

Macromedia and Microsoft have furthered their existing relationship with a commitment to Flash Player support across all Windows embedded platforms. The Flash Player Source Code SDK provides source code and documentation for fast porting to Microsoft Pocket PC 2002 and Windows CE .NET platforms, along with existing support for Windows XP Embedded. As Microsoft moves into new arenas such as console gaming, home automation systems, interactive TV, and smart phones, the partnership with Macromedia will ensure that the applications of today run on the systems of tomorrow.

Scalability

With Flash, we can be screen size agnostic. In other words Flash can scale from the small screen of a smart phone to the large screen of the Jumbo-Tron in Times Square. With minor modification and proper planning, much of your content will never need to be re-authored.

WHAT YOU'LL FIND IN *FLASH ENABLED*

This book covers many of the subjects and content creation guidelines just mentioned. You'll learn how to use type on embedded systems—not only to make type legible, but also to lift the Kimono to see the proper ways for using type. In Chapter 3, "Interface Design for Devices," you'll create and use interfaces in Flash, which can be scaled to multiple devices. Later you'll explore everything—we mean everything—about creating content for the Pocket PC. This book will then move on to creating animation and games for the Pocket PC. Moving from content creation to server side and delivery, you'll learn online and offline applications and creating standalone applications with Flash and Java. You'll then learn about Flash for television and developing content for the Sony PlayStation 2. This great resource then concludes in a bow with server-side Dynamic Flash content, the future of Flash, and appendices that will help you figure out where your Flash content can go.

We've assembled the best authors from around the globe, all who have written many best-selling books and who speak at conferences around the world. We're hoping their experiences in these new and emerging vessels of creativity cannot only inspire, but teach.

PART I: GETTING STARTED WITH FLASH ON DEVICES

2

CREATING CONTENT FOR THE POCKET PC USING FLASH

by Phillip Torrone

Buckle your seatbelts, folks; in this chapter we're going to cover everything you wanted to know about Macromedia Flash 5 for the Pocket PC and even go a bit further and hit some of the other content creation tools and mediums for the Pocket PC, such as Windows Media, Theme Creation, and more! There will be some areas when you need some Flash knowledge, others you will not (because there are millions of people who have Pocket PCs but don't use Flash yet).

Throughout this chapter, you'll see references to files used in the examples. We've included theses source files—as well as many games and extras—on the Flashenabled.com book site (www.flashenabled.com/book/). Likewise, you'll find book-related excerpts and information on the New Riders site (www.newriders.com).

WHAT IS THE FLASH PLAYER FOR POCKET PC?

First, here's a link to download the Flash Player for Pocket PC. There are many people who are looking to dive in right away, so here it is: **www.macromedia.com/software/flashplayer/pocketpc/download/**.

A little background: There are currently over 450 million worldwide users of the Flash Player; it's one of the most downloaded pieces of software in history. It's the low-bandwidth, animation, web application super-scripting darling that has made the web more than static pages of content. Developers have built e-commerce sites, banks, MP3 players, animated series, TV commercials—Flash has been used in some manner in pretty much anything that can display an image. Now with all the devices already here and on the horizon with rich color screens, and speedy processors, Flash has made its way into these new vessels of creativity.

Over the last few years Macromedia has worked hard to create SDKs (Software Development Kits) so hardware vendors and developers can deploy Flash to other platforms. Some of these other platforms, such as TV, gaming consoles, and more are covered later in this book. Also, Macromedia and Microsoft have formed a partnership to distribute the Flash Player with Windows XP and Embedded XP, so expect to see Flash running on many of the platforms Microsoft has its fingerprints on, from tablet PCs to Ultimate TV and the Xbox.

 Windows XP Embedded is the componentized version of the leading desktop operating system enabling rapid development of the most reliable and full-featured connected devices. Based on the same binaries as Windows XP Professional, Windows XP Embedded enables embedded developers to individually select only the rich features they need for customized, reduced-footprint embedded devices. All the device drivers, peripherals, and applications you use on the desktop can easily run on such devices as: set top boxes, home gateways, information appliances, kiosk/gaming consoles, network attached storage, and retail point-of-sale terminals.

Part of Macromedia's Flash Player offering has been the Flash Player for Pocket PC. Basically, the Flash Player for Pocket PC installs to a Pocket PC and behaves just as any other ActiveX control or plug-in. Later in this chapter we'll get to the specifics of what the Flash Player can and can't do, but for now, let's discuss why a designer or developer would want to use the Flash for Pocket PC.

WHY USE FLASH FOR THE POCKET PC?

Money, and making lots of it. Actually there's more to it than pure capitalism, but it's a note-worthy point; many companies and developers are making a fine profit from using Flash on the Pocket PC. Let's discuss why.

Flash enables developers to *develop content once* and deploy it pretty much everywhere, from desktops to Pocket PCs to TVs. With proper planning much of the heavy lifting of a project can be repurposed just by using Flash. If you've ever had to re-create a project from scratch (we all have) you'll appreciate the timesaving high ROI.

This book demonstrates that Flash content is viewable across multiple browsers, platforms, Internet appliances, and perhaps one of the best platforms, the Pocket PC. The nature of the Flash format allows developers to create content for multiple screen sizes, so as Pocket PCs and other devices get smaller or larger screens (and screen resolutions) your content can scale accordingly. With Flash your content can work on multiple Pocket PCs without recompiling the assets or code.

The *speed and ease* of developing with Flash holds true for developing content for the Pocket PC with Flash. Usually, a prototype of an application is needed before actually creating the application. Many development and design shops use Flash to prototype applications to get client approval, feedback from the users, and to work through many of the issues normally associated with device application development. There have been many projects that the only reason that a particular web shop or developer got the gig is because they showed up with something to show. Don't be afraid to wow your clients or prospects. There will be many times where the final project may not involve Flash at all, but its role may be integral to visualizing what an application may do.

Because *storage space* on devices will always be precious, the small footprint of the Flash Player makes it an ideal runtime-like engine for fueling your business, productivity, and learning applications. In other words, you can install Flash on your Pocket PC and still have plenty of room for all your applications. Or in other-other words, smaller is better—at least in this case it is. Where else can you get sound, animation, scripting, images, and high-level interactivity all in one industry standard package? At some point Flash for the Pocket PC is likely to be pre-installed in the Pocket PC operating system, just like it has been in the desktop arena for years—cross your fingers!

Scripting. If you know JavaScript, you pretty much already know ActionScript, Flash's native scripting language, which, like JavaScript, is based on ECMA script.

Connectivity. With wireless networks becoming more and more ubiquitous, Flash, which was designed to deliver high-bandwidth animations over smaller pipes like 9600bps modems (we call that "back in the old days"), is now well suited for viewing content over wireless networks, which are usually less than 19.2kbps. Viewing a full-length cartoon over a wireless modem that usually only gets text and news headlines is both very useful and amazing for demonstrating what's possible with current technologies. Because more and more companies are creating web-based systems, Flash will be an integral part of the desktop and device browsing experience. Also, in the next few years most Pocket PCs will be wireless-enabled out of the box or have wireless connectivity options readily available. Because Flash was designed for the web, most of the plumbing needed to move data around, load screens, and manage memory is already baked in.

Branding. Just like the Internet having so many crummy looking web sites, we're suffering through quite a bit of crappy device applications, gray backgrounds, square buttons—programmer art as they say. As the web evolved, companies figured out that you could have a usable interface and still live up to a brand. Branding is more than logos and fonts; it's part user interface and part "soul" (as cheesy as that sounds). The only thing more memorable than a good user interface is a bad one, and that's a newly emerging part of a brand. Most of the popular destinations on the web use Flash in some manner, and it'll only be a short time until the popular places on the web need to migrate their content to the smaller screen. Because much of the work has been created using Flash and other vector-based tools, it's going to be easier for designers to use the same tools to create content for the Pocket PC. This is opposed to using a more complex (though not necessarily more powerful) programming environment, such as Visual Basic and C++. Many design and development shops are surprised how their existing staff, many of whom are Mac users, can start creating applications now with Flash and the Pocket PC. Flash is one of the only tools that makes it possible to create applications on multiple platforms, including for the Pocket PC.

Content is king, always has been, always will be. There are hundreds of thousands of Flash applications, games, animations, and more on the web. Many of the games, entertainment, and e-learning applications that are available now run on Pocket PCs, sometimes with minor changes, often with none at all. One of the more interesting and recent coincidences with Flash and Pocket PC is the pixel size of some new online ads. The size of the "Cnet" sized ads in the middle of your news stories happens to be almost the same exact size as a Pocket PC screen. There already have been many online ads that have been ported to the Pocket PC by simply making a new HTML file.

Resources and community are just two of the reasons Flash has flourished on the web, and that holds true for the Pocket PC platform now as well. There are over a million Flash developers worldwide. Because of this large developer base and community there is lots of help, inspiration, conferences, classes, and more to help with creating content. Go down any computer aisle of a bookstore and look at all the titles available for Flash. Some titles are design-centric, some are programmer- and developer-centric, and some are both. With that many resources and community sites out there with thousands of example files, you can build applications faster and get the help you need in a jiffy.

Server side and middleware are usually components of a front-end application that are the most difficult to do in the device world. Visualizing data and the return of queries is a daunting task, to say the least. Luckily, many of the issues and challenges have been solved and there are multiple solutions for getting your data into the device using Flash. So whether you're using ASP, JSP, CML, PHP, XML, CSV, or ODBC and JDBC there are many rebuilt solutions that may simply need to be redesigned for a smaller screen. Being able to choose which middleware, standards-based solution and backend database is often not the case with device applications. Flash on the Pocket PC allows the developer to choose the most appropriate solution for the project. One last word on Flash on the Pocket PC and server side. If you are an experienced Flash developer, you've used **loadVariables** to load data into Flash, basically the loaded data in it's name / value pair format is much smaller than loading in HTML tags where in many cases much of that data is never displayed, it's simply for formatting. With Flash on the Pocket PC, you're only loading in the data you need; in wireless environments every byte you can save counts.

There are of course many more reasons to consider Flash for the Pocket PC. This is a just tour of some of the reasons we're going to cover. But what list of benefits would be complete without a top ten list?

Top Ten Reasons to Use Flash for Pocket PC

10. Runs on all the important platforms and devices.
9. High level of interactivity and multimedia.
8. Middleware friendly.
7. Standards based.
6. Branding.
5. Plethora of resources.
4. Humongous community.
3. Plumbing for wireless already built in.
2. Content is king and it's the best authoring tool!
1. Flash won't hurt your feelings.

ON WHICH POCKET PCS CAN THE FLASH PLAYER FOR POCKET PC RUN?

At the time of this writing there are 22 OEMs (Original Equipment Manufacturers) that make Pocket PC devices. Just about all of those devices run the Flash Player for Pocket PC. The Pocket PC operating system currently exists in two different flavors, Pocket PC and Pocket PC 2002. For the folks who have Compaq iPAQs (StrongARM processor and upgradeable ROM), they'll be able to upgrade to Pocket PC 2002. For the folks who have older Pocket PCs with MIPS and SH3 processors, they will not. This gets really confusing really quick, so here is an attempt to help clarify things.

Devices that have MIPS and SH3 use the Pocket PC operating system, and are not upgradeable to Pocket PC 2002. These include older versions of the HP Jornada 540, 545, 547, also the Casio E-115, 125, and EM-500 that are all MIPS based. That means if you want to run Flash for the Pocket PC on those devices you'll need to use the Flash Player 4 for Pocket PC. Many folks out there will never need to use an older device or use an older version of Flash for the Pocket PC, but here's something to consider. On eBay, at the time this was written, you could purchase a Casio E-115 for $40. Using Flash for Pocket PC you can create a high-end Picture viewer, an MP3 player, and other standalone kiosk-like devices.

The Flash Player 5 for Pocket PC will run on all Pocket PC 2002 devices.

See Appendix C, "Flash Device Resources," for a list of links to Pocket PC hardware manufacturers.

If you've used or read about Pocket PC devices, you'll notice that they all have a consistent set of specifications. Microsoft wanted to be sure all the devices have similar specs for ease of development, performance, and quality user experience.

Pocket PC 2002 Specs

206MHz StrongARM processor

32–64MB RAM

Display at least 4,096 colors (most have 64,000)

Expandable memory

Long battery life

It's a developer's and designer's dream to actually know what the performance is going to be on the user's device; in the desktop world it's often a numbers game where some people will simply not have the best experience.

WHAT ISN'T SUPPORTED IN THE FLASH PLAYER FOR POCKET PC?

Flash Player 6 support. At the time of this writing, the Flash Player 6 for the Pocket PC is not yet available, but devices are being deployed with the Flash 5 Player. Developers can use the Flash MX authoring environment to author content, but they must publish for the Flash 5 platform or to whatever version of the player is supported on the specific device. If using Flash MX and above to create content for the Flash Player 5 for Pocket PC 2002, some of the Flash MX ActionScript features may not be present. However, many new ActionScript features are still available.

Remember, the Flash Player for Pocket PC is an ActiveX Control. Registry edit programs for the Pocket PC that turn off ActiveX controls should be avoided because they will not allow the content to play. Also, be sure to keep Fit to Screen selected (see Figure 2.1). This setting is usually selected by default. When Fit to Screen is unselected the Flash content will not scale to a different size, but will produce unpredictable results such as causing scroll bars to appear, as well as moving the Flash movie off screen.

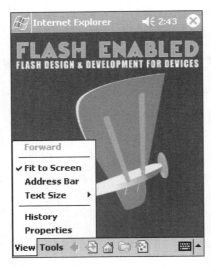

FIGURE 2.1

Fit to Screen option on Pocket PC 2002 should always be selected.

FSCommands are not supported at this time. Internet Explorer for Pocket PC does not yet, and may not ever, support the specific browser calls that are required to invoke the FSCommand. But, you can transfer information between Flash and JavaScript. See Chapter 8, "Data Persistence with Flash, JScript, and HTTP Cookies," for a thorough discussion of this topic.

Contextual menus (right-click menu) are "different." Because there isn't a right-click button on the stylus, holding down the pen will invoke the contextual menu (the right-click menu). This is only true for non-hit areas. If your application requires the contextual menu to never be activated, you can simply put an invisible button underneath the entire application. Later on in this chapter we will demonstrate how to accomplish getting rid of the contextual menu even in non-hit areas.

Movie sizes. Choose the pixels option to set the values of the WIDTH and HEIGHT in the HTML Publish Settings. Internet Explorer for Pocket PC ignores the "%" when defining width and height in the HTML embed tag. For example, defining "width=100% height=100%" is the same as "width=100 height=100".

Yes, there is no standalone Flash Player. The Flash movie must be embedded inside an HTML page. There is no standalone player functionality at this time from Macromedia.

Mobile Favorites with Internet Explorer for Pocket PC for saving Flash content are not support-ed at this time. But Mazingo (**www.mazingo.net**) and MyCasio (**www.mycasio.com**) do support syncing Flash content for the Pocket PC. For more information about how to sync content using Mazingo and MyCasio see the "Distributing Your Flash Content for the Pocket PC" section of this chapter.

Authoring content for the Pocket PC is possible on either the Macintosh and Windows platforms, or any platform that can create SWF files in the Flash 5 format. Transferring the files via an ActiveSync requires a Windows-based system at this time or by using Pocket Mac (**www.pocketmac.net**), which reproduces the functionality of ActiveSync, but for the Apple Macintosh operating system.

So for the most part, all the features you're familiar with in the Flash Player for the desktop are supported on the Pocket PC.

CONTENT CREATION GUIDELINES

So now that you know what the Flash Player for Pocket PC is, what it can and cannot do, and what devices it can run on, it's almost time to dig in and start creating some great content. But first, let's review some of the guidelines for creating content. After that, we'll put it all together and create an application.

Movie Size

When starting Flash, it's usually a good idea to set the movie size right away. To set the size of the movie, choose Modify, Modify Document (see Figure 2.2). In most cases you'll need to set the dimensions to 240×240 (this allows the address bar in Pocket IE to be activated, but the scroll bars will not be visible). Or set the dimensions to 240×263, which assumes that the address bar will not be visible. After a few years of deploying content to Pocket PCs, we've found that most users have the address bar down by default and 240×240 is the safest bet. Later on we'll show you how to use a template to make this easier.

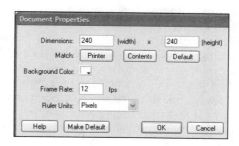

FIGURE 2.2

Setting the document properties.

If you need the extra 23 pixels, be sure to include instructions to the users, which could be something like this: "If the scroll bars are visible, go to the View menu in Pocket IE, uncheck Address Bar and then press the Refresh button."

This of course is pretty confusing and most users will just try to look at your content with big scroll bars, which is often undesirable. If your application's dimensions are too large and will always require scrolling, you can modify the Registry in the Pocket PC to reduce the size of the scroll bars from 20 pixels to something smaller. See the "Advanced Topics" section in this chapter for changing Registry settings on the Pocket PC.

Frames Per Second

Later on in this chapter we'll dig into how fast these little Pocket PCs can run Flash content. Running at 206MHz on a StrongARM processor you can expect 8 to 15 frames per second to be the consistent playback rate. As a general rule, you should set your frames per second to 12 to ensure the most consistent playback.

Now that we're all set up, let's talk about the user interface elements when creating content for the Pocket PC with Flash.

The User Interface

With Flash for the Pocket PC it's sometimes a challenge to create interface elements that are familiar but also do not confuse the user. For example, a home button in your application may be confused with the home button in Pocket IE. If your application is a portable version of a desktop application or web site the user has already used, be sure you're not simply resizing the interface and assets, but optimizing the content for the Pocket PC.

 Be sure to review the Chapter 3 "Interface Design for Devices," for specifics on creating the best user interfaces for your applications.

One of the major differences (or challenges) between user interaction on a device (as opposed to the desktop) is that when users are interacting with a device, they're often in "application-mode" and don't think the content you've created is a web site. It's important to manage those expectations in the applications you create. One of the common phrases you'll hear throughout this chapter is "self-documenting." This means that the interface should be obvious when the user interacts with it. People want to spend time using your application, not learning it. Can your application be handed to a variety of users and can they immediately start using it? Having clearly marked buttons isn't always the sure-fire way to accomplish this. Ideally, after creating your application, break down what tasks are to be performed and test with a group of users to obtain feedback. Usability doesn't mean a bunch of gray buttons with labels on all of them. Usability means a common sense approach to application design. Take a look at ATMs, video game consoles, and appliances where there are limited methods of input and what ways the developers have solved those issues. With Flash for the Pocket PC, the primary way to input information is a stylus. Take a look at other applications on the Pocket PC, as well as Palm applications, for a well rounded view of what developers have created for scrolling lists, icons, buttons, pop-down lists, and other user interface elements.

Also, Flash for Pocket PC isn't the best tool for everything, really. For example, many applications may consist of a Flash menu system and branch off to HTML pages with large amounts of text. Flash isn't best suited for displaying full screens of text and performance can be dramatically affected. Try to avoid more than three or four paragraphs of texts if possible.

Flash can link to HTML pages using the **getURL** actions and HTML pages can link directly to pages with Flash applications; often the best applications are a combination of the two. Pocket Internet Explorer cannot support pop-up windows, so be sure to provide links directly to the page or have some type of device detection scheme.

For tips on usability visit Macromedia's usability section. Although it discusses Flash for desktops, it's good information that spans to the small screen as well: www.macromedia.com/software/flash/productinfo/usability/tips/ contents.html.

Intros—Don't Do Them

Okay, don't use intros, ever. Unless there's an amazing reason to have an intro, it's not needed. Does a user need to see an intro to Microsoft Word before he starts using it? No. So there's a good chance your application does not need one as well. But let's say you had to, and in some cases such as gaming, entertainment, design portfolios, and branding exercises an intro is desired. Be sure to use a cookie so that if the user does decide to skip the intro, that information is recorded. See Chapter 8 for more information on using cookies with Flash.

Build Once

If you've used Flash on a regular basis, you're quite familiar with the Symbol Library. The Library allows developers to store assets that can be used without re-creating the content and thus increasing file size. The nature of Flash allows developers and designers to reuse assets very easily, and when working on a desktop project, it's often possible to reuse many of the same symbols, graphics, and movie clips for the device applications created.

When planning and strategizing projects, break the content into as many standalone pieces as possible. Each reusable piece saves time and can positively impact development, QA, and authoring time.

Some good examples you're bound to use over and over (trust us on this): zoom in and zoom out buttons, scroll bars, progress bars, loading screens, pop-down lists, date and time widgets, radio buttons, forms, keyboards, sliders, volume buttons, and VCR-style controls. Between the examples in this book, Macromedia Exchange (**www.macromedia.com/exchange**), and the flashenabled.com site, many of these are already available.

Input Methods

The Pocket PC supports various methods of input: stylus, software keyboards, hardware keyboards, hardware buttons, and also voice commands with third-party software. The stylus is similar to a mouse in function, but operates like a pen or pencil. Function keys on the Pocket PC are not supported; try to avoid using those when possible. Also try to avoid creating content that requires a key press when possible because popping up the keyboard causes scroll bars to appear over your content (see Figure 2.3).

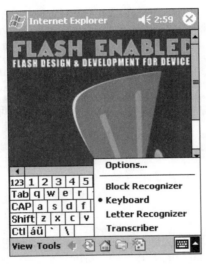

FIGURE 2.3

Some input methods on the Pocket PC cause scroll bars to appear and cover the content.

Buttons

There are two major considerations with creating buttons on the Pocket PC using Flash. First, there is not a pointer or mouse, so everything is considered a mouse click. There aren't rollover states; in fact these should be removed since a rollover state will "stick."

The other important consideration is defining the hit state size. Be sure to make larger-than-normal hit states for the buttons. On the desktop, having to click a few more times is not perceived as a performance issue; on the Pocket PC it would be. Also be sure (when possible) that the buttons can be activated with a finger because that is a commonly used method of input.

Because the Pocket PC, or any PDA for that matter, will always have a less powerful processor and be dependant on batteries, try to avoid blinking, pulsing, rotating, or animated buttons when possible unless it's necessary to the application. Basically, anything that is CPU intensive. Also, stop loops and animation when they are no longer needed.

Many applications created on the Pocket PC will work with other applications on the device, such as email, PIM, calendars, and so on. If you're going to use icons to represent these applications, try to use icons the user is familiar with.

If you're going to use icons to represent functionality, such as send, email, next, back, and so on, try to use well-recognized icons or icons based on often-used iconography, if possible.

 Keep your buttons far from other buttons when possible, this helps to avoid accidental slips and misses of the stylus. It's easier and more natural for users to tap buttons that are against the edge of the screen as opposed to those requiring aim.

Right-Click Menu

Pressing and holding down with the stylus in non-hit areas (areas without a button) will cause the right-click menu to appear in your application (see Figure 2.4). There are two settings for menu items in the Flash Publish settings: Show Menu On or Off.

FIGURE 2.4

The Flash Player menu.

Although it appears the menu can be turned completely off, it cannot. Even with the off setting it will still display "About Macromedia Flash." To turn off the menu completely (in some cases it may be a requirement for a project), place an invisible button under the content area.

To disable the right-click menu:

1. On the stage (without any symbol selected), go to the Insert, New Symbol menu. Choose Button and name the symbol "InvisButton."

2. In the Symbol Edit screen (double-click the symbol in the Library), place a keyframe in the Hit frame of the button (see Figure 2.5). To insert a keyframe, select the Hit frame and go to the Insert, Keyframe menu.

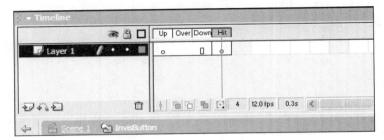

FIGURE 2.5

Inserting a keyframe in the Hit frame.

3. In the stage, place a square in the center of the stage. The size doesn't matter in this example.

4. Go back to the main stage, open the Library, and drag the invisible button to a layer under all the other layers of your content.

5. Be aware if you plan to use this application for the desktop, there will be a mouse over cursor (a little hand with finger) over the entire piece.

We've included the invisible button files on the Flashenabled.com/book web site. Be sure to visit the site if you had trouble following along, or if you'd like to use the button in your project.

"Stacking" the Deck

Because we pretty much only have 240 pixels of both width and height to work with, it's important to have a strategy for displaying information in a useable way. If you've ever developed content for cell phones you may be familiar with the "deck" model. Basically, much like a stack of cards, only one "card" or screen is viewed at any given time. Scrolling could kill a processor, and because Flash needs to move shapes, animations, and more, it's best not to scroll to avoid sluggish performance. Also, unlike the desktop, the Pocket PC cannot pop open new windows inside Pocket Internet Explorer.

Most of the examples in this chapter, as well as this book, use the deck model to create the space needed for the content and applications (see Figure 2.6).

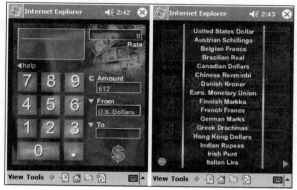

FIGURE 2.6

Stacked example, currency calculator.

One of the many benefits of using Flash for Pocket PC development is that Flash has a built-in deck model—from using scenes, to keyframes, to built-in next and back navigation aids, the authoring environment enables you to create applications fairly easily.

Progress Indicators

Some applications for the Pocket PC will be transferred over a wireless network and others will be loaded from a variety of storage cards. In most cases, you will not know how the content will be accessed, and in some cases, at what speed it may be necessary to create a loading screen. You don't want the user to get a blank screen with no clear indication of what's going on.

In some cases where the movie is very large, a progress indicator is needed, in other cases a flashing loading screen will do, and in others a game such as tic-tac-toe may help to pass the time. Ideally, the best loading schemes are the ones that users never notice.

Forms

If your application requires submitting data through forms, it might make sense to use Flash for the Pocket PC. There are some cases where it makes sense, but in most cases using forms inside HTML forms are usually more effective. Flash does offer acceptable support for forms and for creating elements normally found inside forms, such as drop-down lists, radio boxes, and so on. With pen-based input it may be okay to use Flash, but there are some instances where the user may have a hardware keyboard plugged into the Pocket PC and tabbing between fields in Flash is fairly tricky.

For more information on the tab order of the Flash Player visit: **www.macromedia.com/ support/flash/ts/documents/tab_order.htm**.

One challenge with Flash on the Pocket PC is when developers and designers create custom forms, the users don't always recognize these somewhat form-like interface elements as forms. There are some things you can do when creating forms inside Flash to help the user with the forms you have created.

Try to put a blinking cursor in the first entry field by using the following ActionScript from these steps on an editable text field:

1. Be sure the text field is an Input Text field, and in the variable field give it a name (see Figure 2.7). For this example it is called hocus. Also check the Border/bg checkbox so you can see it on stage.

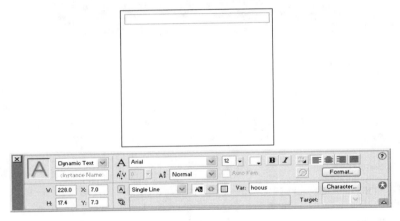

FIGURE 2.7

The input text field.

2. In the same frame as the text field add the following:

    Selection.setFocus("hocus");

3. When you test the movie or use it on a Pocket PC, the field you created will have a blinking cursor in it.

Another tactic is to label the form with a button or label that states "Please fill out this form." When possible try to make web forms in Flash look like web forms in HTML—it'll make the application more usable and less confusing.

One clear advantage of Flash is its ability to submit form data to a server without (re)loading a page. (We like to refer to that as a destructive refresh.) For example, you can have a shopping cart, wireless application, or other data-submitting application and the data can be posted without the page going completely away and a new page loading back in.

Fonts and Text

This is perhaps *the most important* part of your Flash applications and content for the Pocket PC. Flash will anti-alias fonts by default on the desktop and that's usually okay. For a device it's important to know what fonts look good on the screen, which native fonts can be taken advantage of, and when to use other fonts such as pixel fonts for super crisp text display.

This is such an important subject that we've dedicated an entire chapter to it. See Chapter 4 "Typography in Flash for Devices" before reading any further. The information in Chapter 4 is down-and-dirty for Flash and Pocket PC development only, so keep that in mind.

Pocket PC 2002 includes the built-in fonts you see in Figure 2.8.

Tahoma
Tahoma Bold
Courier
📚📖★📖 (Bookdings)
Fruitiger Linotype
Fruitiger Linotype Italic
Fruitiger Linotype Bold

FIGURE 2.8

The Pocket PC 2002 built-in fonts.

When possible, use these fonts when authoring. Also, when using these, check Use Device Fonts in the Text Options panel (Window, Properties), as you see in Figure 2.9.

FIGURE 2.9

Using device fonts in the Properties panel.

When installing the Microsoft Reader for desktop or laptops, these fonts are included when installing the Reader application. To download the Microsoft reader for desktop visit: **www.microsoft.com/reader/download.asp**.

It's worth noting that ClearType does not work on the device fonts inside Flash on the Pocket PC, even when using forms, and the fonts are device fonts. For more information on ClearType visit: **www.microsoft.com/typography/cleartype/default.htm**.

Small Fonts are Blurry and Hard to Read on Pocket PCs in Flash

Small fonts can become blurry in the Flash content on the device, making them difficult to read. By default, text used in Flash is anti-aliased. Anti-aliasing is also referred to as smoothing. Anti-aliasing makes bitmaps and vector graphics display better onscreen, but can make small fonts unreadable in most cases, particularly on devices.

One solution is to use an input text field instead of a type block. Text used in text fields does not anti-alias by default. To use an input text field, highlight a text field on the stage and select Input Text (Window, Properties).

An input text field displays small text much crisper than a type block. Additionally, using text fields to display text will decrease file size, because font outlines are not enclosed in the rendered movie. It's important to note that you'll need to block the user from being able to input text with an invisible button or similar method.

Another technique is to use static text but to use the Use Device Fonts option (Windows, Properties).

Depending on the type of application you're creating, the user may want to select text and cut and paste to other applications on the Pocket PC. To make text selectable, check the Selectable box in the Text Options panel.

This technique should only be used with the included fonts on the device, such as the included fonts with the Pocket PC (Tahoma, Courier, Bookdings, and Frutiger).

As previously stated, Flash is usually not the best medium for displaying large amounts of text, and other media, such as HTML, plain text, Microsoft Reader, Adobe Acrobat, or word processor documents, should be considered.

Pixel Fonts

One of the best solutions is to use pixel or bitmap fonts. These fonts work well at small sizes because they do not anti-alias.

See Chapter 4 for a complete discussion of how to use, and even make, bitmap fonts.

 On some systems, such as Windows XP, the built-in ClearType option may make pixel fonts look slightly smoothed. This only affects the authoring and not the playback, however, which means that the font will be crisp on the device.

Colors on the Pocket PC and Flash

One of the main reasons businesses and consumers are attracted to the Pocket PC is because of its ability to display rich content, such as images and video. All current Pocket PC 2002 devices can display at least 4,096 colors. However, most display 65,535 colors. The grayscale Pocket PCs cannot run the Flash Player. Be sure to check the device manufacturer to see how many colors are supported by the device(s) you're targeting.

Because not all Pocket PC devices have the same display color depths, as a developer/ designer you should be aware of the device limitations. You can be assured that the colors you use from the two color ramp files available on the accompanying CD-ROM will display correctly on devices that can only display 12-bit color (4,096 colors). One of the color ramp files is a color rainbow and the other is a grayscale gradient. There is not much of a need to worry about a palette when targeting devices that display 16-bit (65,535) color.

 The color ramp files are available on the Flashenabled.com/book and www.newriders.com sites as well as Bill Perry's www.Pocketpcflash.net.

When choosing colors and palettes for Flash applications for the Pocket PC, choose highly contrasting colors when possible. The tiny displays are not as advanced as desktop monitors and often have low contrast ratios. Use graphics that have a high contrast ratio between colors and that have crisp edges in the details of the picture. We will go over when and how to use bitmapped graphics in the "Importing a Sequence of Bitmap Images" section.

Vectors and Optimization

The way Flash works (both on the desktop and Pocket PC) is that you're basically getting the recipe of the cake and baking it on-the-fly. This is much faster than trying to jam a big cake down a small pipe, like a 28.8 modem. That said, the more recipes you get, the slower things can get. Because the processors of these Pocket PCs (206MHz) are less than half as powerful than most desktop machines, the processor of the device can be easily taxed when rendering graphics and animations. The more curves in your application, the more processor cycles it will take to display your content.

Limiting the number of curved sections of your shapes and content inside your Pocket PC application will not only reduce the file size, but will also reduce the processor utilization of the application. Flash has a built-in optimizer to help do this.

1. To reduce the amount of curves in a shape on stage, first select the shape, then choose Modify, Optimize from the menu.

2. As you move the slider toward Maximum pay close attention to where the slider is (see Figure 2.10). Check Use Multiple Passes and Show Totals Message. After moving the slider, click OK.

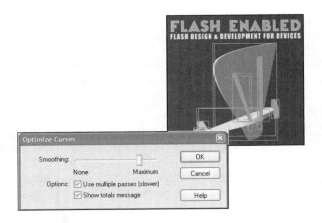

FIGURE 2.10

Optimizing shapes.

3. If the smoothing isn't quite right—too much, or not enough—you can always undo the optimization (Edit, Undo).

Many applications for the Pocket PC might not need all the assets created in Flash. For example, mapping applications are often displayed better and perform more acceptably when importing a GIF. There are a few reasons for this. Flash doesn't need to draw every line, shape, and curve of the map; the GIF is not anti-aliased (smoothed). There are some drawbacks; zooming in and out will make the map appear chunky, so you may want to consider another version of the map for when the user zooms in or out.

In some cases, images or transparent versions of the object you plan to move may be better to use for animations. For large animations with large amounts of motion it's often a good technique to smooth motions and keep the static areas crisper, with more curves. Also, in some cases, it's acceptable to create a "blurred" bitmap of an object in motion to make the Flash shape appear more fluid. Please check out Chapter 6, "Creating Motion Graphics and Character Animation for the Pocket PC Using Flash," for more information.

Setting Image Compression

Flash has built-in global compression settings in the Publish Settings area (File, Publish Settings). To control JPEG compression, in the Publish Settings, Flash tab, adjust the JPEG Quality slider or enter a value (see Figure 2.11).

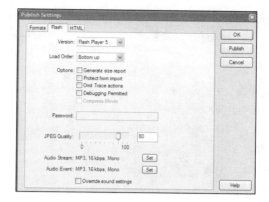

FIGURE 2.11

The Publish Settings image compression.

Lower image quality produces smaller files; higher image quality produces larger files. Try different settings to determine the best trade-off between size and quality. Imported GIFs are not compressed; they retain their compression settings from import. Usually after an application is complete, it's common to export two to three versions with different compression settings to compare the quality on each device. Often you can reduce the file size by 20–30% without any noticeable quality loss. You can compress graphics on a Pocket PC more than the desktop without noticeable image quality loss because the lower quality screens Pocket PCs have as compared to their desktop picture tube / LCD monitors. This is one of the few times a poorer quality screen can be used as an advantage.

 When you import a JPEG image, the image will retain its compression setting prior to being imported into Flash and will not be effected by the Publish Settings. To change the image compression of imported JPEGs, select the image in the Library and use the Property Setting to change the compression settings.

Multimedia Elements

On to the good stuff—the stuff dreams are made of. Well, at least the dreamy rich multimedia elements that make a Pocket PC more than just an organizer when using Flash.

Sound

The Flash Player for Pocket PC is an ideal way to deploy portable music videos, mobile entertainment, learning applications, help systems, language aids, and animations, while also protecting the content by embedding links and purchase information right in the content (see Figure 2.12).

FIGURE 2.12

Multimedia content with sound in Flash for the Pocket PC.

Do plan carefully when thinking of putting all the multimedia content inside your Flash application on the Pocket PC. Sometimes, it's better to use multiple applications together, such as the Windows Media Player for video and music.

For most Pocket PC application-based content, less sound is often better unless the application specifically relies on it. Playback of sound requires large amounts of processing power to uncompress sound data and it also consumes precious power resources. Compressed sound is much like a folded up piece of paper; the more it's folded, or compressed, the greater the effort to unfold it.

Most Pocket PC users have the sound muted or it's turned on and off based on the power settings at the time. It's important to provide instructions to the user if the Flash movie requires the use of sound. Test the device to determine playback quality of the sounds that are to be used and that require very clear playback. Often the tiny speakers of the Pocket PC, as well as not so great headphones, might not be ideal for your application. Also, some Pocket PCs have the speaker underneath the directional pad, which can muffle sound.

The Flash Player for Pocket PC supports volume adjustment as well as panning from right channel to left channel (the user may need headphones for that feature as most devices only have one built-in speaker).

On the Flashenabled.com/book web site we've included volume and balance components to use with your application. Because most users will not want to manage sound in two places, your application and the device's settings, it's not recommended you create your own volume and balance controls unless it's for a standalone Flash application for the Pocket PC. The user must also have the volume turned on for these components to work; Flash for Pocket PC cannot turn on the volume if the device is muted.

Using Sound Inside Flash for the Pocket PC

Flash can import audio to use with your Pocket PC applications in the following formats: AIFF, WAV, and MP3. Generally, AIFF is for Macs, WAV for PCs, and MP3 is universal. For the most part, developers usually use MP3s inside Flash for authoring due to its quality and high compression ratio.

Getting audio from sources requires an audio capture/compression program such as SoundEdit, Sound Forge, QuickTime, and so on. After you get your sound into the format that you want, you're ready to import it into Flash. It's a good idea to start out with the best quality sound when importing the sounds into Flash. The initial compression settings do not matter until the Flash is compiled and the sound setting in the Publish area are applied (File, Publish Settings).

To import a sound into Flash, use the File, Import menu; when imported the sound is placed in the Library (Window, Library). The sound can be used as a streaming sound track on stage or for an event-based sound such as a button click. In most cases you'll want to set the sound to stream for sync'ed playback (see Figure 2.13).

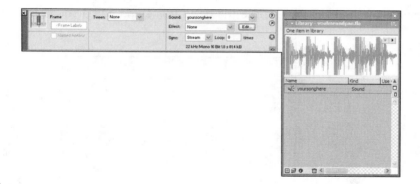

FIGURE 2.13

Imported sound set to stream.

You can use the built-in editing tools inside Flash to manage and edit many of the sounds you import. But, it's often better to do a majority of your sound editing outside Flash in a tool specifically designed for sound.

Flash allows looping, which means you can take a small file and loop it many times to give the appearance of a continuous sound (see Figure 2.14). This saves on file space on the device and/or download times, but it can be really annoying to the user. Make sure to provide a "mute all sounds" button when possible.

FIGURE 2.14

Sound looping.

To kill all sounds, add the following ActionScript to a button in your Pocket PC application:

```
on (release) {
    stopAllSounds ();
}
```

To add a sound to a button in Flash, add a new layer above the button frames. Then, while symbol editing, create a keyframe above the down frame and add a sound to that frame by dragging it from the library (see Figure 2.15).

FIGURE 2.15

The sound will play when the button is clicked on the Pocket PC.

In Publish Settings, you can specify the sound setting of the final Flash application (see Figure 2.16). Set the Sound to MP3, 16 kbps, Mono.

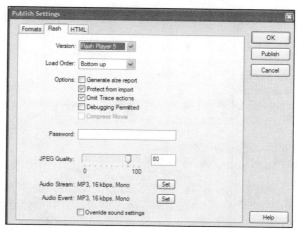

FIGURE 2.16

The Publish Settings dialog box.

You can also set the sound setting of each sound by double-clicking the sound in the sound library. This displays the Sound Properties dialog box for the selected sound (see Figure 2.17).

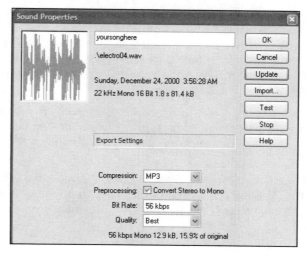

FIGURE 2.17

The Sound Properties dialog box.

Select Override Sound Settings in Publish Settings (File, Publish Settings, Flash tab) if you want to use global settings across the movie and not the individual compressions on each sound.

Which Sound Compression Is Best for Flash for the Pocket PC?

Most developers use some variation of MP3 compression in mono for web delivery. In general, for the Pocket PC a bit rate of 24 kbps, Mono, and Fast compression is a good balance between quality and file size. The most common compression settings are these:

- Audio Stream: MP3, 24 kbps, Mono
- Audio Event: MP3, 24 kbps, Mono

Don't forget, although MP3 sound is very small, it does take up precious processor cycles. Because of this, in some cases ADPCM sound compression may work better for your application. Be sure to perform proper testing and observe file sizes to find the acceptable compromise.

Also, there are many resources that are specifically dedicated to sound and Flash. Check **www.newriders.com** as well as **www.macromedia.com** on a regular basis.

Animation

We dedicated all of Chapter 6 to animation. The following are some general tips and guidelines.

Because you are always trying to conserve processor cycles and power, it's often best to avoid large amounts of animation, tweening, and motion graphics when possible. Also avoid intensive visual effects. This includes large masks, extensive motion, alpha blending, and complex vectors, such as extensive gradients. That's not to say you should use animation at all. In fact, Flash for the Pocket PC is one of the best (and only) ways to animate content on the Pocket PC. The other key benefit, Flash runs on PCs, Macs, Linux, and beyond—so the work you create isn't a "one off."

For some projects, you may want to use ActionScript to animate your content, but intense ActionScript can also drain a processor, so be sure to explore combinations of tweens, keyframe animations, and ActionScript-driven movements. If you test frequently, your results will be greatly improved.

One last thought on animation, mobile computing, and Flash. At the 2002 Sundance Online Film Festival, 12 of the 26 films are animated. Of those, most were created with Flash. This shows that not only is there content, but also demand. The mobile versions of the content you create will surely have a broad audience.

Gaming and Interactivity

We've dedicated Chapter 7, "Creating Interactive Games for Devices Using Flash," to gaming, so be sure to check it before diving into a hardcore game development.

Most industry analysts believe that the Pocket PC is so popular because of its enterprise features, business-to-business applications, productivity tools, and so on. But the real reason for the device's popularity is simple: games and lots of them! Well, that probably is not quite true, but most Pocket PC users have a collection of games that helps them get through meetings, elevators, and airports where they are held hostage to your content. According to some estimates, there will be one billion (yes, *billion*) hours spent in corporate offices playing Solitaire in 2002. As more professionals become mobile professionals, we'll need to fuel their gaming addiction with some portable content. There are many games available for the Pocket PC created in Flash, from adventure and strategy games to old favorites, such as Poker (see Figure 2.18).

FIGURE 2.18

A Poker game for the Pocket PC created with Flash.

If you've kept your finger on the pulse of what's to come in the device world, mobile entertainment is one of the killer apps for local and wireless content. In just one month, over 25 million people visited a gaming site, logging 3.1 billion minutes of playing time. Those numbers were substantially higher than they had been three months before, and ten times more than the year prior. As devices get online, you can expect online gaming for the Pocket PC to become ubiquitous.

Enter Flash, which is already one of the top tools for creating online games. One challenge with creating Flash games for the Pocket PC is being able to save scores and stats within the game. One method is to house the game online and have the user browse to the online game over a connection. From there you would create the game to store information with a variety of middleware and database solutions. Because that's not always possible and the user may or may not have a connection to the web from his Pocket PC, another method is to use cookies on the device with Flash. For more information on using cookies to save data in Flash, see Chapter 8.

VIDEO IN FLASH FOR THE POCKET PC

Often, you'll need to use a video or video-like effects in your project. Or, you'll want to create a standalone video player with your own user interface. Also, many clients will want Flash MX-like effects; this section addresses some of the many video-in-Flash techniques.

Windows Media Player on the Pocket PC

Included on almost all Pocket PC 2002 devices is the Windows Media Player 8 for Pocket PC (see Figure 2.19).

FIGURE 2.19

The Windows Media Player for Pocket PC playing a video.

Windows Media Player supports the organization and playback of Windows Media content through play lists, MP3 audio files, Windows Media Audio, Windows Media Video, FhG MP3, and streamed content in Windows Media format using WM protocols (HTTP and MMS). Most desktop users (over 70%) currently use the Windows Media Player and they're already familiar with the interface, so in most cases using the Windows Media Player for video is often the best choice.

If the user has Windows Media Player 7 or above on his PC, he can use it to easily transfer digital media files to his Pocket PC (see Figure 2.20).

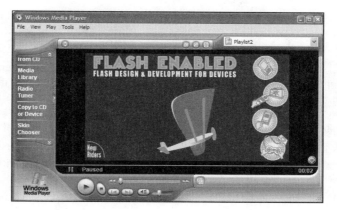

FIGURE 2.20

The desktop Windows Media Player.

Also, with a wave of digital rights–based content, users will soon be playing more content that has been purchased, such as music. Flash works well with other applications, just like the desktop, so it's important to start planning for what is to come with engaging combinations of Flash and Windows media content for the Pocket PC.

 To download the latest version of the Windows Media for Pocket PC, visit: www.microsoft.com/windows/windowsmedia/download/pocket.asp.

Launching a Windows Media file from Flash on the Pocket PC is as simple as linking to a file via **getURL**. For example:

```
on (press) {
   getURL ("video.wmv");
}
```

After the user is finished with the video and closes out of the application, it will return the user to the page he just came from. Actually, let's be a little more specific and mention a few caveats. "Closing" an application on the Pocket PC is actually just placing it in the background. So if you have any sounds or animations in your Flash application on the Pocket PC, be sure to stop the animations and sounds when launching a user to another application. This can be accomplished by using the **stop ();** command on the timeline and **stopAllSounds ();** in the movie. In fact, this is why it's usually a good idea not to have a background track running or intense animations at all times, or to create a timeout.

You can also quit almost any application on the Pocket PC by using the built-in keyboard. To quit an application with the built-in keyboard, tap Ctrl and then the Q key (just like the desktop) and that closes most applications, including Internet Explorer for the Pocket PC.

If you plan to open extremely large documents from Pocket Internet Explorer, you may want to consider deploying an additional ActiveX control with your application if it's permitted. The AppLaunch ActiveX Control from Microsoft makes it possible to open large files more quickly in Internet Explorer for the Pocket PC. It bypasses the temporary cache, resulting in a faster launch of the application—launching as if it is in File Explorer. To download the ActiveX control, visit: **www.microsoft.com/mobile/developer/downloads/powertoys.asp**.

To use this ActiveX control within Flash, call the JavaScript function from within Flash (be sure to consult the ActiveX control documentation as well). To call the AppLaunch Active Control, add the following action to a button inside Flash:

```
on (press) {
    getURL ("javascript:LaunchMe();");
}
```

In this HTML file you have the script that's ready to be called:

```
<HTML>
<HEAD>
<TITLE>exe_tester</TITLE>
</HEAD>
<BODY bgcolor="#FFFFFF" leftmargin="0" topmargin="0" marginwidth="0"
➥marginheight="0">
    <SCRIPT LANGUAGE="JScript">
function LaunchMe()
{
  var Launch;
  var ExeName = "\\windows\\player.exe";
  var ExeParam = "\\My Documents\\video.wmv";

  Launch = new ActiveXObject("AppLaunch.Launch");

  Launch.ExeName = ExeName;
  Launch.ExeParam = ExeParam;

  Launch.Run();        // Launches "player.exe" with "video.wmv" as a parameter

}
    </script>
```

```
<CENTER>
<OBJECT classid="clsid:D27CDB6E-AE6D-11cf-96B8-444553540000"
codebase="http://active.macromedia.com/flash2/cabs/swflash.cab#version=4,0,0,0"
ID=PocketPC  WIDTH=240 HEIGHT=240>
<PARAM NAME=movie VALUE="exe_tester.swf"> <PARAM NAME=quality VALUE=high>
➥<PARAM NAME=bgcolor VALUE=#FFFFFF>
</OBJECT>
</CENTER>
</BODY>
</HTML>
```

We've included this example on the Flashenabled.com/book site if you need to take a closer look at it.

 See Appendix C for links to resources on creating video for Pocket PC.

Video Inside Flash on the Pocket PC

In some cases you may decide that the Windows Media Player for Pocket PC doesn't have the level of control that your application requires. For those instances, as well as design projects which may require "video-like" effects, here are two ways to get Flash content to play video on the Pocket PC.

Importing a Sequence of Bitmap Images
The first technique is basically importing a sequence of bitmap images in a series of keyframes to simulate video. Usually, you import the video into Flash first, export it as a bitmap sequence, then import it back in (with sound track imported as well). Flash will do a pretty good job of making short video clips (usually a few seconds) fairly video-like.

Let's create a short video clip. Set up your movie, 240×240, 12 frames per second, with a white background.

1. Be sure you have QuickTime installed (**www.apple.com**); also use QuickTime Pro (that means you need to pay the $20)—it's worth it. Import a QuickTime movie (File, Import) onto the main stage. Resize the file to fit inside the stage. You can get the sample movie we're using from the Flashenabled.com/book site or use your own. Flash will ask if you'd like to embed video in a Flash document, or link to the video; choose Link to External Video file. Resize the video to 240×180.

Although you can directly embed video inside Flash (Flash 6 Player) using Flash MX, that feature is not supported on the Flash Player 5 for Pocket PC at this time. Use the other methods described here to embed video on the Pocket PC with Flash.

2. Keep inserting frames on the timeline (Insert, Frame) until the QuickTime is fully visible (see Figure 2.21). If you see an X in the QuickTime box, you have gone too far.

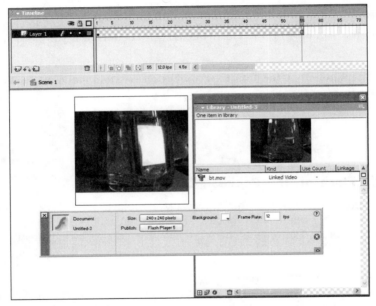

FIGURE 2.21

QuickTime inserted on the main timeline.

3. Now export the movie by selecting File, Export Movie to display the Export Movie dialog box (see Figure 2.22).

4. In the Save As Type field, choose Bitmap Sequence (*.bmp).

5. Choose the folder you want, enter a filename, and click Save.

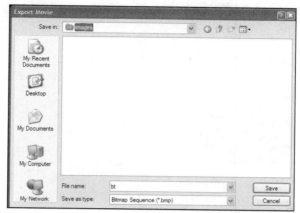

FIGURE 2.22

Exporting the movie as bitmaps.

6. Use the settings in Figure 2.23 for the images. On a Mac, use similar settings for PICTs.

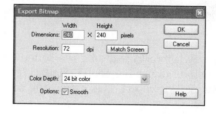

FIGURE 2.23

Export settings.

7. Now in the QuickTime Player application (you should be using QuickTime Pro or another video editing application), export the sound track in Flash as a WAV file or other importable sound file for your particular system.

8. Go back to the Flash movie and delete the QuickTime movie on the stage by selecting it and pressing Delete.

9. Next, import the images (File, Import) and select the first image. When Flash figures out that this is part of a series of images and asks to import them all, select Yes. You may need to move the images for proper placement.

10. Now add a new layer to the Flash movie (Insert, Layer). Import the sound into Flash using File, Import (see Figure 2.24).

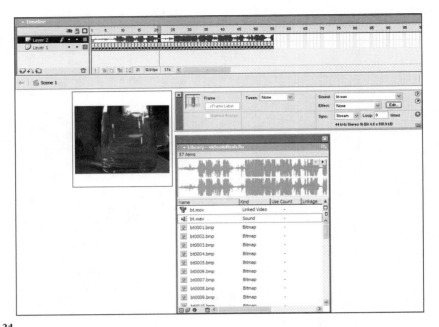

FIGURE 2.24

The sound imported to the main timeline.

11. Open the Library (Window, Library) and drag the sound onto the layer called sound-track. Click the timeline and under the sound panel (Window, Properties) choose Stream under the Sync pull-down list. This makes the soundtrack match up with the movie.

Test your movie (Control, Test Movie). In Publish Settings (File, Publish Settings) under the Flash tab you can adjust the JPEG settings to make the movie smaller or larger in file size and memory. The technique of using imported bitmaps is good in some cases, but be aware that this is extremely memory intensive and can cause the Flash Player for Pocket PC to crash.

Before you transfer the HTML and Flash file (SWF) to the Pocket PC, be sure to review the "Copying Content to the Pocket PC: A Checklist" section of this chapter.

Video with Wildform Flix

The other method of using video inside Flash for the Pocket PC is to use a third-party tool such as Wildform Flix (**www.wildform.com**).

With Wildform, you can avoid 99% of the work of the previously described technique, and get results that are much better (and smaller). Flix is the best video-to-SWF (Flash movie) encoder. It is the most stable, has the best quality, converts the most file types, is available for both PC and Mac, offers great support and resources, and it comes with discounts on royalty free video from the Wildform Video Library (which is useful if you need quick content for your projects). Using Flix, you can also save encoding profiles specifically for the Pocket PC (much like the Windows Media Encoder). Flix converts the following video formats into Flash movies: .mov, .qt, .dv, .avi, .mpeg (PC Only), .wmv, .asf. The Flix screen is shown in Figure 2.25.

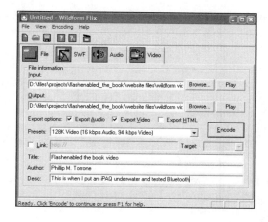

FIGURE 2.25

Wildform Flix is the best video-to-SWF encoder.

Using Flix, encoding video for use in Flash only involves three steps:

1. Choose the input file.
2. Select your preset.
3. Click "encode."

At the main Wildform web site, there is a fully functioning demo of Flix. There are tons of sample movies and custom players to try out. After creating Flash movies with Flix, you can load them into your Flash movie using **loadMovie**:

```
loadMovieNum ("myvideo.swf", 0);
loadMovie ("myvideo.swf", "holder");
```

On the Flashenabled.com site we've included a few samples and source files for integrating video SWFs from Flix into Flash for Pocket PC applications.

As with the first video-in Flash-technique, using large SWFs with bitmaps and sounds can cause the Flash Player for Pocket PC to bring the processor to its knees. Proper testing and planning will prevent your applications from crashing or causing sluggish performance. In the next section, we'll explore ways to manage memory in and out of Flash for the Pocket PC.

MEMORY AND MEMORY MANAGEMENT WITH FLASH FOR THE POCKET PC

If you're an old-timer like some of the authors of this book, you may recall when 64k of RAM was more than you'd ever need and a floppy disk was truly, floppy. Well, now we've gone back in time a bit, not that far to TRS-80s but to a few years ago where Pentium 100s and 64MB of RAM was the norm.

All the devices that support the Pocket PC 2002 operating system have at least 32MB of RAM and sometimes up to 64MB. That's a pretty fair amount of storage. Most users have 5–6MB free at any given time for applications. Also, you may hear the term "flashable ROM," it has nothing to do with Flash, but it's still very cool. Basically, flashable ROM allows all the new Pocket PCs to be upgraded to the next version of the operating system. The Compaq iPAQ was the first to support this and it could be the reason they sold over one million in just under a year!

To see how much memory your Pocket PC has, go to the Start menu on the Pocket PC, Settings, the System tab, and then click the Memory icon (see Figure 2.26). As you create applications, it's important to check this setting often to see how much memory and storage you have on your device. Also check the running programs and quit specific programs when needed.

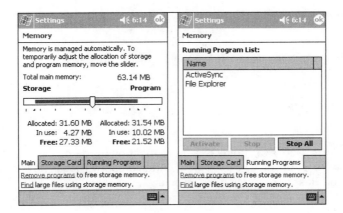

FIGURE 2.26

Storage on the Pocket PC.

Back to physical storage. Flash files are tiny, so tiny that only a few megabytes could contain an entire learning course or dozens of games. For wireless networks, the smaller the size the better; the average connection speed for a wireless device in the year 2001 was less than 9.6kbps. In 2002 there will most likely be faster networks, but not in all areas.

Similar to traditional device application development, one of the many advantages of using Flash for application creation for Pocket PC is that larger applications, which are designed to be stored locally, can have larger file sizes and contain richer content than web-based Flash content. This is because the file is loaded from the file system and not transmitted every time the user interacts with the application.

Also, Pocket PCs usually have many forms of storage built in or additional storage available as an add-on accessory. Formats include: Compact Flash (CF), Multimedia Cards (MMC), and Secure Digital (SD).

Managing Memory

As you create applications for the Pocket PC, you can never test them too often. This is especially important because memory can be scarce and is most likely going to be the main deal breaker in many of your applications. Creating content for any device is a careful balance of sacrifices. Flash allows you to sometimes have your cake, and eat it too. You can use the built in features of Flash and its scripting language to load and purge memory as the user interacts with your applications.

When planning your applications always try to break the components of the application into smaller movies. It's very common to deploy a Flash application for Pocket PC that consists of one HTML page and 7–8 movie files (SWF). For example, if you're creating a learning course, each main section can be a Flash movie (SWF) and all the text can be an external data source like a text file. This enables you to not only update your content on a more frequent basis and use other languages, but by loading content in and out of a main Flash movie you can restore the system memory as you use the application and also after you leave the application.

If you are familiar with multiple timelines and the loadMovie command, you shouldn't have too much difficulty doing the same for your Pocket PC applications. If you're not familiar with the concept, here's a quick overview. Also, don't forget to lean on the thousands of books and resources online for the complete load movie experience.

- The first Flash movie you put into the HTML page on the Pocket PC is referred to as a "base movie." This movie is level 0. The base movie controls the frame rate for all the loaded in movies.

- When loading a Flash movie into a level, the SWF files that are being loaded in should be the same dimensions as the base movie; otherwise you may experience unpredictable results.

- You can load movie files (SWF) into levels, usually 1 and above, as well as targets (other movie clips inside existing levels inside your Flash application).

- When loading a movie into the same level where another movie exists, the newer movie purges the existing movie before the new one can be displayed. If you need to view the movie that was purged, you will need to load that movie in again. After playing a large movie, it's often a good technique to load in a blank or empty movie to free up the memory on the device.

- Loaded movies can communicate to each other by referencing the timelines using relative (**_parent.foo**) or absolute (**_root.foo**) paths, as well as sending variables to and from movies or globally. Root level is also relative, it only references the root of the level; if you need to reference an absolute path, use level 0, level 1, and so on.

- When loading a movie into a target, you're loading a movie into a predetermined location on the stage.

In the sample applications included on the Flashenabled.com/book site we use the loadMovie command to load in content to and from our Flash application for Pocket PC.

LOADING DATA INTO FLASH FOR THE POCKET PC

Let's look at the various ways to load data into Flash applications for Pocket PC. Flash has two main ways to load data:

- loadVariables
- XML

Using loadVariables

loadVariables is the most common way to load in data. It follows a simple name/value pair system. For example, if you had a dynamic text field in your Flash application on the Pocket PC named "message" and loaded in a data source text file called "data.txt" with the following text

&message=your ad here

the text would display "your ad here" inside Flash. Let's take a look at the ActionScript. In some cases, you may need to url encode your data, for example, %20 are url encoded spaces. See the note in this section for specific information about url encoding.

loadVariablesNum ("data.txt", 0);

This loads in the data file located in the same directory as the Flash movie into level 0. You could load the data in from another location (see the "Security" section later in this chapter for specific information) from an ASP, JSP, CFM, PHP, or CGI script, as well as loading the data into another level if needed. In Chapter 10, "Server-Side Dynamic Content for Flash-Enabled Devices," we really dig in to how to use dynamic data sources for you Pocket PC applications; be sure to check it out.

Be sure to separate your name value pairs with &'s and make the values by using the = sign before the value. For example, **var1=value1&var2=val2**.

If you're going to send characters and symbols (like &s and =s), in some cases you'll need to url encode the data as well as using escape characters.

You can also use the built-in escape and unescape functions inside Flash. The escape () function converts ASCII text and encodes it in a URL-encoded format, where all alphanumeric characters are escaped with % hexadecimal sequences. Conversely, the unescape converts a URL-encoded string to ASCII characters.

If you're looking for a great URL encoding chart, visit: http://i-technica.com/whitestuff/urlencodechart.html.

Also, for a Flash-based encoder and decoder visit: www.dommermuth-1.com/protosite/experiments/encode/index.html.

In many of the sample applications on the flasheneabled.com/book site we use loaded data for our applications. Of course, if you are loading data from an external server, then the Pocket PC device must be connected to a network for the Flash movie to work.

See Chapter 10 for some techniques on how to dynamically embed your dynamic data into a Flash movie before it is downloaded or synced to your device.

Using XML to Load Data

Another way to get data into Flash applications in the Pocket PC is Extensible Markup Language (XML). It is called extensible because it is not a predefined language like HTML. Instead, XML is actually a "meta-language," a language for describing other languages, which lets you design your own customized markup languages. With XML you can create your own language definitions or use other XML standards based schemas. The Flash Player for Pocket PC can read XML data the same as the desktop player.

This is exciting for mobile application developers because many of the data sources that are used for applications are XML based, but with Flash for the Pocket PC you have far more design control when presenting the data. The Flash Player for the Pocket PC does not use Document Type Definition (DTDs) files, which are used by other XML-reading applications. Flash allows you to read XML-structure data into a Flash XML object, which has predefined methods and properties associated with it.

Loading XML data into the Flash Player for Pocket PC is a fairly straightforward process.

1. Start a new Flash movie: 240×240, white background, 12 frames per second. Create a text box on the stage; choose the _sans font (that will force the Pocket PC to use built-in fonts). Under Text Options (Window, Properties) make the text Dynamic text, and check off HTML, Word Wrap, and Selectable. Also select Multiline and name the variable _root.HTML. Try to make the text about the same size as the example by resizing it.

2. Create a new layer called actions and in frame actions of that frame add the following ActionScript:

```
function Process (success) {
if (success) {
    _root.Parser.Parse(this);
} else {
    _root.HTML = "XML Load Error<br> XML File Doesn't Exist!";
    }
}
WebXML = new XML();
WebXML.onLoad = Process;
WebXML.load("data.xml");
```

This ActionScript defines the function executed when the data has loaded, and reports an error if there is not an XML document to load. It also tells Flash which function will be used when the data has loaded and lastly it loads the data.

3. Now we need to create a new XML Object. Insert a New Movie Clip (Insert, New Symbol) and call it parser.

4. From the Library (Window, Library) drag that Movie Clip to the stage, select that clip by clicking on it, open the Actions Panel (Window, Actions), and place the following ActionScript in the Object Actions (see Figure 2.27):

```
onClipEvent (load) {
    function Parse (xml) {
    DocumentName = new XML();
        DocumentName = xml.firstChild;
    if (DocumentName.nodeName.toLowerCase() == "data") {
    ChildName = new XML();
    ChildName = DocumentName.firstChild;
    _root.HTML = ChildName.nextSibling.firstChild.nodeValue;
    }
}
}
```

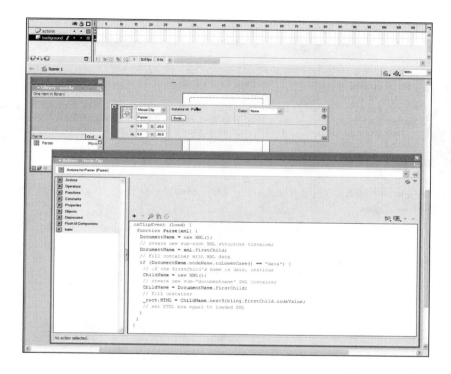

FIGURE 2.27

Putting it all together.

This creates the new XML Object that contains the data and sets test box equal to loaded XML data.

5. What's missing? The XML data. Using Notepad or your favorite text editor create the following XML document:

```
<?xml version="1.0"?><data>
 <info><![CDATA[<p>this is dynamic text, with <b>bold</b>, <u>underline</u>,
➥<i>italic</i>, a <font face="Arial">different font</font>, <font size="20">size</
➥font> and <font color="#0000FF">color</font> with a link to <a href=
➥"http://www.flashenabled .com"><u><font color="#0000FF">
➥http://www.flashenabled.com</font></u> </a>.</p>]]>
 </info>
</data>
```

6. Now test you, movie (Control, Test Movie). You should have the same results as the previous example with all the HTML formatting preserved, but loaded in via an XML data source.

 Parsing XML within Flash can be CPU intensive. This is especially true if you are parsing large or complex XML documents. If you must parse large documents, you may need to parse them in chunks across frames to avoid errors and delays. Also, when parsing large documents, remember to give your user some feedback on what is happening. See the section "Data Loading and Processing Considerations" that follows for more information and optimization techniques.

If you're looking for some great (and free) XML newsfeeds, be sure to visit Moreover at **http://w.moreover.com/**.

There are hundreds of data sources in Flash variable format as well as XML formatted.

Data Loading and Processing Considerations

Using loadVariables and parsing data with the ActionScript XML object can be just as processor intensive as using MP3 files, large images, and complex scripting. Processing large amounts of data can cause slow and sluggish performance on the Pocket PC. Just as you break movies into smaller Flash movies (SWFs) to load in, you should try to process small bits of data when possible as opposed to loading in all the data all at once. However, if loading the data from the network, proper testing will help find the balance against the added time required to load the data from an external source versus loading in the data in one query.

Also, the Flash community has written a number of optimized ActionScript objects that improve the performance of the built-in ActionScript objects:

- **String.as.** An ActionScript library that rewrites some of the built-in string functions, resulting in performance increases. In particular, the **String.split()** method has a significant performance increase. You can download the String.as library from: **http://chattyfig.figleaf.com/~bhall/code/string.as**.

- **XML Nitro.** An ActionScript library that rewrites the parsing of the ActionScript XML object, and in the process provides significant performance increases. You can download XML Nitro from: **http://chattyfig.figleaf.com/~bhall/code/xmlnitro.as**.

- **FLEM.** An effort to add "event engines" to Flash that allows developers to have more application-like features in their projects: **http://chattyfig.figleaf.com/flem/**.

   Although not specific to data processing optimizations, this can greatly ease your ActionScript development workflow.

Data Loading Bandwidth Conservation

Because most Internet connections on the Pocket PC will be wireless and usually less than 9.6k per second, it's important to keep the amount of data you're transferring as small as possible. Only send data that is necessary for your movie. If you have to send large amounts of data, consider loading it in smaller pieces. Not only will this be faster, but also the Flash application on the Pocket PC will appear to be more responsive. Also consider using short variable names and XML tags. For example:

<TitlePageHeader>Your Ad Here</TitlePageHeader>

Should be changed to:

<tp>Your Ad Here</tp>

This can significantly reduce the amount of data that has to be transferred and in some cases make the difference between a good and poor user experience.

Connected and Unconnected Applications

In most cases, the content will be transferred to a device by either "syncing" with a desktop machine or transferring the files over some type of connection. With a connected application (one where the device has a docking cradle for periodic updates) the developer can take advantage of the device having a speedier connection.

With Pocket PC 2002, users can access the web through "Desktop-Pass through." This allows users to surf the web while the device is connected to the cradle or connected to the PC/Mac via IR. While most end users won't use this feature that often, it's an excellent tool for developers to test content online. There is a great opportunity to create "cradle games" where the user is instructed to play the game or content while the device is connected in the cradle. Or a sketch or note pad that can save mobile notes to a server, such as the draw pad example found in the samples on Flashenabled.com/book (see Figure 2.28).

A developer could also make a time-based clock or stock watch that could sit in the cradle and provide information to the user on a regular basis, thus making the Pocket PC into an information display device.

FIGURE 2.28

Pocket Sketch for the Pocket PC uses a server and client side component (Flash on the Pocket PC).

**For more information on Desktop Pass-Through visit:
www.microsoft.com/mobile/developer/technicalarticles/passthrough.asp.**

For the unconnected application (wireless transferring or live querying), the content needs to be as small as possible with only the smallest amounts of information transferred to function. Loading in text files that drive Flash content via Load Variables is a good example of when Flash files cannot be transferred at all. Rather, only the small text files needed for data can be transferred as described in the previous section.

Online Detection

When deploying an application that requires a wireless or LAN connection for the Pocket PC, a developer can "ping" the web server by loading in a text file via an http request. This request contains a value that will trigger the application to allow interaction for online use. Include a timer script that will give the user a message or display content when the application is not connected.

On the Flashenabled.com web site, we created a file that any developer creating Flash content for the Pocket PC can use to test their online connection. You should only use this file for testing, though. If you move your movie to production, you should place a copy of the file on your own server. Here are the steps:

1. To "ping" the server, create a new Flash movie, 240×240, 12 frames per second, white background (see Figure 2.29).

2. Create two layers, one called actions, the other vars. In the vars layer, add a variable text field and call the text field status (Window, Properties).

3. In the first frame of the actions layer, add the following frame action (Window, Actions):

loadVariablesNum ("http://www.flashenabled.com/ping.txt", 0);

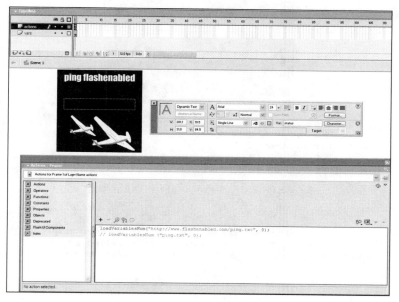

FIGURE 2.29

Let's ping the server to see if we're online.

4. When you test the movie (Control, Test Movie) the Flash file will load the text file and the status variable will be changed to "loaded;" based on that you can write other scripts. If the variable never loads, then you can make decisions and load in other content or instructions so the user knows he needs to be online to use the application. This example assumes the Flash file and HTML are on the local device and the device is connected online (see Figure 2.30).

FIGURE 2.30

Successful ping from Flashenabled.com.

Be sure to read the following section about the security model that you must follow to load in your data.

As a special treat we've also included an advanced example on the Flashenabled.com/book site, which allows developers to detect the Internet connection speed of the device when it is connected to your server!

SECURITY MODEL OF FLASH ON THE POCKET PC

The Flash Player for Pocket PC follows the existing security model of the Flash Player. For security reasons, a Flash movie playing in a web browser and loaded from a URL cannot access data residing outside the web domain from which the SWF originated. This applies to any ActionScript command or object that can send or receive data, including loadVariables, the XMLSocket Object's methods, and the XML Object's send and sendAndLoad commands.

For example, if you're accessing a Flash application from Pocket Internet Explorer at **www.flashenabled.com/**, the application can access any data (TXT, HTML, XML) and files at the Flashenabled.com domain such as sub-directories (Flashenabled.com/mobile/), as well as sub-domains (youradhere.Flashenabled.com).

The application on Flashenabled.com cannot load data from an outside domain like **www.pocketpc.com**. The query will not return any results nor will it provide an error message.

These security features do not affect Flash applications loaded locally from the device, only those playing during browsing via http requests.

A common technique is to store the Flash application on the Pocket PC and use the wireless connection to load data into the application. This has two benefits:

- The "heavy parts" of the application, such as graphics, sounds, and main files, reside on the device.
- Only small amounts of data are transferred over the Internet, in fact the data is smaller than HTML files because the data is specifically formatted for the Flash application on the Pocket PC.

There are two other options if keeping the application on Pocket PC is not permissible for the project:

- Create a "Proxy script." A Proxy script allows the Flash application on the Pocket PC to request the data from a script on the server such a CGI, ASP, CFM, JSP, and PHP middleware on the server, and that script will request and return the data. This can be a fairly slow process and tax the server if not deployed and tested thoroughly.
- The next method is called Domain Name System (DNS) aliasing. With domain name aliasing, the Pocket PC Flash application requests its data from a sub-domain like scripts.Flashenabled.com and the server sends that request to an outside server. This usually is a messy process and generally not supported by most system administrators.

For more information on Flash security, consult the documentation or visit: www.macromedia.com/support/flash/ts/documents/loadvars_security.htm.

Version Detection

It's important to know which version of the Pocket PC Flash Player is on the user's device for deploying specific content. Also Macromedia occasionally creates updates to the Flash Player and it may be part of your application to use the new or updated features. Flash for the Pocket PC has built-in detection so a developer can detect the current version and push content or instructions based on the return.

1. To detect the version of the Flash Player for Pocket PC, create a new movie, 240×240, white background, 12 frames per second.

2. Create a text box on the stage and choose the _sans font (that will force the Pocket PC to use built-in fonts). Under Text Options (Window, Properties) make the text Dynamic text, and check off Word Wrap and Selectable (see Figure 2.31). Select Multiline and name the variable detect. Also, add an additional text block with the same parameters, but name this one playerVersion in the variable field. Try to make the text fields about the same size as the example by resizing it.

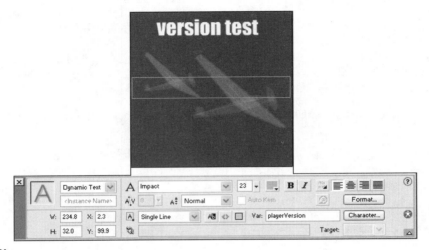

FIGURE 2.31

Text field with playerVersion variable.

3. Add the following ActionScript to the first frame in the movie (you should be in expert mode for this ActionScript):

playerVersion = getVersion();

4. Test the movie (Control, Test Movie). On the desktop, it will return the desktop version of the player you're currently using; and on the Pocket PC, it will also display the current version on the device (see Figure 2.32).

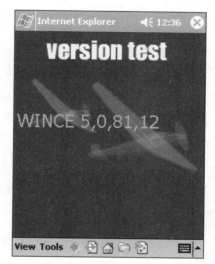

FIGURE 2.32

Flash version detection on the Pocket PC.

When using this ActionScript to detect version information, it is returned as a string in the following format:

(Windows Player) WIN 5,0,42,0
(Macintosh Player) MAC 5,0,41,0
(Linux Player) UNIX 5,0,45,0
(Pocket PC Player) WINCE 5,0,86,1

The string consists of an abbreviation for the platform, followed by numbers indicating Flash Player version number (major version, zero, minor version, zero).

Note that the Pocket PC version begins with "WINCE". Using the code that follows, you can detect whether your Flash movie is being played on a Pocket PC device.

```
/*
* This is a simple function added to the built in String object that checks
* whether a String begins with the string passed into the function.
*/
String.prototype.beginsWith = function(s)
{
return(s == this.substring(0, s.length));
}

var playerVersion = getVersion();
```

```
if(playerVersion.beginsWith("WINCE"))
{
//Pocket PC 2002 <u><b>Detected;
detect = "Pocket PC 2002 Flash player detected";
}
else
{
//Pocket PC 2002 NOT detected;
detect = "Pocket PC 2002 Flash player not detected or version info has changed";
}
```

For more information, consult Flashenabled.com/book or visit: **www.macromedia.com/ support/flash/ts/documents/version.htm**.

It is possible to determine whether the user has the Flash Player 5 for Pocket PC without using JavaScript (as you would normally use JavaScript for detection on the desktop, JavaScript detection is not supported with the Flash Player 5 for Pocket PC).

It's often a good idea to place this type of action in the first 4 to 5 frames in case there are any playback issues on the download to the device.

In your Flash application (which resides on the server), place a getURL action in the first frame that goes to your Flash application on the server.

In the index page of the application on the server, place a meta tag with a 2 to 3 second refresh tag that points to a non-Flash page with instructions on downloading the Flash Player for Pocket PC, for example:

```
<META HTTP-EQUIV="Refresh"
➡content="2;URL=http://www.flashenabled.com/mobile/noflash">
```

For more information, consult the Flash documentation or visit: **www.macromedia.com/ support/flash/ts/documents/scriptfree_detection.htm**.

DEVICE SPEED AND FRAMES PER SECOND

Many of the questions Flash developers ask when first working with the Flash Player for Pocket PC is how many frames per second can the Pocket PC play. This is important because Flash is frame based and much of the content and animations depend on smooth playback.

In general it's a good idea to avoid full screen wipes, full screen fades, and full screen animations. Keep in mind that updating large numbers of pixels at a time can be slow and chunky. You can expect around 8 to 15 frames per second on a device.

Frames per second on the device can vary from device to device and often depends on open applications and free memory. Be sure to check the memory settings as you test your applications and observe the frames per second with various applications opened. In most cases, 12 frames per second is a good frame rate to start at, but results may vary from project to project.

On the Flashenabled.com/book site, we have included a Flash for Pocket PC frames per second detector to aid developers in optimizing content for the wide variety of uses (see Figure 2.33).

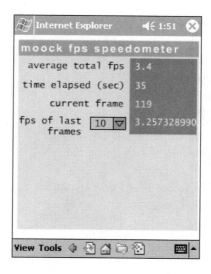

FIGURE 2.33

Moock.org frames per section detector.

DETECTING THE PROCESSOR SPEED ON THE POCKET PC WITH FLASH

There will be times when a user is accessing your content from a variety of Pocket PCs as well as desktop systems. In addition to processor detection, it is also possible to detect the processor speed of the Pocket PC using ActionScript. This can be useful for giving your applications a longer "shelf life." For example, if a new Pocket PC is released with a 400MHz ARM processor next year, you may want to load additional content that can take advantage of the faster processor.

To detect the processor speed of a Pocket PC, place the following script in the first frame of the Flash application on the Pocket PC:

```
n = 0;
a = getTimer();
while (Number(n)<1000) {
  n = Number(n)+1;
}
b = getTimer();
CPUlag = b-a;
if (Number(CPUlag)>100) {
  response = "you're on a device";
} else {
  response = "you're on a desktop";
}

counter++;
```

In the second frame, loop back to the first frame by adding the following action:

```
if(counter < 24)
{
        gotoAndPlay (1);
}
else
{
        stop();
}
```

On the stage, create a variable text field and call the text field CPUlag (see Figure 2.34).

FIGURE 2.34

Variable text field with CPUlag as the variable.

When testing the movie on the desktop, you can expect a return of 10–80 milliseconds. Pocket PC 2002 devices, which are all based on 206MHz ARM processors, should give a result around 225–275 milliseconds. Figure 2.35 shows the result given after the CPU speed has been successfully detected.

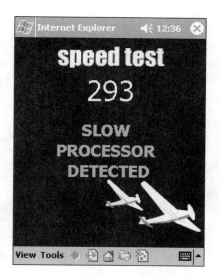

FIGURE 2.35

Successful CPU speed detection on the Pocket PC with Flash.

SCREEN ECONOMY WITH FLASH FOR THE POCKET PC

The theme with developing content for the small screens seems to be "whatever sucked on the desktop, sucks even more." The screen size of the Pocket PC is less than 25% of the average desktop and has lower quality, so every pixel you can squeeze out of your interface is precious.

But it's not all bad news; one of the benefits of Flash for any device, particularly the Pocket PC, is that it can be scaled to new screen sizes without any re-authoring of content. This allows developers to create applications with a large number of the applications scaling to larger or smaller screen sizes, as more devices are available.

Whenever possible, the applications you create should be screen-size agnostic and not require specific screen sizes to function and still be usable. If an application relies solely on the characteristics of the display area and screen size, then the user interface has not been clearly separated from the application.

Not only are there fewer pixels on the Pocket PC, but the legibility of the screens isn't as good as their desktop companions. A scaled down 800×600 web site will be unusable and unreadable in most cases, so proper planning is required, as well as a detailed assessment of the screen elements that you have control over and what you don't. When possible consider using fewer elements on the screen, but with higher informational value. For example, universal icons such as home, mail, and so on not only take up less screen size but also are language independent. Also see Chapter 4 and sections in this book to get the most legible and smallest fonts in your Pocket PC applications.

Fit to Screen

By default, Pocket Internet Explorer has Fit to Screen selected by default; if it is not, be sure it is set.

When Fit to Screen is unselected the Flash content will not scale to a different size, but will produce unpredictable results such as scroll bars appearing and the Flash movie moving off screen (see Figure 2.36).

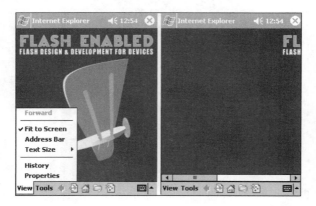

FIGURE 2.36

Fit to Screen checked and unchecked.

By default, Pocket Internet Explorer has Show Images activated by default; if it is not, be sure it is set. When the Show Images icon is depressed, the Flash content will not be viewable in some cases or cause unpredictable results.

Pocket PC Screen Dissection

The Pocket PC has a screen resolution of 240×320 pixels. Unless you're using a full screen Flash Player (See the "Playing Flash Full Screen on the Pocket PC" section in this chapter for more information) you cannot take advantage of the entire screen.

The resolution of Internet Explorer for Pocket PC 2002 is 240×320 pixels. The user interface of Pocket Internet Explorer defines two areas that cannot be used for content, as shown in Figure 2.37:

- The menu bar at the bottom of the screen
- The caption bar at the top of the screen

FIGURE 2.37

Top and bottom Pocket Internet Explorer GUI elements.

Both the menu and caption bars take 26 pixels each off the vertical resolution. Therefore, if designing content for a Pocket PC 2002 that fits on one page, the page must not exceed 240×268, which assumes the address bar has not been activated. Once the page exceeds 268 vertical pixels, the vertical scroll bar will appear and reduce the screen width to 229 pixels, or 252 if the address bar is not activated.

The user can decide to switch off the address bar, allowing for an additional 23 pixels at any time, but you cannot detect if the address bar is activated. Even after the user turns off the address bar he will need to refresh the page if the scroll bars were activated. Because this is a fairly lengthy and complicated process for most users, it should be avoided. There are utilities that get rid of the caption or menu bars, see the "Playing Flash Full Screen on the Pocket PC" section later in this chapter for more information. Generally, end users do not enjoy having to do so much work for a Flash application, and this process should only be considered for power users or standalone kiosks-like applications.

When testing your content to be sure that scroll bars do not appear, make sure that Fit To Screen is turned off in Pocket Internet Explorer. Otherwise, the scroll bars will never appear, which could lead to inaccurate display when the movie is displayed on other devices.

When utilizing the full 240 pixel width, the horizontal scroll bars will also appear because Internet Explorer for Pocket PC 2002 needs to provide a way to reveal the remaining 11 pixels with the vertical scroll bar. You can avoid the horizontal scroll bars by setting the margins of the HTML container page to zero. For example in the HTML used to load the Flash Movie:

<body leftmargin="0" topmargin="0" marginwidth="0" marginheight="0">

This also applies to the vertical scroll bars. In the Flash Player 5 for Pocket PC template located on Flashenabled.com/book, these parameters are already set. See "Using the Flash Player 5 for Pocket PC Template" section in this chapter for more information.

Of course, be sure to properly test your application to cover all the possible viewable content areas. Generally, deploying content with the application size of 240×240 will display without scroll bars, provided all the margins are set to zero. In an informal poll on Flashenabled.com, 97% of 500 Pocket PC users had the address bar active, so keep that in mind or provide instructions if deploying content in another manner.

ROTATING FLASH CONTENT FOR THE POCKET PC

There are many existing applications for the Pocket PC that do not need to be modified at all to play on the Pocket PC. By loading the Flash movie into a movie clip on the stage and rotating the content with ActionScript, you can play Flash content on the Pocket PC in "Landscape" mode, or to put it another way, take advantage of the vertical screen size.

Place an empty movie clip on the stage and give it an instance name of "loader." In the first frame of the movie clip place the following action in the frame actions (Window, Actions):

loadMovie ("rotate.swf", "loader");

This loads the movie into the target movie clip on the main timeline.

Place the movie clip on 240 x coordinate. This places the content in the proper area. We've already created a movie called rotate.swf and it is in the same directory as our HTML and Flash (SWF) files.

In frame 1 on the main timeline, add the following frame action (Window, Actions):

```
loader._rotation = 90;
loader._xscale = 50;
loader._yscale = 50;
```

Here is a simple function that you can use to automate this process:

```
function ppcRotate(mc)
{
mc._rotation = 90;
mc._xscale = 50;
mc._yscale = 50;
}
```

Assuming that the loaded movie is loaded into a movie clip called "loader," you would use the function like this:

```
loadMovie ("rotate.swf", "loader");
ppcRotate(loader);
```

We've included a sample on the Flashenabled.com/mobile. Be sure to review the source files if your results are not as expected.

Most Pocket PCs were designed to work in portrait mode so be aware that there are many disadvantages and caveats. Also, be sure to check out the "Playing Flash Full Screen" section later in this chapter.

In general, HTML frames do not add any value in a Flash application for Pocket PC. Not only do frames take up precious pixels (you cannot turn off the borders) but also they can be resized by the user causing more pixels to be lost to scroll bars. If frames are going to be used, try to avoid more than two panes of HTML.

INTERNET EXPLORER FOR POCKET PC

Many enterprise users of mobile devices have flocked to the Pocket PC because of its software, particularly, the built-in applications and specifically Pocket Internet Explorer.

For a complete list of the features and capabilities of Pocket Internet Explorer, see Appendix D, "Pocket PC Device Detection."

Overall, the Internet browsing experience on the Pocket PC is very much like the desktop. This will not only help your user start using the applications you create faster, but you're creating content for one of the best possible viewing experiences in the mobile computing arena!

HTML AND THE INTERNET EXPLORER FOR POCKET PC

A Flash movie must be embedded inside an HTML page to play on a Pocket PC device, even when using external applications to wrap your content such as custom standalone program. There currently is not a standalone Flash Player from Macromedia, but stand alone-like functionality is possible; we'll get into that later in the "Advanced Topics" section.

Internet Explorer for Pocket PC is HTML 3.2 compliant, with some minor exceptions. In most cases all HTML tags that are defined by this standard can be displayed in Internet Explorer for Pocket PC.

In general, try to avoid complex HTML when possible. It takes up processing time as well as causing scrolling and loss of screen real estate. If you're using frames, nested tables, and multiple instances of ActiveX controls, performance will be sluggish. Also, try to only use supported HTML to avoid unpredictable results.

Multilanguage Support

When using Flash to create content for the Pocket PC, use variables as placeholders for Multilanguage support. This allows you to load in other languages as needed without re-authoring the Flash content. Use the supported character sets for the target device if mixing HTML and Flash. If the device doesn't support multiple languages—but the project demands multilanguage support—you can use Flash and allow the user to select preferred language by creating multiple versions of the content within Flash. For example, the device can be US/English-based, but the content and character sets can be Japanese (see Figure 2.38).

You could do this by using variables as placeholders for all of the content, and then using loadVariables to load the language specific data at runtime.

FIGURE 2.38

Multiple language support with Flash for the Pocket PC.

Flash can also provide the user with a graphical representation of requested content that's independent of the device. For instance, if deploying location-based information such as maps, use variables for the legend and corresponding information in the user's preferred language. This information can also be hard coded into the application in the native language of the user. To deliver exactly what the user wants in the preferred language is value-added personalization that will help make your application an intimate part of the user's life. Keeping the content separated from the design is also a good way to keep development costs and QA times down.

Embedding Your Flash Application into HTML for Pocket Internet Explorer

When putting Flash content on a Pocket PC, just as the desktop, you must provide specific tags in the HTML file so the content can be displayed.

The most important tag is the <Object> tag. The <Object> tag is used by Internet Explorer for Pocket PC to instantiate the ActiveX control (in this case Flash for the Pocket PC). When deploying to a desktop browser, you can use either OBJECT or EMBED tags (EMBED tags are used for Netscape based browsers). However, Internet Explorer for Pocket PC only supports the <Object> tag, and this <Embed> is not needed.

The following is an example of the typical code required to display a Flash 5 movie in the Flash Player 5 on Pocket PC:

```
<HTML>
<HEAD>
<TITLE>Your Ad Here</TITLE>
</HEAD>
<BODY bgcolor="#FFFF00" leftmargin="0" topmargin="0" marginwidth="0"
➥marginheight="0">
<OBJECT classid="clsid:D27CDB6E-AE6D-11cf-96B8-444553540000"
 WIDTH="240" HEIGHT="240">
    <PARAM NAME=movie VALUE="youradhere.swf">
    <PARAM NAME=quality VALUE=high>
    <PARAM NAME=bgcolor VALUE=#FFFF00>
 </OBJECT>
</OBJECT>
</CENTER>
</BODY>
</HTML>
```

Note that the quality and bgcolor params are not necessary to view the file.

If you compare this example to the desktop version, you'll notice that the code base attribute is not required because Pocket Internet Explorer will not download ActiveX controls that it doesn't have installed.

When creating content for the Pocket PC, it's sometimes a good idea and reduces file size to not include tags that you don't need in the HTML file, and thus reduce download time. But, there are sometimes more benefits than saving a few bites by allowing your content to run on multiple systems without modification.

There have been many times when content that developers have created for the Pocket PC has run on other systems such as Linux-based set-top boxes, Sony Direct TV boxes, Compaq home appliances, and more. This is all possible because the content, which was being tested, had all the necessary tags to run on multiple browsers.

```
<HTML>
<HEAD>
<TITLE>Your Ad Here</TITLE>
</HEAD>
<BODY bgcolor="#FFFF00" leftmargin="0" topmargin="0" marginwidth="0"
➥marginheight="0">
<CENTER>
```

```
<OBJECT classid="clsid:D27CDB6E-AE6D-11cf-96B8-444553540000" codebase=
➡"http://download.macromedia.com/pub/shockwave/cabs/flash/swflash.cab#
➡version=5,0,0,0"
ID=PocketPC  WIDTH=240 HEIGHT=240>
<PARAM NAME=movie VALUE="youradhere.swf"> <PARAM NAME=quality VALUE=high>
➡<PARAM NAME=bgcolor VALUE=#FFFF00> <EMBED src="youradhere.swf" quality=high
➡bgcolor=#FFFF00  WIDTH=240 HEIGHT=255 TYPE="application/x-shockwave-flash"
➡PLUGINSPAGE="http://www.macromedia.com/shockwave/download/index.cgi?P1_Prod_
➡Version=ShockwaveFlash"></EMBED>
</OBJECT>
</CENTER>
</BODY>
</HTML>
```

Enclosed between <Object> and </Object>, is the required tag <Param name="movie" value="youradhere.swf"> where "youradhere.swf" should be the actual filename of the SWF movie in the same directory as the HTML file. Also, the margins have been set to zero and the movie is centered in the HTML page. As mentioned previously, do not use "%" when defining width and height in the HTML embed tag. There is one tag in the example that is optional, the ID tag. Back when the Flash 4 Player for Pocket PC was the only game in town the ID tag was needed. In some cases there still may be users using Flash 4 for the Pocket PC, so some developers still include the tag, provided their Flash content is Flash 4 based. The Flash Player 4 for Pocket PC will not play Flash 5 content, so see the "Version Detection" section of this chapter to detect what version the user has on his device. Adding the ID tag will not affect the playback of Flash movies in the Flash Player 5, and thus it is a good idea to include it.

Just as in the desktop player, other tags are available to influence the playback of the Flash movie.

```
<PARAM NAME=quality VALUE=high>
<PARAM NAME=bgcolor VALUE=#000000>
```

Developers can also pass data into the Flash movie to be used with variables inside the Flash application through the HTML file, provided it follows the Flash variable format. For example:

```
<PARAM NAME=movie VALUE="youradhere.swf?mydata1=youradhere">
```

 See the "Loading Data with Flash for the Pocket PC" section in this chapter for more information on the format and the methods to load data into Flash.

Using the Flash Player 5 for Pocket PC Templates

A developer should spend more time creating great applications and content and not toiling in the details of HTML tags. That said, we've created a series of HTML templates that you can use in the Flash authoring environment. To get the templates, visit Flashenabled.com/book and download the templates. Once downloaded, place the templates in one of the following directories on your system:

- Macromedia\Flash 5\HTML folder
- \Macromedia\Flash MX\First Run\HTML

In the Publish Settings dialog box (File, Publish Settings, HTML tab) you can select the file in the Publish Settings (see Figure 2.39). It is called Pocket PC in the pull-down list.

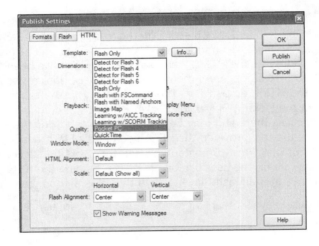

FIGURE 2.39

The Pocket PC template in the Publish Settings dialog box.

This template should be used when your project requires the Flash movie to be 240×240, centered with zero borders. We've also included other templates for other case scenarios such as address bar up and full screen.

If you're manually publishing, choose the Pixels option to set the values of the WIDTH and HEIGHT in the HTML Publish Settings. To avoid undesirable results do not choose Percent.

If your project requires additional information to be included in the HTML file and you would like to automate that process, refer to the details on the HTML Publish Settings in the Flash manual and help documentation.

Copying Content to the Pocket PC: A Checklist

When copying content to the Pocket PC, be sure to do the following:

1. Publish the SWF as a Flash 5 file (File, Publish Settings).
2. Publish with the included Pocket PC HTML template.
3. Transfer the file via the Pocket PC My Documents folder or via browsing to My Computer / Mobile Device.

If enabling Pocket PC content to be viewed via a wireless connection on the Pocket PC, see the "Internet Explorer for Pocket PC" section of this chapter for more information.

Quality Settings

You can set the HTML quality to any of the following: Low, High, Auto Low, Auto High, Medium, or Best (see Figure 2.40). The Quality Setting in the Publish area specifies the level of anti-aliasing, or smoothing, to be used during movie playback. The templates on Flashenabled.com/mobile are all set to High quality.

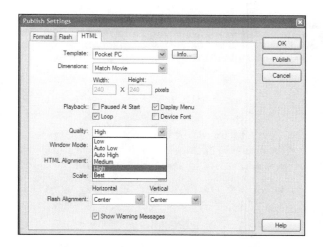

FIGURE 2.40

The Quality settings in the Flash Publish Settings.

Lower-quality settings often improve playback performance but they degrade the quality of the graphics and especially text. Always test the application on the devices to ensure the desired playback. Because anti-aliasing requires a faster processor to smooth each frame of the movie before it is rendered on the viewer's screen, choosing a value based on speed or appearance is always a good idea:

- Low favors playback speed over appearance and never uses anti-aliasing.
- Autolow maps to Low.

- Medium applies some anti-aliasing and does not smooth bitmaps; it produces a better quality than the Low setting and should be used for most content.
- High, Auto High, and Best map to Medium.

Setting the **_highquality** property to true in ActionScript will not force the player to Best mode because the highest possible quality is Medium. The default value for quality is Medium if this attribute is omitted.

Most developers use Auto High for their Flash Pocket PC applications; that way a desktop system will play the content at the best possible quality, as will the device.

USING JAVASCRIPT WITH FLASH FOR THE POCKET PC

You can use Flash methods to send JavaScript calls to Flash movies from the HTML pages. A Flash method is a JavaScript function that is specific to Flash movies. Each method has a name and most methods take arguments. An argument specifies a value on which the method operates.

For a complete list of methods you can use to control a Flash movie from JavaScript on the Pocket PC visit www.macromedia.com/support/flash/ publishexport/scriptingwithflash/scriptingwithflash_03.html.

For our purposes we're going to focus on one technique, SetVariable, to send data from JavaScript to the Flash movie. Inside Flash we use SetVariable to set dynamic data; outside of Flash we'll do the same with JavaScript to send in information.

SetVariable sets the value of the Flash variable specified by variableName to the value specified by value. The argument type for both arguments is string.

For example, an HTML page could have the following:

```
<a href='javascript: window.pocketpc.SetVariable("myvariable","your ad here")
➥'>Click me</a>
```

The HTML looks like this:

```
<HTML>
<HEAD>
<TITLE> Your Ad Here</TITLE>
</HEAD>
<BODY bgcolor="#FFFFFF">
<OBJECT classid="clsid:D27CDB6E-AE6D-11cf-96B8-444553540000"
    ID="pocketpc" WIDTH=240 HEIGHT=240>
    <PARAM NAME=movie VALUE="myflash.swf">
    <PARAM NAME=quality VALUE=high>
    <PARAM NAME=bgcolor VALUE=#FFFFFF>

    <EMBED src="myflash.swf"
        quality=high

        bgcolor=#FFFFFF
        WIDTH=200 HEIGHT=130
        swLiveConnect=true NAME=pocketpc
        TYPE="application/x-shockwave-flash"

PLUGINSPAGE="http://www.macromedia.com/shockwave/download/index.cgi?P1_Prod_
➥Version=ShockwaveFlash">
    </EMBED>
</OBJECT>
<br>
<a href='javascript:window.pocketpc.SetVariable("myvariable","Your Ad Here")'>Send data
➥in!</a><br>
</BODY>
</HTML>
```

This allows you to have a link inside the HTML page and send that information (**myvariable=your ad here**) into the Flash movie (see Figure 2.41). Note the ID tag as well as the **"swLiveConnect=true NAME=pocketpc"** in the EMBED tag. The ID tag is so the Pocket PC knows where to send the data to. The **swLiveConnect** is for the benefit of the Netscape users; while it's not needed for the Pocket PC it's a good idea to put it in there in case you need your content to be viewable on desktops as well as devices.

The Flash movie simply has a variable text field called **myvariable**.

FIGURE 2.41

Sending data into a Flash application from JavaScript in Pocket Internet Explorer.

See Appendix C for links to more information on integrating Flash and JavaScript.

See Chapter 8 for a thorough discussion of using Flash and JScript to store data using cookies.

SNIFFING FOR INTERNET EXPLORER FOR POCKET PC ON THE SERVER

If you are using Microsoft Internet Information Services 4.0 or later, a file named BROWSCAP.INI exists in the directory \WINNT\system32\inetsrv. This file contains descriptions of all known browsers at the time of service pack installation.

Here is the description of the Internet Explorer for Pocket PC needed for the BROWSCAP.INI:

```
; Pocket PC
[Mozilla/2.0 (compatible; MSInternet Explorer 3.02; Windows CE; 240x320)]
browser=Pocket Internet Explorer
version=4.0
majorver=#4
minorver=#0
```

```
platform=Windows CE
width=240
height=320
cookies=TRUE
frames=TRUE
backgroundsounds=TRUE
javaapplets=FALSE
javascript=TRUE
vbscript=FALSE
tables=TRUE
activexcontrols=TRUE
```

Be sure to check this information on a regular basis, as it may change.

Other web servers, such as Apache, support similar configuration files. Consult the web master or system administrator for more information.

Internet Explorer for Pocket PC is actually a mixture of Internet Explorer 3.02 (HTML), Internet Explorer 4.0 (Scripting), and Internet Explorer 5.0 (XML) components. That is why it is identified as Microsoft Internet Explorer 3.02 although it uses version 4.0 inside the properties.

When Internet Explorer for Pocket PC 2002 sends a request to an HTTP server, the following user agent information is sent to the server:

HTTP_USER_AGENT - Mozilla/2.0 (compatible; MSIE 3.02; Windows CE; PPC; 240x320)
HTTP_UA_OS - Windows CE (POCKET PC) - Version 3.0
HTTP_UA_LANGUAGE - JavaScript
HTTP_UA_PIXELS - 240x320
HTTP_UA_VOICE - FALSE
HTTP_UA_COLOR - color16
HTTP_UA_CPU - ARM SA1110

If your existing web application requires the browser of the viewing device to be IE 5.0 and above, you can change the registry to reflect a later version of Internet Explorer. See "Changing Registry Settings on the Pocket PC" in the "Advanced Topics" section of this chapter. That said, you shouldn't rely on the user agent solely to detect devices.

Using Middleware to Detect the Pocket PC

Developers can create special optimized pages with Flash content for the Pocket PC as soon as an Internet Explorer for Pocket PC enters the site by using any middleware language, such as ColdFusion, ASP, JSP, or PHP.

The following example is an ASP script that sends the Pocket PC user to a new page.

```
<%

'    This specifically tests for Pocket IE on Pocket PC 2002 by searching for the "PPC"
➥string within
'    the User Agent field. "PPC" is only included in the USER AGENT header field on
➥Pocket PC 2002.

    userAgent = Request.ServerVariables("HTTP_USER_AGENT")
    isPocketPc = false

'    This checks to see if the browser is any version of MSIE on Windows CE. That way,
➥if the browser
'    gets updated, this should still detect that it is from a Windows CE machine.
    if(userAgent <> "" AND (InStr(userAgent, "PPC") > 0)) then
        isPocketPc = true
    end if
    if isPocketPc then

'    If the user is connecting with a pocket pc, then we redirect them to another
➥page.
        response.redirect("sucess.html")
    else
        response.write("You do not have a Pocket PC")
    end if
%>
```

You can also use middleware for loading in data to the Flash application on the Pocket PC. See the "Using Data with Flash for the Pocket PC" section in this chapter, as well as Chapter 10, which addresses dynamic data.

Using JScript to Detect the Pocket PC

The following is useful for desktop systems for pushing proper content to them while still providing the right content for the Pocket PC. To identify the Pocket Internet Explorer using client-side scripting (JScript), use the following:

```
var strNav = navigator.userAgent;
// Check for Windows CE (Pocket PC, Palm-size PC, Handheld PC, Handheld PC Pro)
    var isCE = strNav.indexOf("Windows CE");
    if(isCE > -1) {
//add Windows CE specific code
```

```
    }
    else {
//add code for other platforms
    }

// Check for Pocket PC
    var isPPC = strNav.indexOf("240x320");
if(isPPC > -1) {
// add Pocket PC specific code
    }
    else {
// add code for other platforms
    }
```

Place your specific code there in the commented areas "//".

DISTRIBUTING YOUR FLASH CONTENT FOR THE POCKET PC

After creating your Macromedia content for the Pocket PC, you'll need to get as many people as possible to view it. There are many places online right now that are content hubs for Flash for Pocket PC content:

Flashenabled.com/mobile (**www.flashenabled.com/mobile**), a collection of inventions, applications, and fun with a Pocket PC focus (see Figure 2.42).

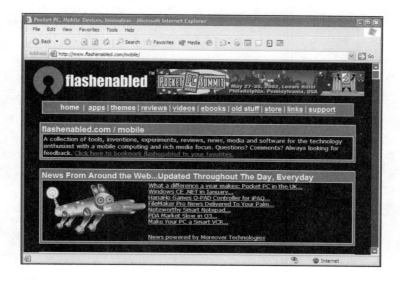

FIGURE 2.42

FlashEnabled.com

PocketPCFlash.net (**www.pocketpcflash.net**), one of the best resources on the web for Macromedia content for the Pocket PC (see Figure 2.43).

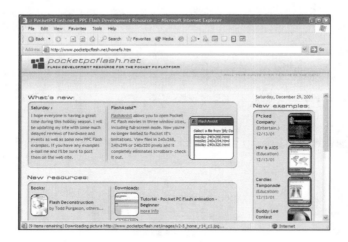

FIGURE 2.43

PocketPCFlash.net

Macromedia Gallery (**www.macromedia.com/software/flashplayer/pocketpc/gallery/**), the place that started it all (see Figure 2.44). Macromedia has one of the best galleries of mobile content for Pocket PCs in the world!

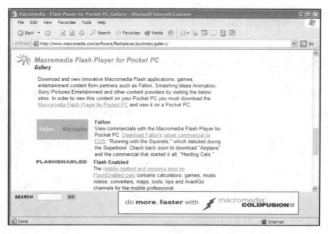

FIGURE 2.44

The Flash Gallery for Pocket PC on Macromedia.com.

Generally, Flash files are distributed as Zip files with three types of files included (see Figure 2.45):

- The HTML file that will contain the Flash application
- The Flash file (SWF)
- A readme.txt file with setup instructions, purchase, and contact information

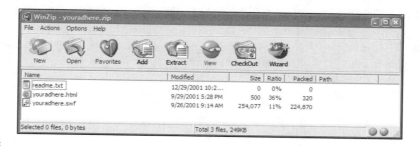

FIGURE 2.45

Zipping the files for distribution.

You may want to include a shortcut to the application (HTML file) to your application, but keep in mind that if the user changes its location to a storage card, the shortcut will not work.

This is often the first interaction a user will have with your content; because this is a part of the total user experience and overall usability, try to make the processes of getting the application up and running as easy as possible. Focus group and QA testing your application should help tease out any installation issues.

Developers also can distribute content with installers such as InstallShield with full-featured install and uninstall features. This is often used for mission-critical projects with budgets. Many developers who create Pocket PC applications for large clients use InstallShield Professional. For more information on InstallShield professional visit: **www.installshield.com/isp/info/ features.asp**.

You can also use Pocket Setup from HelpStudio Software, which has similar features but costs less: **www.pocketsoft.hpg.ig.com.br/pocketsetup/index.htm**.

Pocket Setup comes in both standard and professional versions; review the features to determine which is the most appropriate version for your project.

Another similar application is Pocket PC Install: **www.datamasta.co.nz/ppcinstall.htm**.

And if you'd like to install your applications from the web for the Pocket PC directly, be sure to check out CEWebInstallX: **www.doctorce.com/cewebinstallx_features.htm**.

Lastly, you can also use a CAB file. Self-installing CAB files are provided as an alternative to installers. The CAB files can be placed on a variety of medias or on a Pocket PC directly. With a single tap, the software will self-install. You'll also need to create an INI and Setup executable. After you have your CAB files, SETUP.INI file, and a SETUP.EXE file to invoke the CE Application Manager, you simply need to put the files on a CF card, CD, disk, or in a Zip file for distribution to your users. Understanding the steps required to get these files can be quite a bit to absorb the first time you do an installation, but subsequent installations will go quickly because you can simply change a few values in your source files from any previous installation.

CAB files are very useful when you know the user may be beaming your content (see Figure 2.46). Pocket PCs cannot beam folders or multiple files at once, only one file at a time. If you can make it easier for your users to distribute your content for free, you've won half the battle of a successful application.

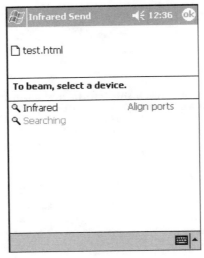

FIGURE 2.46

Beaming files on the Pocket PC.

For more information on CAB files visit: **www.microsoft.com/mobile/developer/ technicalarticles/installation.asp**.

There are also ways to distribute your Flash content through content distributors such as Mazingo and MyCasio. Although AvantGo can be used to distribute some content, we're not going to cover AvantGo because it does not support any rich media and is primarily used for text transfer and some images. For more information about AvantGo visit: **www.avantgo.com**.

And for creating content for AvantGo channels visit: **http://ami.avantgo.com/support/ developer/channels/**.

Mazingo (**www.mazingo.net/**) is a very exciting (and perhaps the best way) to distribute your Flash applications for all Pocket PCs online (see Figure 2.47). The name "Mazingo" comes from the concept of "Magazines to go." Pocket PCs can do some amazing things with text, audio, video, and other rich media, and Mazingo enables publishers and developers to reach readers with a very exciting and easy-to-use form of subscription content.

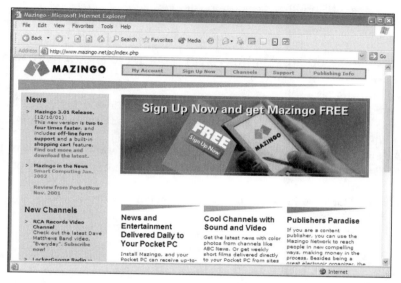

FIGURE 2.47

Mazingo is one of the best ways to distribute your content.

Mazingo offers Flash channels, which allow developers to have users subscribe to your Flash applications. This means that on every sync (or predetermined interval), the (updated) content will be transferred to the device.

Publishing a Flash movie as a Mazingo channel is easy, but it requires a special setup. For starters, the audience needs the following installed:

- Flash Player for Pocket PC
- Mazingo version 1.20 or later

Because Flash for the Pocket PC only plays inside HTML pages, you must transfer an HTML and SWF file by following these steps:

1. Build an HTML cover page (cover.htm).
2. Build an HTML container page with a .fhtm extension (container.fhtm).
3. Make the Flash SWF file (youradhere.swf).
4. Submit your site to Mazingo.

A basic cover page has a link to the container page, and whatever text and artwork you like. You should make it clear to the user that the Flash Player is required to view the animation, and tell your users how to get it.

The container page is loaded into the browser and plays the Flash file. Here's an example of how it would be coded. Notice the special tag near the end of the file, which is necessary so Mazingo can find the SWF and transfer it to the device:

```
<HTML>
<BODY bgcolor="#000000" TOPMARGIN=0 LEFTMARGIN=0 MARGINWIDTH=0
➥MARGINHEIGHT=0
STYLE="margin: 0px">
<OBJECT classid="clsid:D27CDB6E-AE6D-11cf-96B8-444553540000"
codebase="http://active.macromedia.com/flash2/cabs/swflash.cab#version=4,0,0,0"
ID=anystring WIDTH=240 HEIGHT=240>
<PARAM NAME=movie VALUE="youradhere.swf"> <PARAM NAME=quality VALUE=high>
<PARAM NAME=scale VALUE=exactfit> <PARAM NAME=bgcolor VALUE=#000000>
</OBJECT>
<this tag loads the Flash file in Mazingo: href="youradhere.swf">
</BODY>
</HTML>
```

When you submit your site, keep in mind the following fields:

- **Source Location.** Set this to the URL of the cover page.
- **Link Depth.** Set this to 2. One level for the container page, and one level for the animation itself.
- **Submission.** If you need to test your animation channel before submitting it live, email **support@mazingo.net**, and Mazingo will set up a temporary account for you where you can test the animation before submitting it.

Another similar way to distribute content is MyCasio (**www.mycasio.com**). MyCasio gives developers and content providers an easy way to distribute a variety of entertaining rich media content, as well as business and personal services for users (see Figure 2.48). With its unique "grab & go" system, the MyCasio service provides a one-stop-shop for mobile users to easily access and download business applications and information services and includes digital music, pictures, animation, video, and games. This service is a value-added service to owners of Casio Pocket PCs and Casio electronics.

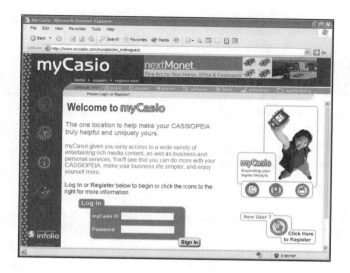

FIGURE 2.48

MyCasio! Another great place to distribute your content.

Creating MyCasio content is a straightforward process, but has some specific requirements. Be sure to check the MyCasio web site on a regular basis as some information may change.

The user will need:

- A Casio device that supports MyCasio
- The Flash Player for Pocket PC
- A MyCasio Account
- Access to the MyCasio content you create

As the content provider you will need to provide the following:

- A server with the proper mime types
- A page with a link to a .infc xml data file that is the location of the content
- Content

You'll also want to work with MyCasio to promote your MyCasio content.

The following is the process in which information from MyCasio content is transferred to a Casio device:

1. User clicks meta-file link (INFC) on content provider's site. The link is to an XML file with an .infc extension. That file contains the location of the files that will be downloaded to the Casio device.

2. The Browser downloads meta-file and launches "Click Agent" due to extension and/or mime type associations. See the mime type information in the next section to set up the mime type.

3. The Click Agent asks user for confirmation to add the content.

4. Click Agent reads contents of meta-file. (Click Agent does not verify contents of meta-file.)

5. Click Agent sends contents of meta-file to the Backpack. The Backpack is where users can store all their content entries.

6. The Backpack reads the XML data from the INFC file.

7. Backpack adds entries to the backpack on the device.

On the server side, proper mime type associations and extensions are required to deploy MyCasio content. A special INFC file is used to tell the MyCasio application on the desktop and device where the content is and then places it on the device. To properly support the new file type, the file must have the .infc extension and all web servers that will host these files must have the "application/infolio-cagent" mime type associated with the .infc extension. If the INFC file is being generated dynamically, then the server script should specify the mime-type in the response header.

- Type: application
- Sub-type: infolio-cagent
- Extension: .infc

The meta file (INFC) that you link to will use the following XML format:

- The root element will be "ITEMS". This element will contain one or more ITEM tags.
- The ITEM tag will designate a record.

The ITEM tag will have these required child tags:

- **TITLE.** The descriptive name of the media file.
- **URL.** The full URL to the media file.
- **CHANNEL.** Destination channel of the media file.
- **PARTNER.** Partner string of the owner of this media file (content partner, not user).

The ITEM tag may also have these optional child tags:

- **EXT.** Final extension of the media file.
- **MIMETYPE.** The final mime-type of the media file.
- **COST.** The monetary cost associated with the media file.
- **SIZE.** The expected size of the media file.
- **MD5.** The expected MD5 checksum of the media file.

 The four required tags are all that is currently implemented. The optional tags will be implemented in the future to support e-commerce and more robust download verification. Check with MyCasio for the latest information.

If a tag is present it must not be empty. (It must at least contain a space.)

Sample XML data (INFC) file:

```
<ITEMS>
  <ITEM>
    <TITLE>Your Ad Here</TITLE>
    <URL>http://www.contentpartner.com/mediafiles/youradhere.swf</URL>
    <CHANNEL>myapp</CHANNEL>
    <PARTNER>Flashenabled</PARTNER>
  </ITEM>
</ITEMS>
```

The following is the meta-file format detail that helps explain the sample XML file tags. Consult MyCasio.com for more information.

Tag name	Format	Required	Comment
ITEMS		Yes	Root tag (no data).
ITEM		Yes	Child of ITEMS. Specifies one file.
TITLE	Plain text field (max length 100)	Yes	Child of ITEMS. Specifies the descriptive title to use for the media.
URL	Encoded URL format (max length 255)	Yes	Child of ITEM. Specifies the URL to the media. The media file must include a valid extension.
CHANNEL	See table below	Yes	Child of ITEM. Destination channel for the media file
PARTNER	Plain text name (max length 20)	Yes	Child of ITEM. The string being used to identify the content partner. This can be any string. MyCasio admin screens will not consolidate records under multiple strings, so pick a string and stick to it!
EXT	Win32 extension	No	In a future release, the extension field can be used to specify the final extension when the URL is a reference to a CGI script.
MIMETYPE	Mime-type	No	In a future release, the mime-type can be used to specify the final mime-type when URL is a reference to a CGI script.
COST	0.00	No	In a future release, the cost field designates the cost associated with the download of this file.
SIZE	Number	No	In a future release, the file size can be provided. This may be useful to users with limited bandwidth.
MD5	MD5 format (max 30 chars)	No	In a future release, the MD5 can be provided to verify a successful download.

The following channels are currently supported, included are the descriptions. Be sure to visit MyCasio for more information:

mymusic   "my music" channel
myanim   "my animation" channel
myebook   "my ebook" channel
mymovie   "my movie" channel
mypic   "my pictures" channel
mygame   "my games" channel
myapp   "my applications" channel
myinfo   "my information" channel

The following is a sample HTML page with link to the INFC file sample as previously described:

```
<html>
<head>
<title>Flashenabled MyCasio Channel</title>
<meta http-equiv="Content-Type" content="text/html; charset=iso-8859-1">
</head>
<body bgcolor="#FFFFFF" text="#000000">
Welcome to the Flashenabled MyCasio Channel, <a href="fecasio.infc">click here</a> to
➥get the latest content from flashenabled.com to your Casio!
</body>
</html>
```

If all works well, the Flash movie will be rendered inside the Backpack application. If you're having trouble getting this to work, visit MyCasio.com or download the sample files.

On the Flashenabled.com/book site we included a MyCasio sample channel page. Be sure to check it out (and subscribe to it) if you have a Casio device and MyCasio account.

Using the Auto Run Feature to Install and Transfer Files on the Pocket PC

This final option is not for the weak of heart; in fact we're not totally sure this works all the time. Pocket PCs can Auto Run files and applications on CF cards inserted into the Pocket PC. Auto Run must be turned on by going to the Start menu, Settings, and clicking the System tab, and then the Auto Run icon. Note: Not all Pocket PCs will have the Auto Run functionality; consult the device documentation for more information.

Creating the Auto Run content is somewhat of a mystery that's not fully documented. That said, we're going to point you to the best places. For more information on Auto Run, search eVB (Embedded Visual Basic) with the "Using Auto Run on the Pocket PC" as the search term. Also, more information can be found about Auto Run by visiting **http://msdn.microsoft.com/library/default.asp?url=/library/en-us/wcesetup/htm/instapps_23.asp**.

On the Flashenabled.com/book site we've included an Auto Run sample that basically allows a developer to install the Flash Player for Pocket PC (CAB file installer), an HTML file, and SWF automatically from a CF card.

EMULATION OF THE POCKET PC FOR TESTING

All device kits usually have a device emulator as part of the development environment. An emulator is a good place to start testing, but it's never as accurate as the real device.

The Pocket PC emulator is part of the Microsoft eMbedded Visual Tools 3.0 that can be ordered or downloaded from **www.microsoft.com/mobile/downloads/emvt30.asp**.

Although the emulator doesn't currently play Flash movies, it can be used to view images and mock-ups of content for layout purposes.

For the emulator to play Flash content, Macromedia would need to create an x86 version of the Pocket PC Player for Pocket PC. If there is enough demand for this, Macromedia will most likely release a version for developers, email: mailto:wish-FlashPlayer-PocketPC@macromedia.com.

But don't worry, you're not out of luck. We've created a series of HTML files and images created to help "emulate" the PDA experience and included them on the Flashenabled.com/book site (see Figure 2.49).

FIGURE 2.49

Using a frame set to test Flash content if a Pocket PC is not available.

You can also use the "Remote Display Control Power Toy" for Pocket PC from Microsoft. The control can be downloaded from **www.microsoft.com/mobile/pocketpc/downloads/ powertoys.asp**.

This program allows you to display and control the screen of the Pocket PC device from a connected laptop or desktop computer. This control also allows you to test Flash Pocket PC content on your laptop or desktop computer. Simply connect the device to your computer and then run the control. You can now copy files directly to the Pocket PC and view the output on the control. This makes it relatively simple to test and develop content for the device.

TEST, TEST, TEST, AND TEST SOME MORE!

Test the application frequently on the actual device. We have said this many times throughout this book, but it's extremely important to properly test your applications. This advice may sound obvious, but this step is often overlooked. It is especially important when developing Flash content for Pocket PC. No matter how much device detection or proactive steps a developer takes, the final delivery remains the most important step in the development cycle.

Developers make the most impact and give the strongest message by delivering a well-designed user experience; remember the only thing more memorable than a good user experience is a bad one. If the application is slow, sluggish, or unviewable, the application becomes diluted.

ADVANCED TOPICS

In this section we're going to cover many things outside the Flash domain; some of this may be interesting, some of it may allow you to do other projects that you weren't able to before. Keep in mind that this section is not for the weak of heart, but that doesn't mean you can't dig in a bit to see what other tools and possibilities there are with Flash.

Embedded eVC and eVB, Gotta Get 'Em!

The Microsoft eMbedded Visual 3.0 delivers a complete desktop development environment for creating applications and system components for the Pocket PC (see Figure 2.50).

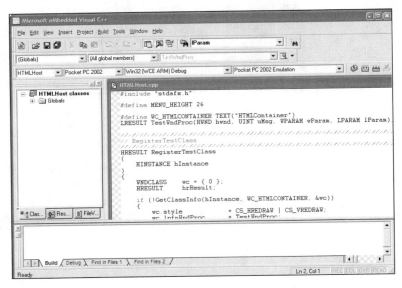

FIGURE 2.50

eVC++ is available free from Microsoft.

The eMbedded Visual includes eMbedded Visual Basic and eMbedded Visual C++, including SDKs for the Pocket PC. The eMbedded Visual Tools are the successor to the separate Windows CE Toolkits for VC++ and VB. This version is standalone and does not require Visual Studio.

In many of the subjects we're going to cover in the Advanced Topics section we'll refer to eVC and eVB. Also, much of the sample code is also in eVC.

Microsoft eMbedded Visual Tools 3.0 can be ordered or downloaded at **www.microsoft.com/mobile/downloads/emvt30.asp**.

Changing Registry Settings on the Pocket PC

There are some times when you may want to turn ClearType on the Pocket PC on all applications, or make the scroll bars smaller so your Flash application gets more real estate. Usually, that requires a complicated Registry modification that can completely screw up a device. The Registry refers to a database of system settings used by all versions of the Windows operating system to store settings. Luckily, there's a comprehensive application called RegKing that helps automate the process. To download RegKing, visit: **www.doctorce.com/regking.htm** (the same folks who make Pocket Mac!).

RegKing can make the following modifications to the Pocket PC Registry; many of them are very useful for creating your Flash and surrounding content:

- Makes Pocket IE pretend to be IE 5.5—This allows users to access secure web sites such as banks or brokerage houses. Right now most sites just check the browser's version and if it is less than 4.02, they do not allow you access. Pocket IE by default reports IE 3.02 so you won't get access.
- Enable ClearType in all HTML Applications including AvantGo.
- Change AvantGo Channels to \Storage Card\AvantGo (must create directory, copy files and resync).
- Set Glyph Cache to 16384—Makes graphics render faster.
- Set Glyph Cache to 26384—Makes graphics render faster.
- Set TCPWindowSize to 65535—Increases the buffer size for TCP/IP.
- Turn off ActiveX Controls in IE— Disables Flash if you have it installed.
- Turn off Scripting in IE.
- Show JavaScript errors in Pocket Internet Explorer—Handy for web developers.
- Increase font to 17 points—Requires Soft Reset.
- Increase font to 16 points—Requires Soft Reset.
- Increase font to 15 points—Requires Soft Reset.
- Decrease font to 14 points—Requires Soft Reset.
- Decrease font to 13 points—Requires Soft Reset.
- Decrease font to 12 points—Requires Soft Reset.
- Decrease font to 11 points—Requires Soft Reset.
- Make the system display font bold—Requires Soft Reset.
- Make the system display font italic—Requires Soft Reset.
- Change font to Frutiger Linotype. The same font as Reader uses—Requires Soft Reset.
- Turn on Battery Warning message when you insert a PC Card or CompactFlash Card—Requires Soft Reset.
- Turn on Windows Animation—Requires Soft Reset.
- Turn Menu Animation off.

- Wakeup Power-Off Timeout.
- Set Letter Recognizer as default.
- Set Block Recognizer as default
- Enable ClearType in all applications.
- Increase Fonts in Inbox.
- Widen the scroll bars.
- Narrow the scroll bars.

You can also view the specific Registry settings at: **www.phm.lu/PocketPC/RegTweaks/**.

Terminal Services

There are some instances in which your application cannot run on a Pocket PC, such as an existing Macromedia Director application. Use the Terminal Services Client to connect to Windows 2000 and Windows XP server products to open up a "window" directly to your server. By simply resizing your application on the server, users can access the content that was created for a desktop system on the Pocket PC (see Figure 2.51). This is useful for managing a server.

All the data storage and processing occurs directly on the server, while you run applications or remotely manage your server from the Pocket PC.

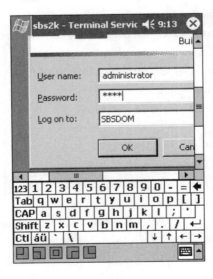

FIGURE 2.51

Terminal services for the Pocket PC 2002 operating system.

Playing Flash Full Screen on the Pocket PC

As long as there have been Flash Players for the Pocket PC, one of the most asked requests is "Can I play Flash full screen?" The following is every way to get more pixels for your Flash applications for Pocket PC.

The first utility is Multi-IE. Multi-IE's most useful feature to Flash applications on the Pocket PC is that Multi-IE can get rid of the top and bottom menu bars and run Pocket IE in full screen mode.

Other features include

- Open the current page in a new window.
- Use the Menu Activation feature to open a link in a new window.
- See a list of all open windows by web page title and switch between them.
- Close the current window, leaving all others open.
- Save HTTP/ HTTPS/FILE web pages as text, html only, html complete. (This saves inline images and frames in same format as used on desktop.)
  Note: AvantGo files can be saved as text only.
- View page in full screen mode, hiding top and bottom menus to use more of the precious screen real estate while surfing.
- Supports all versions of Blue Kite web compression software. The Blue Kite icon is now visible on all open windows.
- Map Multi-IE to a hardware button for quicker access to Menu Activation, or the Windows List menu.
- When browsing with pictures disabled, use the Menu Activation feature to display an individual picture.
- Multi-IE integrates in to the Pocket Internet Explorer toolbar, and is easy use.
- Small size, only takes around 40k of memory.

It should be noted that Multi-IE is an advanced application for power users and should not be considered a method to ensure full screen Flash playback on the Pocket PC.

For more information on Multi-IE visit: **www.zip.com.au/~peterept/**.

FlashAssist from Ant Mobile software (**www.armentaonline.com/antmobile/**) lets you open Flash content on your Pocket PC in three different window sizes (see Figure 2.52):

- 240×268: Standard window with menu bar
- 240×294: Extended window, no menu bar
- 240×320: Full screen

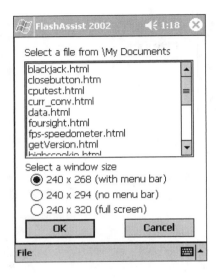

FIGURE 2.52

FlashAssist for the Pocket PC.

FlashAssist completely eliminates scroll bars—you do not need to Fit to Screen to view Flash content clearly.

Also available, FlashAssist PRO. FlashAssist PRO allows you to create fully installable and executable Pocket PC applications from your Pocket PC Flash content. Here are just a few of the features of FlashAssist PRO:

- Flash content runs as its own application, with its own icon and window title.
- Choose from three different window sizes, including full screen mode.
- User can still switch between full screen FlashAssist PRO applications and other apps.
- FlashAssist PRO apps check for presence of Flash Player and notify user if not installed.
- Complete template provided for creating PC desktop installer for your application.
- JScript HTML template provided that checks for correct operation of your Flash movie.

Pocket PC 2002 SDK samples SDK files from Microsoft and Flashenabled that have been modified to play Flash files full screen on the Pocket PC 2002.

The full screen Flash Player and source files are meant to get you started running Flash full screen.

The files use the HTML host control to create an HTML window inside an application. The full screen player plays any file called test.html in the My Documents folder. You exit the application by clicking the white bar at the bottom of the screen.

To download the source files for the Pocket PC 2002 full screen Flash Player, visit the Flashenabled.com/book web site. You will need to have eVC installed before opening the files.

Microsoft eMbedded Visual Tools 3.0 can be ordered or downloaded at www.microsoft.com/mobile/downloads/emvt30.asp.

SysInfo allows the developer to pass in environmental information such as power, battery, memory, disk spaces, volume, processor, and date information to an HTML page or Flash movie. This works with all ARM based Pocket PCs.

After downloading the Trumpet files from the Flashenabled.com/book site, place the regsvrce.exe file in the Windows directory on the Pocket PC. The regsvrce.exe file is located in the trumpet_sdk\regsvrce folder.

Then place the sysinfo.dll file in the windows directory on the Pocket PC. The sysinfo.dll file is located in the trumpet_sdk\arm_sysinfo_dll folder.

Register the sysinfo.dll file by clicking the regsvrce.exe file in the Windows directory of the Pocket PC, type in the name of the dll, sysinfo.dll, and register the .dll (see Figure 2.53).

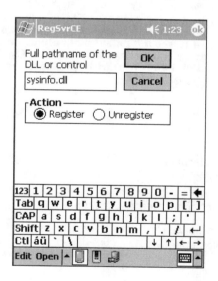

FIGURE 2.53

Using regsvrce.exe to register a .dll on the Pocket PC

Place the folder arm_sys_info_flash in the "My Documents" folder on the device, run the sys.html file to confirm the dll is functioning properly. The Flash movie should show system information (see Figure 2.54). On the desktop and / or the Flash file, view the HTML source and the Flash variable to view how the information is being passed in. It's using a combination of JavaScript and ActiveX controls interacting with Flash.

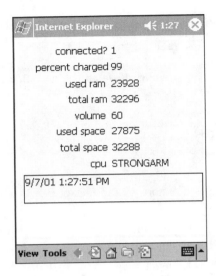

FIGURE 2.54

Getting the system information from the Pocket PC using Flash and sysinfo.dll.

 As with all the data variables (some are not needed for production work) you may experience a 10-second delay; by limiting the amount of data to battery and power the delay is lessened. You may need to tap the Flash movie to gain focus and for the variables to start to populate the Flash movie.

Animated Today

Stephen Eddy of **www.gigabytesol.com/** and I (Phillip Torrone, Flashenabled) are thrilled to bring you Animated Today (see Figure 2.55). What is Animated Today? It allows users to play Flash content on their Today screens. As a developer, you can create and sell content packs and provide useful utilities and net-connected applications.

The Animated Today screens consist of three parts: the .at configuration file, a today screen TSK (theme), and a SWF (Flash file).

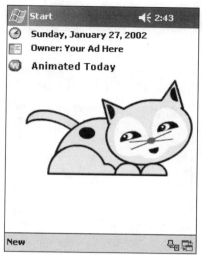

FIGURE 2.55

Animated Today screen of a cat from designer Christian Erickson.

The following is the configuration file. As you can see, it has all the parameters normally associated with an HTML page for Flash for the Pocket PC, with some new parameters such as today skin, scheme name, and description.

// Animated Today skin configuration file

```
[Config]
classid=D27CDB6E-AE6D-11cf-96B8-444553540000
size=120
id=pocketpc
position=top
todayskin=Fire
schemename=Cat Nap
schemedesc=Sleeping Cat
backcolor=#FFFFFF

[Parameters]
movie=cat.swf
quality=high
bgcolor=#FFFFFF
```

After you create the configuration file (cat.at), the Today Theme (TSK), and Flash movie (SWF), transfer them to the device. Using the user interface, select the Animated Today Scheme (see Figure 2.56).

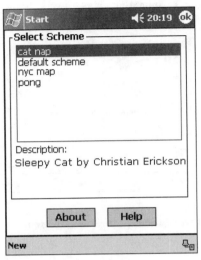

FIGURE 2.56

Select a theme for Animated Today.

For more information and to purchase Animated Today, visit **www.gigabytesol.com/**.

For content packs, visit **www.flashenabled.com/mobile**.

SUMMARY...THAT'S ALL, FOLKS!

I hope this chapter has been useful and beneficial as well as fun. Remember, more failures mean more successes; most of what you've read is a result of many people not being scared to break some eggs to make omelets. Be sure to check Flashenabled.com/book and Flashenabled.com/mobile to see the latest experiments, tips, and, well, broken eggs. Cheers.

3

INTERFACE DESIGN FOR DEVICES

by Branden J. Hall, Fig Leaf Software

It would be an understatement to say that designing good user interfaces is tough. It is, in fact, so difficult that there are numerous Ph.D. dissertations written every year on the subject. However, to summarize all the difficulties with good interface design, you could simply say that people are a problem.

Our attention span is short, our eyesight is in various stages of deterioration, and our hand-eye coordination varies greatly, just to name a few of our maladies. Toss into the mix that we are sometimes plain and simply dense, and you can see the formidable challenge posed to any interface designer.

In this chapter, you are going to learn about common interface issues, certain considerations you need to keep in mind when developing for devices, how to use some specially built interface components for devices, and how to optimize the code that makes up your user interfaces. This chapter won't make you an interface design guru, but it will help prevent you from making some of the most common interface mistakes, as well as give you some tools to help you create good user interfaces for devices.

COMMON INTERFACE ISSUES

Designing an effective interface goes way beyond functionality. You have to be able to meet the needs and expectations of a wide range of users—and you have to do it while juggling the limitations of the device for which you're designing. Some of the common interface issues you'll be facing as you design for devices include these:

- Designing for both haves and have nots
- Providing what users expect to find
- Figuring out how to help humans use what they already know
- Developing desktop functionality for device applications

Most computer-literate folks have, on their PCs, the icons reduced to next to nothing and the resolutions cranked up. Most people who are not computer-savvy have their desktop PCs set to whatever resolution, icon size, and color depth with which the computer came installed. Hence, the still lingering nastiness that is the web 216-color palette (which I hope we can soon regard as quaint, much in the same way that we regard 2400-baud modems these days).

An additional issue is that we interface designers are digitally "tuned-in," sometimes to our own detriment. A good example of this is the current trend of design-oriented web sites to use smaller fonts. Sure, it looks cool, but it is often just plain unreadable. Sometimes, the text written in that small size doesn't mean anything—it's just there for design purposes. However, even then, the small size is detrimental because it's nearly impossible for a literate human being to look at text in this language and not try to read it.

This brings us to a very important point that interface designers can utilize; human beings are, for all intents and purposes, pattern-matching machines. We can pick out a single conversation from a crowded room and know instantly the face of friend we last saw 20 years ago. Our brains are wired to match patterns, so let's use that to our advantage.

A good example of this is what happened when I first started to use my Pocket PC. The interface looked and usually acted like the Windows I was used to, and because of this, I could quickly jump in and start working with it. However, years of working with Windows taught me certain patterns that at the time simply didn't exist in the Pocket PC world—namely closing applications. I must have spent 30 minutes, on and off, looking for the little X to close Pocket Word when I was done writing. I knew and realized that the paradigm of using a Pocket PC was much different from a desktop one, but the continuation of my use patterns between the devices led me to look for a Close button when it just wasn't there.

Patterns are powerful things, and often, even though there might be a more efficient and usable way of creating an interface, it's best to stick with what people know. Yes, a Dvorak keyboard is better than a QWERTY one, but I sure can't come close to the 70wpm I'm currently typing on a Dvorak. You'll notice that this is the reason that the interface widgets that I talk about (and provide later in this chapter) aren't all that different from their desktop counterparts. It is important to know, though, that they are different so that they can deal with the restrictions of devices. Just plopping a regular desktop widget on a device will rarely work well; you almost always need to make some sort of modification.

Typing Made Tedious, or Why QWERTY Stinks

You might be wondering why our QWERTY keyboard is bad. It was actually designed specifically to slow us down! Early typewriters, being mechanical in nature, jammed easily when a typist got up to a decent rate. To avoid this jam-up, the standard keyboard was invented to keep commonly associated letters as far away from each other as needed to prevent the typewriter from jamming. Later, the Dvorak keyboard was invented to be much easier on our poor digits by placing commonly associated letters near each other. Alas, Dvorak has never really caught on, and unless you want to take the time to both find a Dvorak keyboard and learn how to use it, you are stuck typing with the parking brake on. It's also interesting to note that various other keyboard layouts have been designed especially for one finger or stylus-based typing. The best known of these, the Fitaly keyboard (www.fitaly.com) actually claims to enable users to type up to 80WPM using a single digit! The layout is based on both letter frequency in the English language and mnemonics. (The keyboard spells out various words, and by looking for words, it's easy to find letters.)

Many, if not all, of the modifications that were made to the widgets were in the name of simplicity. Even if we weren't talking about devices, simplicity would be the name of the game. However, simplicity is more important than ever when you are developing for devices (if for no other reason than that people use devices much differently from PCs). Devices need to be quick and simple to use or people won't use them. A good example of simplicity in interface design is the venerable Palm Pilot. It took Windows CE devices nearly three generations to begin to become even close to being as accepted as Palm-based devices. Anyone who has owned or used a Palm Pilot knows how simple the devices are to use. There is simply little to no learning curve. The fact of the matter is, if technology is going to try to replace a pen- and paper-based solution, it has to be just as easy, if not easier, to use than pen and paper.

A lot of what has been mentioned so far might have seemed like common sense to you. In fact, that's the point; a good deal of interface design is separating the "cool" from the "makes sense." Here's where a very important problem arises, though. As the person who has designed an interface, you know the program inside out and backward. It will nearly always seem usable to you! However, what you need to do is test your usability on a group of impartial, representative users as early as possible in your application development process. If your application will be used mostly by, say, middle-age housewives, have a group of them test the application rather than a group of hardcore UNIX sys-admins.

When you are doing your testing, watch your users closely. If they get hung up on a particular element, ask them what they were expecting and why. (You'll almost always get a good answer for the "what" part, but don't expect to get too much for the "why" part.) Look for patterns in your users—where they get hung up, where they whiz through, and where they just seem confused. More than likely, you will be able to extrapolate from the results of such testing what needs to be done to your application.

SPECIAL CONSIDERATIONS FOR DEVICES

Interface design for devices is very much a world unto its own. You'll probably glean at least a couple of important rules from both this chapter and from your own common sense; keep it small (but not too small!), and keep it simple.

Although keeping your applications small and simple are valuable core ideas, implementing these rules can be far from easy. Different devices bring different challenges. For example, if you've ever worked on, say, a kiosk, you are well aware of the first big challenge our design group ran into: rollovers, or lack thereof.

Making Buttons Stand Out

Because devices rarely deal with mouse-based input, no actual cursor exists. In fact, the position of the user's "pointing device" isn't known until he actually taps on the screen. This obviously disallows the use of any kind of rollover or rollout effect. Given how simple such effects are to create in Flash, it might take you some time to get used to being without them. Just remember to keep that OVER state of your buttons the same as your UP state.

Besides the obvious cosmetic pleasantries that rollovers provide, they also serve the important role of letting the user know what he can click on. This means that you need to be sure that the user can tell what is "clickable" on devices. Beveled edges and other 3D effects might be tempting, but remember that you only have a limited amount of real estate. Why use those valuable pixels on the interface when you don't have to? Take a cue from the device's OS makers: Some of the best interfaces for devices—Palm OS and Windows CE—are flat in nature. They use shapes, small icons, and certain consistent rules to cue the user to what is a button and what's not.

Surrounding text with a simple border or making it bold works well for denoting something as a button. By making something stand out, you are cueing the user into the fact that it's not just something to read.

Icons work similarly well, as long as they are good icons. Good icons denote an idea or action clearly and with little to no room for confusion. An envelope icon for email and a Clipboard for tasks are both examples of good icons. Good icons don't need text labels, so if you find that you really need some kind of textual label, consider revising your icon.

One of the most important but overlooked ways to denote something as a button is to be consistent in your buttons. Show all buttons in your application the same way, and if possible, show them in the same area of the screen. This way, after the user understands the basic rules for what is a button, he can make intelligent guesses in later parts of your application.

Limited Device Functionality

Besides buttons, another problem when designing interfaces for devices is working with the fact that the user's input has been mostly stripped down to two functions: tapping and dragging.

Tapping by nature isn't extremely precise. With a mouse, you can "aim" with the cursor before clicking. With a stylus-based interface, you either get it right, or you don't. Therefore, you should be sure that all your interface components are large enough for the user to make small mistakes but still hit the target using either the stylus or his fingers. What if the user still manages to miss? If your interface is designed in an intelligent manner, this shouldn't be a problem. Your buttons and other components should be spaced far enough apart that it would be difficult for a user to both miss his target and hit something else.

Zombie Buttons

The fact that you don't have an actual cursor on devices causes one particular bug that you might run into: zombie buttons. That is, if you press on a button and then drag the stylus and lift off the screen while not on the button, it will stay stuck in its **DOWN** state. However, the button will properly fire any on(releaseOutside) statements that are attached to it.

The easiest way to deal with this issue is to make all your buttons invisible and then have movie clips represent the actual graphics of the button. These movie clips can have two frames: one for the **UP** and one for the **DOWN** state. The invisible button can simply tell the movie clip which frame to show.

Dragging can also be a problem for users. Problems mainly arise when you don't let users know they are dragging something. The simple remedy for this is to be sure that all your buttons have a **DOWN** state. Also, if the range of the dragging is limited, you should visually show the user what that range is. These "gutters" help the user get a sense of proportion, which is quite important when manipulating slider-type controls.

 Although not specific to devices, an additional rule you should stick to is keeping the poison away from the milk. That is, keep components that perform destructive actions as far away as possible from your other components. If you design your interface with this in mind, then a user who manages to miss his target and hit something else won't do damage. A good example of poor design in this manner is the Windows icon strip at the top of all applications—Minimize, Restore, and Close. It is easy for a beginning user to accidentally click the Close icon when he just meant to minimize the window.

The Challenge of Typing

Unless a device comes with a keyboard of some sort, typing is far from easy for users. If at all possible, it's best to avoid having users type. If you can't avoid the need for typing, however, you have two options:

- **Let the OS handle it.** Pocket PC devices have built-in software keyboards, but they always appear at the bottom of your screen; therefore, these keyboards could easily block the text field in which the user is typing. If you plan to use the built-in keyboard, be sure that you keep your text fields at the top of the screen and be sure that the keyboard won't block anything the user needs while he types.

- **Make a keyboard in Flash.** If you provide the only method for input in a text field, you can do all sorts of things, such as limiting the user to certain characters or making the keyboard dragable. This option is more flexible than using the OS keyboard, but at the cost of development time and file size. If you do decide to use a custom keyboard, it's often a good idea to "pop up" the keyboard automatically for users. You can do this by attaching the following code to a movie clip in your movie. The code determines (when the mouse is released) what, if any, text field has been selected and then runs the code of your choice.

```
onClipEvent(mouseUp){
    var selected = Selection.getFocus();
    if ((selected != null)){
        // insert code to display keyboard here
    }
}
```

Small Display Area

A major issue that every person who is developing for devices runs into is the extremely small screen real estate. There is only so much you can pack onto a screen at once. In fact, it's best to try to keep as little as possible on the screen at one time. Don't try to pack information onto the screen like you would in a desktop application. Instead, base your system around screens of information. For a good example of this type of design, look at the Windows Media Player for the Pocket PC. Most of what you need to do with it is on the main screen—play, pause, fast-forward, and so on. All the additional functionality, such as playlists and track info, has its own separate screen. This keeps the information accessible, yet the interface remains uncluttered and readable.

With such little space in which to work, it's tempting to scale down fonts to tiny when developing for devices. This can be a real problem with Flash though, due to its built-in anti-aliasing. If you look at text in Flash, it's often fuzzy, which makes small text nearly impossible to read. There are numerous ways around this problem though, from making your movie run in LOW mode to using pixel fonts, such as those available from **http://miniml.com/**.

For more information about using text with Flash on devices, make sure to check out Chapter 4, "Typography in Flash for Devices."

CREATING STANDARD COMPONENTS FOR DEVICES

No matter what you are creating for devices, at some point, you will need a "standard" component of some sort. Whether you need a radio button, checkbox, slider, or drop-down menu, creating and perfecting the infernal little thing will take up too much of your time. Any time you have to reinvent the wheel, it's a painful experience; thankfully, you don't have to do it now. On the web site for this book, (**www.flashenabled.com**) is a full set of components that are made just for devices. Download them now and then come back and learn all about how to use them!

Understanding Smart Clips

All the other components you'll create for devices are Flash 5 smart clips. If you are unfamiliar with smart clips, the idea behind them is actually quite simple. *Smart clips* are just normal movie clips that have a visual interface for setting variables that live within them. Although they are simple, they provide an extremely easy mechanism for configuring reusable components.

Smart clips do have drawbacks, though. Specifically, methods that are defined within a smart clip are not immediately available in their parent's timeline. This is because a smart clip's code runs after that of its parent timeline. As long as you keep this limitation in mind and don't try to access methods within a smart clip immediately, you shouldn't have trouble.

For more information on creating and working with smart clips, check out the Flash Exchange at **www.macromedia.com/exchange/flash/**.

Checkboxes

The checkbox control provides a simple method for allowing users to select Boolean values (see Figure 3.1). It's easy for both users and developers.

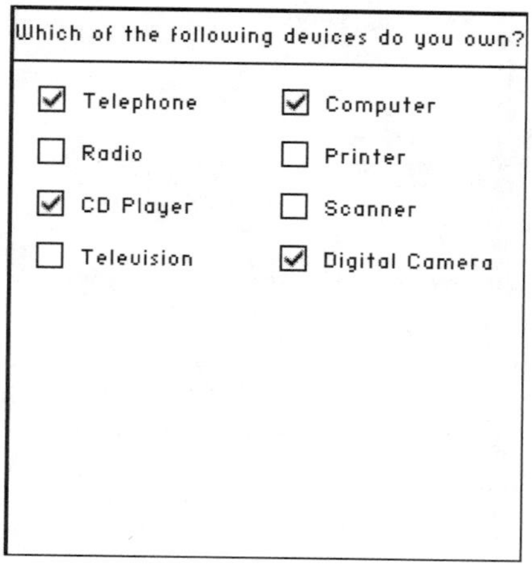

FIGURE 3.1

A simple checkbox control in action.

All you need to do to use the checkbox control is place an instance of the DeviceCheckBox movie clip on the stage and then bring up the Clip Parameters panel. Here you see that the checkbox has three parameters: **varName**, **initialState**, and **enabled**. The first parameter, **varName**, is the name of the variable that this checkbox sets. This variable lives in the same timeline that houses the checkbox component. The second parameter, as it suggests, sets the initial state of the checkbox—on or off. The final parameter, **enabled**, allows you to decide if the component should be immediately usable or if it will have to be enabled in some way before the user can modify it.

After you have set these parameters, you're done! There's nothing else you have to do to use the checkbox. However, there are a few additional methods and callbacks that the component supports (see Figure 3.2).

First, there's the **setVar** method. This method supports a single parameter, a string. When you call this method, you are changing what variable is tied to the checkbox.

Next, there's the **setState** method, which gets passed a single parameter, a Boolean value (true or false). This method allows you to change the state of the checkbox at any time without requiring the user to intervene.

Finally, there are the enable and disable methods. These methods do exactly what you might think they do: They enable and disable the checkbox.

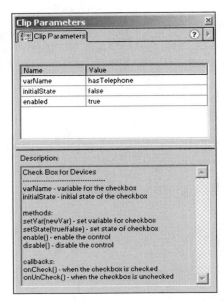

FIGURE 3.2

The Clip Parameters panel for the checkbox smart clip.

Along with these methods, I mentioned that the checkbox also has a couple of callbacks. Callbacks are methods that you can overwrite to allow you to easily capture the point at which a particular event occurs. In the case of the checkbox, there's a callback for **onChecked** and another for **onUnchecked**.

To see how these work, let's look at an example. Let's say that you already have a checkbox on your stage and it has an instance name of checkbox01. Let's also say that when this checkbox is checked, you want a movie clip named ball to appear; when it's unchecked, you want the movie clip to disappear. To do this, you would have the following code on your main timeline:

```
checkbox01.onChecked = function(){
    _parent.ball._visible = true;
}
checkbox01.onUnChecked = function(){
    _parent.ball._visible = false;
}
```

What's happening here is that you are overriding the **onChecked** and **onUnChecked** methods of your checkbox movie clip. That is, the checkbox assumes those methods are in place and calls them automatically. By redefining them with your own code, you are making Flash run your custom code each time it calls those methods.

Radio Buttons

Radio buttons allow users to choose a single option but still see all the options available to them (see Figure 3.3). Actually, calling it the radio button component is a bit of a misnomer. This is because the actual component is the radio button group because there's not a whole lot you can do with a single radio button!

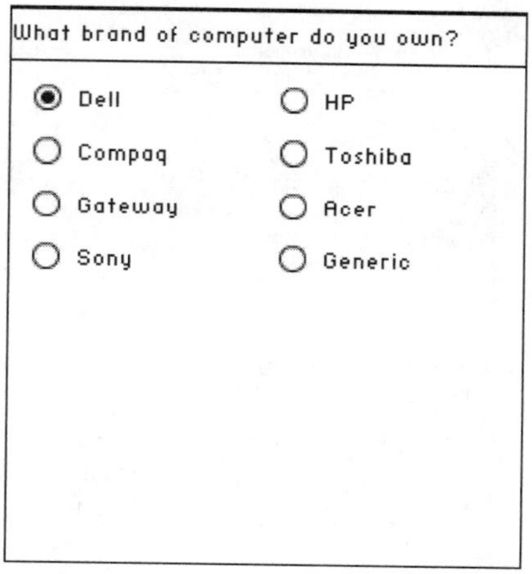

What brand of computer do you own?

- ● Dell   ○ HP
- ○ Compaq   ○ Toshiba
- ○ Gateway   ○ Acer
- ○ Sony   ○ Generic

FIGURE 3.3

A group of radio buttons in action.

However, if the component were to be the radio button group, then you would have to define the layout of the individual buttons within the Clip Parameters panel—not exactly WYSIWYG. Because the component is actually just a piece of a component, there are a few strange things you will need to get used to when using the radio button.

Each radio button instance that you drag to the stage (the DeviceRadioButton movie clip) has a number of properties that you need to set in the Clip Parameters panel (see Figure 3.4). These parameters are **groupName**, **value**, **initialState**, and **enabled**.

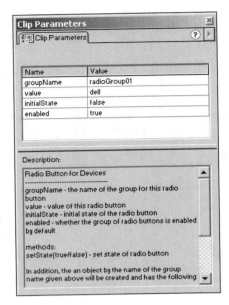

FIGURE 3.4

The Clip Parameters panel for the radio button smart clip.

The **groupName** parameter sets the name of the group to which this radio button belongs. It is actually the name of an object that will be created in the timeline to handle the group as a whole, but we'll get into that later.

The **value** parameter is the value of that particular radio button. The actual type of this value will always be a string, so if you set this to be a number, be sure that the function that will be reading the values changes the type appropriately.

The **initialState** parameter determines if the radio button will be on or off by default. Keep in mind that if you have multiple radio buttons, their **initialState** should be set to true. Only the last one will actually stay true because radio button groups can only have one radio button on at a time.

Finally, the **enabled** parameter sets whether the group to which this radio button belongs is enabled by default. Notice that we are talking about the whole group and not an individual button; therefore, like the **initialState** parameter, it's only the last button in the group that can actually change this parameter.

Radio buttons also support a single method: **setState**. You pass **setState** a single Boolean parameter, which represents the state to which you want to change the radio button.

As you learned earlier, the radio button component creates a radio button group object for working with the group as a whole. However, again due to some shortcomings with the smart clip architecture, you need to create the group yourself if you want to be able to use it immediately.

For example, if you had a group of radio buttons on the main timeline with their group all set to **myGroup**, you would probably want to have the following code in your main timeline:

myGroup = new Object();

After that line, you can use some of the special functionality of the radio button group object.

The radio button group object is where you can enable or disable the group, where the current value of the group lives, and where a special callback lives that lets you capture when a radio button is selected.

Just like the checkbox component, the radio button group supports both enable and disable methods. The most interesting parts of the radio button group are its value property and its **onRadio** callback. The value property of a radio button group always contains the current value of the group. (Remember: The value of the group depends on the values you set for each radio button.) The **onRadio** callback is called any time a radio button in the group is selected. It is passed the value of the button that is selected.

For example, if you just wanted to trace out the value of the **myGroup** radio button group, you would have the following code in your main timeline:

```
myGroup = new Object();
myGroup.onRadio = function(value){
    trace("Radio button group value: "+value);
}
```

If you ever want to disable the entire radio button group, you can simply use this:

MyGroup.disable();

You might want to do this if the availability of a radio button group is dependent on some external variable. For example, if the user has the sound turned off in an application, he can't choose the default sound for the application.

Sliders

The slider control provides a simple method for allowing users to choose from a range of values. It allows users to drag the slider around or simply click on the location where they want it to be (see Figure 3.5).

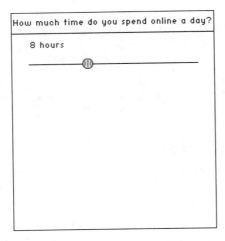

FIGURE 3.5

A slider component in action.

Like the other two previously discussed controls, the slider control is a smart clip and is named DeviceSlider (see Figure 3.6). After you have dragged an instance of it onto the stage, there are a number of parameters you can set for it in the Clip Parameters panel, such as **min**, **max**, **default**, **integersOnly**, and **enabled**.

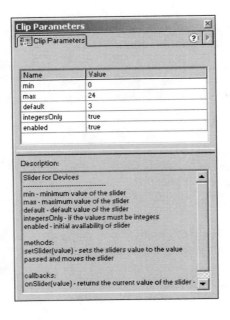

FIGURE 3.6

The Clip Parameters panel of the slider smart clip.

The **min** parameter sets the minimum value that the slider can report. Note that this is inclusive; therefore, if you set this to 0, at its lowest point, the slider produces 0 as its value.

The **max** parameter, as you might have guessed, sets the maximum value that the slider can report. Like the **min** parameter, the **max** parameter is inclusive in nature.

The **default** parameter is the value that the slider will display when it is first shown. The slider will fire off a call to its **onSlide** callback when it sets this initial value.

Finally, the **enabled** parameter works just like the enabled parameter in the other components and allows you to specify whether the slider is initially enabled.

Besides these parameters, the slider supports three functions—**enable**, **disable**, and **setSlider**— as well as a callback, **onSlide**. The **enable** and **disable** functions work just like they do in the other components. They allow you to disable and enable the component any time you want.

The **setSlider** method allows you to set the value of the slider at any time. Note that the value that you pass to **setSlider** must be within the **min** and **max** range you set for the component.

Lastly, **onSlide** is called any time the slider is moved either by dragging it or by clicking on the slider's gutter. The **onSlide** method is passed the new value of the slider. In addition, the current value of the slider is always stored in the value property of the component.

If you want to simply capture the current value of a slider component named **mySlider** and trace it, you would code the following:

```
mySlider.onSlide = function(value){
    trace("slider value: "+value);
}
```

OPTIMIZING INTERFACES

It is a well-known "law" of programming that when you run a program, it will spend 90% of its time in 10% of the code. Determining what that 10% is is literally half the battle of optimization. After you've optimized that 10%, there's little more optimization that needs to be done because mathematically, the rest of the code is just noise.

How does this apply to interfaces? Well, it just so happens that interfaces have a nasty habit of living in that 10% of your code that runs the most. Your interface is always around; therefore, it often has code running to handle it. The last thing you want to do is to waste valuable cycles on your interface on a low-powered device! With that in mind, let's take a look at various ways of tracking down the most wasteful parts of your code and optimizing them.

Non-Coding Issues That Are Related to Optimization

Most of the non-coding issues with developing Flash interfaces for devices (or any platform for that matter) come down to being careful with bitmaps, gradients, excessive vectors, and alpha. By themselves, all four of these can grind a processor into the dirt.

Drawing bitmaps hurts devices in two ways. First, they tend to be large, which is obviously an issue on devices where space is at a premium. Second, blitting bitmaps to the screen takes up a relatively large amount of processor power. This is made even worse if you animate bitmaps. That's not to say that you shouldn't use bitmaps—just use them in moderation.

That's not to say that vectors can't hog the CPU as well. Remember: Vectors are just rules that describe how to draw an image, so if there are a lot of vectors, the processor has to do a lot of work to draw them. In fact, very complex vector images are just as bad—if not worse—than bitmaps. The secret is to find the sweet spot for your particular image. If your image is relatively simple in nature, a vector will probably work best. If your image is complex and detailed, a bitmap will be a better choice. When in doubt, test both options.

Gradients are similarly CPU intensive. This is particularly true if you use gradients that have transparent colors in them. When optimizing a movie for devices, gradients should be one of the first things to go.

If you saw the earlier paragraph on bitmaps and thought that you might be able to use "trace bitmap" to get rid of your bitmaps in a processor-friendly way, you are mistaken. That process produces hundreds—if not thousands—of vector shapes, something that can easily bring a device's processor to a grinding halt. Simplify your vector shapes whenever possible using the Modify, Optimize panel.

If a particular shape or symbol in your movie is using alpha transparencies, then the CPU has to render both behind that object and behind the actual object. Essentially, it's more than twice the work. If you don't have to use alpha, then don't. When possible, consider modifying a symbol's brightness or tint instead of its alpha.

Besides optimizing in this manner, you might also want to look into the possibility of rendering your movie in low quality. When you do this, you are skimping the anti-aliasing engine that's built into Flash and saving quite a bit of CPU power. If that's not possible, try the medium setting. That setting does half of the anti-aliasing and can speed things up a bit.

Code-Based Optimizations

Keep in mind that it is often said that premature optimization is the root of all evil, and I tend to agree. Before you go gung-ho with these optimizations, be sure that your *idea* is optimized. Changing how you think about a problem can easily outstrip any optimizations you can do by tweaking a bad idea.

With that in mind, we are going to cover three optimizations: variable and object optimization, loop optimization, and memory optimization.

Optimizing Variables and Objects

Optimizing variables and objects is actually pretty straightforward. The rule of thumb is to keep it simple. For example, if a variable doesn't need to be a floating point, chop it down to an integer before you do math on it as in this example:

```
foo = x/y;
// if foo doesn't have to be a floating point number, just force it an integer
foo = int(foo);
// you could also use Math.floor or Math.ceil
```

Don't do string operations if you don't have to. The string operations in Flash 5 are actually written in unoptimized ActionScript and can bog down quickly. If you have to use string operations, get the string object rewrite from **http://chattyfig.figleaf.com/**.

You should also try to avoid the XML object, which is naturally pretty slow in parsing. If you have to use the XML object, be sure to also use the XMLNitro package from **http://chattyfig.figleaf.com/**.

One of the biggest optimizations you can do with loops is to use shortcut variables. That is, if you have objects that you need to reference often, like this:

root["item"+I].header["icon"+j]

then create a shortcut to that variable:

var temp = _root["item"+i].header["icon"+j]

Loop Optimizations

All of those array operators and such are CPU intensive, particularly if you are doing it multiple times within a loop. By creating a shortcut, you are only doing that once within your loop.

This also applies to working with the length property of strings and arrays. The following code

```
for (var i=0; i<str.length;++i){
...
...
}
```

is going to be significantly slower than this code:

```
var max = str.length;
for (var i=0; i<max; ++i){
    ...
    ...
}
```

This fact is particularly true if the length of the string or array is large. This occurs because the act of calculating the length of something takes CPU cycles, and by having that calculation in the comparison part of the **for** loop, you are forcing it to be rerun each iteration. By precalculating the length of the string, you are letting Flash do a simple variable lookup rather than a measurement calculation, which quickly adds up to a lot of savings.

Memory Optimizations

Memory optimizations are particularly important on devices due to their limited RAM sizes. When at all possible in your Flash movies, clean up after yourself. That is, remove movie clips that aren't needed, unload SWFs that you aren't using, and use the **delete** operator to remove objects that you are no longer using.

Keep in mind that the **delete** operator does not immediately delete an object; instead, it removes that particular reference to the object. Flash automatically collects its "garbage" by doing what is known as reference counting. When an object doesn't have more variables referencing it (and there is sufficient CPU time), it removes the object and frees up its memory.

SUMMARY

In this chapter, we covered quite a bit about designing interfaces for devices. You explored issues that you have to deal with in all interfaces, as well as specific issues that are common to devices. You learned how to use a small set of components that were created just for devices. You can use these components as a basis for your own interfaces. Finally, you learned about how to optimize your interfaces both from an art and a code perspective.

4

TYPOGRAPHY IN FLASH FOR DEVICES

by Craig Kroeger

The potential of Macromedia Flash for devices—specifically for the Pocket PC—is only as great as the capability of Flash to deliver content effectively. One critical area is the capability of Flash to incorporate typography that is suitable for the limitations of devices—limited screen resolution and size. The best typographic solution to combat these limitations is bitmap fonts that are designed for the screen with these issues in mind. Bitmap fonts, or *pixel fonts* as I prefer to call them, are built using the smallest unit of screen measure: the pixel.

This chapter discusses the complete process—from initial design considerations to how to effectively use the fonts in Flash. Then it details how to create pixel fonts that work in Flash. Finally, it shows some examples of effective typography solutions.

WHAT ARE PIXEL FONTS?

Pixel fonts are letterforms that are constructed from the smallest building block of any display: the pixel. One of the major hindrances to the progress of screen fonts has been the slavish dedication of most traditional type designers in trying to approximate the look of print fonts. It is my belief that you must be true to your media. In the case of screen fonts, it is clear that the letterforms should consist of the screen's unit of measure, which is the pixel.

Because Flash was not originally designed for creating applications for devices, it lacks the innate ability to incorporate pixel fonts. Fortunately, I have developed a way to create bitmap fonts that work gracefully in Flash.

TYPE CONSIDERATIONS

When selecting type to use on a device, function should be your guide. In general, the more stylized a font is, the more space it occupies. Because the maximum screen area available on a Pocket PC is 240 pixels by 263 pixels (see Figure 4.1), you must balance the need for expression versus the need for functionality. When dealing with the practical matter of having legible text, style should be of secondary importance.

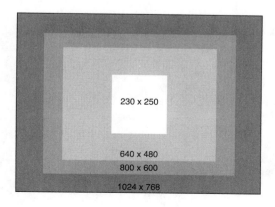

FIGURE 4.1

Comparison of typical Pocket PC screen area with traditional screen formats.

Most fonts are not designed to work at the size that is necessary for a device. At smaller sizes, text tends to blur (anti-alias), making it difficult to differentiate letterforms (see Figure 4.2). Anti-aliasing attempts to smooth the inherently jagged nature of the screen by introducing shades of gray. Not only does this take up more screen space, but it also lessens legibility by reducing contrast. A pixel font remains aliased, offering greater space economy and legibility (see Figure 4.3).

THIS IS ANTI-ALIASED SAMPLE TEXT.

FIGURE 4.2

The effects of anti-aliasing.

THIS IS ANTI-ALIASED SAMPLE TEXT.
THIS IS ALIASED SAMPLE TEXT.

FIGURE 4.3

Notice the difference in clarity.

You can use the device font option within Flash MX to incorporate aliased fonts in your applications. However, because you cannot be assured of which font will be used, you are gambling with variable factors (type style, size, and so on) and compromising your ability to design an application that works, and looks, as good as it should.

PIXEL PROBLEMS IN FLASH

The problem of using pixel fonts in Flash is two-fold. First, Flash wants to anti-alias everything. In general, this is a good thing because it makes graphics look smoother (see Figure 4.4).

Anti-aliased circle

FIGURE 4.4

Anti-aliasing can make shapes appear smoother.

Anti-aliasing also makes it easier to have unwanted anti-aliased, fuzzy text. The only way to globally turn off anti-aliasing is by setting the movie quality to low. You can do this by inserting the following code on your main timeline:

highquality = 0.

However, you usually want to keep the quality at its default value to benefit from the improved graphics rendering. Second, Flash cannot embed a normal pixel font based off of bitmaps. This means that the font you want to use cannot be stored within the movie so that it displays correctly on your end user's device. You can get around this by importing images of the text, but that eliminates the dynamic content capabilities of Flash.

THE SOLUTION TO PIXEL PROBLEMS

The key to allowing Flash to incorporate pixel fonts is to design a font that looks like a bitmap font but works like a regular font built from outlines (see Figure 4.5).

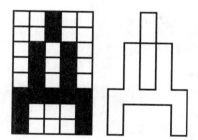

FIGURE 4.5

Bitmap versus vector outlines.

This bitmap emulation can be embedded in Flash and remain aliased in Flash at any quality, as long as it is used properly. The next section discusses how to use my fonts in Flash so that you can start using aliased fonts in your next Flash project.

If you would like to use pixel fonts that work in Flash, please visit my web site at www.miniml.com. On the web site, you will find free versions of my fonts to experiment with for personal purposes as well as professional commercial sets that are available at a reasonable price.

USAGE OVERVIEW

Imagine the screen as a series of pixels. When you place a font on the stage, it must remain "on pixel" for it to remain sharp (aliased). Figure 4.6 shows an example of this.

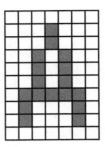

FIGURE 4.6

The font needs to correspond to the screen, pixel per pixel.

Flash makes it easy for you to get lost in the movie, with multiple timelines in the form of movie clips. Because each movie clip has its own set of pixel coordinates, you must be aware of how the movies relate to one another (see Figure 4.7).

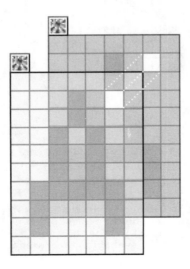

FIGURE 4.7

All movie clips need to stay consistent with the main timeline.

The following guidelines enable you to get the sharp, legible text that is so vital for small screens. Keep in mind that these rules only apply to fonts that you download from **www. miniml.com**. Other fonts will not work because they were not designed for Flash. Miniml fonts work equally well in Flash 4, 5, and MX (see the Note that follows). You can also use miniml fonts in most design applications.

Flash MX condenses all the Flash 5 type panels (Character, Paragraph, and Text Options) into one larger Type Inspector. Despite the visual reorientation, all the usage guidelines are unaffected by this new version.

The fonts will work the same whether the text you are using is static, dynamic, or input. Do not use the bold or italic style options to affect the appearance of the font. Using the superscript or subscript options will anti-alias the type.

- **Font height.** Miniml fonts must be used at the intended point size for optimal results. Set the Font height to 8 point or any multiple of 8 (16, 32, and so on), as you see in Figure 4.8.

FIGURE 4.8

Set the font height to 8 (or any multiple of 8).

- **Paragraph alignment.** Use Left Justify paragraph alignment (see Figure 4.9). Although you can use the other settings, Left Justify is recommended for easier registration.

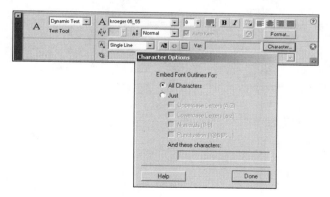

FIGURE 4.9

Set paragraph alignment to Left Justify.

- **Embedding the font.** Embed the font when using it as dynamic or input text (see Figure 4.10). (Static text embeds it automatically.) If you don't embed the text, the font will not display properly on the end user's screen.

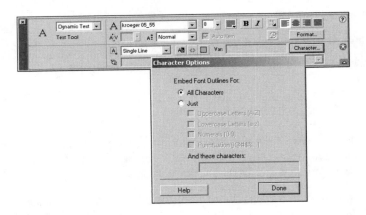

FIGURE 4.10

Embed the font for proper display.

To reduce exported file size, only embed the characters you need. You can also include single characters, which is useful in cases such as the @ symbol for email addresses, instead of including the entire font outline.

- **Font placement.** The font must be placed on a whole pixel. Use the Info panel in Flash to determine the font's _x and _y position (see Figure 4.11). The numbers must be set to a whole integer value (for example, 23.0, not 23.5). You must also set the point of registration to the upper-left corner (see Figure 4.12).

FIGURE 4.11

Use the Info panel to determine coordinates.

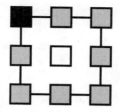

FIGURE 4.12

The point of registration needs to be set to the upper left.

 When you are using the fonts with motion, such as a scrollbar, it is easy to set the font off pixel. To fix this, you need to force the _x and _y values to return to whole integers. Use the following ActionScript code on each instance that will be in motion:

_x = Math.floor(_x);
_y = Math.floor (_y);

- **Symbol registration.** Flash centers the point of registration when you convert an object to a symbol, such as a movie clip. Go into the symbol and make the registration point the upper-left corner. Zero the _x and _y coordinates to reposition the clip for consistent stage placement (see Figure 4.13).

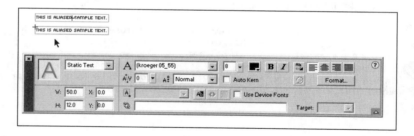

FIGURE 4.13

You need to zero the coordinates to the upper-left registration point every time an object is converted into a symbol.

- **Publishing.** Always view the movie at its intended size (100% scale). Preview the movie in Flash Player 5. Click directly on the exported SWF to open the file in Flash Player 5. The original scale of the movie *must* be keep intact for the fonts to appear correctly. Any scaling introduces unwanted anti-aliasing. This is important to keep in mind when placing movies inside HTML documents. Match the movie dimensions (pixel width and height) of the source Flash movie exactly. If you are using the Pocket PC HTML template, use the Dimensions: Match Movie option under the Publish Settings (see Figure 4.14).

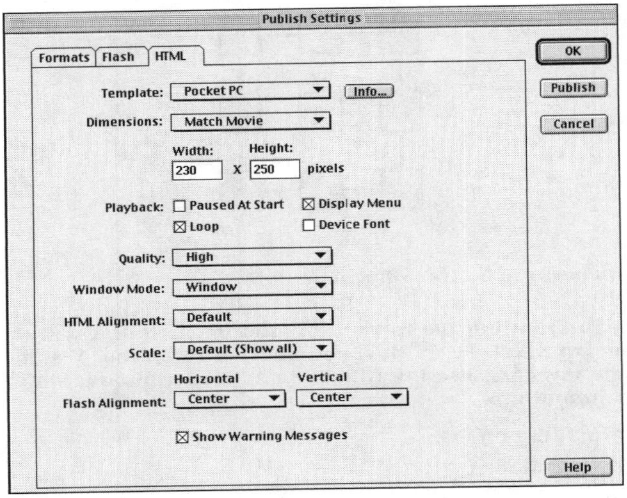

FIGURE 4.14

Settings for the Pocket PC template.

These are the main guidelines to use the fonts. It is best to build with these guidelines in mind because it is often difficult to find the source of trouble if you are in too deep.

 For your information (and to save you some future frustration), there is a known problem in Flash when dealing with bitmaps. I've noticed that when I copy paragraphs of text, sometimes there is an inexplicable blurring of the text. If you are experiencing unreasonable problems, try to copy the text into a new text block. After you get the hang of how to use the fonts, I think you'll find the payoff to be more than worth the trouble.

For your convenience, I've created a Pocket PC–sized PDF mini guide that is available for download from the web site. It's perfect for a quick reference while you're working on your Flash movies. It's available at **http://www.miniml.com/flash/fonts/guide.pdf**.

MINIML FONT NUMBER SYSTEM

This section explains what the last four numbers of my fonts mean. It's a way for the fonts to have a large range of visual style options that make some kind of sense.

The first two numbers correspond to the font height in pixels (hooge **05_**54). A font such as standard 07 would be seven pixels high. Copy 08 would be eight pixels high. This is useful in determining the actual size between fonts because the fonts are always set to the same point size. Remember: All fonts must be set at 8 points or any multiple of 8, as mentioned previously in the guidelines (see Figure 4.15).

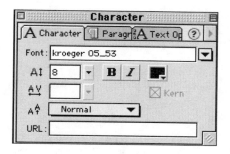

FIGURE 4.15

Quick visual guide to the miniml font naming convention.

The third digit (hooge 05_**5**4) corresponds to the typeface overall weight as follows:

5	Regular
6	Bold

The fourth digit (hooge 05_5**4**) corresponds to the typeface style as follows:

3	Expanded
4	Expanded, More Letterspacing
5	Regular
6	Regular, More Letterspacing
7	Condensed
8	Condensed, More Letterspacing

For example, hooge 05_56 is the typeface I use on **www.miniml.com**. The name means it's 5 pixels tall, regular weight, with more letterspacing than hooge 05_55. Hooge 05_66 would be the bold version of that font.

The reason I include versions of the typefaces with more letterspacing is because Flash does not allow you to set the letterspacing when you are using dynamic or input text. You can modify static text.

MAKING YOUR OWN FLASH PIXEL FONT

After using the fonts, you might be inspired to try to make your own typeface. Or maybe you'll want to modify an existing font to suit your project. Take it from me: It's a lot of work, and it's not for impatient types. However, it can also give your project that extra edge. I will take you over my process so that you, too, can become a pixel master. This process involves these steps:

1. Determining your need
2. Doing the initial setup
3. Constructing the font
4. Importing the font
5. Cleaning up the characters
6. Generating fonts

The sections that follow walk you through the steps that are involved in creating your own fonts.

Determining Your Need

What kind of typeface do you need to build? Based on the project, determining what you need is the most important guide to creating a font that will be usable and aesthetically pleasing. The primary question is what the font is going to be used for. Is the font going to be used for text? Is it for a heading? This will help you determine what size, boldness, and style the type should take. Another big factor when designing for a device is how much room you are going to have for the type to exist on the screen. The line spacing might be one area with which you can experiment to maximize your usable type area. Line spacing, or leading, is the space between baselines in a paragraph (see Figure 4.16).

FIGURE 4.16

Line spacing in a paragraph.

Initial Setup

After you have decided what you want the font to look like, it's time to start building. I build the fonts in Adobe Illustrator 9 because it gives me the capability to quickly change the font design before bringing the final version into a font creation program, such as Macromedia Fontographer. Illustrator 9 also allows you to work in pixels, giving a better sense of what your font will look like as you build. To set up a pixel grid in Illustrator, go to Edit, Preferences, Guides & Grid and change the Gridline Every to 1 px with 1 Subdivision (see Figure 4.17).

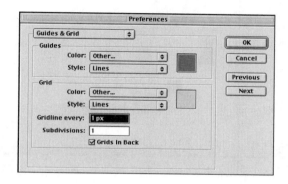

FIGURE 4.17

Setting a 1-pixel grid.

Then, turn on the Snap to Grid feature under View. This allows you to set the pixels on grid.

Construction

You need to make the pixel shapes in which you will construct your characters. Select the Rectangle tool. Click on the artboard to bring up the Rectangle tool options. Set the width and height to 1 px (see Figure 4.18).

You can start to build out the letterforms by copying the pixel shape repeatedly. Sometimes, it's more efficient to build out the form in Outline mode under View to make sure all the pixel shapes are aligned properly (see Figure 4.19).

This prevents more work later down the line when you are working in Fontographer. Be sure you look at the font at 100% scale for any design decisions. This is the size at which your end user sees the typeface, so it's best to make choices based on real viewing conditions. If possible, view the font on the device to make any final design decisions. Be sure to give your eyes a break once in a while. This allows you to see things in a different light and make better overall choices.

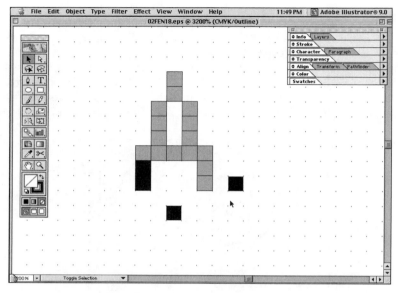

FIGURE 4.18

Using pixel shapes to build characters.

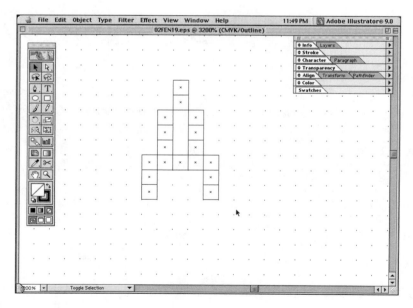

FIGURE 4.19

Use outline mode to check shape alignment.

After you have your final characters, it's time to save them into a format that Fontographer can easily read. Save the file as an EPS with a compatibility of 5.0/5.5 (see Figure 4.20). This reduces importing errors into Fontographer.

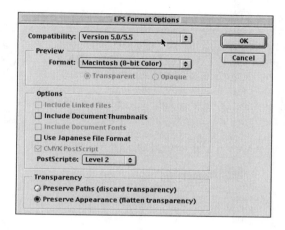

FIGURE 4.20

Illustrator EPS settings.

I usually save characters in batches (A–M, N–Z, a–m, a–z, 1–9, and so on) to keep them manageable. Unless you have a lot of free time, you definitely do not want to import them one at a time into Fontographer.

Determining Font Size

For your font to display at the right size, you need each pixel to correspond to a certain em value in Fontographer. In my case, I want the font to display properly when set to 8 points in Flash. The fonts are set at 8 points because this is the size at which the fonts work best in Flash, especially when used in paragraphs. As I have mentioned before, Flash not only wants to anti-alias everything and has a problem rendering bitmaps, but it also seems to have trouble dealing with bitmap emulations that are set at sizes larger than 8 points. I stumbled on this fact accidentally as I was noticing how one early font prototype phased in and out of focus at 10 points but was perfectly clear at 8 points. Because I couldn't change how Flash renders type, I decided to make my fonts work uniformly at 8 points (which is fairly convenient when switching between fonts).

Pixel fonts work best when they are created to work at 8 points in Flash.

For the font to work at 8 points, each pixel must correspond to 125 em units. This is true when the em square equals 1000 em units. (To figure out the math, 1000 em units divided by 8 equals 125 em units. A 10-point font, for instance, would be equal to 100 em units.) When you import the EPS into Fontographer, it automatically scales up the font to whatever you set the Ascent value under the Element, Font Info option. For instance, if the font you create is 8 pixels tall, you would set the Ascent value to 1000 em units (8×125 em units). If the font is 9 pixels tall, it would be set to 1125 em units (9×125 em units). If you don't, then it will automatically scale the characters to fit whatever Ascent value is set, which creates output problems later. The only other trick is that not all characters are the same height in pixels. For instance, often the Q is one pixel "taller" because it descends below the baseline. In that case, you would want to bring in the "Q" at the right size for that character (125 em units more than the other characters if it was 1 pixel taller). (See Figure 4.21.)

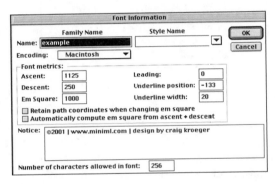

FIGURE 4.21

The Ascent value is based on pixel height.

Importing into Fontographer

Now it's time to transfer the characters you created in Illustrator into Fontographer so that you can make a usable font. To import the outlines into Fontographer, select an empty unused character spot. After the correct Ascent value is set, import the characters under File, Import, EPS and select the appropriate file. Then go into that character spot, select each character, and copy and paste it into its corresponding location. After pasting each character, immediately set the right sidebearing under Set Width. Set that value equal to the width of the character plus 1 pixel of space more so the characters don't touch each other (see Figure 4.22).

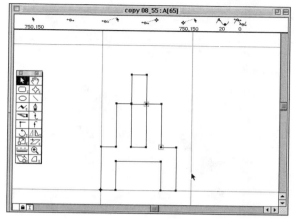

FIGURE 4.22

Setting the right sidebearing.

If the font were 5 pixels wide, the width would be set to 750 em units ((5+1)×125 em units).

Cleaning Up the Characters

After you have all the characters in place, you need to remove any extra information to make the font's file size as small as possible. Do this by selecting all the characters and then selecting Element, Remove Overlap. This joins all the individual pixel blocks. This also creates a lot of unnecessary points. You can eliminate these extra points by selecting Element, Clean Up Paths and setting the range to the maximum setting (see Figure 4.23).

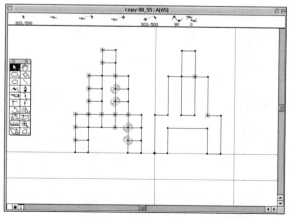

FIGURE 4.23

Before and after cleaning up the forms.

Eliminating Fill-In

There is one problem with pixel fonts that are created from outlines. When forms meet at points, the computer displays the letterforms with the counters filled in, unless you slightly adjust the form (see Figure 4.24).

FIGURE 4.24

Closed character forms can fill in when there is not enough distinction.

You will need to adjust the interior spaces of closed letterforms, such as A, B, D, O, P, Q, and so on, to prevent the forms from filling in. Adjust the interior space by 5 em units until the form is more clearly defined (see Figure 4.25).

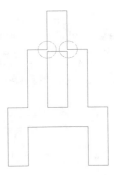

FIGURE 4.25

The adjusted shape prevents fill-in.

The form, although slightly less of a pure pixel form, will render just fine at the intended size.

Generating Fonts

After the characters are cleaned up, you need to make a font. In Fontographer, under File, select Generate Font Files. Select the Computer type and corresponding encoding. Under Format, select TrueType. I use the TrueType type format over PostScript because the fonts are meant for screen use and Flash handles them better. Plus, you can open the fonts without an outside application. Be sure to give the font a unique ID number, especially for PC versions (see Figure 4.26). If the number is the same as an existing font in your system, it won't appear in your menu. Simply change the number to a different value and re-export the font.

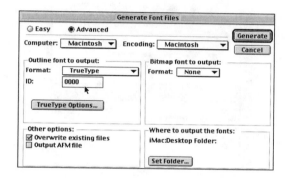

FIGURE 4.26

Settings for generating fonts.

After the font is generated, you can install it and use it in Flash. Wasn't it worth the effort?

FONTS IN APPLICATION

A good example of type that is used in an application created for the Pocket PC is the Pocket PC Summit guide created by Bill Perry. This piece shows the importance of creating graphics and text that work well with each other. Despite the small screen area, white space and clear instructions invite the viewer to engage the piece (see Figure 4.27).

FIGURE 4.27

An example of graphics and text that work well together.

Flash is used as a way to reveal the navigation when you need it by having the menu conveniently accessible at the bottom. This allows the navigation to be both available and unobtrusive to allow other important information to occupy the screen. The navigation choices are clear and consistent (see Figure 4.28). Even when the navigation options become more complicated, the hierarchy remains clear due to division formed by placement, lines, and color as tools to differentiate purpose (see Figure 4.29). No matter how much you edit your copy, there will be a time when you will need to be able to access more text than what fits in the given area. Being able to have a large paragraph of text and still have both graphics and multiple forms of navigation all on the same screen is the luxury that pixel fonts provide (see Figure 4.30).

FIGURE 4.28

You can see the navigation choices easily.

FIGURE 4.29

Placement, lines, and color help make navigation choices obvious.

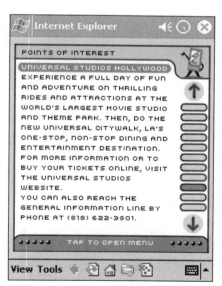

FIGURE 4.30

Pixel fonts enable you to maximize screen area while maintaining legibility.

SUMMARY

As technology becomes smaller and more portable, it is essential to focus on the purpose of this technology. The way we interact with these devices and the effectiveness of the device as a life-enriching tool depends largely on the design of applications that benefit the public. Although the typeface for a device-based application might not change the world, it is a necessity for changing the individual user's experience. Good experiences are powerful.

Typography should not be underestimated, especially when the margin for error is so small. The means for delivering information in a small, legible, effective manner is here. It is up to the developers, like you, to create the kinds of tools that benefit everyone. Attractive typography is only as effective as the quality of the content. We should not focus on the technology, but rather on how the technology can be utilized. Consideration and compassion should be the means to the end. Clear type is considerate. Caring about what you create is compassionate. Everything else will fall into place.

5

FROM START TO FINISH: UNDERSTANDING THE FLASH APPLICATION DEVELOPMENT WORKFLOW

by Bill Perry

At this point in the book, we have covered just about every aspect of creating Macromedia Flash content and applications for the Pocket PC platform. However, the previous chapters have been largely technical, giving you the "how" of development. This chapter focuses on the process, the "what" of development. It attempts to give you an idea of the entire process of creating an application, from concept, to specing out the requirements, to the actual creation, debugging, and deployment of the project. For the project in this chapter, you will create an advanced Flash-based event guide for a conference, which forces you to focus on all aspects of Flash device development (such as UI, navigation, and device limitations).

You can download the files used to create the application from the book's web site, www.flashenabled.com, and from the New Riders site, www.newriders.com.

INTRODUCING THE EVENT GUIDE APPLICATION

We've all been to trade shows and are familiar with the cumbersome-but-necessary printed event guides that show us the conference schedule, presenters, a map of the exhibits, conference sponsors, and so on.

I use a Pocket PC device daily for various purposes including calendar, contacts, notes, and Flash development, among other uses. During these conferences, I find myself using both the event guide and my Pocket PC, which is not easy to do as I'm walking around. So I thought, why not take the same information (or at least the information that I find useful), create a great user experience, and put it on a Pocket PC that I can easily access? Not only can I include information about the event, but I can also include hotel information, local map, points of interest, and anything else that might be specific to the event.

Creating this application for the Pocket PC using Flash seemed like a useful way to present the workflow process in this chapter while at the same time creating a functional—and hopefully fun—model. By using Flash to create this event guide application, we're able to take advantage of the "develop once, deploy anywhere" feature of Flash, which has been mentioned throughout this book. This same event guide that we will create can also be viewed on desktops, WebTV, and other devices that can display Flash with no or little modifications done to the finished files.

As a developer, you will no doubt create a wide variety of Flash projects on many different devices. Each project will have its own quirks and challenges, but there will be similar issues to address in them all. Using Flash to develop an event guide for the Pocket PC serves as an example that requires you to think about the following issues determine the best solutions:

- What stages are involved in developing a Flash application?
- What's involved in specing out a project?
- What's the target audience?
- How do I assess the limitations and plan for them before I begin?
- What resources do I have for troubleshooting?
- What type of connectivity will be required?
- How much time do I have to develop, test, and implement the project?

These questions and more are sure to come up as you plan your own Flash projects (see Figure 5.1). For that reason, the process of developing the Flash event guide will help you anticipate and answer some of the challenges you will find in your own projects.

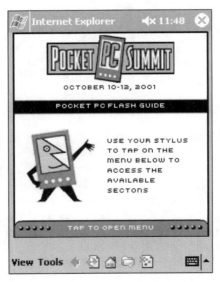

FIGURE 5.1

Completed Pocket PC Flash event guide.

PLANNING YOUR PROJECT

One of the most important things you need to do before, during, and after a project is to be organized. Being organized might seem time consuming, but in the overall picture, it helps you keep focused on what you need to do and keeps you on track. Organization is a good skill to have, and it will help you in other situations.

At this point, you should have an idea of the types of devices you're considering, cost and time estimates for completion, and how you plan to utilize the capabilities of Flash for your project.

Five Things to Ask First

Here is a quick checklist of questions that you should ask in the initial meetings with a client:

- What's the purpose?
- Are there any specific requirements?
- Who will be the end users?
- What's the scope?
- What's your budget?

Remember: This checklist can be used in all types of projects, not just Pocket PC Flash projects.

Understanding Your Limitations

Every project will have its own unique set of limitations—only in an ideal world will we have all the time, resources, functionality, and flexibility to create projects just the way we want them. Here are some limitations I've found that might affect your Flash project:

- Available time for development
- Available resources (which means "cheap is good")
- Ambiguity from the client
- Ignorance about the software
- Hardware (platform?) limitations
- Limited training available
- Lack of IT support
- Internal politics and personality clashes
- Other concurrent projects you might have

In the event guide example that we're following in this chapter, we need to consider many major limitations: the event guide content, the Pocket PC Flash Player, and the Pocket PC devices. For example, consider these issues:

- **Amount of content.** Event guides usually include a lot of information. How do you choose what you need for your Pocket PC application? What's fluff and what's important? You will most likely determine the specifics with your client, but the sifting will have to be done.

- **Information that is hard to reproduce.** Event guides often have large maps that show you city information and where to find booths you're interested in visiting (see Figure 5.2). A large map or a complex table can be hard to display well on the Pocket PC.

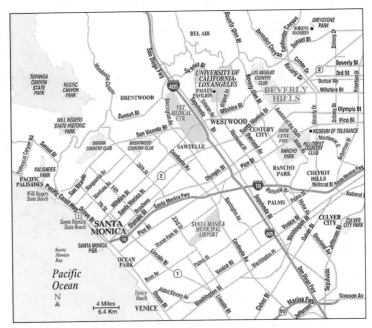

FIGURE 5.2

Map of the city of Santa Monica, California.

- **Flash Player for the Pocket PC.** You've already read in Chapter 2, "Creating Content for the Pocket PC Using Flash," about the Flash Player for the Pocket PC, and you should be aware of the limitations of displaying Flash content on Pocket PCs. Please refer to that chapter for more detailed information.

- **Screen size.** Pocket PC devices have a relatively small screen size that you must take into account when planning your design.

- **Color depth.** Keep in mind color depth limitation when planning your design for display on Pocket PCs.
- **Available RAM.** Another limitation you need to plan for might be the storage space or built-in RAM. Currently, devices have anywhere from 32–64MB, with the latter being plenty for most projects.

When creating your project, you should keep in mind that in most cases, devices have limited storage space or bandwidth; therefore, file size should be a consideration.

Planning the Workflow

Most people are visual learners; they remember things more easily if they're able to see a picture or diagram of a concept as opposed to just reading about it. This is where a project workflow comes into play. It doesn't have to be complex or confusing, but something simple to which you and the client can refer throughout the project. Here is an example of a project workflow for a medium-sized Pocket PC Flash project:

1. Initial meeting with client in which you get your questions answered. [Time estimate: 2 hours]

2. Spec, research, and prepare proposal, with prototype if needed. [Time estimate: 8–16 hours]

3. Confirmation meeting with client—presentation of project plan. [Time estimate: 1–2 hours.] This could be done online to save time.

4. Begin development. Determine the number of developers, make task assignments, and set deadlines, with checkpoints midway through. [Time estimate: 1–4 weeks (depends on complexity)]

5. Walkthrough meeting with client, which can be scheduled once or several times during development. [Time estimate: 2–4 hours]

6. Testing and modification cycle. [Time estimate: 2–8 hours (depends on number of modifications)]

7. Rollout/deployment. [Time estimate: 2–8 hours]

Defining Your Project

This might be the most critical part of your project, so it's important to spend the time to get it right the first time. At this point, you should have already met with the client, asked your questions, and have a good understanding of the purpose of the project, the requirements, the scope, and so forth. Now you need to define what the project will be, what needs to be accomplished, and how your project might be used beyond its intended scope.

Here are a few things to consider as you begin to define the goals and expectations of your project:

- Remember the purpose of the project.
- Research and determine the best solutions.
- Have a device on which to test your project.
- Create realistic goals and deadlines.
- Manage your hours to stay within budget.
- Be prepared for things to go wrong.

Thinking and planning beyond the scope of your project toward how it can grow is a great selling point to a client for follow-up work. Not only will the client get enhanced capabilities, but the development time and costs will also be minimized because you're adding to an existing project. When defining your project, it's best not to think of it as only one project, but instead as the start of several projects. A great way I've found to accomplish this is to present your project in "phases" to the client. Each phase of the project can be built on the other, developed and deployed at different times. This "phased" approach might not be applicable to all projects, but always try to develop projects this way.

Introducing the Event Guide

First, let me define an event guide. For the purposes of this chapter, I'll define an *event guide* as organized content for an event, conference, or summit that allows attendees to find relevant information. In general terms, the purpose of an event guide is to give the attendee a portable overview of information for the event.

Why Flash and the Pocket PC Are a Good Fit

Creating a printed event guide involves numerous steps, and it limits you to when you can add or remove information. It would seem to make more sense to only have an electronic version of the event guide (see Figure 5.3), or depending on the event, to have both versions available.

FIGURE 5.3

Here you can see several screen shots of the Pocket PC Summit 2001 event guide.

There are several advantages of creating an electronic event guide with Flash versus a traditional printed guide. These advantages with the Flash guide include the following:

- Can be changed and updated at any time
- Is quicker to develop and has faster turnaround
- Can be shared with anyone
- Can create mini-communities
- Can be customizable
- Is printable

These are some of the benefits, but the most important one that I'm going to focus on is the interactivity of the application. By using Flash to create the event guide, you can utilize some of the capabilities of the devices, including connectivity. Some of these capabilities include real-time feedback of the current event, conference-specific chat rooms, user forums, and much more. Also, by allowing the application to be dynamic, you're able to push conference updates to users via wireless connectivity (Bluetooth, 802.11b). Now you have a living document that is interactive and can be shared. Pretty cool, huh?

Choosing Your Platform

Now you're thinking, "Okay, with all the different devices that are available to me, how do I choose the best one for my project and for the client?" If you're thinking about developing your project using Flash, then you're limited to devices that have a Flash Player available.

 See the book's web site (www.flashenabled.com) for a list of the latest Flash-enabled devices.

Another feature to consider is which device will give the best user experience. Screen size will be an issue, so you're probably not going to consider a cell phone–sized screen. You want to be sure your project is easily accessible and usable at any time, so a PDA solution is probably your best bet. Currently, there are two main PDA market segments: Pocket PC and Palm OS.

Finally, you need to think about the ubiquity of the device. You want to be sure that enough people have the target device to make development for it worthwhile.

Planning the User Experience

It can be easy to get carried away when designing a user interface (UI) for an application, so it's important to recognize the determining factors for creating the best user experience. You need to remember that the end user will be someone with a Pocket PC device. These devices have a small screen (320 height × 240 width in pixels), so it's not going to be the same as when designing applications for desktop PCs (usually 800×600 or higher). This means that you need to be creative and efficient when designing your application.

In most cases, the users will be using their stylus to access the information on the Pocket PC device, so the navigation needs to be easy to read and simple to understand. Some users might use "snap-on" or "fold-up" keyboards to access and enter information on their Pocket PCs. If you're designing an application that requires a lot of text entry, you might want to consider a "keyboard" solution to work with your application. Using contrasting colors and fonts that are specially designed for small screens is important to remember.

See Chapter 4, "Typography in Flash for Devices," for more information on using fonts with Flash on devices.

Eventually, the user experience will come down to a combination of different factors. These include the following:

- Amount of information
- Type of navigation
- Creativity
- Any special requirements
- Ease of use

Amount of Information

Depending on your project content, you need to determine what stays and what goes. If possible, try not to use information that is irrelevant because it might confuse the user. Organize information in a way that doesn't overwhelm the user. Make information usable.

Type of Navigation

Remember that you're working with a small interface, so you don't want your navigation to hog the screen. Menus that slide out, pull out, or expand and collapse are good solutions. Although these are only a few of the possibilities, it's up to you and your client to decide what the best navigation should be. Don't forget that the majority of your screen should be used to display the content of your application, not the navigation.

Creativity

Some people say you're born with it, and others say you achieve it through everyday experiences. Whichever the case, having some creativity in your application is necessary for several reasons. Creativity helps to separate your work from everyone else's. A client wants to have that standout, unique app that everyone is talking about.

Any Special Requirements

Being aware of and addressing any of your client's special requirements is vital; after all, they chose you because they believed in you and thought you could help them. Your project might require that the application connect to a database and update information nightly, or it may require Bluetooth connectivity between multiple users of your application—each one on a different device. You need to be able to understand what the special requirements are and determine the best solution.

Ease of Use

Try to make your application as enjoyable as possible for the user while maintaining usability. Your goal is to create an inviting GUI that masks the fact that the user is interfacing with an application. Remember: You want your users to spend their time using the application and not learning how to use it.

CREATING THE FLASH PROJECT

Now it's time to start actually making the event guide in Flash. As you go through this example, remember that you can apply these steps to planning, developing, and implementing your own particular projects. If you are interested in creating your own Flash event guide for the Pocket PC, you can download the source files from the book's web site.

Project Requirements

First, you need to identify the specific project requirements, the scope, the target platform, the content to be used, and the technologies to make everything come together. Don't skip this step; if you do, I can guarantee you will run into problems later on in the development cycle. Always remember that if something can go wrong, it probably will. Have a backup plan in place in case you lose your work or your device.

From a development standpoint, you need to have the "right tools" to get the job done. These tools have been covered in the other chapters, but for a quick refresh, they are Flash 5 (or higher) to create the content, a Pocket PC device to test your application, and the Pocket PC Flash Player 5 to view your content on your Pocket PC.

You don't really need a Pocket PC device to complete this chapter, but it helps you to see the completed animation on the target platform.

Organizing the Project

This is what some people might consider a "pre-planning" phase for a project. In any project, it is a good habit to plan ahead so you can try to forecast any problems that might arise during the development phase. You can't predict problems that might occur; however, you can be prepared in case any happen.

One way to plan is to sketch out a flowchart of how the navigation should work and the different sections that you plan to have. By doing this, you'll be able to foresee what resources you will need (artwork, photos, maps, and so on).

Gathering Content

The content you gather for your project can be any material that you need. Whatever it is will have to be converted to a digital format to be brought into Flash (such as scanning artwork, photographs, and so on).

Organizing Your Folders

You will probably have more than one Flash animation or application on your device at any one time, so it's a good idea to create separate folders for each Flash animation or application. Whether they are Flash animations that you've created yourself or ones you've downloaded, it's a good practice to keep each one in its own folder. Here is a screen shot of how I have my subfolders set up on my Pocket PC device (see Figure 5.4).

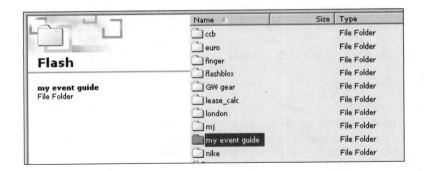

FIGURE 5.4

Setting up your folders before you begin helps keep your project organized.

Making the Event Guide

You might be asking yourself, "What are we making?" and "What content will it contain?" As I discussed earlier in this chapter, I'll be taking what I feel are the "core sections" of a printed event guide and converting them into an easy-to-use, Flash event guide—designed for Pocket PC devices.

For our purposes, I'll be explaining the steps involved for creating the Pocket PC Summit 2001 event guide and how you can apply some of the ideas to your own projects. I've broken down the development into five sections:

- Part 1: Laying the Foundation
- Part 2: Creating the Sections

- Part 3: Creating the Navigation
- Part 4: Testing
- Part 5: Deployment

While I was defining this project, I made decisions to remove certain content that I didn't feel was important from the Flash event guide. For example, my decision to eliminate an advertising section was based on the fact that people who were using the Flash event guide wanted to have immediate access to the core content (conference schedule, map, and so on).

For navigation, I felt that a slide-out type of menu would be the best solution. By doing this, I was able to maximize the available screen area for content, while still providing the user with easy access to the entire application—all from a single tap.

Are you ready? Okay, let's get into the development part of the project.

Part 1: Laying the Foundation

First, I created a new movie and then added and named the layers that I knew I would need for this project. Then, I added labels and some generic ActionScript to establish a working framework. After this was done, I imported and organized all the images I had prepped using Photoshop. Next, I brought in a layout template I had created to use as a template when creating the GUI in Flash. Depending on your project, you might want to consider creating a GUI mockup outside of Flash.

 It's important to note that the type and amount of images that you will be importing will vary. Some of these images might include maps, photos, scanned artwork, and so on. It's best to try to reuse imported images as much as possible to minimize the SWF file size. Also, rename your imported images and put them into library folders so that you can easily identify them.

With a good framework in place, I then moved on to creating the opening sequence animation. Some motion tweens, text, and color tinting helped to create the look I was going after.

Now that I had all of my pieces imported, my timeline in skeleton form, and my opening sequence, I could then move on to Part 2 (see Figure 5.5). Just a reminder: You don't have to do anything too complicated, but just enough work to get you ready for the other parts of the development phase.

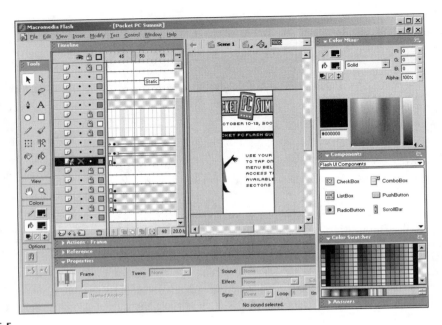

FIGURE 5.5

A pretty good foundation for the event guide.

Part 2: Creating the Sections

For the next part of the development phase I focused on the different sections of the event guide. During the planning part of the project I actually sketched out some ideas for each section along with some ideas of how to present the information to the users. In the case of the Pocket PC Summit event guide I only wanted to create six areas or "sections." Although the steps I used to create and set up each one of the sections are specific to the event guide, it's important to emphasize that if you can reuse elements or MCs throughout your project, you'll be able to save time and minimize testing.

For example, each one of the sections in the event guide looks and functions similarly. Each one fades in and displays the section content; then, when you leave a section, it fades away. It was apparent that once I was able to get one section working correctly, I could duplicate it and change only certain variables and the main content. By doing this, I could create the "shells" for each section and then go back and spend time integrating the necessary content in the appropriate sections (see Figure 5.6). As you can see, by taking this approach to your project development, you can be more efficient with your time and eliminate unnecessary work.

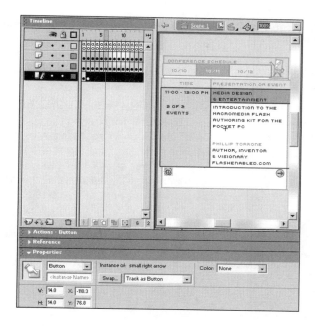

FIGURE 5.6

Now that the section "shells" are complete, you can add the section-specific content.

When creating content for use on small devices, choosing the right font, size, and color are important. If the end user is unable to read the information you're presenting, then you've failed at your job of creating useful content.

See Chapter 4 for more information on using fonts within Flash on devices.

With the opening animation and sections pretty much complete, I needed to move on to the third part of the development cycle: the navigation.

Part 3: Creating the Navigation

You can have the best Flash application with all the necessary content, beautiful pictures, and useful information—but if the user does not understand how to use the navigation, your application is not useful. You need to put as much attention into your application navigation as you do with the other aspects of development.

An easy-to-use and understand navigation structure is essential to your application.

As I mentioned earlier, I felt that a sliding menu would offer the maximize screen area for the content. I could "open and close" the menu by simply tapping on the visible portion of the menu bar. To do this, I created the navigation as an MC and accessed it on the main timeline via ActionScript (see Figure 5.7). Creating the ActionScript for the menu wasn't difficult because the menu was similar to the sections. If you can get one of them to work, then you can get all of them to work. I applied the same "template" approach to create the navigation logic that I used for creating the sections; by doing this, I saved time and minimized my mistakes.

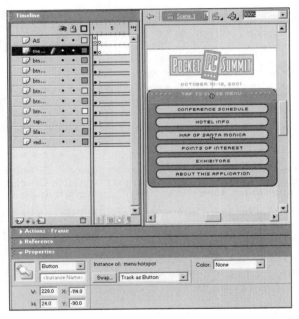

FIGURE 5.7

Here you can see how the navigation is contained in one MC and is controlled by ActionScript.

For your projects, try experimenting with different types of navigation, keeping in mind that the user will be touching the screen with a stylus or his finger. I've seen several Flash applications created for the Pocket PC with interesting navigation solutions. Whether it's the "sliding method," "drag and drop," "expand and contract," or others, try different styles with your application or take a look at what other Flash developers have created to get some ideas. However, remember that when designing your navigation, usability is your number one priority.

After successfully integrating the navigation with the rest of the event guide application, you must test it on a Pocket PC 2002 device. There are only two parts left to the development and we'll be done.

Part 4: Testing

You're done with the FLA file. Now you need to test it on a Pocket PC 2002 device. To do this, you need to export the final versions of the SWF and HTML files that will be synched to the Pocket PC 2002 device. From Flash MX, choose Publish Settings (File, Publish Settings) and click on the HTML option. In the HTML tab, choose the Pocket PC 2002 template from the drop-down list and accept the default settings (see Figure 5.8).

Be sure that you set the Flash movie to publish as a Flash 5 movie. This is done by going to File, Publish Setting, Flash and setting the Flash movie to Flash 5.

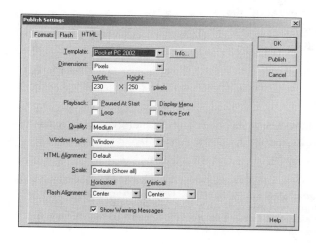

FIGURE 5.8

Flash MX offers the "Pocket PC 2002" HTML template for publishing your Pocket PC 2002 Flash content.

However, before you copy the HTML file over to the Pocket PC, you need to tweak the HTML file. You want to do this so that you can have the maximum amount of space for your Flash movie. To do this, you need to put the following code into the <Body> portion of your HTML code:

leftmargin="0" topmargin="0"

Keep in mind that if your Flash movie size is larger than the recommended maximum size for Pocket PC 2002 devices, adding the preceding tweak to your HTML code won't get rid of the scrollbars in Pocket IE.

As you can see here, I've stripped out all the code that Pocket IE doesn't need. The event guide plays fine using this HTML code on a Pocket PC 2002 device. (Notice that there aren't a lot of lines of code to worry about.)

```
<HEAD>
<TITLE>Pocket PC Summit</TITLE>
</HEAD>
<HTML><BODY bgcolor="#FFFFFF" topmargin="0" leftmargin="0">
<OBJECT classid="clsid:D27CDB6E-AE6D-11cf-96B8-444553540000"
 WIDTH="230" HEIGHT="250" id="Pocket PC Summit">
 <PARAM NAME=movie VALUE="Pocket PC Summit.swf">
 <PARAM NAME=loop VALUE=false>
 <PARAM NAME=menu VALUE=false>
 <PARAM NAME=quality VALUE=medium>
 <PARAM NAME=bgcolor VALUE=#FFFFFF>
</OBJECT>
</BODY>
</HTML>
```

Be sure that you test the Flash movie on your Pocket PC 2002 device after tweaking the HTML code. You don't want to end up doing more work because you're missing a line of code in your HTML file.

If you want to put up your project on a web site where people can access the same SWF and HTML files, then having a preloader is a good idea. If you're creating your project only for the Pocket PC, the SWF and HTML files are stored locally on the Pocket PC device; streaming isn't an issue.

After copying the files to the Pocket PC 2002 device, I thoroughly went through and tested all the sections, the navigation, buttons—everything in an effort to break it. I found only a few minor things that I was able to quickly fix.

One good way to test your application is to have someone else test it for you, someone who hasn't been involved with the project or is not familiar with the application. Give this person tasks to accomplish using your newly created Flash app and see how he uses it. Here are several things you should look for while observing others using your application:

- Do they look confused when they first see the application?
- Are they having difficulty navigating?
- Do they lose interest quickly?
- Are they happy using the application?
- Do they ask a lot of questions?
- How long does it take them to accomplish an assigned task?

You can use and modify this list any way you want to, but if you study people's reactions and behaviors when using applications, you can really learn a lot. Depending on the scope and budget of your project, you might be able to incorporate some user feedback before actually deploying your application.

Part 5: Deployment

This is the fun part of the project—actually seeing the completion of all your efforts culminate in the delivery and deployment of your application.

After you have distributed your Flash content, you might be called on to help with problems that arise from certain users—it's inevitable. There's always at least one little problem that sneaks by when developing a project. It's a good habit to keep track of these little problems because if they happen again on another project, you'll know right away how to fix them.

If you're just messing around and you've created something that you think other people might find interesting, be sure to get it out there for people to use and provide feedback. There's nothing more exciting than finding a really cool Flash app that is made for the Pocket PC. You can post your work at several sites. Check Appendix C, "Flash Device Resources," for more information.

After your project is complete, archive all your source and completed files in case you need to reference something in the future. There are several ways of doing this, including burning a CD, saving to a Zip disk, or backing up to tape.

SUMMARY

As you can see, creating applications in Flash for Pocket PC devices takes preparation, planning, development, and testing—each of these having its own requirements. The important thing is that you should now understand the process and limitations for developing a Flash application for Pocket PC devices. You can modify this project development process to fit your own Flash projects. There isn't an absolute right or wrong way of working on a project; it's different for each person. What's similar is the fact that we can share ideas for developing projects, thus learning from each other.

PART II: ADVANCED FLASH DEVELOPMENT FOR DEVICES

6

CREATING MOTION GRAPHICS AND CHARACTER ANIMATION FOR THE POCKET PC USING FLASH

by Glenn Thomas

One of the great features of Macromedia Flash is its ability to develop "create once, change it around a bit, and play it anywhere" media content. Motion graphics and animation created for the web can also be shown on CD-ROMs, DVDs, broadcast television, interactive television, and now handhelds and embedded devices.

Using Flash to create animation and motion graphics provides high-quality entertainment and motion design for handheld devices that can't be created with any other technology. Flash's vectors allow the development of movies with small file sizes and stunning production qualities to play back within the limitations of a broad range of devices (see Figure 6.1).

FIGURE 6.1

Great entertainment for multiple devices can be created in Flash.

With the advent of Flash for handhelds and embedded devices, there's a chance to develop for almost every major platform in the digital world. This great opportunity requires designers and animators to understand how to create movies for deployment on multiple platforms (see Figure 6.2). Although developers can easily create content for multiple devices, it does take planning, an understanding of what device limitations will do to content files, and a balancing act between the limitations of file size and quality to create great content.

FIGURE 6.2

Cartoons and motion graphics with distinctive styles can play back on a variety of devices for many audiences.

In this chapter, we'll explore how to create motion graphics and character animation for devices by following the creation of a short cartoon based on a previously drawn comic strip called "The Prague Years." The project allows us to go step-by-step through the process of creating and optimizing a movie specifically for device playback that can also be shown on other platforms.

- **Planning, Organization, and Optimization.** How to think about and set up a motion graphics or animation project for embedded devices.
- **Device and Platform Realities.** The possibilities and limitations of both the devices and platforms that Flash will play on at this time and in the future.
- **Keys to Motion Graphics.** The step-by-step way to create motion graphics that play well on devices.
- **Keys to Character Animation.** The step-by-step method for creating character animation that plays well on devices.

PLANNING, ORGANIZING, AND OPTIMIZATION

To understand the best approaches to creating animation and motion graphics for handhelds and other devices, it's important to realize the current limitations of devices, as well as how these limitations will affect current content and new content.

Character Animation and Motion Graphics for Devices

Animation in Flash falls into two distinct categories—motion graphics and character animation. Each type of animation relies on techniques that can be problematic on many devices and platforms.

Great motion graphics design often contains intense motion tweening applied to fonts and photographic elements, while also using a mixture of transparency and color effects (see Figure 6.3). Character animation relies on nuanced acting to convey story and emotion. It's created using keyframed drawings placed in front of rich, stylized backgrounds. When combined with music, dialogue, and sound effects, both types of animation are brought to life.

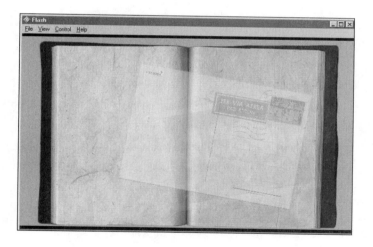

FIGURE 6.3

Using alphas and motion tweens with large photos can cause problems during playback on devices.

Unfortunately, all the mentioned animation elements cause problems because of the limitations of current embedded platforms. Devices have variable playback performance, file size limitations, and hardware capabilities. In many cases, processor speeds are low, so animation frame rates drop on playback, graphic refresh is slow, file sizes need to be small because storage is limited, MP3 sound isn't always supported, and display sizes are so different that one movie can't fit all of them.

Currently the limitations of these devices and displaying animation and motion graphics are fairly severe so it's important to define a lowest common denominator and adhere to it during the production process. The main specifications to define are

- The target processor speed
- Storage capacity
- Sound playback capability
- Screen size
- Player version implementation (Flash 3, 4, or 5)
- The connectivity of the device

Once these aspects are taken into account, it's amazing to be able to create cartoons and motion graphics that people can watch on any device capable of displaying Flash content.

Repurposing Content

Many animators and companies already have Flash animation or motion graphics developed for the web. This material can be repurposed for alternative devices or the same content can be modified with device limitations in mind. Repurposing or modifying content is the quickest way to get content on devices, but must be done carefully to ensure proper playback.

The key points to consider whether repurposed content will look good on devices are

- Is the frame rate too high to play well on devices?
- Are there lots of complex vector lines in the movie? If yes, will the lines overwhelm the visuals when played back at a smaller size or will they slow playback on devices?
- Will the graphics look okay when played back on small screen sizes? Is there too much detail that will be lost on smaller screens to make the content unintelligible?
- Is the file size too large to fit on devices' smaller hard drives or memory cards (see Figure 6.4)?
- Does the content rely on long shots, close ups, or both? If the screen for playback is small, will viewers understand what is happening?
- What player version does the movie require and will the target device support it?
- Does the content require a persistent connection from a device? If so, do target devices have the capability to have a persistent connection?
- If it does require a persistent connection and the device doesn't realistically support this, can the content be changed to play locally?

FIGURE 6.4

This digital photo album of Alaska would not be a good project to repurpose because it contains 18M worth of photos, much too large a file size for the average handheld user.

After questions like these have been answered, it's possible to decide whether it's worth the time to repurpose content from the web to devices. The simplest possible way to repurpose content is to output it in a compatible version of Flash, change the movie dimensions in the HTML page, and play the files on a device. Although this works at times, it's often necessary to open the file, further optimize symbols, and simplify animation so that files play back at the proper frame rate.

Animation and Motion Graphics Styles that Work on Devices

Due to the variety of device capabilities, the best styles of animation and motion graphics for devices are ones that use strong, simple elements without too much complex movement or applied color/transparency effects.

Animation with simple characters and backgrounds, animated comic books, and animation relying on a few characters delivering short, punchy lines work best. The display size of devices really works against creating dramatic atmosphere or developing great depth in emotional feelings. It's difficult to get drawn completely into a story that's only a couple of inches square when normally it would be seen on a monitor, a television, or a film screen. Screen size does affect what people will enjoy watching.

Animation styles that work extremely well are cut paper animation like *South Park* or *Blue's Clues*. Photographs can also work well for stop motion-style animation, but it's easy to end up with large files due to the raster images. Photos also don't scale up or down well, so it's important to bring the photos in at the size they'll normally be shown at in the movie.

Because screens are small, cartoons with lots of close-ups on characters' faces will deliver the story better because the character's emotion will register visually the best (see Figure 6.5). Strong character movement also works better than subtle movement because of the screen size. One way to think about character movement at this size is that if the animation wouldn't be strong and understandable if done in silhouette, then it won't work when lines and color are added.

FIGURE 6.5

Cartoons with close-ups work extremely well for handhelds that support Flash, such as the Pocket PC.

Character animation styles that don't work nearly as well are ones with complex lifelike motion and ones that contain characters with lots of vector lines and details (see Figure 6.6). Complex lifelike motion requires so many drawings and symbols that it doesn't play back well. In testing a complex character's walk cycle, playback on devices fell to 1–2fps from a set rate of 10fps. Because the character wasn't even walking in front of a background, playback within a cartoon would have been even slower.

FIGURE 6.6

Complex line drawings won't animate well in Flash.

Although handheld devices that support the Flash player will undoubtedly become more powerful over time, with faster processors, more memory, and better screens, the developer needs to target current playback reality for the target audience. As the target audience device improves, designers will be able to use more complex animation and effects.

Camera moves like zooms, pans, and trucks, as well as editing effects such as cross-fades don't work well on devices due to processor limitations and graphic refresh problems. Frame rates can decline by 50–75% when these kinds of techniques are used in movies. If they absolutely have to be used, then try to ensure that backgrounds and symbols are as simple as possible. As an example, panning with a simple character running in front of a complex city background plays back well below the set frame rate, but the same sequence with the camera's point of view repositioned to show the character running against the sky plays back at the correct frame rate.

In common with character animation, motion graphics styles that rely on strong, powerful movement and images work best on devices. Panoramic effects, subtle motion, small fonts, and minor graphic effects get lost at the reduced screen size of devices (see Figure 6.7). In addition, using lots of transparency effects, full screen motion, large text blocks moving at the same time and lots of color effects will cause the frame rate to decline or cause the movie to drop frames in playback to keep up to the set frame rate. It's also important to keep motion limited to the movie display area because any motion occurring outside the display area will affect the processor and thus the movie playback.

FIGURE 6.7

Panoramic photos shot at a distance may display too small on handhelds or other devices to effectively convey meaning.

Although more complex styles of animation will play back better as devices improve over time, it's useful to always think about the lowest common denominator in terms of playback and the small screen size to make great animation for devices.

THE REALITIES OF DEVELOPING FOR DEVICES AND PLATFORMS

A variety of issues affect developing animation and motion graphics for handhelds and other devices. The four main areas that developers need to face and that will be discussed in the following section are

- Processor speed
- Sound compression
- File size: connectivity and storage space
- Displays

The Limits of Processor Speed and How It Affects You

A device's processor speed affects the playback of the Flash movie because the processor mainly determines whether the device can keep up with the movie's defined frame rate. The processor has to maintain the graphic refresh rate of the device's screen at a speed equal to the set movie frame rate. If the processor can't do that, then the Flash movie will play back at a lower frame rate or begin dropping frames when sound is set to stream. Slow frame rates ruin the effect of motion graphics and character animation, so it's important to keep in mind what can be done to minimize these problems.

Flash redraws graphics based on a bounding box that surrounds the area on the screen where movement occurs (see Figure 6.8). To decrease the load on the processor, it's possible to develop a storyboard with movement that keeps the area of the screen that has to be redrawn at any one time to a minimum (see Figure 6.9). When this is done, it's possible to create more complex movements and effects because less of the processor is being used to redraw the background and other unnecessary graphics.

FIGURE 6.8

The bounding box that contains motion can include the whole screen.

FIGURE 6.9

The bounding box can become much smaller if thought is given to the layout.

Techniques and items that take up too much of your device's processor speed—and therefore cause your Flash movie to creep along—include the following:

- Pans, zooms, and cross-fades
- The use of alpha and gradient effects
- The complexity and size of the vector shapes animating at any specific time
- The number of symbols animating concurrently
- Shape tweening
- The number of changes (color, size, rotation, and so on) applied to symbols
- The number and complexity of motion tweens
- The use of complex, animated masks
- The use of complex lines, especially the nonstandard lines such as ragged, dashed, and dotted
- The motion of fonts, especially resizing and scrolling large text blocks
- Intense use of ActionScript that controls MCs or creates complex visual effects
- Combining many of these techniques makes things even worse

By minimizing the use of these techniques and items, animators and designers gain greater control over the frame rate playback of movies. Using too many of these techniques will ensure that movies play back poorly on current devices (see Figure 6.10).

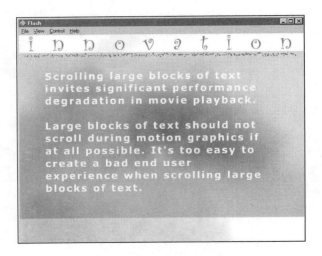

FIGURE 6.10

Alphas, photos, complex fonts, and scrolling large blocks of text slow down Flash movie playback.

Sound Compression

Audio, whether music, dialogue, or sound effects, is crucial to the success of any cartoon or motion graphic because audio brings visuals to life. Without audio, most visuals are stiff and dull.

 Adaptive Differential Pulse Code Modulation (ADPCM) compresses sounds by recording only the difference between samples rather than the entire sample. MP3 stands for MPEG (audio layer 3) and compresses sounds in a more sophisticated manner that creates much smaller audio files. MP3 uses perceptual audio coding and psychoacoustic compression to discard all audio information that the human ear can't hear.

The new multimedia-focused devices are configured to provide high-quality sound playback using MP3 audio. Because Flash 4 and above support MP3 it seems automatic to use this type of sound compression. MP3 provides smaller file sizes, greater audio clarity, and higher audio fidelity; but sometimes it makes sense to resist using this audio technique when deploying content to devices, for the same reason certain graphic techniques should be avoided.

The problem is that MP3 sound compression dedicates a lot of a device's processor to decompress and play the audio. Because MP3 audio uses so much of the processor, it can negatively affect the playback of the animation. Frames are either dropped to keep up with the sound or the playback frame rate declines dramatically. As a result, developers must reconsider using ADPCM, Flash's other audio compression format, because it is much less processor intensive.

It's important to test animations using both formats on different devices to see if MP3 compression ruins the animation. If it does, then it's possible to deliver movies that use ADPCM audio (see Figure 6.11). Unfortunately these files will be much larger than the same files with MP3 sound and the audio won't sound as clear, but the animation will play properly.

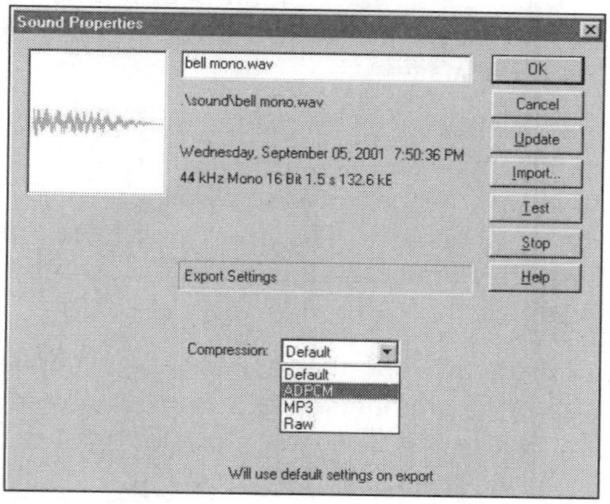

FIGURE 6.11

Some sounds can be compressed using ADPCM to improve animation playback by lessening the audio's use of the processor.

Using a mixture of both formats is often the best solution in these cases. ADPCM can be used where the audio affects the animation and MP3 can be used where it doesn't. Animations can be storyboarded with this sound problem in mind from the start of the project so that bad sound doesn't ruin the movie.

 Another sound issue to keep in mind is that the speaker quality on most devices is poor. This will undoubtedly change in the future, but getting the best possible audio quality requires a viewer to use headphones. Without headphones, a lot of the audio on devices sounds as if it's being played through old car speakers from a static-filled AM radio that doesn't get any stations very clearly. Because this is the case, be sure audio levels are set extremely well or else the dialogue will get lost in background music and sound effects.

File Sizes: Connectivity and Storage Space

Devices and handhelds have file size limitation issues because both storage space and connection speeds affect what people can download and view.

Many connection options available for handhelds and devices are fairly slow. Speeds for wireless connections can be slower than 14.4kbps. Fast connections are still fairly rare so it's important to keep movies as small as possible. A 1M cartoon could take 10 minutes or more to download over a slow connection. It's difficult to imagine people waiting that long to download an animation that they may or may not enjoy. Although future wireless network technology may alleviate this problem, that appears to be in the distant future.

It's almost as if handhelds and embedded devices return developers to the beginning of the web when connection speeds averaged under 14.4. Because this is the problem that Flash was created to solve, it's the perfect tool for developing content for devices.

Many devices are not connected directly to the web and instead get files by synching with a personal computer. Because users are downloading files over a network or modem connection, storage space is what limits file size the most on these devices. The problem is that most devices don't have a lot of storage space.

Many handhelds only have 8–64 megabytes of built-in storage space, so there isn't too much room for big files. A lot of handheld owners own expansion cards that allow them to carry more files with them, but this is by no means universal. Because many viewers only have a few megabytes of storage space for noncrucial files, they might not want to download and store large animations. This immediately limits the audience, so it's important to take every opportunity to decrease the file size.

If vector graphics are used for the artwork, then it's usually dialogue and music that have the largest impact on the file size of an animation. Because sound is so crucial for the success of any animation, it's important not to cut back too much in this area, but a few things can be done to reduce the file size of the movie. If at all possible use small looping sound clips under the animation and insert shorter musical effects for specific emphasis.

Given all the uncertainties of built-in memory sizes, expansion cards, and connection speeds, it's best to keep animation files around 500 kilobytes for cartoons and less than 100 kilobytes for motion graphics projects. Each project will be different, but these are reasonable rules of thumb. If these file sizes are going to be exceeded, then it's important to consider whether a viewer is going to be willing to wait for the file to download.

Developing for Different Displays

Devices have different aspect ratios, screen sizes, display resolutions, and color display settings. These differences provide one of the greatest challenges in developing for multiple devices. Movies have to be created with all the possible future platforms for deployment firmly kept in mind.

Because the goal is to develop content that is "create once, tinker with a bit, and play everywhere," it's imperative to decide at the earliest possible stage of the production process what the movie size should be and how that will affect its display on different devices. Important animation and titles have to be kept within the smallest display size-safe area. To accomplish this, place a simple rectangular frame template that defines the smallest display size on a layer over the movie work area in the Flash authoring environment (see Figure 6.12). Referring to this template during production will keep crucial animation within the safe area.

For more information about device screen size, see Appendix B, "Flash Device Matrix."

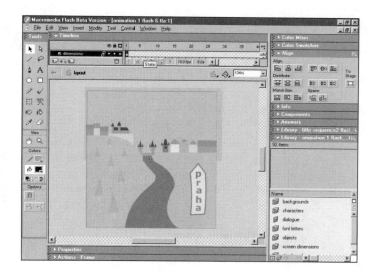

FIGURE 6.12

Adding a rectangular frame template inside Flash will help define where the animation safe area is for the smallest display size.

The aspect ratio of a screen defines the rectangularity of the screen as it compares the horizontal image dimension to the vertical dimension. The traditional aspect ratio is rectangular, for example television screens are normally 4:3 (or more commonly shown 1.33:1).

The aspect ratio and display size of devices vary widely. While the standard aspect ratio for computers and televisions is around 4:3 in a landscape mode, many devices have an almost square or even slightly vertical display size in a portrait mode. The actual display sizes of devices vary from the television displays of set top boxes at 640×480 (1.33:1) to Pocket PCs at 240×260 (1:1.083). This means that movies need to be resized and possibly rotated.

It's possible to create movies at a horizontal aspect ratio and then play them back on vertical displays like those of the Pocket PC devices. The trick is to create a Flash movie in a horizontal aspect ratio and then load it into a movie with a vertical aspect ratio. The loaded movie is then rotated 90 degrees to display in the handheld screen area. This technique requires the viewer to turn the device, but this shouldn't be a problem for viewers with handhelds and it's certainly much easier than reformatting a horizontal movie into a vertical aspect ratio.

Vectors are useful in creating content for multiple display sizes because they usually look good when resized. To make vectors that resize well, it's best to create movies at the smallest targeted display size and then increase the final size movie in the HTML code or by loading it inside another Flash movie. This is because vectors scale better going up then going down. Sometimes the anti-aliased edges on vector lines will overlap when scaled down. If a movie is created at the smallest display size and then scaled up to larger display sizes, it won't have these problems.

Photos aren't nearly as good for this "create once, play everywhere" philosophy because they don't scale up or down very well. If photographs are used, then it's best to create the movie at the largest intended display size and then scale downward. This decreases pixelation in the photographs, but photos that are shown at anything other than their exact size often look bad in Flash. Creating at the largest possible size also increases file size significantly. When using photos, it's often better to create content for specific device display sizes.

Besides sizes and aspect ratios, displays also provide a wide range of color and resolution options. Television displays have very low resolution and text needs to be large to be clear. Thin lines often jiggle nauseatingly during playback on televisions. This is a problem because hairlines work best in Flash for animation. Handhelds have higher resolution and are sharper for reading text, but small display sizes means that text needs to be fairly large to be readable for these devices.

To find out more about developing Flash applications for televised display, see Chapter 11, "Flash Content for Television." Additionally, you can learn about using fonts on devices by reading Chapter 4, "Typography in Flash for Devices."

Colors on displays can range from 256 colors to thousands of colors. The web-safe color palette, which is the standard palette when opening the Flash authoring tool, is generally acceptable for use, but it's incredibly limiting to creative expression in animation. Television displays provide a separate challenge because colors such as reds blow out and bleed over lines. However, the TV-safe color palette can be used for animation that will be viewed on television displays to avoid these problems.

KEYS TO MOTION GRAPHICS

Now that there's an understanding of the challenges in creating animation for devices, let's develop a motion graphics title sequence to investigate the keys to motion graphic design for devices. The following title sequence is from a cartoon project called "The Prague Years." The cartoon is about a couple of twentysomething characters named Godpy and Podie that move to Prague in the early '90s to enjoy the expatriate experience in the recently freed communist city. The title sequence needs to quickly imply the foreign setting, define the style of the cartoon, and attempt to impart the idea of Prague's rapidly changing society—all in 10 to 15 seconds and at a miniscule file size so that it doesn't impede the download of the rest of the cartoon.

Making Motion Graphics that Work

Because the cartoon is aimed at handhelds, and currently only Pocket PCs, the movie size is set at 230×250. Although the available display size on Pocket PCs is 240×260 (full display size is 320×240), it's prudent to develop movies at a slightly smaller size. This is because scrollbars may appear in the browser and take up about 10 pixels vertically and horizontally if the Flash movie is set to 240×260. Although it's possible to set the margins to 0 in the HTML document to solve this problem, this doesn't always seem to work. The pragmatic solution is to develop at a slightly smaller file size.

The first choice to make in developing this title sequence is the main font. Although a classic art nouveau or socialist constructivist font would imply Prague's setting and the comic strip's ethos, neither kind of font would impart the whimsical and capricious nature of the story. The original comic strip used a handmade title font so in the end it makes the most sense to create that font in Flash and animate the motion graphic title sequence with the resulting artwork (see Figure 6.13).

FIGURE 6.13

The hand drawn font used in the original comic strip title was re-created for the Flash cartoon.

 Flash handles fonts in a way that can seriously degrade the animation playback of a motion graphics sequence. Fonts require more of the processor to play, so it's often useful to convert a font to curves and import the artwork into graphic "font" symbols in Flash. Using these symbols often allows motion graphics to play more smoothly.

The color palette for the entire cartoon, as well as the title's motion graphic sequence, contains flat colors that adhere as closely as possible to the web-safe color palette. The end result of this decision is that the project has a lot of strong colors like red that really pop out from the screen. Although this is useful on smaller screen sizes like handhelds, it does cause a problem because a lot of the more vibrant colors won't display well on television. The choice of colors ends up limiting where the project can display properly.

 If possible, use alpha transparencies and masks sparingly in motion graphics sequences. They are processor intensive and will slow down the playback of the movie.

The next choice to make is what kind of music to use during the motion graphics title sequence. Because Prague has a long fascination with Mozart and the city's link to his classical music heritage (Mozart premiered *The Magic Flute* in Prague), let's use a clip of classical music from a sound library. Because we want to imply a changing society with the title sequence, let's find a piece of rock or grunge music to imply the new era of freedom that was ushered in with the fall of communism.

Although it's always best to have a composer create music specifically for a motion graphic, this kind of original music is often out of reach due to budgetary restrictions. Musical clips are available from a variety of sound libraries on the web or through mail order on CD. Some favorite sound libraries include the Fresh library (**www.freshmusic.com**) and the Music Bakery (**www.musicbakery.com**). If a production team member has any musical talent, then it's possible to create soundtracks with software tools like ACID. This tool provides small chunks of music that can be built up to create a musical composition. It's basically a drag and drop timeline that allows you to create in a WYHIWYG (What You Hear Is What You Get) manner.

After the musical choices have been made, it's important to think about what kind of animation will be used to create the motion graphics. Flash supports two main kinds of animation—keyframe animation and motion tweening (see Figure 6.14). Keyframe animation is the classic way to animate characters by creating a new drawing in successive frames, while motion tweening lets the software program move objects around the screen automatically after defining a beginning and end point.

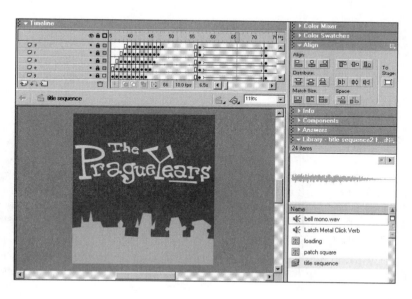

FIGURE 6.14

Flash supports both keyframe and motion tween animation.

Because the software does so much of the work with motion tweening, it's considerably faster than keyframing. Motion tweening does have a tendency to look a bit mechanical. Motion graphics designers use motion tweening to rough out the movement and then use keyframe animation to give more emotion to a motion graphics project.

The type of animation that will predominate throughout a movie also impacts the choice of a movie frame rate. Motion graphics play back best when the frame rates are set to 20 and above. The movement of letters and graphics is much more fluid at higher frame rates. Unfortunately, character animation in Flash can't keep up at those frame rates so a choice has to be made.

One solution is to put the title sequence in a movie with a higher frame rate and develop the character animation in a completely different movie set to a lower frame rate. When the title movie ends, a command then brings up the character animation movie as a new URL link. This is an awkward solution because the cartoon doesn't get a chance to load while the title sequence plays.

The standard approach is to animate the motion graphics at the character animation frame rate of 10–12 frames per second and use strong movement that still looks good at the lower frame rate (see Figure 6.15). It's always important with Flash to create the motion graphic effect with the lowest common denominator in mind and develop a solution that looks good for that viewer. Because pans, zooms, and cross-fades don't work well for playback (and look even worse at slow frame rates), it's important to concentrate on finding a motion treatment that doesn't use these techniques.

FIGURE 6.15

Set the movie frame rate to 10–12 fps to get decent playback.

In the case of "The Prague Years," the solution is to drop the text onto the screen in a wavelike sequence, to give the title an interesting movement at a small file size, while also implying that change is coming to the setting of the cartoon. The other useful aspect of this motion technique is that the bounding box around the changing animation elements never contains the whole screen. This allows the animation to play back at the intended frame rate because the entire screen never has to refresh completely.

After deciding how to animate the title into the scene, it's important to consider the background that will appear behind the title. The simpler the background, the better the playback of the title sequence (see Figure 6.16). The worst backgrounds for playback are complex vector graphics.

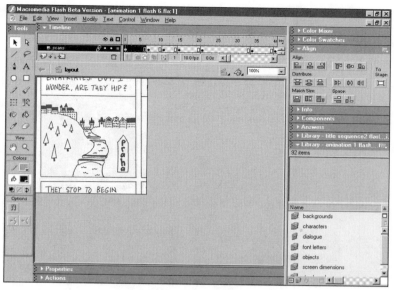

FIGURE 6.16

The simpler the background in the title sequence, the better.

Following up the text motion, the title and background will change from grayscale to color. This helps give a sense of the setting's impending change at little file size cost. Because this technique requires the entire screen to change in each frame, the animation does play back slowly on some devices.

Although this title sequence ends up being quite simple graphically and somewhat limited in its motion graphics, it does the job for a title sequence that will work on devices. The title sequence plays back at the proper frame rate at a small file size, and gives a fair sense of the coming cartoon.

Movie Creation Step-by-Step

Now that the decisions on how to create the motion graphics title sequence for "The Prague Years" have been made, the following section goes through the sequence step-by-step to show how to create it in Flash.

The Title Sequence

The title sequence files are available for download at the book's web site (**www.flashenabled.com**). These files include the font scan, the traces of the letters, the symbols, the animated title sequence, and the loading code. The scratch soundtrack also is provided. Use these files to follow along or put together your own motion graphic sequence.

Because the title sequence for "The Prague Years" uses a hand-drawn font for the title, the first step is to scan and trace the letters. The secret to getting the absolutely smallest file size and most efficient playback with any tracing in Flash is to use the Line tool or the Bezier curve tool. Using these tools creates the smallest number of points in the traced drawing.

 A drawing tablet such as a Wacom tablet is the most important tool for any digital animator to use. Wacom tablets allow a more natural way of drawing digitally. Using the pen on the tablet is more efficient and gives better line quality than using a mouse. See these products at www.wacom.com.

1. Scan and place the image of the title on a bottom layer and name it scan.
2. Lock this layer because there's no need to select the image again (see Figure 6.17).

FIGURE 6.17

Place the title font scan and lock the layer.

3. Create a new layer and name it traces.
4. Select the Line tool (keyboard shortcut N).
5. Select hairline in the Stroke panel. This allows the line in the scan to be seen easily as it's being traced.
6. Select red to differentiate the drawn line from the scanned line.
7. Set Snap to on by selecting View, Snap to Objects (Ctrl+Shift+/).

8. Draw straight lines over the scan from point to point of the font outline. The best way is to draw from each corner point back to the end of the last line. This is because Flash can force the line to snap to pixel points in the grid rather than to the place you want it to end. Snapping to the end of a line overrides the points in the grid.

9. When there is a curve in the scanned drawing, create straight lines for each part of the curve. As an example, there may be three lines for a sharp curve, one for each distinct part of the larger curve.

10. First draw all the straight lines, then select the Arrow tool and pull the lines into curves (see Figure 6.18). Deselect the Snap tool before starting this step or it will be difficult to get the curves to pull out properly. It's easier to do all this work at the end of the process because it's more efficient than always changing back and forth between the tools and toggling snap on and off.

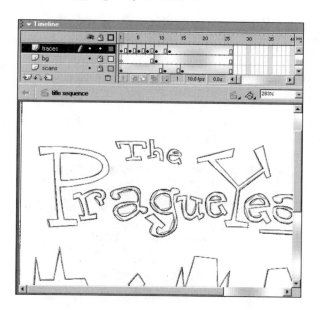

FIGURE 6.18

Trace over the entire font with the Line tool.

11. Review all the points in the lines you've drawn by selecting all the lines and then selecting the Subselect tool (keyboard shortcut A). It may be possible to optimize the lines further by deleting some of the points in the lines at this time.

12. After all the lines have been created and reviewed, select all the lines and change them to the desired line size of .75 and change the line color to orange (the font outline color). See Figure 6.19.

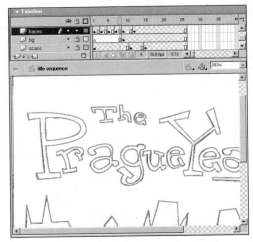

FIGURE 6.19

Pull out the curves with the Arrow tool and then make the line width wider.

13.   After the final line size and color are selected, turn the lines into fills using Modify, Shape, Convert Lines to Fills (see Figure 6.20) and save your project.

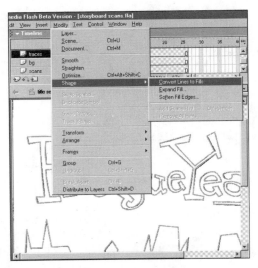

FIGURE 6.20

Convert the lines to fills to control the line width while resizing.

Another way to do this would be to use the scanned raster images of the individual letters as graphic symbols and animate them. The problems with this are that the file size would be too large and it would be almost impossible to have the letters move against a background because it would be so difficult to cut out the scanned letters.

It's important to turn the wider lines into fills because line widths in Flash do not resize as expected. Line widths change unexpectedly as symbols scale up and down. Letters that were created at the same time with the same line width and then put into different symbols might have completely different line widths when they're resized. The only way around this aesthetic disaster is to turn thicker lines into fills. Hairlines do resize properly, but hairlines are often the wrong graphic choice for a project. Hairlines also jiggle when displayed on televisions so they are somewhat limited.

Compare the efficiency of the hand-drawn lines to the lines created using Trace Bitmap or a program like Streamline. Trace Bitmap or Streamline creates vector lines with much larger file sizes because they contain many more points. Because there are so many points, graphic refresh is much slower and frame rates decline.

Now that the title font has been traced into Flash, each letter can be made into a symbol. Decide on a naming sequence, in this case it's "t-a1" where the "t" stands for title, the "a" stands for the letter and the "1" stands for the first instance of that letter (see Figure 6.21). Select each letter and turn it into a movie clip symbol. In general, it's best to make all symbols movie clip symbols (F8). This allows ActionScript to work with the symbols more easily.

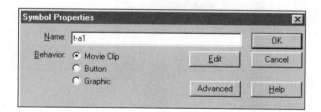

FIGURE 6.21

Decide on a symbol naming convention and stick to it throughout the project.

At this point it's also useful to move all the letters onto distinct layers. Because each letter will be animated with a motion tween, which only affects one object per layer, each letter has to have its own layer. Add layers for each letter and then name them accordingly. Cut and paste each letter onto the appropriate layer.

Adding Sound to the Title Sequence

The next step in the project is to digitize and import the audio files into Flash. The music and effects for the title sequence are pulled from a royalty-free CD. Syntrillium Software (**www.syntrillium.com**) makes a good, and inexpensive, audio editing program called Cool Edit 2000. A 64-track audio editing program called Cool Edit Pro also is available. Using Cool Edit, it's possible to record dialogue using a simple microphone, digitize audio clips off CDs, and edit clips.

It's preferable to record the clips at the highest possible quality, generally 44KHz, stereo and 16-bit. After the audio is recorded, it's then possible to convert the audio to mono before bringing the files into Flash (see Figure 6.22). The reason for doing this is that higher quality stereo audio will be on hand in case it's possible to use it in the future, but it's easier to work with smaller size audio files (less than 3M) in the Flash authoring environment.

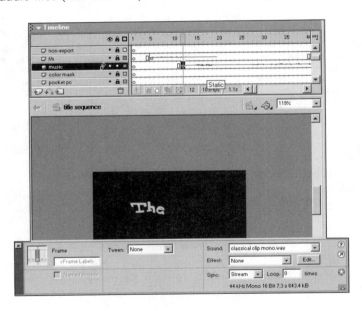

FIGURE 6.22

Importing sound into Flash as mono is useful for keeping working file sizes small. If needed, it's easy to update to stereo in the future.

Adding Animation to the Title Letters

After the music is inserted, it's time to create the "wave" effect on the title letters. This is done by resizing each letter and applying a standard motion tween to each. As an example, the P that starts Prague will begin much larger than the movie area, drop quickly into place, get a bit smaller than the final symbol size, and then ease into the correct size. Try to minimize the amount of motion that happens outside the screen area. This motion still affects the processor and screen redraw.

The drop into place will take three to four frames and then the easing in from the smaller size will take three frames. The reason for adding the small motion at the end is so that the overall motion doesn't appear too mechanical.

Flash 4 allowed users to select a sequence of frames and insert keyframes into each one of them at the same time. Subsequent versions of Flash changed this behavior and inserted only one keyframe at a time into the keyframe at the playback head. This behavior was moved to the Modify, Frames, Convert to Frames drop-down menu.

It's possible to change back to the Flash 4 behavior by going to Edit, Keyboard Shortcuts and duplicating the current Flash keyframe set. Once the keyframe set has been copied, switch F6 from the command Insert Keyframe to Modify, Frames, Convert to Frames.

First, insert a series of keyframes in the P layer after the first instance of the P symbol (see Figure 6.23). Resize the P by selecting the symbol with the arrow tool (keyboard shortcut "V") and the Scale option in Flash 5 or the Free Transform Tool in Flash 6 (see Figure 6.24). The other way to do this is to select Modify, Transform, Scale and Rotate (Ctrl+Alt+S). When the dialog box comes up, enter a numeric value for the resize (see Figure 6.25). This can be useful in doing title sequences that require all the changes to be exactly the same because it's much easier to apply numeric value changes across multiple letter symbols.

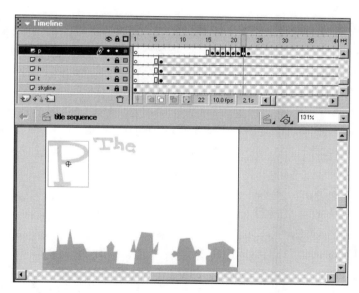

FIGURE 6.23

Insert keyframes into the P layer.

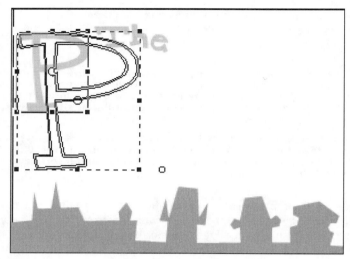

FIGURE 6.24

Resize the P using the Free Transform tool.

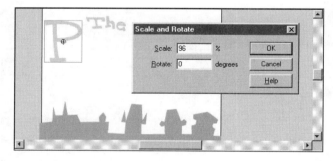

FIGURE 6.25

It's possible to resize using the Scale and Rotate tool as well.

Review the motion by playing through the frame sequence. If the motion seems off, turn onion skinning on and look at the outlines of the letter (see Figure 6.26).

After review, the P in the second frame is a little too small for the rest of the movement. With onion skinning on, it's possible to go to that frame and resize in comparison to the letters in the other frames (see Figure 6.27).

FIGURE 6.26

Compare the size of the symbols using onion skinning.

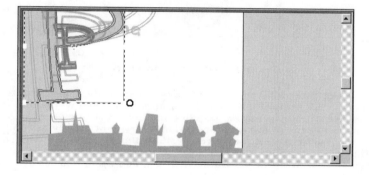

FIGURE 6.27

Resize the symbols in the sequence as needed using the Edit Multiple Frames feature of onion skinning.

Once the feel of the movement is right for the P symbol, go through all the rest of the symbols and create the same sequence of frames and resize the symbols appropriately (see Figure 6.28).

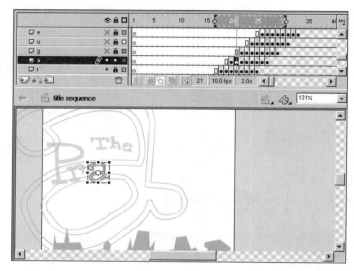

FIGURE 6.28

Resize all the other letter symbols to create the motion sequence.

If you're using a lot of motion tweens, then try to make sure the symbols are movie clips rather than animated graphics or, even worse, groups of objects. The file size for animated graphics and groups is calculated in a different way in tweens so the graphics inside the symbol usually get counted multiple times, while in most movie clip symbols the graphics are only counted once. This will take some trial and error. It's also useful to keep in mind that large tweens add 12 bytes per frame. This can add up to a lot of bytes so it's important to use tweens cautiously.

There are several programs that simplify the creation of motion graphics and title sequences. The most commonly used program is Wildform SWfX available at **www.wildform.com**. SWfX provides hundreds of built-in text animations at a reasonable price, but be aware when using these programs because they can create larger than usual Flash movie file sizes. This is because symbols aren't always created in the most efficient manner in these software programs. It's important to import the resulting SWF into Flash and review the symbols and structure to see if it's possible to optimize the file size as well as the playback speed.

Adding Color with Motion Tween

The next part of "The Prague Years" motion title movement is a transformation from black and white to color using a motion tween on all the symbols.

1. Create the color change by selecting all the layers where the color change will end and inserting a keyframe.

2. Select each layer's end keyframe that you just created and choose the Tint option from the Effect panel. Select a color to tint the selected object and be sure the value is 100%.

3. Repeat this for the other layers.

4. Select all the layers in a frame before the end frame of the tween (see Figure 6.29).

FIGURE 6.29

Select all the layers to create a motion tween on all of them.

5. With a frame selected, the Property Inspector in Flash 6 will show a Tween option. Select Tween/Motion (see Figure 6.30).

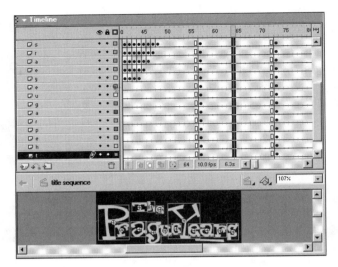

FIGURE 6.30

Add a motion tween to all the layers.

6. The color will now change from grayscale to color.

7. Fine-tune the color change by Easing In or Easing Out the tween (see Figure 6.31). This makes the color change begin more slowly than it ends (Easing In) or end more slowly than it begins (Easing Out). In this case, Ease Out by keeping all the layers selected and move the Easing slider down to a negative number. It's also possible to type in a negative number in the Easing text field to get an Easing Out effect.

8. Save your file.

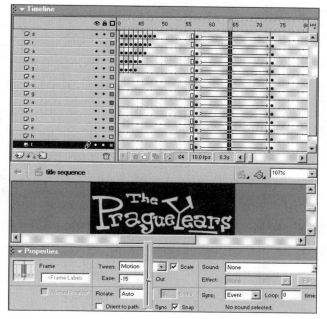

FIGURE 6.31

Ease the motion in over the layers.

Adding a Picture Frame

Don't forget to put a "picture frame" around the movie to mask the work area outside the viewable display (see Figure 6.32). Without a frame to mask the work area, this whole area can be seen if the movie is placed in an HTML document incorrectly or if the movie is sent out as a standalone movie that is resizable.

It's important to add the picture frame because the final movie is often shown from sites that the designer or animator has no control over. Because other people might make mistakes in the HTML code or even distribute the movie as a standalone file that can be resized to show the work area, it's best to cover the area up so that it can't ever be seen. Adding the picture frame allows the creator to know that the viewer will only see the intended movie area.

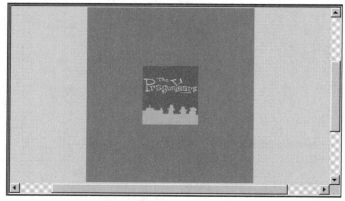

FIGURE 6.32

Add a picture frame on the top layer to cover the movie's work area.

Designing the Loading Sequence

The final step in creating the title sequence is to make sure that there is a loading sequence so viewers will know if they have to wait for the cartoon or motion graphics to download before they can view anything (see Figure 6.33). This can often be accomplished visually by using a progress bar. It's easy to see filling up on a Pocket PC and is readily understandable.

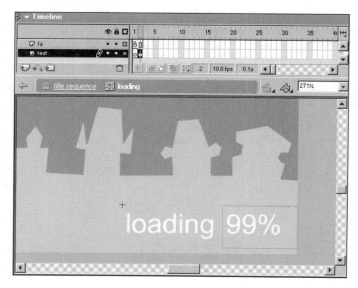

FIGURE 6.33

The loading sequence should tell the audience when the cartoon is loaded and viewable.

The most important thing to remember is that waiting is bad. People hate to wait. This should not only influence the creation of a loading sequence but also the entire development of movies in Flash.

Because some viewers of the finished cartoon will watch it over a direct wireless connection, enough of the cartoon will need to load so that it doesn't stop during playback. Depending on the connection speed, this might be anywhere from 20–80% of the cartoon.

 A progress bar is a useful way to visually see how quickly the file is downloading. It's easier to see a progress bar "filling up" on a Pocket PC or other small screen device than it is to read text.

It's also important that the loading sequence doesn't come up if the cartoon is being accessed off a hard drive or if it's being downloaded over a really fast connection. In these cases there will be no loading time, so it is poor information design that allows the load sequence to be seen. Because the load sequence won't be seen by a lot of the audience on Pocket PCs, the file size should be kept small.

Some of the best practices for loading sequences are to tell the viewer how long the cartoon will take to load at different connection speeds and to show the viewer what percentage of the file has loaded. It's important to give viewers as much information as possible so that they don't get frustrated and leave. If it's at all possible to integrate a game, a quiz, or some other kind of time killer while the cartoon loads, then that should be done as well.

It's also imperative that the font that is used in the loading sequence isn't used later in the movie. Flash loads an entire font family the first time any characters are used in a movie. The letters for "loading" and the numbers for the percentage of the movie that is loaded will only add a few K to the file size, but an entire font family can be up to 20K. If the font used for "loading" were the same font as one used later, the entire font family would have to be loaded. It's completely unnecessary to load all those bytes at the start of a movie and make people wait; so use a separate font.

The basic steps in creating a loading movie are to find out how large the file is and whether it's already downloaded. If it's already downloaded, then it's possible to skip the loading sequence and go directly to the title sequence. If it's not already loaded, then it's possible to find out how quickly the movie is being downloaded.

This general connection speed test will define how much of the movie needs to be downloaded before the loading sequence should start the movie playing. On a slow connection (14.4K and below), 80% of the movie might need to be downloaded before it will play without a hitch. On a faster connection (56K and above), only half of the movie or less might need to be downloaded. The amount that is loaded will need to be determined per project and for each connection speed, but this more detailed loading code provides the audience with the least amount of waiting based on the connection and thus the best possible viewing experience.

Rather than go through the load sequence ActionScript code used in this project in this book, the code is available in the files that can be downloaded from this book's web site. The file also includes the scanned and traced letters, as well as the motion graphic sequence.

KEYS TO CHARACTER ANIMATION

Now that the title sequence is finished, it's time to start on the animation for "The Prague Years" itself. Animation uses the mechanics of motion to create characters that come to life. Although it's impossible to teach the ins and outs of animation in this short chapter, it's still important to consider the traditional principles of lifelike character animation.

The principles of character animation include important ideas such as Squash and Stretch and Arcs and Anticipation. Developed over many years of trial and error by the animators at the Disney Studios, these principles have stood the test of time. Because developing animation for devices can be fairly limiting, it's useful to remember that these principles still apply and that following them will make for better animation.

Squash and Stretch

The key to lifelike animation is emphasizing the contraction and extension of forms. The classic example from Disney's animators is to consider a half-filled flour bag that is squashed when it's dropped on the floor and stretched when held up by two corners. The squash and stretch shown by that simple flour bag is no different than the squash and stretch shown by any nonrigid object, such as a part of the human body or a bouncing ball (see Figure 6.34).

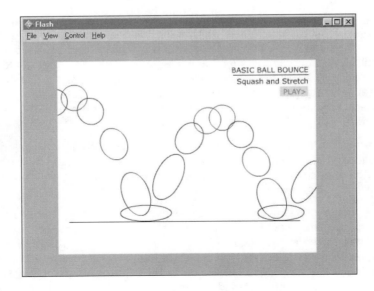

FIGURE 6.34

The classic ball bouncing shows both squash when the ball hits the ground and stretch when it bounces off the ground.

Anticipation

It's important to anticipate a character's actions with a movement, a look, or some other device to prepare the audience for the action. As an example, people gather themselves and lean back slightly before they begin to run forward. When people pick up an object, they normally glance at it before moving toward it. If this kind of anticipation isn't in the animation, then the movement will appear lifeless. Using visual clues to show anticipation rather than verbal clues leads to stronger animation.

Follow Through/Overlapping Action

The key point here is that characters never stop all at once. Different parts of the body move at different speeds and stop at different times. The way a character stops also adds to the character's personality. A character can stop in a loose, relaxed way or with tight control over every part of the body. Either way of stopping shows the audience a different aspect of the character's personality.

Arcs

Character movements follow a slightly circular path. Character actions made on straight lines appear stiff and mechanical. In a walk cycle, the character's body must move up and down, rising and falling in an arc with the rhythm of each step (see Figure 6.35). Animators that rely on motion tweens for character movement usually end up with lifeless motion because tweens rely on straight lines rather than arcs.

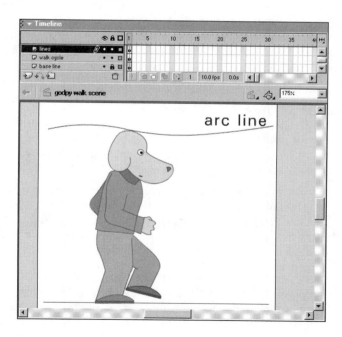

FIGURE 6.35

Use arcs when animating characters to get lifelike movement.

Secondary Action

Secondary actions are actions that support the primary action of the scene. Secondary actions drive home the emotion of the primary action. If a character begins to cry quietly, then an appropriate secondary action might be to slowly wipe away one of the dripping tears.

Timing

Timing in animation, as in any other acting discipline, is crucial to the development of a scene. In animation, timing depends on the number of frames that contain drawings and how many frames each drawing stays on the screen. Film animation is normally done at 24 fps with most drawings staying on the screen for two frames, called animating on twos; although some actions such as lip synching require drawings to stay on the screen for one frame, called animating on ones. Because frame rates are well below 24 fps in Flash, it's normal to animate everything on ones, and animation timing will reflect this.

Exaggeration

Exaggerating action so that it's strong and clear, yet still believable, is one of the keys to successful animation. Exaggeration allows animation to be happy, funny, sad, or any other emotion. In general, animation benefits from slightly exaggerating all the emotions and movements in a cartoon.

Ease In, Ease Out

The idea behind ease in and ease out is that the key poses are the most important to convey in an animated sequence. The drawings on each side of these key poses create a movement that moves slowly away from that key pose. In consequence, there are only a few "in between" drawings between the two key poses that link these two poses. Because so many drawings are close to the key poses, the key poses are on screen for the longest possible time. This makes the animation appear to flow more smoothly.

Straight Ahead Animation and Pose to Pose Animation

Animators work in two distinct ways. In straight ahead animation, animators begin at the start of a scene and animate frame to frame. This keeps the animation fresh and full of action. Straight ahead animation rarely works in layouts with strong perspective because it's too easy to lose focus on the overall scene, but it does work very well for any fast, free-for-all action.

In pose to pose animation, animators create key frames to show the most important actions and then return later to fill in the frames in between these key poses with drawings (in betweening is where Flash gets the terminology for motion and shape tweening). Animating pose to pose keeps tight control over the development of scenes that need clear action because the individual poses can be worked out carefully in relation to each other.

Staging

Staging means presenting each story idea in a clear and immediate visual manner. Staging is important in the storyboard phase because it defines what kind of layout or camera shot will work best to convey the story idea. It means that every attempt is made through layout, action, and design to focus the audience's attention on the unfolding of the story.

These are the key principles that have guided character animation over the years. They have worked for feature films, television shows, and independent shorts. Although developing character animation for devices means that animation must be simplified to play back well, adhering to the basic premises of these principles will allow animation for devices to approach the quality of these other display formats.

The animation of "The Prague Years" requires two main characters, a few backgrounds, and a half dozen minor characters. Because the graphic style is simple, the number of symbols and graphics needed to create all the animation and settings is fairly small. This is useful because storage space on devices varies so widely.

In thinking about developing for device screens, the main overall decision that was made with the cartoon was to add as many close-ups as possible of the characters. Because the screen size is small, it's important to keep a tight focus on the characters to convey emotion and expression (see Figure 6.36). Another decision that affected the development of the cartoon was the choice to move forward with a close-to-web-safe color palette. The goal was to use bright colors to help the cartoon pop on the screen.

FIGURE 6.36

Use close-ups on the characters when possible to ensure that emotions are visible.

Movie Creation Step-by-Step

The following section goes through a step-by-step example of how to get "The Prague Years" storyboard into Flash, create and symbolize characters, optimize animation for playback on different devices, and then export for display on multiple devices. Files for this cartoon are available for download at the book's web site. These files include the storyboard scans, the traces of the characters, the symbols, and the storyboard. The scratch soundtrack also is provided. Use these files to follow along or put together your own cartoon.

Creating the Storyboard

The first step in creating any cartoon is to have a written script and a set of drawn characters that can be developed into a storyboard (see Figure 6.37). A storyboard is a series of illustrations that tell the action of a story in pictures. The original comic strip of "The Prague Years" was more or less created in a storyboard format so the comic strip provided the storyboard for the cartoon.

FIGURE 6.37

"The Prague Years" storyboard based on the original comic strip.

To create a storyboard, standard paper storyboard forms are available for purchase from animation supply houses or are simple to create and photocopy. Each storyboard page provides space for several drawings of the scene and lines for the dialogue associated with each drawing. Some animators prefer vertical storyboard forms while others prefer horizontal forms, but either format works fine to create usable storyboards. The goal with the storyboard is to place characters in a strong layout so that the animated action will be clear and strong. It's important to have a dynamic "line of action" in the individual character poses and between the characters (see Figure 6.38). To understand this, put an imaginary line through the main action of the figure. Is it a strong curve with direction? If it's impossible to decide the main line of action, then it's time to rethink the character layout.

FIGURE 6.38

Strong lines of action improve the dynamic quality of animation.

 Beware of "twins" while laying out the storyboard (see Figure 6.39). Twins are drawings in which the character's body is presented symmetrically. Think, for example, of a character standing at attention in the military—the shoulders are at the same height, the feet stick out at the same angle, and so on. Twinned characters like this have no life to them because living creatures are never so static.

FIGURE 6.39

Drawing symmetrical figures ("twins") creates stiff characters.

The storyboard is the point in the production process where the animation director and the storyboard artist figure out the pacing and flow of the movie. The length of scenes and the cuts that will be made internal to scenes and between scenes also are defined.

In developing for devices, many types of standard cuts used in animation have to be discarded. Standard fade ins and fade outs are possible but must be carefully tested on devices. Cross fades or dissolves are almost impossible to make work. Fancy editing effects such as using animated symbols in masks to reveal the next scene "through" the current scene are also difficult to make work. "The Prague Years" relies on straight cuts between scenes with a few fade ins and fade outs.

It's also necessary to think about how scenes will be laid out within the Flash authoring tool. In general, it's good to keep any shots with a continuous background in one Flash scene and then add another scene when the background changes. Breaking animation up into many scenes inside of Flash helps keep the animation organized and the number of layers per scene to a reasonable number. The only problem with using lots of scenes is that it can be difficult to work with long streaming sounds that go across multiple backgrounds. In that case, keep all those sections of the animation together in one Flash scene.

A good way to create a fade in or out in Flash is to place a black rectangle symbol on the top layer (see Figure 6.40). For a fade out, make it transparent in the first frame and black in the end frame. Create the color fade by adding a motion tween (see Figure 6.41). This is much simpler to do than fading all the individual symbols to black and also plays more smoothly.

FIGURE 6.40

Add a rectangular box symbol and make it transparent in the first frame of the fade out.

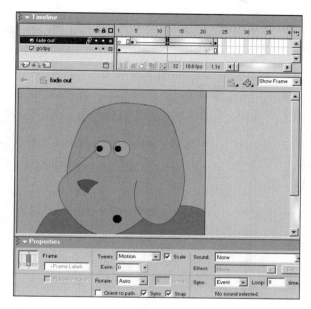

FIGURE 6.41

Create a motion tween to make the scene fade out.

Next, put the animation narration and dialogue in a two-line text block at the top of the frame (see Figure 6.42). This allows a quick review of the dialogue in the movie at the storyboard stage and also gives you the capability to quickly and easily create a close-captioned movie for the hearing impaired. Although this isn't something that's commonly done, it really doesn't add a whole lot of production time, and it's not only useful when reviewing the cartoon but also is considerate to all the possible fans of animation.

The next step is to create a dialogue scratch track to place over the storyboard (see Figure 6.43). This scratch track might not even include the proper character's voices, but will give animators a sense of the cartoon's timing. With scratch track voices added, it's often possible to catch layout errors at this point rather than much later in the production.

FIGURE 6.42

Add lines of dialogue to the storyboard for review and for close captioning.

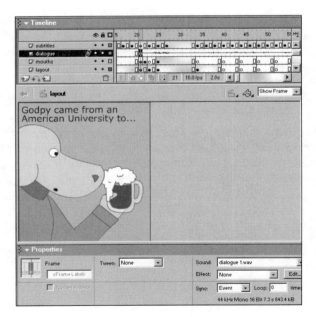

FIGURE 6.43

Add a scratch track to the storyboard to review timing.

Creating the Characters

In the same way as the traced font in the title sequence, characters in Flash can be drawn freehand, traced from scans or vectorized using Trace Bitmap. In general, tracing from scans provides the smallest file size, but many animators prefer drawing straight into Flash or drawing over a reference scan. Because the line of the character is so important to the success of the cartoon, it's important to let animators draw however they prefer. Using Trace Bitmap of scanned pencil or ink drawings will get characters into Flash the quickest, but the file size will be large and the line quality really suffers.

The line width and line quality is extraordinarily important to whether a character comes to life or is mechanical and flat when animated. The way Flash deals with lines has serious ramifications on how characters are created in Flash. As mentioned before, hairlines don't change in size when symbols are resized, while larger line widths do. Using larger line widths is extremely frustrating when resizing symbols because the line weights will not match up from symbol to symbol. Because character symbols are always being resized in Flash, this is a huge problem. It's possible to get around it by making all the lines into paint fills, but hairlines are generally the best choice for Flash animation.

Another type of line to consider is the thick/thin line. Animators love the look of thick/thin lines because these lines impart motion and a sense of life to characters. In Flash, this look normally requires using the Paintbrush tool. Unfortunately, the paintbrush creates lines with huge numbers of vector points, so the file size is large and playback is slow. If the Paintbrush is used, then the lines need to be optimized as much as possible. It's also possible to create this thick/thin line effect by creating parallel lines, pulling them into curves, closing the ends, filling the resulting "line" with a paint fill and deleting the original lines. This is an extremely time-consuming process, however, and should be limited to extremely important graphic elements.

The key to creating character symbols is figuring out the least number of symbols that are necessary to create a character and then give it life through animation (see Figure 6.44). Think about how to cut up a character into the least number of pieces that will allow motion. This usually means creating a new symbol for parts of the body where there are joints, where different parts of the body can turn and twist.

The standard symbols include

- a shoe or foot
- an upper and lower leg
- a waist
- a torso
- an upper and lower arm
- a hand
- fingers
- a neck
- a head

- a nose
- eyeballs
- pupils
- eyebrows
- a variety of mouths

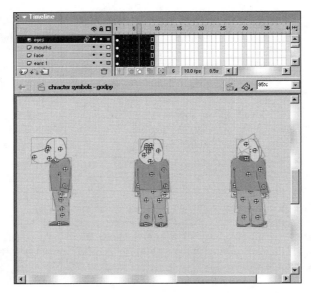

FIGURE 6.44

The symbols for Godpy's standard perspectives allow him to be fully animated.

Symbols need to be created for these parts of the body for different perspectives of the character, but symbols from one perspective can often be used on another perspective. Although there will have to be lots of other fill in symbols to make a character complete, these are the most common symbols that every character should have.

Decide on a symbol naming convention (see Figure 6.45) and set up folders in the movie library for each character. In this case there are so few characters that it's possible to start symbols with the first letter of the character's name and then add a name, point of view and number for the body part, for example, "g – eye front 1" stands for the first example of Godpy's eye viewed from the front. It's common to add a number for various body parts because there may be multiple versions of the body parts created over the course of production.

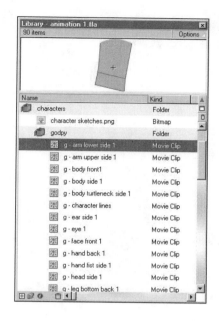

FIGURE 6.45

The symbol naming convention helps keep the animation well organized.

 Flash normally doesn't let a new symbol have the same name as a symbol that already exists. However, if a symbol is in a folder, then Flash does allow symbols to have the same name.

The length of symbol names does affect the file size of the movie, so it's important to keep them short. The names for this cartoon would normally have been made quite a bit shorter by using abbreviations, but for the sake of clarity longer names have been used. As an example of how to cut up a character and create symbols, let's make Godpy's shoe symbol.

1. Create the shoe by copying and pasting the traced shoe part of Godpy's character onto a new layer called shoe.

2. Create a new movie clip symbol called "g – shoe front 1" (see Figure 6.46).

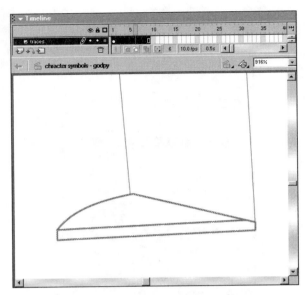

FIGURE 6.46

Select the traced shoe to create a new symbol.

3. Fill the shoe with the intended color, in this case a general web-safe brown, and change the lines to the proper color and weight, in this case dark gray and hairline.

4. Make the graphics smaller in file size by selecting everything on the layer and select Modify, Optimize Curves (Ctrl+Alt+Shift+C).

5. Shift the slider in the Optimize Curves dialog box close to the left side and select Show Totals Message (see Figure 6.47). Selecting Use Multiple Passes will reduce points over several passes and help maintain the integrity of the graphics. In this case the shoe is so simple that it's unnecessary to use Multiple Passes.

6. Select OK and optimize. Flash removes points from the lines and shows how many points have been removed. File size can often be decreased by half without much loss in graphic quality by optimizing artwork in this way.

7. If the artwork loses too much quality, then choose Edit, Undo and redo the optimization with the slider moved further toward the left.

8. It's also possible to retain more control over the graphic optimization by choosing the Subselect tool, selecting lines and removing points individually.

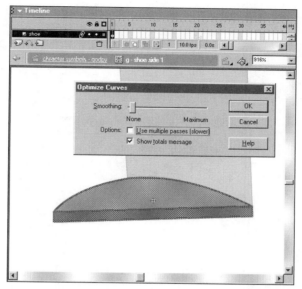

FIGURE 6.47

Optimize the finished artwork using the Optimize Curves tool.

Place the new symbol in the Characters/Godpy folder in the library. It's easier to do this as the character is created rather than when all the symbols have been created. This is because it's impossible to scroll up and down in the library when symbols are selected in Flash 5. This makes it impossible to place symbols in folders that aren't near the symbols.

 As each symbol is created, it's important to add an "arc" to the end of a symbol if it's not completely enclosed with lines and will overlap with other symbols. As an example, do this in an arm symbol by dragging out the fill color into an arc at each end. When symbols are rotated to create movement, these arcs will create better "joins" between the symbols.

It would be possible to minimize the number of symbols in a movie by sharing common body parts between characters. As an example, one round circle could be used as the pupil for every character. In general, this type of sharing is not the recommended way to create symbols for characters because it may be necessary to edit a character's features after symbols have already been created. If symbols are shared across characters, then this will be a difficult change to make because it will require finding and changing every instance of the shared symbol.

It's also necessary to create a series of patches that can be used to place over symbols that don't entirely join otherwise. One of the ways to do this is to create a few symbols of different sizes that are filled black shapes. Common shapes are a circle, a square, and a lozenge shape (see Figure 6.48). Remember to delete the lines around the shapes because they're unnecessary. These patches can be used for all the characters' bodies by placing the patches where needed and then changing the symbol's tint.

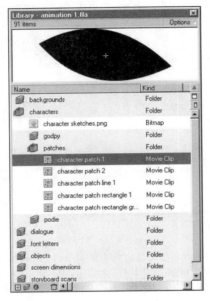

FIGURE 6.48

Create patches to fill in holes between the character symbols.

In feature film animation, every mouth would be drawn separately, but in Flash animation, and especially in animation for devices, it's enough to have the main vowel and consonant shapes to create realistic lip-synching. Because device screens are so small, the mouths won't read as any specific pronunciation when viewed from a distance, but are crucial when viewed in close up.

Character animation in Flash uses a standard minimum set of mouth symbols—the consonants are l/th, f/v, m/p/b, and one for the rest of the consonants, while the minimum mouth symbols for vowels are a/i, e/i, and o (without tongues), and a/e/i, and o/u (with tongues). There's also a standard, nonspeaking mouth plus mouths expressing emotions such as happiness and sadness. Create all the mouths at a similar size so they're easy to replace when lip-synching (see Figure 6.49).

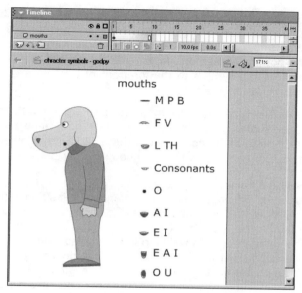

FIGURE 6.49

Godpy's various mouths are created at the same size to aid in lip-synching.

The characters in "The Prague Years" are created in such a simple manner that they almost don't need all the standard mouth symbols. In Podie's case, a simple circle stretched, skewed, and rotated in various combinations can pass for almost all the mouths. Even though this is the case, all the mouth symbols are still created at the start of the project in case they're ever required.

Creating the Background

At some point in the development process, backgrounds based on the scanned storyboard must be created in Flash. This can be done at this stage of the production or it can wait until after the characters have been laid out on the storyboard. Backgrounds should definitely be completed prior to the start of animation. If they aren't completed, then it's easy to develop an animation that gets lost in the backgrounds and ruins the effect of the cartoon.

The backgrounds in "The Prague Years" are kept simple on purpose because the cartoon is aimed at the handheld market. If the backgrounds were complex line drawings of the amazingly detailed architecture in Prague, then the animation playback would drop below the intended frame rate. If detailed backgrounds are a definite stylistic requirement, then it's probably better to bring those backgrounds into Flash as raster graphics.

The backgrounds for "The Prague Years" are based on a cut-out paper graphic style and are extremely easy to produce. In some instances, the backgrounds use gradient colors to add some depth to scenes, but most are purely flat colors. It's important to minimize the amount of gradients on screen at any one time because it will cause the frame rate to drop.

One trick to creating smaller and more efficient files is to re-use one symbol of flat color multiple times. For example, a solid blue sky behind a city skyline and the gray road at the base of the city can be the same symbol. Create a movie clip symbol with a solid black rectangle and place this symbol on a bottom background layer. Tint the symbol to a blue color for the sky. Then copy and paste the same symbol to the forefront of the city and tint it gray. Creative re-use is the key to small Flash movies.

After placing the storyboard scans, quickly trace the background with the Line tool. Create symbols for various background elements if possible. In "The Prague Years," there are many buildings that are reused more than once. A set of these buildings in different colors becomes standard building blocks to create any outdoor scene in the cartoon.

Adding the Characters to the Movie

With the backgrounds and the dialogue scratch track in place, it's finally time to add the characters into the cartoon. Open the character movie and begin copying and pasting characters onto the storyboard (see Figures 6.50 and 6.51). Try to put parts of the character's body that move together onto the same layer. This will help in editing individual keyframes in the animation in the future. For example, put the hand and finger symbols on a separate layer from the other symbols. They'll almost always move together, while other parts of the body, such as the head, might not be moving. It's imperative that the mouth symbols are placed on a separate layer. Having the mouth symbols on a separate layer makes lip-synching and editing a much easier process.

FIGURE 6.50

The scanned storyboard before the character symbols are added on layers above it.

FIGURE 6.51

The storyboard after Godpy's character symbols are added to it.

When placing symbols over a storyboard to create characters, it's often helpful to use the layer outline color feature in Flash. Turn this on by clicking on the color swatch at the right of the layer or double clicking the layer symbol and selecting Outline Color (see Figure 6.52). The outline of the black box above all the layers will turn all layers into outlines. This is incredibly useful in animation because it becomes easy to see the storyboard layout underneath all the layers.

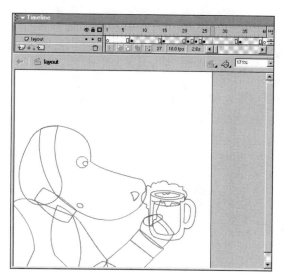

FIGURE 6.52

Select the Outline Color to show the lines that make up the symbols in the character.

There will undoubtedly be missing pieces, shapes, and objects after the characters have been laid onto the storyboard. New symbols will definitely need to be created, but be creative and use as many current symbols as possible. It's amazing that a character's leg symbol can easily become part of another character's hat, but it does work most of the time.

This storyboard with dialogue, some animation, and some effects added is known as an animatic. It's a useful stage for animators and the cartoon director to go back and play with the sense of timing in the cartoon. Most production studios and agencies put a lot of effort into reviewing the animatic carefully and making significant changes at this stage.

Now that the characters are placed, objects are created, and backgrounds drawn, it's time to animate. Re-using symbols to create animation is what makes Flash such a powerful tool for creating animation for the web and devices with small file sizes, but high production values. Symbols can be skewed, stretched, rotated, and flipped to create as much life in each character's motions as possible. Symbols can be made semitransparent to create the effect of blurs to add a sense of movement to quick motions (see Figure 6.53). Avoid using alpha effects too much because they can slow down the playback of the animation.

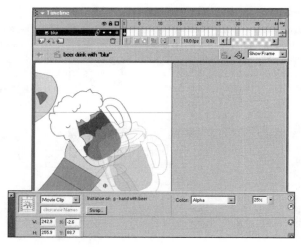

FIGURE 6.53

Partially transparent symbols can be used to create blurs to add to the sense of motion.

One of the ways to add real weight and proportion to animation in Flash is to give proper perspective to characters. One of the standard ways to add depth to characters is to properly foreshorten parts of the body. When the character Godpy picks up a glass in front of him, his arm needs to get shorter and broaden out slightly toward the viewer. In the same way, when

Godpy reaches away from himself, his arm needs to get thinner as it goes back in the distance. Perspective through foreshortening can be achieved in Flash by skewing symbols. Although this isn't as good as drawing each individual perspective, it will usually work fairly well and helps keep file size to a minimum.

One of the standard movements that will have to be created for most characters is a walk cycle. The basic walk cycle contains two steps. The two steps can usually be accomplished in 10–12 frames (see Figure 6.54). The quick way to create a complete walk cycle is to develop one step (see Figure 6.55) and then, after copying and pasting the sequence of frames, switch the opposing hands, arms, legs, and feet from back to front (see Figure 6.56). If the cycle starts with the left arm in back, then bring it to the front of the body and make it the right arm. Once the switch has been made, tweak the symbols a little so that the walk isn't too mechanical from step to step.

FIGURE 6.54

Walk cycles can usually be completed in 10–12 frames.

FIGURE 6.55

The first part of the step in a walk cycle can be copied.

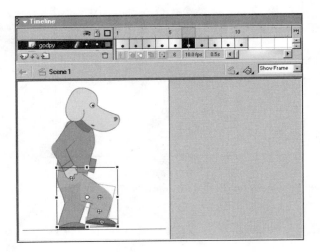

FIGURE 6.56

The copy of the step can be modified to show the next step.

It's possible to change the Edit points of a symbol so that it rotates from that point rather than from the regular symbol center point (see Figure 6.57). This can be useful because most parts of a character have a natural rotation point. A human forearm moves from the elbow, while the upper leg moves from the hip. Changing the edit point like this helps because the symbols move with a more natural arc (see Figure 6.58), but it can cause problems when resizing symbols because the scaling is based on the new edit point.

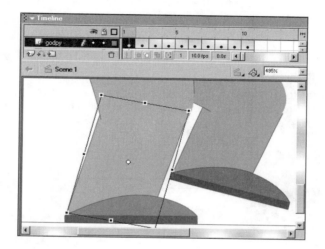

FIGURE 6.57

Select a symbol, click on the Free Transform tool and choose the edit registration point.

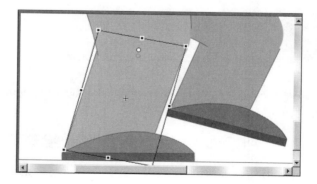

FIGURE 6.58

Move the edit registration point to the natural joint position to aid in creating motion with arcs and rotation.

Turn the completed walk cycle into a movie clip. This allows the character's movement to be reused in many different parts of the cartoon. Analyze the characters for other standard movements that can be turned into movie clip cycles, such as running, jumping, and in the case of "The Prague Years," drinking beer at the local pub.

Adding Dialog

After the broad character movement in the cartoon has been animated, it's time to synchronize mouths to the dialogue. This is a fairly automatic process in Flash, so it's often best to keep it for the end of the animation process.

1. Be sure all the dialogue audio tracks are set to stream sound or it will be impossible to figure out the lip sync.

2. It's often easier to understand what's happening frame to frame by making the frames use Preview mode. This shows the mouth symbol that's in each frame (see Figure 6.59).

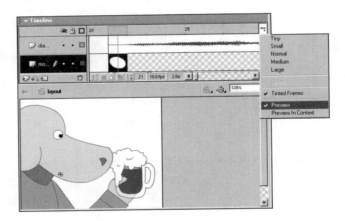

FIGURE 6.59

Select Large frames and Preview to see the mouth symbol that occupies each frame.

3. Scrub across the dialogue soundtrack by selecting the playback head and moving across the timeline.

4. Determine the mouth symbol that is needed in each frame, in this case the standard consonant for D.

5. Set a keyframe for this new mouth symbol.

6. Select the current mouth symbol in the animation (see Figure 6.60).

FIGURE 6.60

Select the mouth symbol to replace it.

7. On the Property Inspector, choose Swap Symbol (see Figure 6.61).

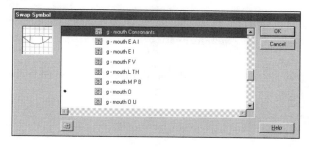

FIGURE 6.61

Replace the mouth symbol in the Swap Symbol dialogue box.

8. Select the consonants mouth symbol and select OK.
9. The correct mouth symbol is now in place. Make sure it's the right size (see Figure 6.62) and then move on to the next position where you will need to make a keyframe.

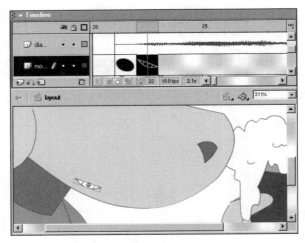

FIGURE 6.62

Review the placement of the new mouth symbol.

After all the mouths have been synched, play the animation back and review the synching carefully. There will undoubtedly be rough patches in the synching that require mouths to be resized, rotated, or skewed slightly.

Programmatic lip-synching is theoretically possible in Flash, but doesn't work in reality. It's possible to type in a sentence, analyze it with ActionScript, and match mouth symbols to the dialogue in Flash, but it's too processor intensive on regular computers so it doesn't stay in synch with the audio.

Adding Details

With the mouths synched, it's now time to return to the animation and add subtle details. Eyebrow movement, head shakes, and hand gestures can be timed to the dialogue more closely to add an emotion and a depth of feeling to the characters. There's nothing more useful than a raised eyebrow to drive home the point of a sarcastic comment; without it the line can easily fall flat.

Finalize the animation and move on to adding the final musical score and any final sound effects. Be sure to balance the audio levels properly between dialogue, music, and effects. If levels aren't balanced properly, then the sound becomes muddy and it can be impossible to hear important lines of dialogue.

Balancing audio can be done inside of Flash (see Figure 6.63), but it's preferable to do it outside of Flash in a dedicated audio editing program prior to importing the sound files into Flash. If it's impossible to use an outside program, then decide on a standard level for the dialogue and change the levels of the music or sound effects accordingly.

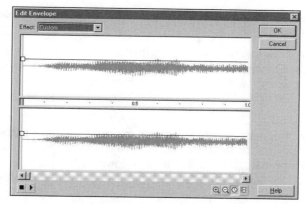

FIGURE 6.63

Balance audio in Flash using the Edit Envelope.

Optimizing the Movie File

Although optimization has been a key throughout the animation process described in this chapter, it's crucial to make a final pass over the cartoon to see if anything can get smaller.

The most important tools a designer or animator has in understanding what constitutes the file size in a movie are the Size Report and Bandwidth Profiler.

The Size Report shows the movie's file size in a frame-by-frame display (see Figure 6.64). It's useful to export the movie, rename the Size Report, optimize further, and then export the movie again. This gives size reports that can be compared over time to understand how the movie's file size is changing.

title sequence2 flash 6 Report.txt - Notepad

Movie Report

Frame #	Frame Bytes	Total Bytes	Page
1	957	957	title sequence
2	2	959	2
3	2119	3078	3
4	2	3080	4
5	3465	6545	5
6	762	7307	6
7	2	7309	7
8	2	7311	8
9	2	7313	9
10	2	7315	10
11	2	7317	11
12	428	7745	12
13	220	7965	13
14	220	8185	14
15	220	8405	15
16	552	8957	16
17	235	9192	17
18	571	9763	18
19	244	10007	19
20	641	10648	20
21	148	10796	21
22	725	11521	22
23	243	11764	23
24	537	12301	24
25	229	12530	25
26	524	13054	26
27	220	13274	27
28	220	13494	28
29	220	13714	29
30	220	13934	30
31	220	14154	31
32	220	14374	32

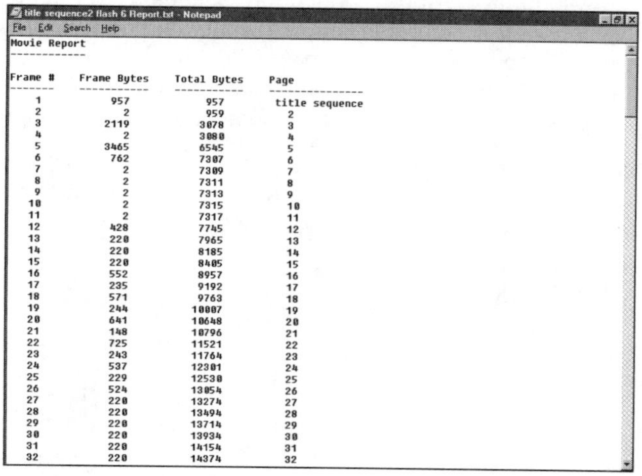

FIGURE 6.64

The Size Report shows a frame-by-frame report of the movie's file size.

Besides the frame-by-frame report, the file size of each symbol, in both shape and text bytes, is shown. Review symbol file sizes for large symbols and try to optimize these symbols.

After the symbols, each event sound is shown, with both the original size and compressed byte size displayed. Review the compression on different sounds to see if they can be lowered. Remember that most sound effects can be exported at an extremely low quality without too much loss in the overall quality of the cartoon. This is an easy way to reduce the file size of the movie.

Streaming sounds don't appear as separate items in the Size Report because they are broken into frame-by-frame packets of information. To review the file size associated with stream sounds, place all the streamed audio files into a separate movie and export as event sounds. It's sometimes possible to find large dialogue audio files that can be further compressed.

Also be sure at this time that audio files are the smallest possible files and that unused sound at the start and end of audio files has been clipped. This is best done in an external audio editing tool.

Imported raster images are shown, with the compressed size, the original size, and the quality setting displayed. Review the quality settings for graphics to see if lower quality settings would be possible to use. Also be sure that the images have been brought in at lowest possible cropped size. Sometimes images are brought into Flash and then cropped inside of Flash. This adds to the file size and should never be done. It's always better to do image editing outside of Flash and bring a graphic with the proper dimensions and resolution into Flash.

Each font family and the characters included with that font family in the movie also are shown. If there is dynamic text in the movie, be sure that only one font family is being used and that only the necessary characters are included. If the only dynamic text is numbers, then the entire font family doesn't need to be included.

The Bandwidth Profiler visually shows where the file size is located in a movie and also shows how a movie will download at various connection speeds (see Figure 6.65). Using the View/Show Streaming option, the animator can see what will happen with the cartoon at any connection speed. If the cartoon won't load on a 56K connection for 10 minutes, then the animator will sit and wait for 10 minutes by using Show Streaming. This is an important test to make at the end of the production cycle and also is useful to make throughout the process.

After the file size has been reduced as much as possible, export the cartoon and an HTML document based on the Pocket PC template. The cartoon is now ready for placement on the web for viewers to download onto a synched device or to view online.

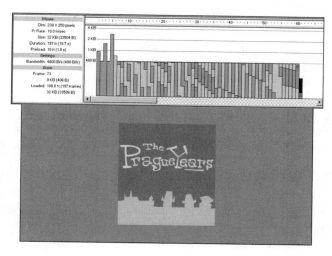

FIGURE 6.65

The Bandwidth Profiler shows how a movie will download over a variety of connections.

Exporting the Movie

Now that the movie is completed and exported for the Pocket PC, it's possible to export it for other devices. There are two main ways to change the display size of the movie for the playback device—in the HTML document or inside another Flash movie. The key to resizing for display is to be sure that the aspect ratio never changes or else the cartoon will look squashed or, alternatively, stretched.

If the cartoon is being loaded into another Macromedia Flash movie, then it's easiest if this loader movie contains a **loadMovie** command in a symbol. Because the cartoon is loaded into a symbol it's easier to target and resize than if it's loaded into a layer. Resizing the cartoon this way gives the most possible control over the sizing and placement of the cartoon for playback because display sizes can easily be tested dynamically and used to change the size of the cartoon. In contrast, it's also possible to resize the cartoon in the HTML page using the HEIGHT and WIDTH properties, but there is less control over placement and dynamic resizing.

In either case, it's crucial to make sure that the picture frame covering the work area of the cartoon matches the background color of the HTML page. This is an issue because Flash often displays hexadecimal colors at slightly different values than the browsers. The color red, as used in Flash, might display differently than the exact same color used in the HTML document. Because this is a problem, it's normally best to use black for the parts of the Flash movie, that is, the picture frame over the work area, that will touch against colors in the HTML document.

SUMMARY

Using Flash to create animation and motion graphics provides a solution for high-quality entertainment and motion design for devices that no other technology offers. Creating with vectors allows movies to combine small file sizes with stunning production qualities that play back within the limitations of a broad range of devices.

Creating character animation and motion graphics in Flash allows designers and animators to develop content that can be played seamlessly in multiple locations—from computers to televisions to handhelds and other devices. Because audiences are beginning to access creative programming from multiple locations now and will do it even more so in the future, it's imperative to understand the limitations of developing for multiple platforms.

When developing for devices, be organized and think ahead about what the device processor can display and at what frame rate, consider what the display size will do to the content, and decide whether it matters that the viewer might not be connected to the web.

Although there are significant limitations in display sizes, hardware speeds, storage capacity, and connectivity, it's definitely worth understanding this balancing act so that content that's developed now can be viewed successfully not only on the web, but on any one of a dozen digital devices now and in the future.

7

CREATING INTERACTIVE GAMES FOR DEVICES USING FLASH

by Andreas Heim

Pocket PC devices are perfect for small, fun games that users can kill time with while traveling or waiting. Because Macromedia Flash runs on the Pocket PC, anyone who is a Flash game developer on the desktop now can develop device games.

This chapter covers categories of games that work well on this platform such as card games, thinking games, and games that are played against the device. Additionally, we will go over the constraints of the platform and what this means for creating games using Flash. The second part of the chapter is all about creating an actual card game for the Pocket PC, including a computer opponent.

The source files for this book are available on the book's web site at www.flashenabled.com/book. You can find the files you need for the examples in this chapter at http://flashenabled.com/ book/chapter7/.

CONSTRAINTS OF THE GAME PLATFORM

When building Flash games for the desktop, we are pretty spoiled. There is plenty of everything: processor power, RAM, powerful video accelerators, and big screens. When you look at the box of a regular game for sale, you will usually see minimal and recommended specifications. When developing a game for the web, either you or your client defines minimal requirements, such as target machine. That target machine, however, is often much slower than the one you do the actual developing on. Still it is often considered acceptable even if the game doesn't run perfectly smooth on the target machine—as long as it is playable, because features required to be in the game are not necessarily compatible with the minimal system. Most users are expected to actually have a faster machine.

This does not translate to the Pocket PC. With the introduction of Pocket PC 2002, all devices equipped with it are currently based on the same processor, the Intel strongARM processor running at 206MHz. In the future, there may be differences in speed between devices and processors, but currently there is one common platform. That makes testing easier for you—if it runs well on your testing device, it will run well on all devices. If it doesn't, it won't work well for anyone else either.

Processor Speed

Pocket PCs are slower than desktop PCs. Although the CPU clock speed does not determine the actual speed of a device, it is an important indicator. Desktop CPUs are now way beyond 1GHz. The CPU currently used in a Pocket PC 2002 runs at 206MHz. The performance of a device is a compromise of size, speed, and power consumption.

What does this mean for Flash games on the Pocket PC? You will meet the limits of processor power much more quickly than on a desktop. A great deal of movement on the screen and intense ActionScript are not your Pocket PC's best friends. Optimization for good performance on the device will accompany most projects. You will find that it's often hard to port a game developed for the desktop to the Pocket PC platform because of processor constraints.

The more actions you try to execute per frame, the more the processor has to work. Loops, and especially nested loops, are not very processor friendly. Recursion is similarly intense—the more levels deep you go the more intense. Some actions take more processing time than others. String operations are generally among the most intense ones, so try to avoid them if you can. Looping through an XML object tree is a combination of looping and string operations; handle with care on devices.

Flash renders graphics in a way that relies mostly on the processor. This is true for devices such as a Pocket PC, where most computing is handled by one single processor. Certain graphical operations are more intense than other ones. The most intense ones are alpha effects, gradients, especially radial gradients, and masks. The more vector lines Flash has to draw, the harder it makes the processor work. Text usually consists of complex lines, so animating text is a bad thing to do on the Pocket PC. Flash tries to reduce the amount of calculation by not redrawing the entire stage every frame, but only the rectangular area within which change occurs. If you have something changing constantly in two opposite corners of the screen, you force Flash to do a full stage redraw every frame, even if not much else is changing.

Alpha effects add even more to that because Flash has to redraw the area that an alpha effect is applied to, even if only a small part of it is actually affected by change. All these effects add up to use more processor power when used together or when used multiple times.

The frame rate of a movie also has an effect on the processor use. The frame rate you set is the maximum rate the movie can run. If Flash can't keep up with it, it tries to catch up—using as much processor power as it can. I recommend 10 frames per second for Pocket PC games. At this rate you still see change as movement. If you set the frame rate higher, your game will probably not run faster anyway on the Pocket PC.

Developing games from the beginning with low processor use in mind will save you a lot of pain. If a game runs fine on the Pocket PC, it will run perfectly smooth on your desktop computer.

Don't Count on Connectivity

Out of the box, the only connections a Pocket PC has are the sync cable to the desktop and the infrared connection. Although most Pocket PCs can be expanded to have an Internet connection of their own—you cannot expect it to be there. With Pocket PC 2002, you can now get to the Internet through the sync cable. That is nice for testing, but is not the typical game-playing situation on a device.

You generally want to play on the Pocket PC when you are away from your desk, when you have only the device with you. If you had a broadband wireless connection, you could just browse to your favorite game site and play. That is not reality yet. Most wireless connections are slow (*really* slow; such as between 1.0 and 1.5KB per second), and you pay for airtime. And most Pocket PC owners do not have one. Downloading a few hundred KB to play a casual game on the road is not really an option for most users.

So for games, as for most applications, it is best to package them so that they can be downloaded onto the desktop and then synched with the Pocket PC.

For some games, then, it might make sense to load small amounts of game data from a server while on the road. Still you should try to design your game so that it can run without a connection.

Saving Game States

The Flash Player for the Pocket PC does not provide you with any kind of file input/output (I/O). Thus you can't save and receive a game state directly.

You can use **loadVariables** (and with the Flash 5 Player, the XML object) to send and receive game states to a server. This, however, requires the device to have an Internet connection.

It is possible to store a game state using cookies. Although FSCommand is not supported by PIE (Pocket Internet Explorer), you can use JavaScript, pseudo URLs in >getURL actions to store data from Flash. However, due to the temporary nature of cookies, you cannot guarantee that the cookie will still exist the next time the user opens the game and wants to continue with the saved game.

Death of a cookie can be caused by its expiration date, or when the user decides to clear his or her temporary Internet files. The browser may also drop cookies if it runs out of allowed space for temporary files. With the limited amount of internal storage space, this can happen much faster than on a desktop. And on top of that, the user may have chosen to only allow session cookies or to not to allow cookies at all. Any other approach to saving game data requires the installation of other software. This can be done by installing or creating a web server on the Pocket PC (see Chapter 9, "Standalone Application Development Using Flash and Java").

If you don't want to rely on cookies, you don't have a real option to save a game state when you use Flash by itself. If you want to be on the safe side, develop games that don't need to save a game state to be playable.

File Size for Games

Pocket PCs have a limited amount of internal storage space—ranging from 32MB to 64MB RAM for Pocket PC 2002 devices. This memory is used for storage and to run programs, usually split in half. The storage space can be expanded with memory cards and micro drives, but you can't assume that your user will have extra memory available.

The Flash Player was originally created with small file sizes in mind. Yet it is still capable of handling files that are several megabytes on desktop systems. On the Pocket PC you shouldn't rely on the same capabilities, simply because there is much less overall memory available.

If you try to play back a 2MB SWF on the Pocket PC, Flash will not only have to keep those 2MB in memory while running as an ActiveX control within PIE, but PIE will also store a copy in the temporary Internet files. The Small Web Format (SWF) is a compressed format and during playback it gets uncompressed. This is especially the case when using bitmap graphics and playing back sound. If your device is equipped with 32MB of storage, of which 16 are reserved to run programs, you can easily run low on memory with larger files, especially when you also have other programs open.

You can help Flash with its memory management by splitting your files into smaller pieces and loading and unloading them as needed.

As you share a limited amount of available space with everything else the user has on his Pocket PC, it is a good idea to carefully watch out for the file size of your game.

Game Sound

Sound is an important part of the gaming experience. There are some limitations to the device, however, that you will have to keep in mind when creating games for the Pocket PC.

The built-in speaker has a naturally limited quality. The headphone outlet provides a decent audio quality. It is likely that the user, at some point, will be in an environment where audio from the device is unwanted. So any game using audio should have a quick option to mute the sound.

On the Compaq iPaq, the speaker is on the joystick. This means that your game audio could be muffled if the joystick is being used.

On the technical side, Flash can export raw, uncompressed sound as well as ADPCM and MP3 compressed audio. The Flash 4 Player that was released for the Pocket PC could only handle raw audio and ADPCM compression. The Flash 5 Player for the iPaq also can play MP3 sounds. Versions for other platforms might or might not be able to handle MP3 sound.

Raw audio means uncompressed sound. This leads quickly to huge files, so you don't want to use it in most cases. Although MP3 offers better compression and better sound quality than ADPCM, it is more processor-intense to play back and is thus competing for resources with the screen redraw and ActionScript. For some games this can make the difference between playing smoothly or not. At this point I recommend mainly ADPCM compressed audio for Pocket PC games.

This might change as more versions of the Flash Player support MP3 and the devices become more powerful. The backdrop is that ADPCM audio adds significantly to the file size compared to MP3 audio, so use it wisely and re-use event sounds where possible and use short loops where needed.

Display Size for Games

All Pocket PCs have the same display size of 240×320, a vertical format. The maximum area that can be used by Flash within Pocket Internet Explorer is 240×260. This area can be reduced if the user has the browser's address bar open.

 To use Flash's entire screen real estate as described here, the margin widths need to be set to "0" in the embedding HTML document:

<BODY marginheight="0" marginwidth="0" leftmargin="0" topmargin=0 ➥rightmargin="0" bottommargin="0" >

This means you have only that amount of screen real estate—and not one pixel more. For game design, this means you have to be sure you have enough space for the game area itself, while reserving space for necessary status displays during the game. Additional framing artwork should be kept to a minimum.

Game Controls

The user interacts differently with the Pocket PC than with a desktop PC. There is no mouse, but rather a stylus and a touchscreen. Sometimes fingertips are used to play instead of the stylus. So depending on the game, it might make sense to have buttons and hit areas large enough so that they can be used with a fingertip.

With the stylus as pointing device, the "mouse" movement doesn't get tracked until you press on the screen. For Flash development, this means buttons do not receive rollover and rollout events.

The Pocket PC doesn't come equipped with a physical keyboard, thus you can't build complex game controls using the keyboard. The directional pad of the Pocket PC, however, functions in Flash as the arrow keys.

GAME CATEGORIES—WHAT WORKS ON THE POCKET PC, AND WHAT DOESN'T?

Games fall into different categories. Each category has certain characteristics, which affect how well a specific game will work on the Pocket PC. In the following section, we analyze different categories and their characteristics. Some games may fall into more than one category.

Card Games

Card games fit well on the Pocket PC. The user usually already knows the rules or can easily learn them, which allows him or her to start playing immediately after installing the game. Card games are usually turn-based, which allows creating multiplayer games where the device is passed around. The game will wait for the user to take a turn—so user interaction doesn't compete with heavy ActionScript running at the same time. Figure 7.1 shows an example of a well-known card game.

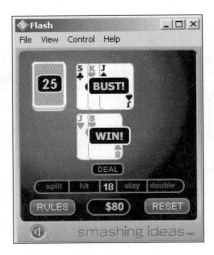

FIGURE 7.1

Blackjack in Flash for the Pocket PC.

The fairly simple rules of most card games also make creating computer players rather straightforward. The number of choices per turn is generally limited. Different levels of "computer smarts" can be developed by having the program keep track and thus predict the moves of the human player—similar to what you do when playing yourself. Based on this, you can even develop different types of strategies for a set of computer opponents.

Thinking and Strategy Games

Thinking games, such as puzzles, work well on the Pocket PC and other such devices. The user is given a fair enough amount of time—if not unlimited—to consider and make his or her next move.

The user and the game developer both benefit from this situation. The user doesn't lose a game if he or she gets distracted while playing. And because there are defined breaking points between when the user can interact and when the game is calculating, writing the code is not as time critical as if those events had to happen at the same time.

Yet you have to be careful to not have the game look frozen after a player makes a move. The first step in achieving this is to give the user an immediate feedback. For example, changing the button he just clicked to a visually different selected state. Because Flash updates the screen only once per frame, the user won't see that instantly if you continue making calculations based on his input. Instead, you have to wait until the next frame to do so.

If the calculations you need to do take up a lot of time, you can display an animation of some sort. However for the timeline of the animation to move, your calculations have to be split over frames as well. Depending on the type of calculation you attempt to do, you may take different approaches to this. If you have to process a sequence of 10 function calls, you might place each call in one frame. If you are running an extensive loop, you might measure the time when you started the loop, and at its next iteration, you check if you have time left to run it again. If you don't, you wait until the next frame. That gives the animation a chance to update itself on the screen. Figure 7.2 shows an example of a tic-tac-toe-like game called FourSight.

FIGURE 7.2

A Flash 3-D tic-tac-toe variant called FourSight for the Pocket PC.

Action and Reflex Games

On the desktop, more and more action games get developed in Flash. It is often hard to believe what can be done with Flash—from arcade-style games to 3D. Unfortunately these games often don't translate well to the Pocket PC. Even on modern desktop systems, Flash action games, especially those running at high frame rates, consume a lot of processor power. On the Pocket PC this becomes even more evident, making it difficult to create games that run smoothly and that allow the user a fair chance to react to game events.

Action games often have a lot of movement on the screen. Sometimes the entire background moves. The more Flash has to redraw per frame, the more processor power is used.

In the same way, the more complex a game becomes, the more code has to be executed per frame. Although ActionScript is very powerful, it does not get executed directly on a system level. This does not affect most Flash applications, but when you try to port an action game to the Pocket PC, you will quickly run into the limitations of CPU power.

This does not mean it is impossible to create an action game for the Pocket PC. You just have to be aware of the limitations from the beginning—the basic rule being to reduce the number of calculations and graphical movement. Transparency effects and radial gradients also eat up a lot of processor power—plain graphics often work better on the Pocket PC.

MAKING A CARD GAME

As the example application for this chapter, I picked a card game called Swimming. The rules are not too complex and are easy to learn and to translate into ActionScript. Although I programmed the game, Shannon Ecke (**http://www.shannonecke.com**) helped me out with the design.

The Rules

Swimming is a game for two or more players. It is usually played with a 32-card deck (card values worth seven and higher). Each player starts with three chances. After he or she loses all three, he or she is *swimming*. On the next loss, the player drowns and is "out."

The goal of the game is to get the highest score with three cards on hand. Each numbered card counts for its value: cards 7 through 10 have their numbered value, the face cards (jack, queen, and king) all count 10, and the ace counts 11. Only cards of the same suit can be added up. Thus the maximum score that can be reached is 31 (for instance, if someone has the 10, king, and ace of spades). As an exception to the same suit rule, three of a kind (for instance, 3 eights) will count as 30.5.

The Game Play

Each player gets dealt three cards, and there are three cards open next to the stack. The person to the right of the dealer gets the first turn (see Figure 7.3). You have four options for your turn:

1. Drop one card and pick one card from the deck.

2. Drop all three cards and pick all three cards from the deck.

3. Pass. If all players in one round decide to pass, the three cards on the deck get discarded and replaced with three new ones from the stack. In case you run out of cards, the discarded cards get shuffled again, and the top three cards get picked from the new deck. The player that first passed gets the chance for the first pick.

4. Knock. If you feel as if you have the highest score in the game, you can knock. Then all other players get one more turn before the game ends. If you don't have the sole highest score, you lose. If you decide to knock, you cannot pick a card anymore.

FIGURE 7.3

Swimming after the initial deal.

The game ends as soon as someone has 31 in his hand or after someone has knocked and all other players have their last turn.

There is one loser per round—either the one player with the lowest score or the player that knocked if he or she did not reach the highest score. A draw means he or she does not have the highest score and loses. Otherwise if two players have the same score, both lose.

As the game goes on, more and more players lose their chances, drown, and have to drop out of the game. Finally, there are only two players left to play the final rounds.

The game ends when there is only one player left.

Programming the Game

The following sections of this chapter walk you through the construction of the game step by step.

- First, we will introduce the programming technique used for this game—an object-oriented approach, which will first be applied in an atypical way using buttons.
- Then we'll show how this programming technique is used to create different screens, starting with the title screen, then all the screens used in the game, and then combining them into one game screen's movie clip.
- The different parts of the actual game are next—a card, a hand, and a player.
- Based on the generic player, we will build a human player, which lets you interact with the game.
- Finally, we put the parts together and add the rules.
- The last step will then be to build and include a computer player into the game.

The computer player comes last because it is easier to test if the game rules are implemented properly with a human player. It also doesn't make much sense to have the computer play against itself, while you can already play the game with two human players. To play against the computer, you also need a human player.

The Foundation

This game was written in Flash 5 using an object-oriented programming (OOP) technique that was made possible in Flash by Branden Hall. This technique allows you to define classes and to have movie clips implement them.

 A *class* is a template to create objects with a certain behavior. In this case, the objects are movie clips into which we "inject" the behaviors of such a class. For example, a movie clip can implement a card class, and now has a value and a suit.

The movie clips need little to no ActionScript placed inside of them. You can separate code and graphics this way, which makes it a lot easier to recycle parts or an entire game—so you could create a game once and then brand it for different clients. You can do this with Flash already, but now you can keep the code in one place and maintain it. Changes to the artwork are less likely to break code accidentally.

Branden Hall contributed to this book as well. See his work in Chapter 3, "Interface Design for Devices."

By defining classes for specific tasks, you increase the modularity of your project. You can extend the functionality of the game by building on top of existing classes. In the case of this game, it will be easy to create new screens by basing them on an existing one with a predefined behavior. And as the icing on the cake, a computer player will be derived from a generic player class.

Classes let you use a higher level of abstraction than traditional Flash programming—for instance, a card class or a hand class. From there on you can modify these classes for different types of games, and can still reuse a lot of the existing code.

The card class used in this game turns a movie clip with a visual representation on a playing card into a card object that is part of a suit, has a face, and values associated with the suit and the face. Let's assume you have a movie clip called myCard that has been made an instance of the card class. If you look at it, you will see an ace of spades.

With some ActionScript you could do, for example, the following:

```
trace ( myCard.getFace() );
trace ( myCard.getDesc() );
trace ( myCard.getValue() );
```

The output window will show this:

Ace
Ace of Spades
11

Now you can create some completely different artwork—and reuse the exact same code. A new game of yours may need more functionality for a card than the class used here provides. For example, you may need to show the back of the card first and then flip it. You can either extend the existing class to accomplish the task, or write a new CardFlip class based on the Card class and add the new flip feature. You don't have to start all over again.

Flash allows the creation of classes using the prototype property of a function object. The prototype is an object with properties and methods that are used as a template to create instances when the function is used as constructor. A function turns into a constructor when it's used in conjunction with **new** to create an instance. By modifying the prototype, you can add properties and methods to the constructor of an object. All instances of this object will inherit what you add. For example:

```
function Say () {
  trace ("Instance of Say created");
}
Say.prototype.hello = function () {
  trace ("hello world");
}
mySay = new Say();
mySay.hello();
```

Now all instances of **Say** will have a **hello** method.

Advanced inheritance is made possible by using the **proto** property of an instance of an object. While prototype is being used to define the class, **proto** points back to the constructor object of an instance. This is how Flash will look up inherited methods and properties.

An instance usually does not have only one **proto**. If you define a new array with

var foo = new Array ();

Then **foo.   proto** will be **Array.prototype**.

Array is based on the mother of all objects—**Object**. So, **foo.   proto   proto_** will be **Object.prototype** (see Figure 7.4).

proto is a read and write property. When used carefully, this fact can be used to create classes that inherit from super classes. Multiple inheritances also are possible, so a class can become a member of two independent super classes. This works by inserting the new class at the right point in the **proto** chain.

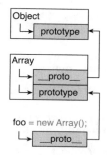

FIGURE 7.4

The proto inheritance chain of an array called foo.

Implementing Classes for Movie Clips

Movie clips also have a **proto** property, which points to **Movieclip**. Because a movie clip should remain a movie clip after implementing a new class, its original **proto** needs to be saved first, and then the new class will be attached as the new **proto** before adding the original back at the end:

```
Movieclip.prototype.implement = function (classObject) {
var temp = this.__proto__;
this.__proto__ = classObject;
this.__proto__.__proto__ = temp;
}
```

By assigning the **implement** method to the **Movieclip.prototype**, it becomes available to all movie clips, no matter what timeline they are in (see Figure 7.5).

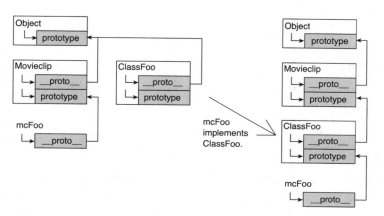

FIGURE 7.5

Inserting a class for a movie clip with the implement method.

I stored this method in an external file, implement.as, and it will be used throughout the examples in this chapter.

If you try to check if a movie clip's proto is actually **MovieClip.prototype**, by trying the following in a new movie

trace ((this.__proto__ == MovieClip.prototype));

you will be surprised to see that it returns false when you do a test movie. If you try the same line a second time, the result will be true, however:

trace ((this.__proto__ == MovieClip.prototype));
trace ((this.__proto__ == MovieClip.prototype));

This is a bug in the Flash 5 Player; however, it does not have a negative effect on the implement method. If you try this in Flash MX, you will see that it is fixed there.

A class object to be used as **proto** of a movie clip needs to be built from the ground up. It can have methods, but it cannot be an instance of a class created with a function as constructor.

The following example will *not* work:

```
foo = function () {
}
foo.prototype.hello = function () {
  trace ("hello");
}
this.implement ( new foo() );
this.hello();
```

Here is how to do it instead:

```
foo = {};
foo.hello = function () {
  trace ("hello");
}
this.implement ( foo );
this.hello();
```

First, you need to create a blank class object. You can attach any number of methods to this object. Then a movie clip can implement the class object and will have the class's methods available.

To make the class objects from anywhere in your movie, it is a good idea to attach them to the Global Object object:

```
if (Object.foo == null) {
  Object.foo = {};
}
Object.foo.hello = function () {
  trace ("hello");
}
this.implement ( Object.foo );
this.hello();
```

Storing Code in .AS Files

In Flash 5 you can store code to be used in your Flash movies in external AS (ActionScript) files, similar to JS files for JavaScript.

You can then make use of these AS files by using the #include statement, for example:

```
#include "implement.as"
```

Different from loadMovie or loadVariables, the code found in an AS file will be compiled into the SWF when you publish your movie. You do not need to distribute the AS files with your SWF. Hence if you make changes in an external AS file, you have to publish the Flash movie again to see the changes in the SWF.

By using AS files, it becomes easier to share code over several projects. If you ensure the code in one such file belongs together and will always be used together, you create reusable modules of code. Don't be afraid to just place a single method into an external file, such as the implement method that we defined earlier. The implement method is complete by itself, so you don't need to carry other unrelated methods with you if you don't need them in your project.

You can update the code for more than one Flash movie at a time if you need to make modifications to the code. You have to be careful, however, to modify the code in a way that still works everywhere you use it.

When working with classes, it makes perfect sense to store each class in a separate file. You will see that I use this concept throughout the examples in this chapter.

Defining Classes—A Button Class

Button is a fundamental class that is being used throughout the game. For better overview and better modularity, I store each class and other key code in their own AS files.

Regular buttons in Flash lack the ability to have off states. You often want a button to be grayed out or highlighted but not be able to click on it. Maybe you even want to make the button invisible.

You can achieve this by wrapping a button inside a movie clip. To illustrate how this works, I have prepared button_class.fla for you. Open it and you will see a Start Game button placed on the main timeline. Double-click it to enter in place mode. You will see that it is actually a movie clip with frame labels indicating the different states: off, active, over, down, and selected.

You also can see that an invisible button is spawned over the active, over, and down keyframes, indicated by a turquoise rectangle. The off and selected frames show artwork only, no button—because the movie clip button will be inactive in these states (see Figure 7.6).

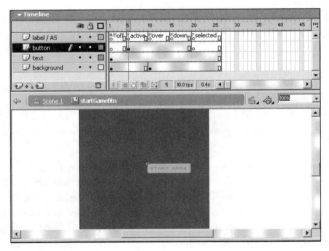

FIGURE 7.6

The timeline of a movie clip button with an invisible button inside.

If you examine that invisible button by double-clicking it to edit it in place, you will find out that it is actually a movie clip with the invisible button inside. This time it is a button for real, with the following actions attached to it (see Figure 7.7). By wrapping the actual button inside a movie clip, it can be reused over and over again, but the button event handlers need to be defined only once. In this example the ActionScript is directly placed on the button—later on it will be used from button_handlers.as. This way you can use the same code on a differently shaped button; for example, if you need a round button instead.

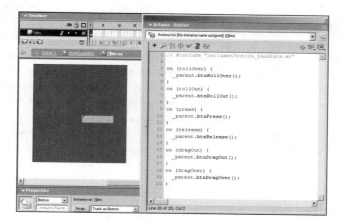

FIGURE 7.7

The invisible button is actually inside another movie clip.

```
on (rollOver) {
  _parent.btnRollOver();
}
on (rollOut) {
  _parent.btnRollOut();
}
on (press) {
  _parent.btnPress();
}
on (release) {
  _parent.btnRelease();
}
on (dragOut) {
  _parent.btnDragOut();
}
on (dragOver) {
  _parent.btnDragOver();
}
```

All possible button events are taken care of, even if you don't need them for now and get passed on to the outer movie clip, which will become a "movie clip button."

Why Not onRelease?

onRelease sounds like a more natural name for an event handler in the surrounding movie clip. So natural that it became a reserved keyword in Flash MX, where you can now directly apply button event handlers this way to buttons and even movie clips. Along with some other new features, this makes it much easier to define more powerful buttons; however, this does not work with the Flash 5 Player, which we are using here. To be sure there is no interference when played back in a Flash 6 Player, I chose "btn" as the prefix for my button event handler names.

The outer movie clip—the movie clip button—can then implement the **button** class (button_ppc.as):

```
if (Object.Button == null) {
  Object.Button = {};
}
Object.Button.initButton = function (mode) {
  this.states = {
    off       : "off"
    ,active   : "active"
    ,over     : "over"
    ,down     : "down"
    ,selected : "selected"
    ,hide     : "hide"
  }
  if (mode != null && this.states[mode] != null) {
    this.set ( mode );
  } else {
    this.set ( this.states["off"] );
  }
}
Object.Button.set = function (mode) {
  if (mode != null && this.states[mode] != null) {
    this.state = this.states[mode];
    if (this.state != this.states.hide) {
      this._visible = true;
      this.gotoAndStop (this.state);
    } else {
      this._visible = false;
      this.gotoAndStop (this.states.off);
    }
  }
```

```
}
Object.Button.hide = function () {
  this.set (this.states.hide);
}
Object.Button.get = function () {
  return this.state;
}
Object.Button.btnRollOver = function () {
  this.set (this.states.over);
}
Object.Button.btnRollOut = function () {
  this.set (this.states.active);
}
Object.Button.btnPress = function () {
  this.set (this.states.over);
  _parent.buttonPress (this);
}
Object.Button.btnRelease = function () {
  _parent.buttonRelease (this);
}
Object.Button.btnReleaseOutside = function () {
  this.set (this.states.active);
}
Object.Button.btnDragOut = function () {
  this.set (this.states.active);
}
Object.Button.btnDragOver = function () {
  this.set (this.states.over);
}
```

First, you must define the button class object. Next you should define an **initButton** construc-tor method, which will have to be called after implementing the class. A constructor initializes all the properties of an instance of a class, based on the parameters passed to it. Here **initButton** defines the states the button can have, matching the frame labels we saw earlier, plus a hide state. Then we set the initial state of the button, which can be passed in as a parameter. If nothing is specified, or an invalid state is trying to be set, the button will go to an off state. The set method will be called a lot—it sets the state of the button. That means going to a certain frame label in most cases, and setting the **_visible** property to false if the state is hide.

There are methods to set a button state and to receive the current button state. And there are the handlers for each button event. At this point, only two of them actually interact with the outside world—**btnPress** and **btnRelease**. They will pass the button movie clip (this) on to the parent timeline. If you need the other handlers to react in a different way, you can either overwrite them for a specific instance or create a sub class of the button class with different behaviors for some or all handlers. More about overwriting inherited methods later.

This button class has been created to suit the environment of a Pocket PC. There is no rollover on a Pocket PC because the stylus can only be tracked when pressed on the screen. The content you create should work on both the desktop and the handheld device, so we keep a rollover state; however, it is identical with the down state, and we will not react to the rollover event other than showing the rollover state.

To emulate a rollover on the Pocket PC, you can use **btnPress** to go to the over state and have the button react on **btnRelease**. **btnReleaseOutside** reacts like a rollout here. By using **btnDragOut** and **btnDragOver** to switch between the active and over states, there is always a visual indication of whether the button will react when you release the stylus at the current position.

In button_class.fla we have placed a movie clip button on the stage. We already examined the inside of it. To access it via ActionScript, it needs an instance name—**startButton**.

To bring the button to life, you need a few lines of code on the main timeline:

```
#include "includes/implement.as"
#include "includes/button_ppc.as"
startButton.implement (Object.Button);
startButton.initButton ("active");
buttonRelease = function (button) {
  if (button == this.startButton) {
    trace ("start button released");
  }
}
```

First, you include the implementer and the button class. Then you have the **startButton** implement and initialize the button class. And finally you define a **buttonRelease** handler, which will be able to react to all release events of all movie clip buttons in this timeline (see Figure 7.8).

At this point, what we did just to track a button release might seem like overkill. This button does, however, already react in certain ways to stylus actions and has predefined behavior of our choosing. This is just the beginning. Now that we did that part, we only need to implement all future movie clip buttons without having to edit any ActionScript placed on them or inside their timelines. To create new movie clip buttons they need to have a certain timeline structure with frame labels for the button states, and the inner movie clip with the invisible button inside placed in the active frames. The beauty of this construct is that all the code you need to worry about is in the timeline on which you placed the movie clip button—where you usually want to deal with it.

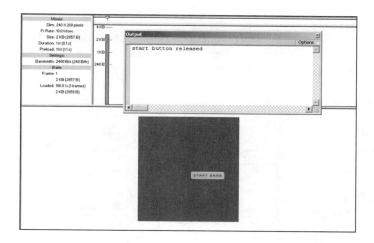

FIGURE 7.8

Test the movie to see the movie clip button in action.

Inheritance—A Screen Class and a Child Title Class

When programming in Flash, you often have to program similar code for different objects before diverging into specific tasks. So you want to have a quick way to integrate the common tasks. The class model described here allows this.

To illustrate how inheritance works, we'll showcase a generic screen super class (screen_generic.as) and a sub class of it that will be used for the opening title screen of the game (game_screens_title.as). To make inheritance work, the sub class needs to be closer to the movie clip instance in the **__proto__** chain than to the super class:

myMovieClip.__proto__ = subClass;
myMovieClip.__proto__.__proto__ = superClass;

This way, the sub class can inherit from the super class. The way the implementer works is that it will always insert the class object you specify as the first **__proto__** of the chain. So to get to this structure, you could include the following:

myMovieClip.implement (superClass);
myMovieClip.implement (subClass);

Finding a Super Class

The super class will be shifted to the right with the second implement. However, it is not very convenient to have to manually implement the super class. It should be possible to just implement the sub class. To do that, the sub class needs to implement super class on its own (see Figure 7.9).

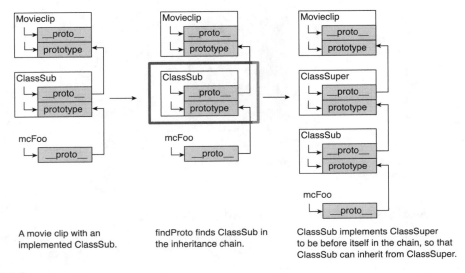

A movie clip with an implemented ClassSub.

findProto finds ClassSub in the inheritance chain.

ClassSub implements ClassSuper to be before itself in the chain, so that ClassSub can inherit from ClassSuper.

FIGURE 7.9

Implementing a super class with the help of findProto.

Therefore, a little helper function is needed to find the **__proto__** of the sub class, after which you want to insert the super class (findProto.as):

```
Movieclip.prototype.findProto = function (classObj) {
  var myProto = this.__proto__;
  while (myProto != null && myProto != classObj) {
    myProto = myProto.__proto__;
  }
  return myProto;
}
```

An abstract example of using **findProto** (findProto.fla):

```
Object.superClass = {};
Object.superClass.initSuperClass = function (foo) {
this.foo = foo;
}
Object.subClass = {};
Object.subClass.initSubClass = function (foo, bar) {
  // find myself in __proto__ chain
  var myProto = findProto (Object.subClass);
  // insert super class
  myProto.implement (Object.superClass);
  this.initSuperClass(foo);
  this.bar = bar;
}
myMovieClip.implement (Object.subClass);
myMovieClip.initSubClass ("foo", "bar");
trace ("foo: " + myMovieClip.foo);
trace ("bar: " + myMovieClip.bar);
```

Defining a Screen Super Class

After the sub class is defined, you only need to implement the sub class and don't have to worry about implementing the super class. It will happen implicitly after you call the constructor.

Let's move on to the generic screen class, **Screen.Generic** (screen_generic.as). You can define a screen as any kind of display that can appear on the screen. Thus a few generic methods won't hurt: **show**, **hide**, and because a screen will often have buttons, **buttonPress** and **buttonRelease**.

```
if (Object.Screen == null ) {
  Object.Screen = {};
}
if (Object.Screen.Generic == null) {
  Object.Screen.Generic = {};
}
Object.Screen.Generic.initScreenGeneric = function (showMe) {
  (showMe) ? this.show() : this.hide();
}
```

```
Object.Screen.Generic.hide = function () {
  this._visible = false;
}
Object.Screen.Generic.show = function () {
  this._visible = true;
}
Object.Screen.Generic.buttonRelease = function (buttonName) {
}
Object.Screen.Generic.buttonPress = function (buttonName) {
}
```

In case you're not familiar with the ternary operator (?), you can read it like a question:

(showMe) ? this.show() : this.hide();

If the expression on the left (showMe) returns true, the first action on the right will be executed (this.show()), otherwise the action after the column (this.hide())

This is a convenient shortcut to replace an if-then-else construct with only one action in each clause. This is equivalent to writing:

```
if (showMe) {
  this.show();
} else {
  this.hide();
}
```

The generic **show** and **hide** methods change the just **_visible** property. The **initScreenGeneric** constructor has a **showMe** trigger, which determines whether the screen instance will start off visible. **buttonRelease** and buttonPress don't do anything—they are just placeholders. Although Flash doesn't complain if you try to call a function that doesn't exist, it is preferable to have a placeholder in place. It was discussed earlier that on devices such as the Pocket PC, **buttonRelease** would be the preferred handler. There may, however, be reasons for which you will need **buttonPress** as well. For example, if you want to drag a movie clip or if you want to create a scroll bar, **onPress** is still needed.

Creating a Sub Class

You implement this super class in a title screen sub class (game_screens_title.as), which will be referred to as **Screen.Title** for the remainder of the chapter:

```
if (Object.Screen.Title == null ) {
  Object.Screen.Title = {};
}
Object.Screen.Title.initScreenTitle = function (showMe) {
  var myProto = findProto (Object.Screen.Title);
  myProto.implement (Object.Screen.Generic);
  this.initScreenGeneric(showMe);
  this.startGameBtn.implement (Object.Button);
  this.startGameBtn.initButton ("active");
}
Object.Screen.Title.buttonRelease = function (button) {
  if ( button == this.startGameBtn ) {
    _parent.startGame();
  }
}
```

The **Screen.Title** class will implement the **Screen.Generic** class after you call the constructor. It will also implement the Button class for a **startGameBtn** movie clip button placed inside.

Implementing the Screen Classes

In **screen_class.fla** you make use of **Screen.Generic** and **Screen.Title**. We moved the start button inside a title movie clip. **Screen.Title** inherits the **show**, **hide**, **buttonPress**, and **buttonRelease** methods from **Screen.Generic** (see Figure 7.10). To be able to react to the Start button's release action, it needs its own **buttonRelease** method, which will overwrite the default one that was inherited from **Screen.Generic**.

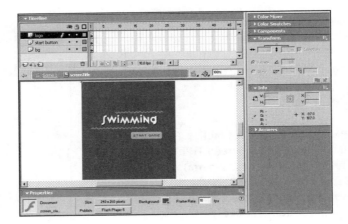

FIGURE 7.10

The elements of the title screen on its timeline.

The title screen is just a screen. It doesn't really do anything else for a living but let the user click the Start button. After this happens, it just passes on the event to the parent timeline, which will then react appropriately.

The button event handlers that are placed on the invisible button inside the start game movie clip button is the only ActionScript that has to be directly placed on an object or as a frame action inside a movie clip (see Figure 7.11). All other code is placed on the main timeline, which makes it easier to overview the scripts in your movie.

```
#include "includes/implement.as"
#include "includes/findProto.as"
#include "includes/button_ppc.as"
#include "includes/screen_generic.as"
#include "includes/game_screens_title.as"
title.implement (Object.Screen.Title);
title.initScreenTitle(true);
startGame = function () {
  trace ("start game");
}
```

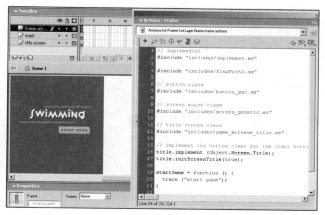

FIGURE 7.11

All the ActionScript to make the title screen work is placed on the main timeline.

First, you include the **implement** and **findProto** methods. These two methods extend the Movieclip.prototype and are the essential helpers to enable classes for movie clips here. This is followed by including the classes needed for this example—**Button**, **Screen.Generic**, and **Screen.Title**.

Then, you implement **Screen.Title** for the title movie clip instance on the main timeline. Calling the constructor **initScreenTitle** makes title inherit **Screen.Generic**, and implements and initializes the Start button inside.

All that is left to do is to define a **startGame** method that will be called by the title screen after the user releases the Start Game button (see Figure 7.12).

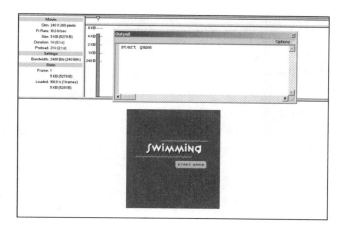

FIGURE 7.12

The title screen with the Start Game button at work.

The Main Screens of the Game

For the game we created four major screens: the title screen, the game screen, the screens for the end of a round and the end of the game, and the help screen. All these are based on the **screen** class. You move from one screen to another either by certain events in the game, or by clicking buttons within the screens, which are all based on the **button** class. The different screens are brought together in a screens movie clip, for which we defined a **Screen.GameScreens** class.

The screens movie clip uses frames to place the sub screens (see Figure 7.13). Each sub screen is an individual movie clip and will be initialized by calling the constructor for each of them when you go there. The visual elements, including buttons, are inside the individual screens, except for the Help button. Because the Help button is available everywhere except on the help screen, it is placed directly on the screens timeline.

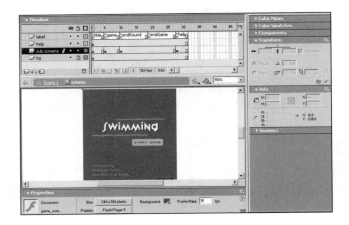

FIGURE 7.13

The timeline of the screens movie clip.

Let's go over the individual screens and the class files associated with them:

- The title screen is the same as before but now is inside the screen's movie clip (game_screens_title.as).
- The game screen just provides the background for the game and holds a Reset button (game_screens_game.as).

- The end screens need to display the game information. Actually, there is only one end screen with different modes. It has a **showEndScreen** method to display the correct header, a message, and the game stats. The game stats will, of course, not work yet without the game in place. At the end of a round, you'll get a Reset button to start over and a Deal button to go to the next round. At the end of a game, you can start a new game with a New Game button (game_screens_end.as).

- The help screen that explains the rules of the game has a Close button, which will take you back to the previous screen (game_screens_help.as).

The individual screens are structured similar to the title screen. They show up on the screen, and if you release a button, that event is passed on to the parent timeline. If there was any sub navigation, it would happen within that screen. For example, if there were more than one help page, navigating through the help pages would completely happen within the help screen. This example, however, has only one help page.

Because the code for the individual screens is so similar to the title screen, it will not be covered here. Instead, please explore the following files on your own:

- game_screens_title.as
- game_screens_game.as
- game_screens_end.as
- game_screens_help.as

Defining a Class to Hold the Game Screens

The **Screen.GameScreens** class in game_screens.as brings the screens together. Because the code in the individual scripts becomes lengthier with increasing functionality, we will focus on the key methods from this point on. The other methods will be displayed in table form for a quick overview. For details of the implementation, please look at the source code provided.

The following is an excerpt from the **Screen.GameScreens** class:

```
Object.Swim.GameScreens.initGameScreens = function (page) {
  var showMe = true;
  findProto(Object.Swim.GameScreens).implement(Object.Screen.Generic);
  this.initScreenGeneric(showMe);
  this.pages = {
    title     : "title"
    ,game     : "game"
    ,endRound : "endRound"
    ,endGame  : "endGame"
    ,help     : "help"
  }
  this.helpBtn.implement (Object.Button);
  this.helpBtn.initButton ("active");
```

```
    this.activate();
    this.gotoPage (page);
}
Object.Swim.GameScreens.gotoPage = function (page, msg, rounds) {
  var myPage;
  if (page == null) {
    myPage = this.pages.title;
  } else {
    myPage = page;
  }
  if (myPage != this.currentPage) {
    this.gotoAndStop(myPage);
    if ( myPage == this.pages.title ) {
      this.screen.implement (Object.Screen.Title);
      this.screen.initScreenTitle(true);
    }
    else if (myPage==this.pages.endGame || myPage==this.pages.endRound) {
      this.screen.implement (Object.Screen.End);
      this.screen.initScreenEnd(true);
      this.msg = msg;
      this.rounds = rounds;
      this.screen.showEndScreen (_parent, myPage, msg, rounds);
    }
    else if (mypage == this.pages.game) {
      this.screen.implement (Object.Screen.Game);
      this.screen.initScreenGame (true);
      _parent.showGame();
    }
    if (myPage == this.pages.help) {
      this.screen.implement (Object.Screen.Help);
      this.screen.initScreenHelp(true);
      this.helpBtn.set ("hide");
    }
    else {
      this.helpBtn.set ("active");
    }
    if (this.currentPage != null) {
      this.lastPage = this.currentPage;
    }
    this.currentPage = myPage;
  }
}
```

The **initGameScreens** constructor defines the pages to exist within its timeline that will hold the individual screens, much like the **button** class defines the different button states. For each page there is a matching frame label in the timeline. The Help button gets implemented and activated.

gotoPage is the dispatcher method that takes care of opening and initializing the correct screen. If no screen is specified, it defaults to title. Then it goes to the frame for that screen and implements the screen. In the case of the end screen, it will remember the additional parameters **msg** and **rounds**—if you go to the help screen, you want to restore the end screen with the same content when you come back. Table 7.1 provides an overview of the methods used in **Screen.GameScreens**.

Table7.1 Overview of the Methods of *Screen.GameScreens*
Class: Screen.GameScreens
SuperClass: Screen.Generic

Method	Arguments	Description
initGameScreens	showMe, page	Constructor. Initializes the screens movie clip, goes to the screen found at page.
activate		Allows the screens movie clip to react to button events.
deactivate		Disallows button events.
gotoPage	page, msg, rounds	Sends the screens movie clip to the screen found at **page** and initializes that screen. Passes **msg** and rounds on to the screen if it is one of the end screens.
startGame		Goes to the game screen and calls **_parent.startGame()**.
resetGame		Goes to the title screen, calls **_parent.resetGame()**.
buttonRelease	button	Goes to the help screen if the Help button is clicked. Calls **_parent.hideGame()**.
backPage		Goes back to the last open page (called by the Close button on the help screen).

There are calls to **_parent.hideGame()** from **buttonRelease** and **_parent.showGame()** if a **gotoPage** ("game") is issued. This is due to the coexistence of the game elements and the screens. When a screen needs the entire screen, it has to hide the game elements first and show them again when returning to the game screen.

Implementing Screen.GameScreens

To make use of the **Screen.GameScreens** class, you need to include the new classes, after the usual implementer and **findproto** methods, and the button and screen generic classes are included (see Figure 7.14). Then methods to be called by the screens are defined, before we have the screens movie clip implement **Screens.GameScreens**.

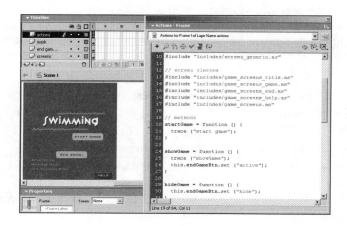

FIGURE 7.14

The ActionScript to bring the screens to life is, again, all placed on the main timeline and not inside the movie clips.

```
#include "includes/game_screens_game.as"
#include "includes/game_screens_end.as"
#include "includes/game_screens_help.as"
#include "includes/game_screens.as"
startGame = function () {
  trace ("start game");
}
showGame = function () {
  trace ("showGame");
  this.endGameBtn.set ("active");
}
hideGame = function () {
  this.endGameBtn.set ("hide");
}
resetGame = function () {
  trace ("resetGame");
  hideGame();
}
```

```
endGame = function () {
  trace ("endGame");
  var msg = "You pressed the end game button!";

  this.screens.gotoPage("endGame", msg);
  hideGame();
}
buttonRelease = function (button) {
  if (button == this.endGameBtn) {
    endGame();
  }
}
this.endGameBtn.implement (Object.Button);
this.endGameBtn.initButton("hide");
this.screens.implement (Object.Swim.GameScreens);
this.screens.initGameScreens(true, "title");
```

showGame hideGame turns the End Game button on and off, which is all you have for a game right now. Releasing the End Game button shows the end game screen, from where you get back to the title screen with the Reset button (see Figure 7.15). Opening the help screen will work as well.

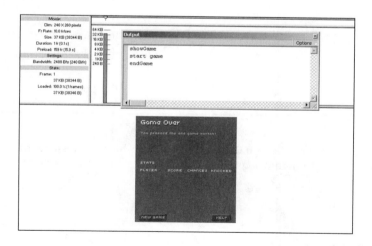

FIGURE 7.15

Test the movie to see how the screens work and to confirm that the navigation for the game is in place.

The Cards

The cards get their own class. They don't get placed on the timeline but rather get stored in the library and then initiated using **attachMovie**. This requires less maintenance in the timeline—you don't have to name the instances manually, and only cards that you actually make use of will be created. This could also come in handy if you wanted to play with a double deck, for example. You don't have to duplicate each card on the timeline and give it a new instance name, but rather create the cards dynamically as needed. Instead of creating symbols for every card, we chose to create one master symbol, which contains the images for all of them—one card per frame. This makes it easier to edit the cards together if necessary, for example if you want to change the background, and it also is easy to ensure they are all the same size and aligned properly. Table 7.2 introduces you to the methods used in the **Swim.Card** class.

Table 7.2   The Methods of the Swim.Card Class
Class: Swim.Card
Super Class: Screen.Generic

Method	Parameters	Description
initCard	**id**, **suit**, **value**, **suitDesc**, **face**	Constructor. Shows a card visual based on **id**. Stores **suit**, **value**, **suitDesc** and face for further use.
getSuit()		Returns the suit value, 1 for example, which will represent hearts in this game.
getValue()		Returns the card value, 7 for instance.
getFace()		Returns the face, "seven" for instance.
getSuitDesc()		Returns the suit's description, "hearts" for instance.
getDesc		Returns the description of the card, "seven of hearts" for instance.

The card class implements **Screen.Generic**, so it has **hide** and **show** methods. Because **Screen.Generic** defaults to **hide** when initializing, the card will be invisible at first.

To create a card, as shown in Figure 7.16, use the following code after including the methods and classes used before:

```
#include "includes/card.as"
this.suits = [
  { desc : "Hearts",   value : 1 }
  ,{ desc : "Diamonds",  value : 2 }
  ,{ desc : "Spades",    value : 3 }
  ,{ desc : "Clovers",   value : 4 }
];
```

```
this.values = [
  { face : "Seven",  value : 7 }
  ,{ face : "Eight",  value : 8 }
  ,{ face : "Nine",   value : 9 }
  ,{ face : "Ten",    value : 10 }
  ,{ face : "Jack",   value : 10 }
  ,{ face : "Queen",  value : 10 }
  ,{ face : "King",   value : 10 }
  ,{ face : "Ace",    value : 11 }
];
var suit = suits[0];
var value = values[0];
var id = 1;
this.attachMovie ("card", suit.desc + value.face, id);
card = this[suit.desc+ value.face];
card.implement (Object.Swim.Card);
card.initCard (id, suit.value, value.value, suit.desc , value.face);
trace ( card.getDesc () );
card.show();
```

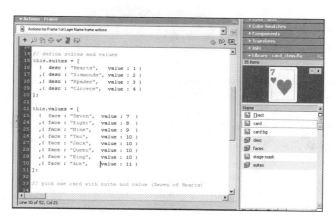

FIGURE 7.16

Creating a card.

First, you define the suits and card values used in the game. Each gets a numeric representation as well as a description. The card value is used to add up scores and to compare scores. The suits are compared using the numeric representation, because this is faster and less processor-intensive than comparing strings

Only the **face** is used later as a string to find three-of-a-kind in a hand. In another card game, the suit may actually have a value according to the rules; for example, a seven of hearts could be worth more than an ace of diamonds. By associating both a numeric value and a descriptive string to a suit in this card class, you will more likely be able to reuse it as is.

You pick one card—in this case the seven of hearts (see Figure 7.17). First create a card movie clip instance on the stage and then have it implement the card class.

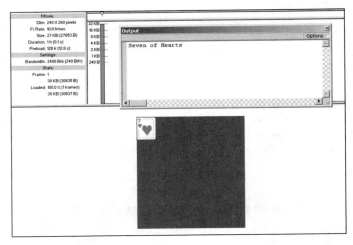

FIGURE 7.17

The first card has been created with Swim.Card.

At this point, the card is in the upper-left corner of the screen—at the position (0,0). You could move it by modifying its **_x** and **_y** properties directly. This, however, always requires two actions, and the position is relative to the parent timeline—in this case **_root**.

Instead use a **placeClip** method attached to the **Movieclip** prototype to set a movie clip to a certain position that can optionally be relative to another movie clip, even in a different timeline. This means you could independently from layer depth set up a slot movie clip and quickly align any other movie clip with it. In some cases this can save you some calculating and headache because you can visually define the spot where the clip needs to go. This is achieved by first converting the target clip's coordinates to global coordinates. Then those get converted to coordinates relative to the parent's timeline of the movie clip because that is the space the movie clip is positioned in.

```
Movieclip.prototype.placeClip = function (point, clip) {
  if (clip != null) {
    var clipPos = { x: clip._x, y: clip._y };
    clip._parent.localToGlobal (clipPos);
    this._parent.globalToLocal (clipPos);
  }
  this._x = clipPos.x + point.x;
  this._y = clipPos.y + point.y;
}
```

The new position has to be passed in as a point object, which has the form of an object with an **x** and a **y** property:

point = { x : xPosition, y: yPosition };

This method also is stored in an external file so that it can be included and so you can place the card almost in the center of the screen, as shown in Figure 7.18.

#include "includes/placeClip.as"
card.placeClip ({ x:120, y: 130 } , this);

this is optional in this case because the card's parent timeline is this, representing _root.

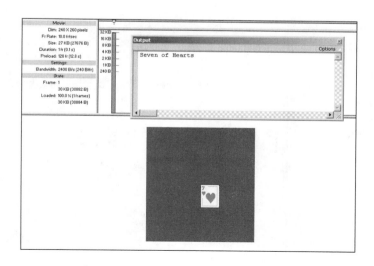

FIGURE 7.18

The card has been placed in the desired position with the placeClip method.

Holding Cards in a Hand

As defined by the rules in Swimming, a hand consists of three cards. Cards can be set one at a time or all three at once. You define **Swim.Hand** as a class to offer all the functionality needed by a hand. Table 7.3 gives you a look at the methods used here.

Table 7.3   The Methods of the *Hand* Class, as Defined in hand.as
Class: Swim.Hand
Super Class: Screen.Generic

Method	Parameters	Description
setCard	slot, card	Places **card** in one of the three slots.
setAllCards	cardArray	Three cards are passed in array form. Set them into all three slots.
getCard	slot	Returns the card found in slot number 'slot'.
getAllCards		Returns all three cards in an array.
Reset		Clears the slots.
analyzeHand		Analyzes the score of the hand and stores it.
getScore		Returns the current score.
showHand		Shows the cards in the hand.
hideHand		Hides the cards in the hand.
Show		Shows the hand and the cards.
Hide		Hides the hand and itself.

The cards are movie clips. They will be created and owned by the game. A hand is another movie clip within the game; it can hold cards, but they don't get transferred into the hand's timeline. Thus to show and hide them, you have to call their own **show** and **hide** methods.

More on Overwriting Methods

The **Swim.Hand** class is a sub class of **Screen.Generic**. Thus it inherits a **show** method from **Screen.Generic**. The generic show method inherited by the hand doesn't take care of our needs; it only turns the hand itself visible. You need to define your own **show** method to fulfill the task. The act of defining a new method with the same name in a sub class is called *overwriting* a method. Instead of the inherited class, the sub classes' own method will be used.

Let's take a look at the **showHand** and **show** methods of **Swim.Hand**:

```
Hand.showHand = function () {
  for (var i=0; i<maxCards; i++) {
    this.cards[i].show();
  }
}
```

The cards of the hand are kept in the cards array. To show the hand, you loop through the array and call the show method of each card.

```
Hand.show = function () {
  this.showHand();
}
```

By defining a **show** method in the **hand** class, the inherited **show** function is overwritten. At this point all it does is call **showHand**, which will show all the cards. If the hand itself had visual elements, they would not be shown yet. Because you overwrote show, it doesn't get called any more.

Now we could look up what code is in the original **show** and just copy and paste it. Then the **show** method would act like a normal show, plus it would show the hand. However, if the formerly inherited **show** method would ever change, you would have to manually update it in the hand class as well.

Luckily, there is a better way to do this. The inherited method does still exist—but it's hidden. Let's look at how Flash finds inherited methods. When you call the **show** method, Flash first looks at whether there is a **show** method defined in the current object. If not, it checks whether the **__proto__** has a **show** method. If it finds it, it will call it and stop the search. Otherwise it checks the **__proto__** of the **__proto__** and so on until it gets to **Object.prototype**, where there is no more **__proto__**.

Because Flash stops looking for an inherited method once it finds one, you have to look up the inherited one yourself, if you want to still use it after overwriting (see Figure 7.19). Because the super class of the hand class is **Screen.Generic** you will look it up using the **findProto** method used to implement it at the right spot in the **__proto__** chain.

var handSuperClass = findProto (Object.Screen.Generic);

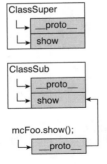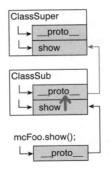

If a ClassSub has its own show method, Flash will only look for it there if the instance mcFoo calls it.

To use the show method of ClassSuper, the show method of ClassSub has to go up the __proto__ path and find it.

FIGURE 7.19

Looking up an overwritten method.

Now **handSuperClass** is actually the class object. If you tried to call a method of it, it would execute it within the class object, not the instance that you want to run it in. So you need to assign it temporarily to the method of the instance and then call it. Afterward you remove it again.

```
this._show = handSuperClass.show;
this._show();
delete this._show;
```

Because another sub class could overwrite the **show** method again, the inherited method needs to be looked up inside of the new method. Completed it looks like this:

```
Hand.show = function () {
  this.showHand();
  this._show = findProto (Object.Screen.Generic).show;
  this._show();
  delete this._show;
}
```

Implementing the Hand Class

Now that we have covered how to overwrite an inherited method and still call the original method, let's move on and make use of it by implementing the **Swim.Hand** class for a sample hand in hand_class.fla, again by using the implement and findProto methods (see Figure 7.20).

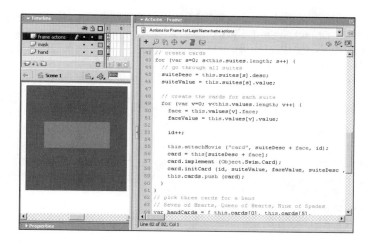

FIGURE 7.20

The hand_class.fla and how we implement **Swim.Hand**.

```
#include "includes/hand.as"

this.cards = [];
this.cardsPerHand = 3;

var card, suitDesc, suitValue, face, faceValue;
var id = 0;
for (var s=0; s<this.suits.length; s++) {
  suitDesc = this.suits[s].desc;
  suitValue = this.suits[s].value;
  for (var v=0; v<this.values.length; v++) {
    face = this.values[v].face;
    faceValue = this.values[v].value;
    id++;
    this.attachMovie ("card", suitDesc + face, id);
    card = this[suitDesc + face];
```

```
    card.implement (Object.Swim.Card);
    card.initCard (id, suitValue, faceValue, suitDesc , face);
    this.cards.push (card);
  }
}
var handCards = [ this.cards[0], this.cards[5], this.cards[18] ];
this.hand.implement (Object.Swim.Hand);
this.hand.initHand (this.cardsPerHand);
this.hand.setAllCards (handCards);
this.hand.analyzeHand();
this.hand.show();
trace ("Score of the hand: " + this.hand.getScore() );
```

To fill the hand with cards, you need more cards. Instead of just creating two more, you create all the cards needed for the game. Then you pick three cards that you want in the hand (for example, seven of hearts, queen of hearts, and nine of spades) and place them in a **handCards** array. You implement the **hand** class for the hand movie clip instance on the stage and set the cards. You can then analyze the score of the hand before showing it. Finally, you display the score. As Figure 7.21 shows, it will show 17, the added values of the seven of hearts (7) and the queen of hearts (10).

Please see the source files found on the book's web sites (www.flashenabled.com/book and www.newriders.com) if you want to view the complete commented code.

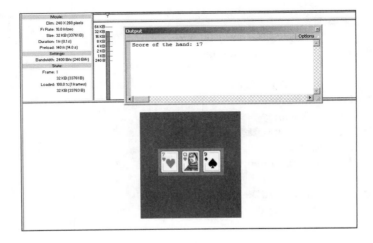

FIGURE 7.21

The hand holds its three cards and can analyze the score of its cards.

The Player Class

A player needs to be able to do more than hold cards—so you define a player class that uses the hand class as super class. If a class B inherits from another class A, that class A becomes a super class for class B. At the same time B becomes a sub class of A. Because Swimming is a turn-based game, there is a **yourTurn** method to begin your turn. You add methods to let the player perform the actions defined in the game's rules—take one card from the stack, take all three cards, pass, and knock. After making a move, **endOfTurn** will be called to report the move back to the game. You also store the chances a player has and define methods (as shown in Table 7.4) to return the chances a player has left and define one that causes the player to lose a chance.

Table 7.4 The Methods of *Swim.Player*
Class: Swim.Player
Super Class: Swim.Hand

Method	Parameters	Description
initPlayer	id, maxCards, chances, showMe, playerName	Constructor. To be called after implementing. Implements **Swim.Hand** as super class. Stores **id** and chances. **PlayerName** is optional. Will be set to **"Player" + (id+1)** if not specified. For instance, **playerName** will be **"Player 1"** if the id is 0.
Reset		Resets everything—hand, chances, and hides.
StartRound		Makes the initial settings for a round of play. Sets **firstTurn** to true.
YourTurn	lastMoves	Receives the activities that have taken place since the last move. Stores the cards that are currently in the stack. Needs to be overwritten by sub classes for specific actions, such as enabling buttons.
EndOfTurn		Gets called by the four game actions. Makes sure **firstTurn** is false and lets the game continue with the next turn (**_parent.nextTurn()**). To be overwritten by sub classes to do their cleanup work.
ChangeCard	slot, stackSlot	Exchanges the card in slot with the card found in the stack at **stackSlot**.
ChangeAllCards		Exchanges all cards with the slot.
TakeOne	slot, stackSlot	Calls **changeCard** with slot and **stackSlot**. Notifies the game of the move (**_parent.recordMove()**) and calls **endOfTurn**.
TakeAll		Calls **changeAllCards**. Notifies the game of the move and calls **endOfTurn**.
Pass		Notifies the game of the pass move and calls **endOfTurn**.

Method	Parameters	Description
Knock		Notifies the game of the knock move and calls **endOfTurn**.
GetChances		Returns the current number of chances.
LoseChance		Takes away one chance.
ResetChances		Refills chances to the maximum allowed.
GetPlayerName		Returns the player's name.

As you can see in Table 7.4, there are two calls to the game after each move: **_parent.recordMove()** and **_parent.nextTurn()**. For Swimming, these calls could be combined into one, as you can only make one single move per turn. Other games, however, might let you do multiple moves per turn—for instance, you could move again in a dice-based game after you throw a six. So to be able to reuse this code or parts of it more easily for other games, it's a good idea to keep the two events separate.

player_class.fla uses the exact same symbols as hand_class.fla—the hand movie clip now has two instances on the stage, stack and player. In the frame actions for Frame 1, you need to make some modifications. Because the two movies are very similar, we will only describe the changes. The player will look for two methods to call back, **recordMove** and **nextTurn**. For now we'll define placeholder methods that will show that they get called and which arguments got passed on to them (see Figure 7.22).

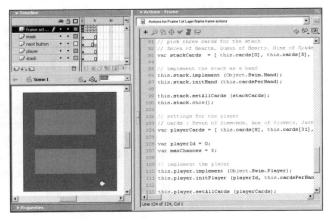

FIGURE 7.22

Implementing **Swim.Hand** for the stack and **Swim.Player** for the player.

```
#include "includes/player.as"
recordMove = function (move, arg1, arg2) {
  trace ("recordMove " + move);
  if (move == "takeOne") {
    var stackSlot = arg1;
    var card = arg2;
    trace ("takes card " + stackSlot + ": " + card.getDesc() );
  }
  else if (move == "takeAll") {
    var cards = arg1;
    for (i=0; i<cards.length; i++) {
      trace ( cards[i].getDesc() );
    }
  }
}
nextTurn = function () {
  trace ("Score of the player: " + this.player.getScore() );
  trace ("next turn");
}
```

Instead of a hand, you now define the stack—the **stack** being an instance of the **hand** class followed by implementing the player:

```
var stackCards  = [ this.cards[0], this.cards[5],  this.cards[18] ];
this.stack.implement (Object.Swim.Hand);
this.stack.initHand (this.cardsPerHand);
this.stack.setAllCards (stackCards);
this.stack.show();

var playerCards = [ this.cards[8], this.cards[31], this.cards[28] ];
var playerId = 0;
var maxChances = 3;
this.player.implement (Object.Swim.Player);
this.player.initPlayer (playerId, this.cardsPerHand, maxChances);
this.player.setAllCards (playerCards);
this.player.analyzeHand();
this.player.show();
trace ("Score of the player: " + this.player.getScore() );
```

So far this doesn't look much different than initializing the stack. Only **initPlayer** requires more arguments. Because the **Swim.Player** is intended to be the foundation for the actual player being used, it doesn't have any methods for a user interface. To test its functionality, we need to remote control it.

To illustrate the changes that happen when the player makes his moves, you stop the movie at this point:

stop();

To demonstrate the functionality of the player class, we added a new layer to the main timeline for a regular button with the following action on it:

```
on (release) {
  nextFrame();
}
```

The main timeline got extended to five frames compared to previous examples, so that we can trace through different actions the player can take frame by frame. In each keyframe, we placed a few lines of ActionScript to control the player.

Frame 2:

```
this.player.yourTurn();
this.player.takeOne (0,1);
```

Frame 3:

```
this.player.yourTurn();
this.player.takeAll ();
```

Frame 4:

```
this.player.yourTurn();
this.player.pass();
```

And Frame 5:

```
this.player.yourTurn();
this.player.knock();
```

If you now test the movie, you will see the cards of the stack and the cards of the player, along with the Arrow button. Click the button, and you see how one card changes (see Figure 7.23).

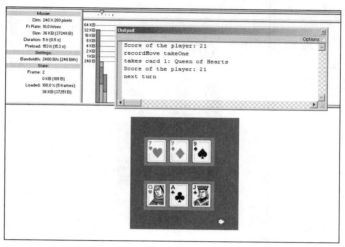

FIGURE 7.23

After taking one card.

If you press Next again, all the cards get swapped, and the move gets traced into the output window (see Figure 7.24). You can do two more moves for **pass** and **knock**. There the cards don't change, but you still see the moves traced into the output window.

This is a simulation to test the player class by itself. We will not use the frame-by-frame code shown here in the actual game.

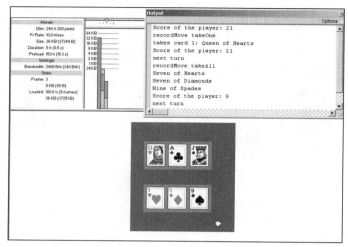

FIGURE 7.24

After taking all three cards.

The Human Player

The **player** class does not have any visual elements that let you interact with the game. The **humanPlayer** class adds the functionality for that. In a turn-based game such as Swimming, where the device gets passed around between turns, you don't want to reveal the hand right away. Rather than that, you want to show an opening screen that stays on until you get the device and press the Start button.

Next, the hand and the stack get shown, along with buttons for the actions you can take, and the score of the hand and remaining chances are displayed. When you look at the **humanPlayer_class.fla**, you will find a new player movie clip instance on the stage with all these elements in it. Double-click the instance to see inside of it (see Figure 7.25). On the top layer, there is an opening screen with a Start button inside. The Start button is setup to implement the **button** class. Make the layer with the opening screen invisible to see the other elements.

There are dynamic text fields that will display the player name, the moves of the other players, and the score of your hand. There is a chance meter movie clip with different states. By using a movie clip here instead of a text field, you can use a graphical representation instead. And last but not least, there are buttons for Take One, Take All, Pass, and Knock.

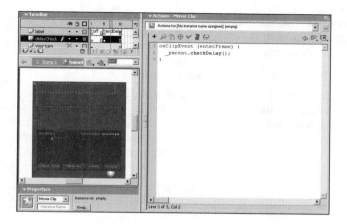

FIGURE 7.25

The inside of the human player movie clip with the opening screen hidden.

In Frame 5 you will find an empty movie clip with the following on it:

```
onClipEvent (enterFrame) {
  _parent.checkDelay();
}
```

This is being used to keep the screen visible for a little bit after you make a move so that you can see the changes you made before it closes. Table 7.5 shows the methods of **Swim.HumanPlayer**.

Table7.5 The Methods of *Swim.HumanPlayer*
Class: Swim.HumanPlayer
Super Class: Swim.Player

Method	Parameters	Description
initHumanPlayer	id, maxCards, chances, showMe, playerName	Implements **Swim.Player** as super class. Implements action buttons. Creates and implements buttons to select cards from the hand and the stack. Implements **Swim.HumanPlayerOpening** for the opening screen.
showLastMoves		Transforms the passed in last moves array into one string for the last moves text field.
showScore		Sets the score display.
looseChance		Calls the inherited **looseChance** method then sets the chances display.
resetChances		Calls the inherited **resetChances** method then resets the chances display.
reset		Deactivates the buttons, clears the score display, and calls the inherited reset method.
yourTurn	lastMoves	Calls inherited **yourTurn**. Shows itself, hides the hand, and shows the opening screen.
startTurn		Closes the opening screen. Activates the action buttons. Updates score and last move displays. Resets previous slot selections. Shows the hand. Shows the stack and the game screen.
endOfTurn		Deactivates action buttons. Analyzes and displays the score. Sends the timeline to **checkDelay**.
checkDelay		Checks whether enough time has passed since **endOfTurn** to give the player a chance to review the move. Calls **humanEndOfTurn** if time is up.
humanEndOfTurn		Hides the stack and itself. Calls inherited **endOfTurn**.
activateButtons		Enables Take All and Pass buttons. Enables Knock button if it's not the first turn. Disables Take One button. Enables buttons to select cards from hand and stack.
deactivateButtons		Turns off all buttons.
selectSlot	buttonName	Sets one card from hand as selected. Enables Take One button if a card from the stack is selected too.

Method	Parameters	Description
selectStack	**buttonName**	Sets one card from the stack as selected. Enables Take One button if a card from the hand is selected, too.
buttonRelease	**button**	Handles all button release events and distributes to the respective methods.

To make the human player work, you need less code in the main timeline than when we used the generic player class by itself in player_class.fla (see Figure 7.26). The human player class takes care of most of it.

First, you need to include the class objects needed. The Next button has changed to a movie clip button. So, you need a **buttonRelease** method. The **nextTurn** method has to be modified to re-enable the Next button when the player is done with his turn.

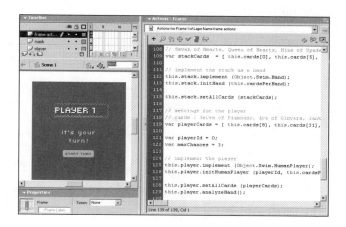

FIGURE 7.26

Implementing the human player on the main timeline.

```
#include "includes/button_ppc.as"
#include "includes/human_player_opening.as"
#include "includes/human_player.as"
buttonRelease = function (button) {
  if (button == nextBtn) {
    player.yourTurn();
    nextBtn.set("hide");
  }
}
```

```
nextTurn = function () {
  trace ("Score of the player: " + this.player.getScore() );
  trace ("next turn");
  nextBtn.set("active");
}
```

To implement the human player class for the player and the Next button with the arrow, the following code is placed after var maxChances = 3;:

```
this.player.implement (Object.Swim.HumanPlayer);
this.player.initHumanPlayer (playerId, this.cardsPerHand, maxChances);
this.player.setAllCards (playerCards);
this.player.analyzeHand();

nextBtn.implement (Object.Button);
nextBtn.initButton("active");
```

Now when testing the movie, you will only see the Next button. When clicking on it, the opening screen for the player will show up (see Figure 7.27). After clicking the Start Turn button, you will see the hand, the stack, the action buttons, and your score. You can select a card from your hand and a card from the stack. After you do so, the Take One button becomes active. You can Take One, Take All, or Pass. The Knock button is disabled because you can't knock on your first turn. After you choose a move, the move will be made, and the player hides.

The Next button becomes visible again. You can click it, and the player comes back up. This time you also can knock if you choose.

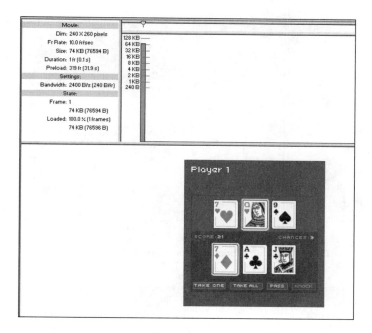

FIGURE 7.27

The human player is active—you can make all moves.

Bringing the Pieces Together—The Game

It's time to put all the pieces together. Instead of one player, we need two. The game screens—title, help, and end screens need to be brought in. And finally the game needs to deal the cards, set the players' turns and determine game ending situations.

In swimming.fla I put all the items just listed into one game movie clip (see Figure 7.28). On the main timeline, there is not much left (see Figure 7.29).

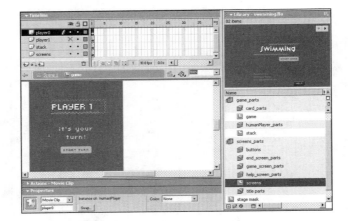

FIGURE 7.28

The game movie clip with all the game elements placed on its timeline.

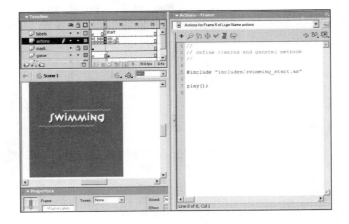

FIGURE 7.29

A small and clean main timeline for the game.

The ActionScript in the Main Timeline

In the first frames we have a little load check in the frame actions layer—in Frame 3:

```
if (getBytesLoaded () == getBytesTotal () ) {
  gotoAndPlay ("start");
} else {
  play();
}
```

Frame 4:

prevFrame();

This is just to be sure the game is really loaded before you go to the start layer.

 This game was created with the intention of distributing it for download and then synching it with the desktop computer. If you intend to deploy a game for web play, you should create a loading bar to show the download progress.

Here the preloader is only a security feature—to prevent the game from choking by jumping right into it without giving the Flash Player on the device enough time to initialize the movie. I recommend from experience not to trust in everything being initialized in Frame 1.

At frame label "start" (Frame 5):

#include "includes/swimming_start.as"
play();

This includes all the classes and methods needed for the game. Inside swimming_start.as you will find all the includes we have used so far as well as:

#include "includes/game.as"

Game.as holds the **Swim.Game** class for the actual game. The methods are listed in Table 7.6.

Table 7.6 The Methods of *Swim.Game*
Class: Swim.Game
Super Class: Screen.Generic

Methods	Parameters	Description
initGame	**playerCount**	Constructor of the game class. **playerCount** will set the number of players in the game. Defaults to 2. Creates the cards for the game. Initializes the players and the deck. Initializes the game screens.
resetGame		Resets all game data. Resets players and the stack. Hides all cards.
getNextPlayer	**currentPlayer**	Finds the next player still in the game after **currentPlayer.**
deal		Initializes and shuffles the deck. Deals each player three cards and puts three cards into the open stack.
startGame		Initializes game data for a round of play. Notifies all players still in the game at the beginning of the new round. Deals and determines the player to make the first turn.

Methods	Parameters	Description
hideGame		Hides the currently visible game elements—the current player and the stack.
showGame		Shows the current player and the stack.
getNewCards		Discards the current cards in the stack, draws three new cards from the deck, and places them in the stack. Returns the new cards in an array.
getKnockPlayer		Returns the player that knocked in this round. Will be null if nobody has knocked yet.
getCardsDesc	cardsArray	Returns the description of all cards in the array in string form.
trackGame	myType, arg1, arg2, arg3, arg4	Keeps track of all events during a round of play, including moves and when new cards get placed on the deck.
recordMove	move, arg1, arg2	Called by a player when making a move. **arg1** and **arg2** depend on the type of move. Not used when the move is pass or knock. **arg1** will hold the cards taken by the player if the move is take all. **arg1** will be the card number from the stack, and **arg2** is the card if the move is take one. Keeps track of the number of players that passed and the player who knocked. Calls **trackGame**.
finishGame	msg, loser	Gets called when **nextTurn** or **firstTurn** determines a game ending situation. Analyzes the winner(s) and loser(s) of the round unless the loser is already specified. Passes the result of the analysis and the passed in message on to the end screen. Shows the end screen.
firstTurn		First turn of a round. Checks if any or all players got dealt a winning hand. Shows the end screen if a winning hand is found. Otherwise finds the player after the dealer and gives the turn to that player.
nextTurn		Gets called when a player is done with his or her move. Checks if the current player has reached the winning score. Checks whether the game has ended after one player has knocked and all other players had one more turn. Checks if all players in a round have passed and replaces the cards on the stack if necessary. If there is no game-ending situation, it gives the turn to the next player.

Putting the Cards into the Deck

The game has a sub object for the deck, with its own methods to shuffle the deck, draw cards, and to keep track of any discarded cards.

The deck object is defined as *object* within the game class. This means all instances of the game will have the same deck, and they will actually share it. Because there is only one game here at any given time, this doesn't have any influence here. Table 7.7 provides the methods.

Table7.7 Methods of *Swim.Game.Deck*

Method	Parameters	Description
initDeck	cardArray	Receives the cards of the deck in the card array. Stores them in its own array and shuffles them.
shuffle	cardArray	Shuffles the deck.
drawCard		Returns the first card from the deck. If the deck is empty, the discarded cards get moved into the deck, shuffled, and the first card gets returned.
drawCards	amount	Draws amount cards from the deck and returns them in an array.
discardCard	aCard	Puts a card to the discarded array.
discardCards	cardArray	Adds the cards in **cardArray** to the discarded array.

Because devices have limited processor power, you give the processor a little break before implementing the game in Frame 6:

```
game.implement (Object.Swim.Game);
game.initGame();
```

Living with the Contextual Menu

The contextual menu: On the desktop it comes up with a right-click or on the Pocket PC when you hold the stylus down for a bit over a non-hit area. Because the contextual menu of the Flash player lets the user control the main timeline with forward and back commands, you send the movie into a "sandbox" where this doesn't have effect, by adding the following to the end of the script in Frame 6:

```
nextFrame ();
```

And in Frame 7 another:

```
nextFrame();
```

And in Frame 9 you place the following:

```
prevFrame ();
```

So, the main timeline ends up in Frame 8. If the user clicks forward or back, the timeline gets sent right back into Frame 8.

Unfortunately you can't block the rewind command, but you can limit the damage by placing a play(); action in Frame 1 of the movie. This way, rewind will just restart everything but not leave the game stuck in Frame 1.

Running the Game

game.initGame(); in Frame 6 initializes the game. It creates the cards as seen before and implements the players and the stack. Then it implements and initializes the game screens, which will bring up the title screen.

Now the game will wait until you click the Start button. The screen's **buttonRelease** method will call the game's **startGame** method.

startGame resets all the game data and tells all active players to get ready for the beginning of the first round. Then it calls the **deal** method.

deal initializes and shuffles the deck. It gives each player three cards before placing three more cards on the stack.

Then **startGame** begins the first round with a call to **firstTurn** (see Figure 7.30). The first turn is special in so far as one or more players could have been dealt a winning hand—which would end the round immediately. If no winner is found, the first player of the round will be picked, and that player's **yourTurn** method will be called.

FIGURE 7.30

Playing the game.

This brings up the opening screen of the player. After clicking the Start Turn button, you can make your move. When you make your move, the game's **nextTurn** method will be called.

nextTurn checks whether the player won or if the game is over after one player knocked and all other players had their last move. It also checks if new cards need to be placed on the stack.

If the game is not over yet, it will find the next active player and call its **yourTurn** method.

In case the game is over, it checks if only one player is left in the game. If so, it will bring up the end game screen, otherwise the end of round screen (see Figure 7.31).

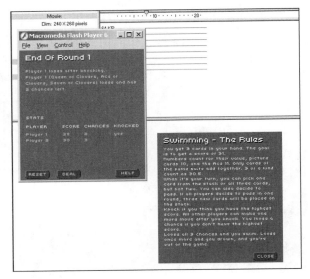

FIGURE 7.31

End of playing a round of Swimming—Player 1 wins.

Playing Against the Computer

The majority of the work has been done. Adding a computer player is a piece of cake now. First you need to add a new screen to the screens movie clip in swimming_computer.fla so that you can choose whether you want to play against the computer or against another human (see Figure 7.32).

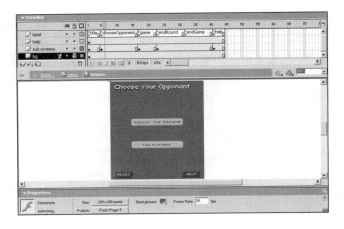

FIGURE 7.32

Introducing the screen that lets you choose whom you play against.

The title screen class gets a slight modification so that it calls **initGame** instead of **startGame** in the screens movie clip. The screens movie clip will then show the choose opponent screen instead of starting the game right away.

There the Against The Machine and Two Players buttons will call **gameComputer** and **gameTwoPlayers** methods in the screen movie clip. These two will call a new **setOpponent** method in the game. **setOpponent** picks the second player based on the parameter passed.

```
GameObj.setOpponent = function (opponent) {
  if (opponent != null && opponent == "computer") {
    this.players = [ this.humanPlayers[0], this.computer0 ];
  }
  else {
    this.players = this.humanPlayers;
  }
  this.startGame();
}
```

For the computer player, you can place a new computer player movie clip inside the game movie clip. It is a very stripped-down version of the human player movie clip. All that is left is a text field indicating the player name and the delay movie clip (see Figure 7.33).

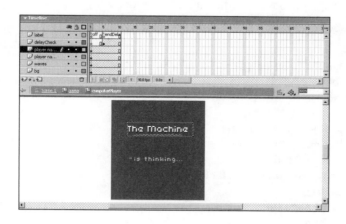

FIGURE 7.33

The inside of the computer player movie clip—not much to look at.

In the **initGame** handler in game_computer.as, you implement the **computerPlayer** class for the computer player.

```
this.humanPlayers = [];
var myPlayer;
for (i = 0; i<this.playerCount; i++) {
  myPlayer = this["player" + i];
  myPlayer.implement (Object.Swim.HumanPlayer);
  myPlayer.initHumanPlayer (i, this.cardsPerHand, this.maxChances);
  this.humanPlayers.push (myPlayer);
}
this.computer0.implement (Object.Swim.ComputerPlayer);
this.computer0.initComputerPlayer (2, this.cardsPerHand, this.maxChances, false,
➥"The Machine");
```

Now let's look at what happens in the computer player. Like the human player, the computer player is based on the generic player class. So it already has all the methods to make a move. It doesn't need all the visual elements that the human player has, so the methods for handling those drop out.

All the computer player needs to do is wait for its turn, calculate and make its move, and then, like the human player, stay on for a little bit so that it doesn't just Flash.

The core of the move calculation is the **think** method (computer_player.as):

```
ComputerPlayer.think = function () {
  var stack = _parent.stack;
  stack.analyzeHand();
  var stackScore = stack.getScore();
  var stackCards = stack.getAllCards();
  var myCards = this.getAllCards ();
  var myScore = this.getScore();
  var stackSlot, changeSlot, mySlot, stackCard;
  var anCards, anScore;
  var hiStackSlot, hiChangeSlot;
  var hiScore = myScore;
  for (stackSlot = 0; stackSlot<this.maxCards; stackSlot++ ) {
    stackCard = stackCards[stackSlot];
    for (changeSlot = 0; changeSlot < this.maxCards; changeSlot++) {
      anCards = [];
      for (mySlot = 0; mySlot < this.maxCards; mySlot++) {
        mySlot != changeSlot ?
          anCards[mySlot] = myCards[mySlot] :
          anCards[mySlot] = stackCard;
```

```
    }
    analyzeHand (anCards);
    if (this.getScore() > hiScore) {
      hiStackSlot = stackSlot;
      hiChangeSlot = changeSlot;
      hiScore = this.getScore();
    }
  }
}
if (hiScore > myScore || stackScore > myScore) {
  if (hiScore > stackScore) {
    this.takeOne (hiChangeSlot, hiStackSlot);
  } else {
    this.takeAll ();
  }
}
else {
  var knocking = false;
  if (!this.firstTurn && _parent.getKnockPlayer == null &&
        myScore >= 27) {
    var rnd = Math.floor (Math.random() * 3);
    if (rnd < 1) {
      knocking = true;
    }
  }
  knocking ?
    this.knock() :
    this.pass();
}
this.analyzeHand();
}
```

This is a straightforward computer player. It checks the score of its hand and the score of the cards on the stack. Then it tries to replace each card from the stack with each card in the hand and remembers the highest score. At the end it will make the move that offers the best score improvement. If it can't improve its score, it passes or might knock if the score is high enough.

The intelligence of the computer player could be further improved. It could try to go prepare a three-of-a-kind if it can't improve otherwise. Right now it will only pick three-of-a-kind if it already has a pair. It also doesn't check whether it leaves a high score on the stack by making a move. And neither does it keep track of the moves of the other player. I leave this up for you to explore on your own. But first play against the computer—and try to beat it (see Figure 7.34).

FIGURE 7.34

Player 1 wins...

SUMMARY

Mobile devices such as Pocket PC have become fairly powerful machines. Now that these can play back Flash, the door is wide open to develop rich Flash games for these platforms. If you keep the constraints of the devices in mind, you have the opportunity to entertain a fast growing group of mobile users.

In the second part of this chapter we developed a game that is well suited for the platform—a card game with fairly simple rules that you can play against the computer or against another human player. We used a programming technique that lets you edit code and artwork separate from each other—so that you can easily reuse parts of either code or artwork for another project, or simply reskin the game to brand it for someone else. I hope you will be able to use it as a base to create your own games for devices.

PART III: CREATING APPLICATIONS FOR DEVICES WITH FLASH

8

DATA PERSISTENCE WITH FLASH, JSCRIPT, AND HTTP COOKIES

by Christian Cantrell

Macromedia Flash is one of the most advanced technologies that is available for user interface design and client-side scripting. It is also becoming an increasingly important component in large-scale, multitier application development as each version of Flash provides better and more sophisticated support for back-end integration. But what if your application falls somewhere in the middle? What if you need to be able to quickly store and retrieve relatively small amounts of information and have them persist from one session to the next, but don't want all the complexity and overhead of integrating a back-end server and database? What if you want your application to run locally, without requiring a network connection? Perhaps you just want to be able to save a few high scores, or store a few simple user preferences. Where you might write out a text file in other languages, or serialize a few simple objects and save them to disk, Flash, combined with JScript (the Pocket Internet Explorer version of JavaScript), can store and retrieve data on client devices using HTTP cookies.

To illustrate the concept of using the browser's cookie database to save data on behalf of a Flash application, we are going to explore FlashTone. FlashTone is a relatively simple and small Flash application I wrote which, by playing tones of the exact same frequency as those generated by touchtone phones, can actually dial numbers for you when you play the tones on your mobile device into the receiver of any touchtone phone. What's interesting about FlashTone, however, is the fact that it also allows users to store up to 10 frequently dialed numbers using nothing but Flash, JScript, and cookies.

WHAT ARE HTTP COOKIES?

Before we jump into Flash and JScript, let's take a moment to really understand cookies and the function they serve in the world of HTTP and web applications. It is actually not entirely necessary for you to understand cookies before you can use them for data storage with the code I have provided here; however, the section that follows will help provide you with a broader perspective on the technology we will be exploring.

First of all, one of the biggest challenges developers face when designing applications for the web is the fact that HTTP is inherently stateless. In other words, HTTP defines a protocol for clients (usually browsers) to make requests to servers and for servers to respond to those requests. That's essentially it. How can a server know that two consecutive requests were from the same client? Why is that you can enter a username and password once, and not have to re-authenticate every time you make a new request? A server cannot depend on clients' IP addresses being unique because any number of users could be using a single proxy server and therefore all appear to have the same IP address. Netscape's answer (which has since become a widely adopted standard) was cookies.

A cookie (named as such for no particular reason) is a relatively small piece of data—about 4 kilobytes or 4,096 characters—that servers can store locally on clients' computers. The most common usage of cookies is storing session or shopping cart IDs and user authentication information. Ad servers also sometimes use cookies to help identify or target viewers. Without getting into too much detail (the HTTP cookie specification is quite complex in its entirety and well beyond the scope of this chapter), let's consider a simple application of cookies.

Let's say one day you get tired of typing in your username password at your favorite news site, and you finally check the checkbox below the password field labeled "Remember my login information." When you click the Submit button and the server finds that checkbox checked, it will send back a cookie header in the HTTP response, which might look something like this:

HTTP/1.1 200 OK
Set-Cookie: credentials="cantrell;lucy"; Version="1"; \Path="/"; expires=Wednesday,
➥01-Jan-03 00:00:00 GMT

The first line of the header specifies the protocol and version (HTTP/1.1) and the response code (**200 OK**) indicating to your browser that the request was processed successfully on the server. The next line of the header is telling your browser to set a cookie named **credentials** to the value of **"cantrell;lucy"** (**cantrell** being the user name, **lucy** being the password).

When your browser parses that portion of the header, it will make an appropriate entry in its cookie database, and from then until midnight on January 1, 2003, it will send the cookie name/value pair in any request to the domain that originally set the cookie. For instance, if the cookie was set by the domain planetearthgazette.com, then any request back to **http://www.planetearthgazette.com** using the same browser that was used at the time the cookie was set will contain a request header with the cookie information. The server then watches for the cookie in certain requests and, where it finds it, automatically uses the user-name and password to authenticate the user.

DATA FLOW BETWEEN FLASH, JSCRIPT, AND COOKIES

The flow of data between Flash, JScript, and a browser's cookie database is probably the most important concept in terms of understanding not just FlashTone, but client-side data storage in general. Because it is so crucial, I am going to take a moment to outline data flow outside of the context of FlashTone where it is free from distractions.

After I have described the concepts at a high level, we will zoom in and see them in action as we explore the FlashTone application.

Using JScript to Retrieve Cookie Data

Using HTTP headers is one way to get and set cookies; however, because our Flash application is running locally without a server component, this technique does us no good. Fortunately, JScript allows us to make and retrieve entries in the browser's cookie database right from the client without even having to communicate with a server or even understand anything about HTTP.

Because one of the most convenient times to pass data into a Flash movie is at the time the movie loads (more on this to come), the flow of data must start with the loading of the HTML page in which your Flash movie is embedded. As the page loads, therefore, we will use JScript to access the browser's cookie database, find the exact cookie we are interested in (in this case, the cookie containing the user's 10 most frequently dialed phone numbers), and save that data to a JScript variable. Step one accomplished. The next challenge is getting that data from a JScript variable into Flash.

Using JScript to Pass Data to Flash

It seems we have a problem. We want to pass data into our Flash movie at the time the movie loads; however, the data is contained in a JScript variable and the movie is loaded from the HTML <object> tag. To get the data from JScript to HTML and finally into our Flash movie, therefore, we will apply the technique of actually using JScript to construct the HTML tags which load the movie, slipping our data in at just the right moment where it will get passed into the Flash movie and become available as an ActionScript variable.

Flash Passing Data Back to JScript

Now the user's 10 most frequently dialed phone numbers have been loaded into the Flash movie and can be accessed easily. But what if the user wants to change one of the phone numbers? Or what if he only has five slots taken and wants to add a sixth number? Not only does the new number have to be stored in Flash, but also it somehow has to make its way back into the browser's cookie database so that it will be there the next time the movie is loaded. Because JScript has the ability to read and write cookies and Flash does not, we will see how Flash can pass data to Jscript functions.

JScript Saving Data as Cookies

Now that the new phone number has been passed from the Flash movie to JScript, it is time to complete the data flow cycle. Figure 8.1 shows how JScript, in addition to reading cookies, can write cookies to the browser's cookie database.

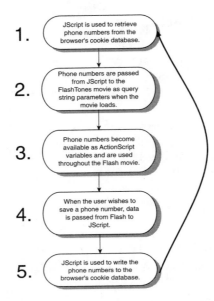

FIGURE 8.1

The JScript data flow cycle.

DISSECTING FLASHTONE

FlashTone is an application written in about 90% Flash and 10% JScript, which both stores and dials phone numbers. Much like a cell phone, numbers are stored in association with the numbers in the number pad (see Figure 8.2). In other words, you might assign your home number to the 1 key, your office number to the 2 key, your spouse's cell phone number to the 3 key, and so on. To save a number that you have already entered, simply tap on the Save button. The number pad reveals all the numbers you have saved so far and which slots you have empty (see Figure 8.2). You can then tap on either an empty slot or an existing number to over-write it. To dial a saved number, tap on the Load button. Again, all the numbers that you have previously stored are revealed through the number pad. Just tap on the number you want to recall, then tap Dial.

FIGURE 8.2

FlashTone running on a Pocket PC device.

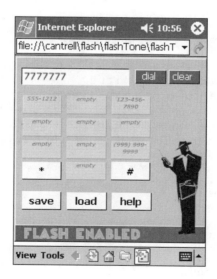

FIGURE 8.3

Notice that previously saved numbers are revealed when the user taps Load or Save.

Touchtone Pads

Touchtone phone number pads are typically arranged in three columns and four rows. Each row and column has a unique tone, which sounds at a unique frequency. When you press a number, the tone you hear is actually a combination of the row frequency and the column frequency. Tones are combinations of two frequencies rather than simply a single frequency in order to reduce the chance that ambient noise might, by chance, match the frequency of a particular number and cause you to misdial your phone. We see, therefore, that the sounds we hear when dialing a number are the actual sounds that place a call. All you have to do to dial a phone, therefore, is to make the correct sounds. In fact, it is merely a convenience that phones have number pads built in at all because all a number pad really is a very precise noisemaker. FlashTone is now exposed for what it really is: nothing more than a Flash movie that plays back WAV files that happen to be recordings of the right combinations of frequencies needed to dial a touchtone phone.

As you can see, dialing phone numbers turns out to be the easy part; it's storing them and retrieving them that requires explanation. Let's examine FlashTone at the beginning of the data flow process as we use JScript to load saved data.

Using JScript to Load Saved Phone Numbers

JScript is typically executed in response to an event. For instance, a developer might use JScript to validate information typed into a web form at the time the form is submitted. Or he might validate each field in the form at the time the field loses focus (a field is said to lose focus when the cursor leaves the field). It is not required that JScript be executed in response to a user event, however. As with ActionScript, any JScript code existing outside of the scope of a function will execute from top to bottom as the code is loaded. Let's start, therefore, by looking at flashTone.html from the top down.

```
<html>
<head>
  <title>FlashTone</title>
  <script language="JScript">
    // Constants.
    var COOKIE_NAME = "_tones";
```

The first thing we do (other than open the HTML document with an <html> tag and open the head of the document) is open a script tag and define a single constant, COOKIE_NAME.

COOKIE_NAME is the name of the cookie in which FlashTone's ten-number memory is stored. We then define the functions **getCookieValue()**, **setCookie()**, and **saveNumbers()** (which we will discuss momentarily) before actually calling the function **getCookieValue()** with the following piece of code:

var tones = getCookieValue(COOKIE_NAME);

 Note that the function getCookieValue() must be defined prior to attempting to call it. Remember, code outside the scope of functions executes as the page loads, so code that executes is unaware of functions that have not yet been loaded.

To see what the value of tones will be, let's examine the function **getCookieValue()**:

```
function getCookieValue(name) {
    // Retrieve saved numbers.
    var allCookies = document.cookie.split("; ");
    for (i = 0; i < allCookies.length; ++i) {
        if (allCookies[i].split("=")[0] == COOKIE_NAME) {
            return unescape(allCookies[i].split("=")[1]);
        }
    }
    return null;
}
```

getCookieValue() starts out by retrieving a list of cookies from the document object. The browser only returns cookies from its cookie database that were set from the same domain from which the current page was served. Because the page was loaded locally rather than served from a server, all cookies that were set locally—whether they were set by FlashTone or some other application—will be returned in one long semicolon delimited list. The first thing we must do, therefore, is split them and sort through the result looking for the exact cookie we are interested in, which is the cookie named **_tones** as defined as the value of constant **COOKIE_NAME**. After we find the correct cookie, we pass the value through the native JScript **unescape()** function, which URL decodes it, and we pass it back to the caller where it is assigned to the variable tones. Notice how if the cookie does not exist (as in the case where the user has either never saved any numbers or is loading the FlashTone application for the first time), null is returned rather than a string. This is by no means a problem or an error condition, and you will see how we deal with it appropriately when the time comes.

As you will see when we go over the process of saving data to the browser's cookie database, all 10 of the phone numbers are stored as a single colon (:) delimited string to save us from having to store and retrieve 10 different cookies. Because 4K is plenty of space (the minimum amount of space a browser must allocate for a single cookie), it is much more efficient to store them together rather than take up more entries in the cookie database by saving them individually.

Now that we have extracted our saved phone numbers from the browser's cookie database, it is time to pass them into the FlashTones Flash movie. The best and easiest way to pass data into a Flash movie from the HTML page in which the movie is embedded is as query string parameters at the time the movie is loaded, like this:

```
<object ...>
  <param name="movie" value="someMovie.swf?name=this+is+a+value">
</object>
```

From the time the movie loads, you will have access to an ActionScript variable called **name** with a value of **this is a value** from the main timeline (_level0). The only remaining problem we must solve is that an object tag is HTML, but all the saved data is in the form of a JScript variable.

Passing the Phone Numbers from JScript to Flash

The only way to pass data from JScript to HTML and then into Flash at the time the Flash movie is loading is to use JScript to generate the HTML tags that load the movie, like this:

```
<body bgcolor="#ffffff" topmargin="0" leftmargin="0">
  <script language="JScript">
    document.write('<object classid="clsid:D27CDB6E-AE6D-11cf-96B8-444553540000"');
    document.write('ID="PPC"');

document.write('codebase="http://download.macromedia.com/pub/shockwave/cabs/flash/
➥swflash.cab#version=5,0,0,0"');
    document.write('width="240"');
    document.write('height="240">');
    document.write('<param name=movie value="flashTones.swf?'+COOKIE_NAME+
    ➥'='+escape(tones)+'">');
    document.write('<param name=quality value=high>');
    document.write('</object>');
  </script>
</body>
```

By using JScript to write out the HTML, we can easily append our saved numbers to the movie's URL, and use JScript's native **escape()** function to URL encode the data. We are then guaranteed that Flash will have access to all the phone numbers on the main timeline in the form of an ActionScript variable from the time the movie starts playing.

Now that our movie has loaded, let's see how the FlashTone movie handles the data we just passed in.

Inside the FlashTone Movie

FlashTone is not particularly complex as far as Flash applications go (see Figure 8.4). It consists of twelve layers over only four frames and does little more than respond to buttons getting tapped and play WAV files. The application does contain a fair amount of ActionScript, however, which, while not overly complicated, does merit detailed explanation.

FIGURE 8.4

FlashTone in the Flash authoring environment.

 At one time, FlashTone was actually much more complex than it is today as I started out building the number pad programmatically as opposed to simply arranging movieclips on the stage. In other words, I used ActionScript to create instances of movieclips and, in a for loop, placed them at specific x-and y-coordinates on the stage to form a number pad. The advantage of building the interface programmatically as opposed to simply placing 12 movie clips on the stage is flexibility—I was able to change their position and distance from each other just by changing the values of a few ActionScript variables. Additionally, I could change the look of all the buttons just by redesigning the one button I used to duplicate all 12 of the others. Unfortunately, when I moved the application over to my Pocket PC device for testing, I discovered that it took between 5 and 20 seconds to actually render, depending on how many other Pocket PC applications I had open. It turned out that the work of building the interface programmatically was too much for my device's processor. So after all that work, I had to refactor the FlashTone movie and place the buttons on the stage the old-fashioned way. I learned the hard way that one must sometimes sacrifice elegance for efficiency when designing for mobile platforms.

Most of the ActionScript in FlashTone is contained on the top-most layer labeled "control." I like to keep as much ActionScript together in one place as I can to simplify development (no searching through your movie looking for one particular function or variable declaration), and because I believe it simplifies and promotes code reuse (using functions more than once from different places in the code).

As with JScript, when ActionScript exists outside the scope of a function, it executes from the top down as it loads. The first thing that happens in the FlashTones movie, therefore, is a call to the native ActionScript **action stop()**; because our movie is more of an application that responds to user actions than an animation, we want to carefully control the flow of the movie rather than simply let it play through from start to finish. We then define a few constants and other global variables before reaching the point where we deal with the string of saved numbers that was passed in from the HTML file as the movie was loaded.

```
// Array that holds the stored numbers.
var savedNumbers = new Array(10);
if (_tones != null && _tones != "null") {
    var allTones = String(_tones).split(":");
    for (var i = 0; i < allTones.length; ++i) {
        savedNumbers[i] = allTones[i];
    }
}
```

We create a new array containing 10 elements (for our 10 phone number memory) and assign it to a global variable called **savedNumbers**. We then check to see if the variable **_tones** has been defined before trying to operate on it (recall that **_tones** is the name of the query string parameter that we appended to the name of the movie while loading FlashTone—it translates directly into the name of an ActionScript variable). The only case in which **_tones** would not be defined is if the user had never saved any phone numbers before, in which case all 10 elements of **savedNumbers** would remain null (a situation we will deal with shortly). Assuming some numbers had been saved in the past, we split the numbers on the colon character into an array called **allTones** (remember that the phone numbers were passed in as a single colon-delimited list), and iterate through them, adding them in their appropriate places to the **savedNumbers** array. At this point, we have successfully retrieved data from the browser's cookie database, passed it into a Flash movie, and made the data available in a useful data structure to the rest of our application. Quite an accomplishment.

Although there is no more code that relates to data persistence until we get to the point in the data flow of wanting to save phone numbers, I will continue to describe the ActionScript in the control layer to make the inner-workings of the FlashTone application clearer.

```
// Create all the sound objects for playing tones.
var tones = new Array();
for (var i = 0; i < TOTAL_NUMBERS; ++i) {
    tones[i] = new Sound();
    tones[i].attachSound("tone_"+i);
}
```

This is the first time we deal with the tones that are eventually used to dial phone numbers. We create an array, assign it to a variable called tones, and then populate the array with new ActionScript Sound objects. Calling the function **attachSound()** attaches a sound from the library to the **Sound** object from which you call the function. Note that for this technique to work, the symbol in the library has to be specially linked. To link a symbol in the library, right-click the symbol and select Linkage. In the resulting box, give the symbol a name and select Export This Symbol. The symbol will then be exported into the SWF file and available for dynamic loading.

The next piece of code completes FlashTone's initialization sequence (as defined by all the code outside of functions that is executed as the movie loads) and is responsible for attaching the saved phone numbers to their appropriate numbers on the number pad.

```
// Populate the number pad with saved numbers.
for (var i = 0; i < BUTTON_EFFECT_NUM; ++i) {
    eval("numberPad.button_"+i).savedNumber =
        (savedNumbers[i] == null ||
        savedNumbers[i] == "")?"empty":savedNumbers[i];
}
```

The main timeline contains a movie clip called "numberPad." The numberPad movie clip contains 12 buttons, one for every button on a touchtone phone. Numbers 0–9 contain dynamic text boxes called "savedNumber" that get assigned to their associated elements in the **savedNumbers** array. As you can see, if an element is null or blank (meaning no number has been saved in that slot), the string **"empty"** is assigned instead.

The rest of the code in "control" exists inside of functions and only executes in response to user input. Before discussing the processes of entering and saving phone numbers, however, it's important that you understand FlashTone's concept of "modes."

At any given time, FlashTone can be in one of three different modes: "enter," "load," or "save." The mode is simply dictated by the value of the global variable "mode," the default mode being "enter" (as you can see from the way in which the mode variable is initialized).

var mode = "enter";

The application's mode dictates the behavior of certain buttons. For example, tapping on the 1 key in enter mode simply sounds the proper tone and appends a one to the value in the numberInput text box. In load mode, however, tapping on the 1 changes the value of the numberInput text box to the stored phone number associated with the 1 key. Finally, in save mode, tapping on the 1 key will save whatever number is in the numberInput box in position 1 of the array of saved phone numbers. (All these process we will look at in more detail shortly.)

Modes are changed from "enter" to either "load" or "save" by tapping on the "load" or "save" buttons, which calls the function **handleAction()**, passing either the string "load" or "save" depending on which button was tapped.

```
// Handles actions like load and save by delegating to the appropriate
// function.
function handleAction(action) {
    // Must be in "enter" mode to use an action. If not, bail out.
    if (mode != "enter") {
        mode = "enter";
        buttonEffectOff();
        return;
    }
    if (action == "save") {
        saveMode();
    } else if (action == "load") {
        loadMode();
    } else {
        help();
    }
}
```

Essentially all the **handleAction()** function does is delegate to **saveMode()**, **loadMode()**, or **help()**, depending on which button initiated the call. **saveMode()** and **loadMode()** do little more than set the value of the **"mode"** variable to either "save" or "load," then call **buttonEffectOn()** (which causes the buttons in the number pad to reveal the saved numbers they have associated with them). The **help()** function simply makes the help movieclip (where all the help copy is stored) visible by setting its **"_visible"** property to true.

The beginning of the **handleAction()** function is interesting, though. As you can see, you are required to be in "enter" mode before switching into another mode; otherwise, the mode is set to "enter" and the function returns. This is to allow users to go from "load" or "save" mode by tapping on the appropriate button back to "enter" mode by tapping on the button again, essentially accomplishing a toggle effect.

So, now that we know how modes are changed, let's explore how being in different modes effects the application. Tapping on any other button in the number pad besides "load," "save," or "help" calls the **buttonPressed()** function.

```
// Handle the event of a button being pushed.
function buttonPressed(input) {
    if (mode == "enter") {
        // User is simply entering a phone number.
        if (numberInput.length < MAX_INPUT_SIZE) {
            soundTone(input);
            numberInput = numberInput + String(input);
        }
    } else {
        buttonEffectOff();
        // Illegal operation.
        if (isNaN(input)) {
            mode = "enter";
            return;
        }
        if (mode == "save") {
            // User wants to save a phone number.
            saveNumber(input);
        } else {
            // User wants to load a phone number.
            loadNumber(input);
        }
        mode = "enter";
    }
}
```

The first thing **buttonPressed()** does is check the application's mode. This is how we know to give the keypad different behaviors depending on which mode the application is in. For example, in "enter" mode, tapping on the 1 key calls the **soundTone()** function (which essentially just calls **start()** on the appropriate Sound object so that the tone actually plays), then appends the number 1 to the numberInput text box. If the mode is "save," the process of saving a phone number is initiated (which we will soon explore in detail). If the mode is not "enter" or "save," it is assumed that the mode is "load," in which case the **loadNumber()** function is called.

```
function loadNumber(num)
{
    numberInput = savedNumbers[num];
}
```

loadNumber()'s only job is to change the value of the numberInput text box to the associated value stored in the **savedNumbers** array. The effect is that a number was just "loaded" from the application's memory.

There are a few other things going on inside **buttonPressed()** that are worth mentioning. Let's take a moment to look more closely at the following code:

```
buttonEffectOff();
// Illegal operation.
if (isNaN(input)) {
    mode = "enter";
    return;
}
```

The call to **buttonEffectOff()** restores the number pad to its normal appearance of obscuring the saved phone numbers. The check to be sure that the value of input is actually a number is to handle the "*" and "#" buttons getting tapped in any mode other than "enter." In "enter" mode, tapping on the "*" or "#" is perfectly fine because they are treated just as any other number in the number pad. In "save" or "load" mode, however, they are illegal options because they are not slots in which phone numbers can be saved or from which numbers can be retrieved. If an illegal operation is detected, therefore, the mode is simply set back to "enter" and the function returns without performing any other operations.

Before we talk about the process of saving phone numbers (which is the last step in the data flow process), let's look at the two remaining buttons in the FlashTone interface which we haven't yet explored: "clear" and "dial."

The clear button is easy; tapping on it calls the **clearInput()** function, which just sets the value of numberInput to an empty string (giving it the appearance of being cleared). Dial is a little more involved, however. Tapping on the dial button calls the following function:

```
// Handle the dial event.
function dial(num) {
   toDial = new Array();
   var numStr = String(num);
   var len = numStr.length;
   for (var i = 0; i < len; ++i) {
      curNum = numStr.charAt(i);
      if (curNum == "*" || curNum == "#" || !isNaN(curNum)) {
         toDial[toDial.length] = curNum;
      }
   }
   gotoAndPlay(2);
}
```

The dial function has two jobs. The first is to break apart the phone number that is to be dialed and assign it to the global array **toDial**. The second is to use the ActionScript action **goToAndPlay()** to play the movie starting from the second frame. On the second frame of the dialing layer, the following code actually dials the phone number:

```
var nextTone = getNextTone();
if (nextTone == -1)
{
   stop();
}
soundTone(nextTone);
```

The **getNextTone()** function is defined in the control layer and does nothing more than iterate through the global **toDial** array, returning one number at a time, and finally –1 when there are no more numbers to return. The code on the "dialing" layer sends the number it got back from **getNextTone()** to the **soundTone()** function in control (which plays the tone), unless –1 is returned, in which case the movie is stopped again. Assuming the movie does not get stopped, it is allowed to continue playing until reaching the fourth frame where there is ActionScript on the "dialing" layer which calls **goToAndPlay(2)**, causing the movie to continue looping until all the numbers have been accounted for and played. The loop between frame 2 and frame 4 is what causes the necessary pause between tones.

Passing Phone Numbers from Flash to JScript

Let's go back and take a closer look at the process of saving phone numbers since it is the final step in the data flow process. The user tapping on a number while in "save" mode initiates the process. As we discussed before, the **buttonPressed()** function is called, which delegates to the **saveNumber()** function as shown here:

```
function saveNumber(num)
{
    savedNumbers[num] = numberInput;
    eval("numberPad.button_"+(num)).savedNumber = (numberInput == null ||
            numberInput == "")?"empty":numberInput;
    var allNumbers = savedNumbers[0];
    for (var i = 1; i < savedNumbers.length; ++i) {
        allNumbers += (":"+savedNumbers[i]);
    }
        // Save the numbers as a cookie.
        getURL("javascript:saveNumbers('"+allNumbers+"')");
}
```

The **saveNumber()** function is not actually as daunting as it may appear at first glance. The first thing it does is replace the appropriate element in the **savedNumbers** array with the number currently in the numberInput text box (the number the user wants to save). The next thing it does is set the number that the user wants to save on the button in the number pad that the user has chosen to associate with the phone number so that the newly saved number can be revealed when the **buttonEffectOn()** function is called. The third thing the **saveNumber()** function does is iterate through all the phone numbers in the **savedNumbers** array and concatenate them all into a single colon (:) delimited string. Finally, **saveNumber()** performs the magic of communicating the string of numbers to JScript where they can be written to the browser's cookie database.

As I mentioned earlier, JScript is usually executed in response to an event, and events are usually captured through event handlers. To capture the event of a form being submitted, you use an **onSubmit** event handler as an attribute of your form. To capture the events of a field either gaining or losing focus, you use an **onFocus** or **onBlur** event handler as an attribute of your input field. The most common event to capture is probably the click, which you can do in two ways; as you might expect, you can use an **onClick** event handler as an attribute of either a button or an anchor tag, or you can use the following syntax:

```
<a href="javascript:someFunction('data')">Click here!</a>
```

Clicking on the **Click here!** link calls the function **someFunction** passing it the string **'data'**. The importance of being able to execute JScript in this manner as opposed to strictly using an event handler is that it is exactly like telling your browser to follow a URL, only the URL is a set of JScript instructions rather than an actual URL (which the browser knows by the **javascript:** prefix. That means any application, process, or plug-in that can tell your browser to follow a URL can also execute JScript, which, using the ActionScript action **getURL()**, gives Flash exactly the hook we need to pass ActionScript data into JScript.

Look again at the last line of the **saveNumbers()** function:

getURL("javascript:saveNumbers('"+allNumbers+"')");

We use the ActionScript action **getURL()** to tell the browser to access a URL; however, prefixing the URL with the keyword **javascript:**, the browser knows to interpret the rest of the URL not as a URL at all, but as JScript. The result, therefore, is the execution of the JScript function **saveNumbers()** with our string of phone numbers being passed in as an argument.

Using JScript to Write to the Browser's Cookie Database

The final process in the data flow between ActionScript, JScript, and cookies has us back where we started: between the <script> tags of the HTML document in which the FlashTone movie is embedded. This time, the relevant function is **saveNumbers()**.

```
// Saves a : delimited list of phone numbers for three years.
function saveNumbers(numbers) {
    setCookie(COOKIE_NAME,numbers,(365*3));
}
```

Remember that this function is now a Jscript function in the HTML page, and not an ActionScript function.

As it turns out, **saveNumbers()** is a very simple function that simply delegates to a more generic function called **setCookie**. I decided to put the code, which actually does the work of saving the cookie, in its own generic function to make it more re-usable. In other words, because there is nothing specific to the FlashTone application in **setCookie**, I can re-use the function for saving cookies on behalf of other applications, as well.

The first thing **setCookie** does is create a new JScript date object, which it then calls **setDate** on, passing it a new future date derived from the current date plus 365×3 (for a total of 1,095) days, which was passed in from **saveNumbers()**. As you will see, the Date object is what we use to generate the date string that gets used as the value of the "expires" attribute of the cookie. By setting it to 1,095 days from the current date, the FlashTone's memory will last for three years from the last time any number was saved. After three years, the browser will remove the cookie from its database and FlashTone's memory will be deleted.

Feel free to redefine 1,095 because it is an arbitrary number. Be sure you include an expiration date, however, as the absence of an expiration date indicates to the browser that the cookie only needs to persist for the life of the current session, which expires the moment the browser is closed.

The last thing **setCookie** does is set the cookie in the browser's cookie database. JScript handles cookies as properties of the document object; however, setting cookies only overwrites cookies of the same name as existing cookies. The JScript syntax is a little misleading, therefore, because you are actually adding to the document's cookie property as opposed to redefining it.

The value of the cookie is passed through the native JScript function **escape()** to make sure the entire cookie is properly formatted. **escape()** returns a URL encoded version of whatever string you pass to it, thus ensuring that there are no quotes or semicolons that will make parsing the cookie again later impossible. Finally, we call **toGMTString()** on the Date instance which just happens to return the expiration date in the exact format the browsers require, and we have completed the data flow cycle from the browser's cookie database to JScript to Flash, then back to JScript, and finally, back to the browser's cookie database. And the whole process happens instantly and completely transparently to the user.

SUMMARY

As developers and designers turn more and more toward Flash as a front-end application solution, data persistence will increasingly become an issue. Large-scale applications will use sophisticated middle-tier code on remote servers to store data in a variety of ways from databases to text files to serialized objects. Such complex architectures are obviously not an option for smaller-scale applications, such as games and simple tools that are becoming easier and faster to create in Flash than in traditional programming environments. As you have seen, JScript and cookies provide an excellent and practical solution.

9

STANDALONE APPLICATION DEVELOPMENT USING FLASH AND JAVA

by Christian Cantrell

Two of the most prominent themes in application development today are *n-tiered architecture* and *platform independence*. Though the terms might come across as impressive if daunting pieces of technical jargon, they are actually fairly straightforward concepts, and integral to understanding the integration of Macromedia Flash and Java on embedded devices. Designing around an n-tiered architecture and aiming for complete platform independence not only makes for a smoother development process, but will also make your work more reusable, portable, and extensible.

DEVELOPING WITH AN N-TIERED ARCHITECTURE

Rather than cramming all your application's code into a single interdependent mass, an n-tiered architecture mandates that you divide it up into sections—or tiers—which talk to each other through a (hopefully) simple, well-defined protocol or API (application programming interface). In a relatively simple web application, your topmost tier might be responsible for generating dynamic HTML content and processing requests from clients (usually browsers). The tier below that might validate that data, and the bottommost tier is generally responsible for data persistence (usually using a database).

Let's say, for example, in the process of creating an account for an e-commerce application, you enter a login name and a password (see Figure 9.1). The top tier hands your registration data to the middle tier, which determines that the login name you chose is not unique, so the top tier is told to rerender the registration form with a message asking you to choose a different login name. The second time the form is submitted, the middle tier confirms that the name is unique this time, so the data is handed to the bottommost tier where it is stored in a database and used for authentication purposes each time you log in to your account.

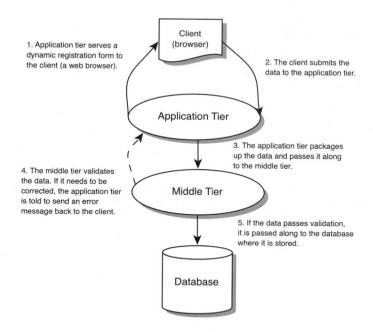

FIGURE 9.1

The n-tier structure.

There are three primary advantages to an n-tiered architecture:

1. If each layer of code is insulated well enough from the layers around it (in object-oriented programming, this is usually referred to as "encapsulation"), then changes in one layer should have little or no effect on other layers.

2. By having distinct boundaries between layers of code, it is easier to allocate developers and designers, allowing teams to specialize in their respective areas.

3. With a well-understood protocol between layers of code, it becomes possible to implement different tiers with completely different technologies.

This chapter is primarily concerned with the third advantage of n-tiered application development because it allows us to combine the strengths of two very different technologies—Flash and Java—to arrive at a single, fully functional application.

Note that if your expertise lies primarily in the realm of Flash rather Java, there is still plenty to be gained from this chapter. Not only will you find Java remarkably similar to Flash 5 ActionScript, but the higher-level architectural concepts presented here apply to software development in general, whether you are using Java, C++, or Flash by itself.

PLATFORM INDEPENDENCE

The idea of building an application without regard to the hardware and operating system it is designed to run on is a relatively recent concept, though one that is having a tremendous impact on software development. It is also a concept that is getting more and more important with the proliferation of intelligent devices. Clearly, it is a far more prudent allocation of resources to build an application that can run on dozens of platforms and configurations rather than having to rebuild and maintain the application for every device market. Flash and Java (the two technologies I used to build TextTool, the application we will be analyzing in this chapter) are models of platform independence and perfect for the mobile and embedded worlds.

 **It is important to keep in mind that platform independence is still a somewhat relative term. Generally speaking, it is unrealistic to develop an entire application with absolutely no regard to hardware in the mobile space simply because mobile devices are all so unique. CPU, memory, and screen size on mobile devices have not yet been standardized to nearly the extent desktop computers have.**

WHY USE DIFFERENT TECHNOLOGIES FOR A SINGLE PROJECT?

Although the ability to implement different layers of an application using different technologies is one of the biggest advantages of n-tiered development, it also introduces additional complications. For example, the protocol used for communication between different tiers needs to be generic enough that both technologies can implement it practically. Additionally, a wider range of expertise is required to build and maintain the application. Before a development team commits to using different technologies, the advantages must clearly outweigh the costs. In other words, one technology must be the most practical solution for one area of functionality while clearly lacking in another, and the other technology must duly compensate for the deficiencies of the first.

THE TEXTTOOL APPLICATION WE ARE BUILDING

The application demonstrated in this chapter, TextTool, is divided into two tiers: the user interface (or UI) and the back-end. It is a Flash- and Java-based text editor, which allows a user to write, save, load, and delete simple text files on any device that supports Flash 5, Java 1.1.8 or higher, and TCP/IP socket connections. Although TextTool is almost completely platform independent, I have chosen to demonstrate the application on a Compaq iPAQ H3630 running Microsoft Pocket PC.

Why Use Flash for TextTool?

Although Java generally provides a comprehensive set of interface design tools with the Swing Java extension, the versions of Java that we are confined to on the Pocket PC platform limit us to the decidedly less functional Advanced Windowing Toolkit (AWT). Even if we were to have Swing at our disposal, however, it would be hard to imagine any interface programmatically built in Java measuring up to the rich, dynamic, interactive creations that are possible with Flash. Additionally, interface designers are rarely programmers (and in my experience, hard-core programmers are rarely designers of intuitive, interesting user interfaces), so implementing the UI in Flash allows us the most effective allocation of expertise.

Why Also Use Java?

Unfortunately, Flash only gets us so far. Through the UI, users can enter and edit text, click (or in this case, tap) buttons, and manipulate dialogue boxes; however, when it comes time to do the actual work of saving, loading, or deleting a file, Flash has no choice but to defer to a back-end capable of file IO (input/output). Although I could have used any language capable of accepting socket connections, I chose to implement the back-end in Java primarily because of its platform-independent nature, general ease of use, wide ranging support, and exploding popularity. Because both Java and Flash are platform-independent, I was able to do the majority of my development and testing on my PC without having to install any special emulators. Additionally, the fact that Java is executed in its own virtual machine meant that I could concentrate on application logic rather than such platform-specific details as memory allocation and de-allocation. And finally, because of Java's relative simplicity and accessibility, it currently enjoys the largest developer community of any other programming language in its class, which means it's going to be around for a long time.

JAVA ON THE POCKET PC

The topic of Java specifications and JVMs designed for embedded and portable devices is a long and involved story, which is clearly beyond the scope of this chapter. I would like to touch on a few of the highlights, however, in order to give you an idea of how the implementations on which this chapter is based fit into the overall scheme of Java Virtual Machines.

Between Sun's official and ever-evolving specifications and the growing number of proprietary third-party solutions, clearly defining the myriad specifications, profiles, and configurations out there is not a simple task. From a high level, however, Java is divided into three editions:

1. Java 2 Enterprise Edition (J2EE), meant for powerful, high-end, distributed computing.
2. Java 2 Standard Edition (J2SE), which supports a rich collection of APIs suitable for small to medium-sized enterprise applications.
3. Java 2 Micro Edition (J2ME), designed specifically for limited embedded and portable devices.

Naturally, this chapter is primarily concerned with J2ME; however, due to the immense diversity of embedded and portable devices (cell phones, set-top boxes, PDAs, pagers, and so on), it is necessary that J2ME be divided into various "configurations." Sun defines two configurations within J2ME: the Connected Device Configuration (CDC) and the Connected Limited Device Configuration (CLDC). The CDC makes use of the same JVMs typically run on desktop devices, while the CLDC uses the KVM (Kilobyte Virtual Machine—a VM whose size is measured in the tens of kilobytes rather than megabytes), a virtual machine designed for devices with more limited resources. Each configuration is then further subdivided into profiles that attempt to group devices based on common or similar functionality and attributes and define platform-appropriate APIs. As if classifying and categorizing devices were not difficult enough, the matter is further complicated by devices' rapid evolution and the increasing number of third-party solutions meant for faster CPUs, larger memory footprints, and longer battery lives.

That said, the question remains: How do you run Java on a Pocket PC device? For the purposes of demonstration, my device of choice is the Compaq iPAQ 3630, and the best Java solution I've found (and the implementation on which the code in this chapter is based) is PersonalJava, which, in J2ME-speak, falls under the Personal profile of the Connected Device Configuration. Sun's 1.1 implementation (3.0 in terms of application environment) is essentially a scaled-down version of Java 1.1.8, which means not all 1.1.8 packages are fully implemented. It is still in beta, but seems to work well enough. And, most importantly, it is completely free. The StrongARM implementation can be downloaded from **http://developer.java.sun.com** after a quick and free registration process.

There are several other PersonalJava implementations available for the more adventurous among you. Most notably, there is the Jeode platform built by Insignia Solutions (**www.insignia.com**) and the Kada VM from Kada Systems (**www.kadasystems.com/ kada_vm.html**). At the time of this writing, Kada's Pocket PC JVM was still in beta—or as they like to say, "debug"; however, you will want to go have a look for yourself because embedded Java technology is moving at an extremely rapid pace. Without much effort at all, I uncovered over a dozen more PersonalJava implementations, so there are plenty to choose from and experiment with. Again, I can only personally speak for Sun's (free!) implementation.

I'm not going to cover installation of PersonalJava here on the off chance that Sun releases a new version or otherwise alters the process. I will mention, however, that it is as straightforward as unzipping, copying, and tapping. Once installed, you can run PersonalJava either from the command line, or simply by tapping on class files copied over from your PC.

To access the command line on a Compaq H3630, hold down the center of the direction pad, then tap and hold on the clock in the upper-right corner.

FLASH ON POCKET PC

Thankfully, Flash is a far simpler matter when it comes to wading through versions and platforms. Go to **www.macromedia.com/software/flashplayer/pocketpc/2002.html**, download the Flash 5 Player for Pocket PC onto the computer you use to synch your iPAQ, be sure the device is connected, and double-click the application. The rest is nicely automated. Unfortunately, you cannot tap on Flash files and have them open in Pocket IE like you can on your desktop; rather, all Flash files have to be embedded in HTML documents. Otherwise, Flash works much the same on your Pocket PC as it does on your desktop PC. (For more information on installing the Flash Player on the Pocket PC, see Chapter 2, "Creating Content for the Pocket PC with Flash."

BUILDING THE TEXTTOOL BACK-END

As stated previously, the TextTool project is divided into two parts: the back-end and the UI. Because the back-end is actually somewhat functional without the UI (the opposite of which is not true—the UI is useless without the back-end), let's start by building the back-end.

There are a few emulators you can use during the development process to simulate the Pocket PC environment on your PC. I haven't used any of them. In fact, you could say I'm fundamentally opposed to the whole idea of emulators in the context of Java development because one of the main points of Java is that I can write code on my PC and run it on any platform with a similar profile. True, there are always one or two surprises in store for me the first few times I try to run the software on my iPAQ, but for the most part, it is not difficult to stay within the bounds of the hardware and the JVM. Go the emulator route if that provides a more comfortable environment for you; however, I believe that you are just as well off looking through the PersonalJava specification to get an idea of what is supported and what isn't, then simply building as lean an application as you can.

The first problem I had to consider when designing this project was how I has going to get the Flash UI to communicate with the Java back-end (see Figure 9.2). Users interact with the UI— enter text, tap buttons, and so on—and eventually that data has to be handed off the back-end so that files can be saved, read, or deleted. The answer I came up with was to use Flash's ability to, in turn, use the browser's ability to make socket connections through the XML ActionScript object. The point where the UI ends, therefore, is the moment it opens a socket connection, and the point at which the back-end starts is where that connection is handled.

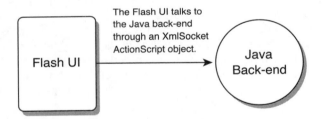

FIGURE 9.2

The Flash UI talking to the Java back-end.

Fortunately, the client-server paradigm is an old one (in computer terms), and has proven itself over time to be useful and reliable. Time has also provided us with countless examples and models, which go a long way toward simplifying the design phase of any client-server application. Clearly, the TextTool back-end needed to consist of a Java process listening for socket connections on a specified port, then parsing and interpreting the content sent over those connections to determine what services to perform and how to perform them. Enter PocketServer.

The back-end of TextTool is divided into two parts: the server and the services that run inside the server (see Figure 9.3). If you're familiar with the JSDK, the PocketServer is analogous to a servlet engine (Tomcat, Jserv, Resin, Jrun, and so on), while the Pocket services are not unlike the servlets that run inside the engine.

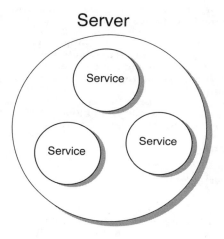

Server

FIGURE 9.3

The server is responsible for dictating the life cycle of the services running in it.

Most people don't really care about how the server works (unless it does not work as designed) as long as they know how to write code that will run inside of it, and some people want the broader picture. If you are interested in how the server works, read on. If you don't care how the server works, but just want to be able to write custom services to run inside the server, feel free to skip to the section entitled "Understanding PocketServices."

Understanding the PocketServer

I chose the name PocketServer rather than something more specific such as TextToolServer to demonstrate an extremely important concept in object-oriented design. The wrong way to design this project would have been to write a TextToolServer that only knew how to service requests from the TextTool UI. Although that would have seen us safely through to the end of this chapter, it is a shortsighted and ultimately limiting approach to application development. What would you do when you then wanted to build a messaging application for your Pocket PC? Would you have to start from scratch and write a ChatServer, half of which would be duplicating code already written and well tested from the TextToolServer? The key here is to *abstract out* (a favorite term among programmers of object-oriented languages meaning, essentially, to separate) the concept of a server from the specific intent of the application, so that the server can be reused in the context of any application that requires the same architecture as TextTool. Hence, the more generic name *PocketServer*.

To make the PocketServer capable of performing any type of service for any type of application, the concept of a service must be abstracted out into either an interface or an abstract class. I chose to go with the abstract class PocketService rather than an interface because I was able to identify some common code between all PocketServices.

If it hadn't been for the fact that I was trying to keep this example relatively simple, I actually would have probably implemented a class between PocketService and SaveFile, ReadFile, and RemoveFile called something like FileService. Specifically, FileService would have extended PocketService and SaveFile, ReadFile, and RemoveFile would have all extended FileService where all my file-specific code would have gone. For example, I might have put code in FileService to check to make sure the paths passed in through the config file pointed to valid directories, and that the Java process had permission to write to and read from those directories. I would have abstracted SaveFile's, ReadFile's, and RemoveFile's initialization codes out into FileService because all three are initialized in the same way. Remember that the more code you can move into base classes, the less there is to maintain and fix.

TextTool required the implementation of three specific types of PocketServices: SaveFile, ReadFile, and RemoveFile.

If you are at all familiar with Sun's Java Servlet API, you will find this passage quite familiar (and it will only get more familiar from here), because I have borrowed several key concepts from the extremely well-designed servlet specification. PocketServer and PocketService are far simpler and "thinner" than the servlet specification, both for the sake of demonstration and because it is designed to run on a handheld device rather than server hardware.

Most servers have three milestones in their lives: one initialization, several (hopefully) instances of servicing requests, and one period of shutting down. For the sake of simplicity, I chose to include PocketServer's initialization routine in its constructor; however, an **init()** method would have worked just as well.

For those of you approaching this chapter from more of a Flash background, do not be deterred or discouraged by the Java code that follows. It is relatively simple, and I think you will find it similar enough to ActionScript that you will not have difficulty following along.

```
public PocketServer() throws PocketException {
    props = new Properties();
    // Use the ClassLoader to load the Config file.
    try {
        InputStream configStream = ClassLoader.getSystemResourceAsStream(CONFIG_FILE);
        props.load(configStream);
    }
    catch (Exception exception) {
```

```
    throw new PocketException("Problem loading the configuration properties.",
    ➥exception);
}


// Get the "verbose" property. If verbose is true, I periodically
// output information about the server. If false, I'll output nothing.
String verStr = props.getProperty("verbose");
verbose = (verStr == null) ? false : Boolean.valueOf(verStr).booleanValue();
logger = PocketLogger.getInstance();
if (verbose) logger.log("PocketServer created.");


// Get a ";"-delimited list of the PocketServices this server will support.
String allServices = props.getProperty("PocketServices");
if (allServices == null) {
    throw new PocketException("No PocketServices were specified in  your config file.");
}
StringTokenizer servicesTokens = new StringTokenizer(allServices,  ";");
// Initialize the Hashtable we keep the services in.
services = new Hashtable();
while (servicesTokens.hasMoreTokens()) {
    String className = null;
    try {
        className = servicesTokens.nextToken();
        Class serviceClass = Class.forName(className);
        PocketService pServ = (PocketService) serviceClass.newInstance();
        pServ.init(props);
        services.put(className, pServ);
        if (verbose)  logger.log(className + " successfully initialized.");
    }
    // So many different exceptions that can happen here that I'm just
    // going to catch a single Exception.
    catch (Exception exception) {
        throw new PocketException("Problem loading and initializing " + className + ".",
        ➥exception);
    }
}


// Set the isolated property. If the server is configured to be
// isolated, it will not service requests from any machine other
// the one it is running on.
String isolatedStr = props.getProperty("isolated");
if (isolatedStr == null) {
```

```
      throw new PocketException("Cannot find \"isolated\" property in config file.");
   }
   isolatedStr = isolatedStr.toLowerCase();
   if (!isolatedStr.equals("true") && !isolatedStr.equals("false")) {
      throw new PocketException("The \"isolated\" property must be either \"true\" or
      ➥\"false\".");
   }
   this.isolated = new Boolean(isolatedStr).booleanValue();
   if (verbose) {
      String v = (isolated) ? " " : " not ";
      logger.log("PocketServer is" + v + "isolated.");
   }

   // Start to set up the actual server.
   String portStr = props.getProperty("port");
   if (portStr == null) {
      throw new PocketException("Your config file does not specify a port on which to
      ➥listen.");
   }

   int port;
   try {
      port = Integer.parseInt(portStr);
   } catch (NumberFormatException exception) {
      throw new PocketException("The config property \"port\" must be numeric.");
   }
   if (verbose) logger.log("PocketServer listening on port " + port + ".");
   ServerSocket server;
   try {
      server = new ServerSocket(port);
   }
   catch (IOException exception) {
      throw new PocketException("Problem opening a socket on port  port + ".");
   } catch (SecurityException exception) {
      throw new PocketException("Problem opening a socket on port " +
                        port + ". Try using an unprivileged " +
                        "port above 1024.");
   }

   // Start the actual server.
   while (true) {
      try {
         new SocketHandler(server.accept());
```

```
    } catch (IOException exception) {
        throw new PocketException("An IOException was thrown while waiting for a
        ➥connection.");
    }
  }
}
```

Notice that the first thing that happens during initialization is the loading and parsing of the configuration file—a simple text file containing parameters to configure the server. Don't worry about how each property affects the application just yet—they will all be explained when their values become relevant.

```
verbose=true
port=2000
isolated=false
PocketServices=SaveFile;RemoveFile;ReadFile
SaveFile.saveBaseDir=\\TextTool\\Files\\
RemoveFile.removeBaseDir=\\TextTool\\Files\\
ReadFile.readBaseDir=\\TextTool\\Files\\
```

This configuration file makes PocketServer far more flexible and easier to work with. The idea of a configuration file in general (often called a *properties file*) is to externalize those aspects of an application that are likely to change most often or that need to be customizable from one piece of hardware to another. The port on which we run the server, for example, is much more likely to have to change (due to conflicts with other servers, perhaps) than the implementation of the code which writes a file to disk (assuming the code was written in the proper platform-independent manner). Because it would be inconvenient to have to recompile the entire server just to change the port number, that value gets stashed in an external text file.

 Currently, most configuration or properties files I deal with are written in XML rather than simple name/value format. For the sake of simplicity, however, I decided to use the Properties object's ability to parse straightforward Windows style ini files.

You should also notice the way in which the config file is loaded—as a system resource stream rather than just a file—because this method goes a long way toward making the code more portable. We already know that the end result of TextTool will be at least three files—the jar file containing PocketServer, the Flash file representing the UI, and the HTML page in which the UI is embedded—therefore the last thing we want is to add a fourth with a configuration file. Using the ClassLoader to find the config file allows us to jar it up with the rest of the class files, which saves us from somehow having to tell the PocketServer where the file is and from having to worry about platform-specific file structures (because development can actually happen on any type of machine that supports Java and Flash rather than on your Pocket PC device itself).

Now that we have our configuration object, we can initialize our logging facility. It's imperative that we have some type of output mechanism in place so that we know what's happening inside the server. As anyone who has written any kind of software can attest to, it is virtually impossible to develop and debug without frequent visibility into the execution of your work.

The tools the PocketServer uses to log are as lightweight as possible, both for the sake of simplicity for this example, and to keep resource consumption to a minimum. In fact, the PocketLogger is really nothing more than a singleton—an object that allows only a single instance—that wraps up a static call to write to stdout. The verbose flag is simply a Boolean as opposed to the more complex and flexible approach of specifying one of a set of integers referring to various levels of logging. You will notice that at least the PocketLogger is encapsulated, however, so you can change the implementation throughout the entire application to be more sophisticated if you need it to be just by re-factoring a single file.

Stateless Versus Stateful PocketServices

There were two approaches I considered when I designed the PocketService model: stateful and stateless. A stateful PocketService is one that is instantiated at request time, has various properties set on it, and eventually is called on to perform some service. Conversely, the stateless PocketService doesn't have a concept of properties, but rather has a single method you pass all your data into, and then that single method also performs the specified service.

The advantage of the stateless model is that as many threads can access the same instance of the service simultaneously as is needed without fear of clobbering other thread's data. For example, if one thread set a property called **fileName** on the SaveFile PocketService to **"my_file"**, then another thread set the same property to **"your_file"** before the first thread could call the method on the PocketService that actually wrote the file, then the first value could be overwritten with the second and the file would be saved as **"your_file"**. To make your code thread-safe, you would either have to synchronize access to your PocketService (meaning only one thread could access it at a time), or have a different instance of SaveFile for every thread, which is not an efficient use of memory (especially on a handheld device), or time, for that matter, because object instantiation is one of the most expensive processes in Java.

The stateless approach, however, allows you to instantiate all the PocketServices at initialization time (which happens only once) and reuse them as much as you want. The configuration parameter **"PocketServices"**, therefore, refers to a semicolon-delimited list of services that the PocketServer supports. They are all, in turn, loaded by name, initialized, and put into a Hashtable for use at request-time.

 If my intended platform were a PC rather than a handheld device, I would use a HashMap because a HashMap is unsynchronized and a Hashtable synchronizes access. However, PersonalJava is based on the Java 1.1.8, which does not support HashMaps.

The "isolated" property addresses a potential security risk inherent in running any type of server on any type of device that could be connected to a network. Setting the isolated property to true ensures that if your device is connected to a network, the server will ignore all requests from clients other than the one the server itself is running on. You will learn more about the significance of isolating the PocketServer in the next section.

Using ServerSocket to Create the Actual Server

The final initialization task is to create the actual server. Without getting into too much server theory, the concept of "starting" a server in Java is really nothing more than calling **accept()** on an instance of ServerSocket configured to listen on a specified port. ServerSocket will automatically block while waiting for requests and queue them up if more than one arrives simultaneously. The idea is for the server to hand off connections to other processes (preferably in other threads) as quickly as possible so it can spend as much time listening for connections as possible, because that is its primary job. Realistically, the PocketServer is far more robust in terms of handling connections than it really needs to be because it will probably only service a single client—the UI—which is unlikely to be making more than one request at a time. However, you certainly could use the PocketServer to provide services to multiple UIs, and any given UI could conceivably request more than one service at a time. I found that creating new threads at request time did not adversely affect the performance of the application, so I decided to go with the multi-threaded approach.

When the ServerSocket receives a connection and the **accept()** method returns, the resulting Socket object is passed to the constructor of the following inner class called SocketHandler:

```
/**
 * An inner class for handling the socket connections. It extends Thread
 * because we want our server to be multi-threaded, meaning it can service
 * multiple requests simultaneously.
 */
private class SocketHandler extends Thread {
    // The socket we are going to read from and write to. It's ok to
    // declare member variables at this point because a new instance of
    // a SocketHandler is made for every request.
    private Socket socket;
    private SocketHandler(Socket socket) {
        InetAddress address = socket.getInetAddress();

        // If the isolated property is set to true, make sure the request
        // has come from 127.0.0.1.
        if (isolated) {
            if (!(address.toString().endsWith("127.0.0.1"))) {
                System.err.println("Rejecting request from [" + address + "].");
                return;
            }
        }
```

```
        }

    this.socket = socket;
    if (verbose) logger.log("Connection from [" + address + "] accepted.");
    start();
}

public void run() {
    String fullRequest = null;
    PocketResponse response = null;
    try {
        // Get the InputStream from the Socket and read it in.
        InputStream in = socket.getInputStream();
        response = new PocketResponse(socket.getOutputStream());
        byte[] buffer = new byte[1024];
        ByteArrayOutputStream byteArrayOut = new ByteArrayOutputStream();
        for (int cnt = in.read(buffer);cnt != -1;cnt = in.read(buffer)) {
            byteArrayOut.write(buffer, 0, cnt);
            if (in.available() == 0) {
                break;
            }
        }
        fullRequest = byteArrayOut.toString();
        if (verbose) {
            logger.log("Full request: ");
            logger.log(fullRequest);
        }
    } catch (Exception exception) {
        logger.log("Problem reading in a request.", exception);
        response.badRequest("An unknown error occurred while reading in the request.",
        ➥exception);
        return;
    }

    // Extract the portion of the request which pertains to service
    // instructions. Handle the StringIndexOutOfBoundsException as an
    // error.
    String service = null;
    PocketRequest request = null;
    try {
        String serviceRequest = fullRequest.substring(fullRequest.indexOf("/"),
                                    fullRequest.indexOf(" ",
                                    fullRequest.indexOf("/")));        // Check to see if the
                                    ➥server should exit.
```

```
if (serviceRequest.indexOf("?") == -1 &&
   serviceRequest.endsWith("KillServer"))
{
   System.exit(0);
}



   // Now parse the service instructions.
   service = serviceRequest.substring(serviceRequest.indexOf("/") + 1,
   ➥serviceRequest.indexOf("?"));
   if (verbose) logger.log("A request was made for service [" +service + "] with the
   ➥following " +
                     "arguments: ");
   String allArgs = serviceRequest.substring(serviceRequest.indexOf("?") + 1,
                        serviceRequest.length());
   StringTokenizer argTokens = new StringTokenizer(allArgs, "&");
   request = new PocketRequest();
   while (argTokens.hasMoreTokens()) {
      String arg = argTokens.nextToken();
      String name = arg.substring(0,arg.indexOf("="));
      String val = arg.substring(arg.indexOf("=") + 1,  arg.length());
      val = URLDecoder.decode(val);
      if (verbose)  {
         logger.log(name + "=" + val);
      }
      request.put(name, val);
   }
} catch (StringIndexOutOfBoundsException exception) {
   logger.log("A malformed request was made. Requests should " +
         "look like: http://<ip>:<port>/<PocketService>?" +
         "<argName>=<argValue>&<argName>=<argValue>");
   response.badRequest("Malformed request.", exception);
   return;
}


// Now get the requested PocketService from the Hashtable of
// PocketServices and call service() on it.
PocketService pServ = (PocketService) services.get(service);
if (pServ == null) {
   logger.log("Error: A request was made for the unknown PocketService [" + service
   ➥+ "]");
   response.notFound("Resource not found. [" + service + "] does not exist on this "
   ➥+ "server.",null);
```

```
        return;
    } try {
        pServ.service(request,response);
    } catch (PocketServiceException exception) {
        logger.log("The PocketService " + service + " threw a PocketServiceException.",
        ↪exception);
        response.internalServerError("Internal Server Error. ", exception);
        return;
    }
  }
}
```

Notice that the first thing the SocketHandler does when it is instantiated is to check the IP address of the machine the request came from and, if the configuration parameter **isolated** is true, to make sure it is 127.0.0.1. The IP address 127.0.0.1 always represents the machine on which the server is running, or the **localhost**. If **isolated** is set to true, therefore, only requests coming from the machine the server is running will be serviced. As mentioned previously, this is a security measure put in place just in case you ever have your device connected to a network. An iPAQ or other Pocket PC device can be seen during a port scan just like any other computer, so if you are not careful to isolate the PocketServer, other machines can run PocketServices remotely on your device (which also happens to be a pretty cool feature—especially during testing and debugging—but one you would certainly want to control).

The SocketHandler's job is essentially to start a new thread in which to do its work, determine which PocketService is being requested, package up the data sent in the request, and pass it along to the requested PocketService (see Figure 9.4). In order for it to understand what the client is telling it to do, however, there must be a protocol established between the SocketHandler and the client (the Flash UI).

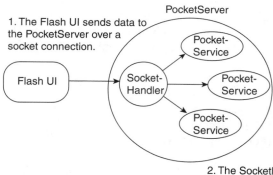

FIGURE 9.4

The SocketHandler and PocketServices.

Because I was already borrowing concepts from the JSDK, and because my architecture is a relatively simple client-server one, HTTP seemed like the natural choice for a protocol for the client and server to use to communicate. Not only is it fairly simple, but also by making the PocketServer understand HTTP, it would be fully testable from a browser or any other client capable of making HTTP requests. Likewise, the UI could be tested against a regular web server (albeit, to a much lesser extent than the PocketServer) or other process capable of servicing HTTP requests.

Notice how the PocketServer will call System.exit(0) if it finds that the request was for a service called KillServer. This is to compensate for an issue I ran into while testing the PocketServer under Sun's PersonalJava on an HP Jornada 568 running PocketPC 2002. Consistently when I tried to close the server, I got a message stating that the program was not responding and giving me an option to close it immediately. Even if I chose "yes", however, I found that although the OS thought the process had been killed, it was actually still running in the background, allowing me to continue using TextTool. Adding the PocketServer's ability to exit, all you have to do to be sure the PocketServer has been stopped is to make a request through Pocket Internet Explorer to http://127.0.0.1:2000/KillServe.

The details of parsing the request are probably best left to the code itself. At this point, an HTTP request, which comes in to the PocketServer either from a browser or from a Flash ActionScript **LoadVariables** action, looks something like this:

GET /SaveFile?fileName=myFile&fileContent=Hello%2EWorld&append=false HTTP/1.1
Accept: /
Accept-Encoding: gzip, deflate
User-Agent: Mozilla/4.0 (compatible; MSIE 5.5; Windows NT 5.0)
Host: 192.168.1.5:2000
Connection: Keep-Alive

This code results in a PocketRequest object containing the name/value pairs from the query string (**fileName=myFile**, **fileContent=Hello World**) and a PocketResponse object containing the output stream from the socket connection getting passed into the SaveFile PocketService object through the abstract service method. The rest of the headers in the request are ignored. Once **service()** is called, assuming no exceptions get thrown, the PocketServer and the SocketHandler have done their jobs and it is up to the PocketService to do its job.

Once again, my methodology is borrowed directly from Java Server Development Kit; however, this is a much simpler, lighter weight implementation suitable for devices with limited resources.

Understanding PocketServices

A PocketService is any class that extends the abstract class PocketService and implements the abstract **service()** method. As long as the **service()** method is properly implemented (and the optional **initSupport()**), the PocketServer doesn't care what the particular service does. It could send email, make database queries, write to a file, or even act as a proxy and simply make another socket connection to someplace else.

It just so happens that the TextTool application requires three simple PocketServices: SaveFile, ReadFile, and RemoveFile. I don't want to waste space describing the particulars of these three implementations as they are simple examples and are easy enough to understand by looking through the code. I will, however, discuss the configuration of the PocketServices before moving on and describing how to implement your own.

Each of TextTool's three PocketServices requires one configuration parameter each: **saveBaseDir**, **removeBaseDir**, and **readBaseDir**. Notice in the configuration file how the name of the relevant PocketService is prepended to (comes before) the parameter name, separated by a dot.

Starting your parameter name with the name of the PocketService it applies to is not required, but it does help preserve a namespace and keep parameters from overwriting each other's values.

Because you can assume that all PocketServices—whether you write them or you get them from some other source—will have a unique name, including that unique name in the parameter, ensures that all parameters will be unique. If two people write PocketServices that both require a property called **randomSeed**, for example, they can both simultaneously hold different values because the name of the two PocketServices would be different. In the case of TextTool, each PocketService has a different configuration parameter, but they all have the same value, which obviously specifies a directory. The values of all three parameters indicate the directories in which files are saved, read, and deleted during use of TextTool. Be sure the parameters are appropriate for the platform on which you are running, and because backslashes are escape characters in Java, don't forget to double escape in the context of the Windows directory structure.

It's important to keep in mind that these properties are not meant to control file access on your device because it is actually possible to save, load, and delete files outside of these specified directories. For example, if you created the directory \Windows\Java\TextTool\Files for storing files, you could actually save a file by the name ../../../MyFile.txt and have that file be written to the Windows directory. A malicious application of this functionality might be to save a text file in the Windows directory as the same name as a dll file already there, thereby replacing the dll and probably doing serious harm to your device's operating system. More robust versions of SaveFile and RemoveFile might use the java.io.FilePermission object to specify which directories users can write to and delete from.

It is decidedly inconvenient that Windows uses backslashes as file separators. Whenever you are referring to the file system in a language that uses backslashes as escape characters, you have to remember to use two backslashes to indicate that you mean a literal backslash as opposed to trying to escape the character after the backslash. On a Pocket PC device, you end up with directories that look like this: TextTool Files.

Writing Your Own PocketService

For the sake of simplicity, neither the PocketServer nor any of the PocketServices are in any type of a package structure, so don't worry about a package declaration in your PocketService. All you have to do is extend the abstract class PocketService and implement a **service()** method. Keep in mind that by extending PocketService, you automatically have access to the Properties object, which contains all your configuration information (so remember to externalize parameters that are likely to change).

Creating a package structure would mean having to maintain a classpath on your device, and because Pocket PC does not have a concept of environment variables, you have to edit the Registry. There are some nice tools out there for both remote and local editing of the Pocket PC Registry, but to avoid that digression here, I've simply opted not to use any packages.

If your new PocketService needs custom initialization, you can override the protected support method **initSupport()**, which will get called once at the time the **PocketService()** is loaded (which occurs during PocketServer initialization) and never again. Now compile the source, be sure your new PocketService is included in the semicolon-delimited list of PocketServices in the config file, and you're ready to go.

Running the PocketServer on Your PC

I definitely recommend running the PocketServer on your PC first because running it on your Pocket PC device may require some additional steps and tinkering, especially if you are writing your own PocketServices. Running the PocketServer on a PC is as simple as compiling the source in whatever manner you are accustomed (either through an IDE or from the command line), making sure the binaries are in your classpath, and running the PocketServer with a command such as **java PocketServer**.

If anything goes wrong, there should be enough information in the exception for you to debug it without too much difficulty. The error you are probably most likely to get is a **NoClassDefFoundError**, indicating that the PocketServer simply was not correctly added to your classpath. Assuming the code compiled and your classpath was successfully configured, there is not much else that can go wrong, so you should see output similar to this:

PocketServer created.
SaveFile successfully initialized.
RemoveFile successfully initialized.
ReadFile successfully initialized.
PocketServer is isolated.
PocketServer listening on port 2000.

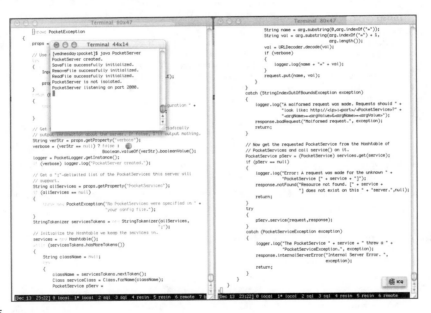

FIGURE 9.5

PocketServer running on my Mac. This is the exact same code that will be copied over and executed on my iPAQ.

You can then exercise the code by making requests from your browser. For example, typing the following in the location bar

http://127.0.0.1:2000/SaveFile?fileName=myFile&fileContent=this+is+a+test

results in the string **"this is a test"** getting saved in a file called "myFile" in the directory specified as the value of the configuration parameter **SaveFile.saveBaseDir**. The request

http://127.0.0.1:2000/ReadFile?fileName=myFile

returns the string **"this is a test"** (which may or may not actually be displayed in your browser depending on the browser you are using because it is not HTML). Finally, you can remove the file with the request

http://127.0.0.1:2000/RemoveFile?fileName=myFile

If all three operations work on your PC, it's time to try running PocketServer on a Pocket PC device.

Running the PocketServer on Your Pocket PC Device

Before you do anything else, be sure to adapt the directories specified in your config file to the directory structure of your Pocket PC device. Again, if your PC is a Unix derivative, don't forget to turn the forward slashes into backslashes and escape them.

The next thing you need to do is get all the class files over to your device. By far the easiest way to move and execute class files on Pocket PC is to jar (Java archive) them up into a single file. To be able to simply tap on the jar file and have the right class automatically execute, however, you have to include your own custom MANIFEST file in the archive (jar file) that tells the JVM which class it should load first. The following MANIFEST file tells the JVM to load the class PocketServer and start it by calling its **main()** method.

Manifest-Version: 1.0
Main-Class: PocketServer

A Java archive is similar to a zip or a tar file. It is primarily a convenient method for packaging up class files, moving them, and executing them. To learn more about jar files, check any Java reference, or simply type jar from the command line of any computer that has Java installed.

Navigate to the directory where all the PocketServer class files are and type the following command from the command line:

jar –cfm PocketServer.jar MANIFEST.MF *.class config

This builds a jar file with all the classes in the current directory and the config file, and replaces the default MANIFEST.MF file with your custom version. You may want to type the command the first time just to test it; however, I strongly recommend you eventually automate the process with an alias, a batch file, or a shell script. Here is the bash script (for Unix platforms) I used while developing the PocketServer:

#!/bin/bash
jar –cfm PocketServer.jar MANIFEST.MF *.class config

Create a folder on your Pocket PC device where you want to store your TextTool files (for example, \TextTool\Java\) and copy PocketServer.jar into it. Assuming you have PersonalJava (or the JVM of your choice) installed properly, tapping on the jar file should start the JVM and load the PocketServer. As a testament to Sun's "write once, run anywhere" motto, you should see the exact same output on your Pocket PC device that you saw on your PC.

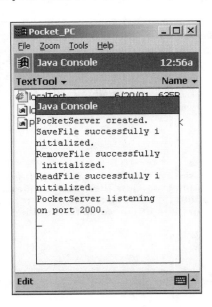

FIGURE 9.6

The same code I ran on my Mac now running on my iPAQ. Notice how the output is nearly identical.

If you are using Pocket PC 2002, you should now be able to make the same requests to test the PocketServer through Pocket Internet Explorer that you made through the full version of Internet Explorer to test the PocketServer on your desktop. If you are using the original version of Pocket PC, however, such requests will yield the message **The page you are looking for cannot be found**. This is a result of an undesirable feature (some might say bug) of PIE on the original version of Pocket PC that prevents the browser from even attempting to make a socket connection to any server (even itself) if there is not some sort of network connection to the device already established. If you were to put your device in its cradle, therefore, your requests would be successful, as even a serial connection is sufficient. Likewise, any type of Ethernet connection will do the trick, as well.

Fortunately, I am not the only one to have ever run into this problem on Pocket PC, and a company called Cambridge Computer Corporation has actually solved it. Cambridge sells a full web server for the Pocket PC platform called vxWeb, which is both multi-threaded and supports CGI. To use it locally (from your Pocket PC device), they provide a tool called ieFix, which, when you start it, makes the device believe it has established a connection. ieFix can be downloaded from the Cambridge Computer Corporation web site (**www.cam.com**) and although there is a licensing fee for vxWeb, ieFix can be used free of charge (you will not need the actual vxWeb web server). Once the ieFix process is started, the PocketServer works perfectly.

I found that it was necessary to use ieFix.exe on an iPAQ running Pocket PC; however, it may not be necessary on other platforms or with other operating systems or clients. For example, using my Jornada 568 running Pocket PC, the PocketServer works perfectly by itself. You might want to take the time to determine that you have a problem on whichever platform you are using before you attempt to solve it.

I found that my iPAQ was easily confused when I swapped between the three forms of network connections I had available to me—Ethernet adapter, cradle, and ieFix.exe—and I sometimes found that a soft reset was the only way I could get the device to behave properly. I have had much better luck with Pocket PC 2002 and would highly recommend upgrading if you have not already.

UNDERSTANDING THE FLASH USER INTERFACE

Fortunately, the TextTool user interface is a much more straightforward than the Java back-end. Flash players have been around for a long time, and my experience has been that the ports from one platform to another are relatively trouble free and surprisingly consistent. Additionally, having access to the advanced functionality of Flash 5 makes life much easier because we can leverage the elegance of true object-oriented programming.

TextTool is a simple application for entering, saving, recalling, and deleting short notes on any device that supports both Java and Flash. The entire interface consists primarily of a main area in which to enter text, three command buttons (Save, Load, and Delete), and three floating prompt boxes that expect input (filenames) from users. If you open the Flash file and look at the main timeline, you will find that the top layer (labeled "control") contains or includes most of the UI's ActionScript while the layers below it contain various graphical elements. You will also notice that everything exists on the first frame of the timeline (even all the movieclips use nothing but their first frames); because the application functions solely through ActionScript responding to user input, you can see that Flash 5 is as much a programming environment as it is an animation tool.

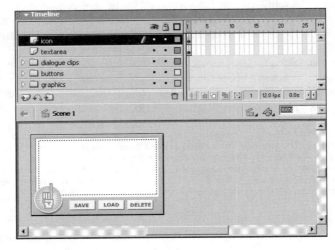

FIGURE 9.7

TextTools Flash user interface under development in the Flash authoring environment.

Let's start by looking at the UI's initialization code, which is any code in "control" that is not inside of a function.

```
#include "ServerConfig.as"
#include "SaveFile.as"
#include "ReadFile.as"
#include "RemoveFile.as"
stop();
// Create a ServerConfig for everyone to share.
var config = new ServerConfig("127.0.0.1","2000");
// Instantiate all our services. We can reuse the same instances.
var save = new SaveFile(config);
var read = new ReadFile(config);
```

```
var remove = new RemoveFile(config);
// Create a new listener. Each service will override the setResponse before
// passing it in.
var listener = new Object();
// Hide all the dialogue boxes.
hideAll();
```

Interestingly enough, the first thing TextTool does after you start it (other than include external ActionScript files) is to call the **stop()** function because the application's job is essentially to allow the user to enter as much text as he likes while waiting for him to tap a button. Once an event is detected, the appropriate prompt box becomes visible while any others, which might be visible, are hidden. The file name entered by the user is then used to either save text, load previously saved text, or delete previously save text. Each action is initiated through a call to a corresponding function in "control".

In the true spirit of object-orientated design, the UI configuration is encapsulated in a single ActionScript object called ServerConfig. Unlike its PocketConfig counterpart, however, its configuration is not loaded from an external file because the ServerConfig contains only two properties: server and port. Because the PocketServer is designed to run locally, the server needs to be 127.0.0.1 (localhost) and the port can be whichever one you configured your PocketServer to listen on.

If it weren't for the fact that I don't want to unnecessarily complicate this example, I would probably load the configuration from an external XML file despite the fact that, at least initially, it would contain only two parameters. Externalizing configuration is almost always good application practice regardless of the size of your project because small applications often have a tendency to grow into much more involved ones.

The next piece of code that is executed in "control" loads and initializes the three objects that are the workhorses of the UI: SaveFile, ReadFile, and RemoveFile. Notice how they are loaded once at initialization time and then reused in much the same way as the PocketServices were loaded once and cached by the PocketServer. Even a generic object called "listener" is reused for maximum efficiency (more on the listener later). Finally, we call the **hideAll()** function that sets the **visible** property of all three prompt boxes to false until such time as they are needed.

Rather than taking you through the UI code one line at a time, I'm going to proceed by describing the object model I chose and how it relates to the PocketServer's object model. I will then take you through a single process (saving a file) in its entirely to demonstrate how all the various pieces fit together.

Because the PocketServer is modeled as a server, the processes that the UI uses to perform tasks against it are modeled as requests. In fact, as there are three primary actions the UI is capable of performing, there are precisely three different types of request objects to ask the PocketServer to perform them. Each request—SaveFile, ReadFile, and RemoveFile—inherits functionality from a base object called PocketServiceRequest. There is obviously a direct correlation between the three PocketServices on the back-end and the three PocketServiceRequests implemented in the UI.

Just as SaveFile, ReadFile, and RemoveFile inherit functionality from the base class PocketServiceRequest, PocketServiceRequest itself inherits from the native Flash 5 XML object. The XML object has the capability to open, read from, and write to sockets from the client (browser), which is how the communication occurs between the UI and the back-end. PocketServiceRequest also provides additional services too, such as functions to initialize and format data.

The Flash 5 XML ActionScript object can only open connections back to the server from which it was served if the Flash file it is in was initially retrieved through a URL (see Figure 9.8). Because the UI Flash file is loaded from the local file system in this case, you will not have to worry about such security restrictions.

Understanding the SaveFile Object

To really give you a sound understanding of the architecture of the UI, let's follow the SaveFile PocketServiceRequest through from its initialization to the completion of a request. Initialization occurs with the following line of ActionScript from the top layer labeled "control":

var save = new SaveFile(config);

A constructor is a function that automatically gets called wherever a new instance of an object is created. The function must have the same name as the object itself (in this case, SaveFile) and, as in the case of SaveFile, can take in arguments.

SaveFile's constructor contains the following code:

this.super(serverConfig.getServer(), serverConfig.getPort());
this.setService("SaveFile");

The first line initializes the superclass PocketServiceRequest, passing it the server and port number from the ServerConfig. The second line tells the superclass which PocketService it is responsible for requesting from the PocketServer. From this point on, nothing happens until the Save button gets tapped, at which point the ActionScript associated with that button gets executed (see Figure 9.8):

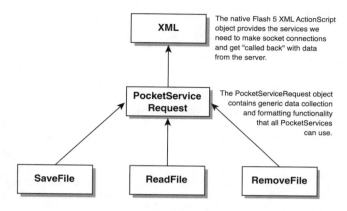

SaveFile, ReadFile, and RemoveFile contain functions
and logic specific to their individual jobs.

FIGURE 9.8

The Flash 5 XML ActionScript object.

```
on (release) {
   if (loadDialogue._visible = true) {
      loadDialogue._visible = false;
   }
   if (deleteDialogue._visible = true) {
      deleteDialogue._visible = false;
   }
   saveDialogue._visible = true;
}
```

After making sure both the Load and Delete prompt boxes are hidden, the **_visible** property of
the Save box is set to true, causing it to show. The user enters a filename and taps on the OK
button, which does nothing but call the **executeSave()** function back in "control".

```
function executeSave(){
   var mainText = textArea.mainText;
   var fileName = saveDialogue.genericDialogue.fileName;
   if (!isValid(mainText) || !isValid(fileName)) {
      return;
   }
      save.clearParameters();
```

```
        save.setFileName(fileName);
        save.setFileContent(mainText);
        save.append("false");
   listener.setResponse = saveResponse;
   save.execute(listener);
}
```

The first thing **executeSave()** does is copy the values of both the file prompt box and the main text area into local variables. It then uses a simple function called **isValid()** to determine whether the user entered useful data. If not, execution is halted by immediately returning; however, as long as at least one character was specified for each input, execution continues.

My implementation of isValid simply determines whether the filename is null or an empty string; however, you can provide a more robust, sophisticated implementation at your digression. The key is to encapsulate that logic in its own function and to reuse that function in as many places as possible so that changing it in one place changes the behavior of the every piece of code using it.

Because the SaveFile object is stateful and gets reused over and over, it is important that the **clearParameters()** method is used to reset any values that have been previously set so that we don't accidentally save old data or, more likely, some combination of the old data and new. We then configure the SaveFile object by telling it the name of the file to save, the content to save, and whether to append the new content to the old file (if a file by that name already exists) or overwrite it instead.

From the perspective of the back-end, it may seem pointless to even have the ability to append data to a file rather than overwrite it if the append property is going to be hard-coded to false in the client. Although TextTool does not really have a need to append text to files, when I wrote the SaveFile PocketService, I did so with the idea of keeping it generic. In other words, there is no reason why PocketServer cannot service requests from multiple clients, each with its own set of functionality and requirements, one of which possibly being to append text to a file rather than overwrite it.

Before we can call **execute()** on the SaveFile object, we have to prepare the listener we use to alert us to when SaveFile has either finished or quit because of an error. Using the callback approach as opposed to simply having the **execute()** function return an exit status, response code, Boolean, or error message is necessary because the SaveFile PocketServiceRequest behaves asynchronously. This means that the **execute()** function will return almost immediately rather than blocking until all its work has completed. I will explain asynchronous execution in more detail shortly.

We specify **saveResponse()** as our callback method by assigning it to **setResponse()** on the listener before passing the listener in to the **execute()** function. Essentially, we have told SaveFile to tell us that it is done by calling **setResponse()** on the listener, which points to the **saveResponse()** method contained in "control".

SaveFile.as is a relatively short and simple file because the majority of its functionality is contained in the PocketServiceRequest super class (several short files as opposed to fewer longer files are generally an indication of good object-oriented design). In fact, the **execute()** function is even contained in the PocketServiceRequest so that all three PocketServiceRequests don't have to implement their own.

It's important to remember that when we talk about sharing code in the context of object-oriented programming, we almost always mean sharing the source code as opposed to sharing the same instances of objects. In other words, although SaveFile, ReadFile, and RemoveFile all extend PocketServiceRequest and all use the execute() function contained therein, they are not calling the same instance of the execute() function, so there is no chance of concurrency issues.

```
function execute(listener) {
    this.listener = listener;
    var req = "http://" +
            this.server + ":" +
            this.port + "/" +
            this.service +
            this.getQueryParameters();
    this.load(req);
}
```

execute() builds a URL and a query string that will be used to make a request to the PocketServer. Notice how it is kept generic (and hence reusable) by not having the service name or any portion of the query string hard-coded. Rather, it uses the service that was previously set through the **setService()** method on SaveFile's constructor, and a method called **getQueryParameters()** to build the query string from the properties that were set within **executeSave()**. Finally, **execute()** calls **load()**, passing in the URL and query string containing the data the user entered from the UI (the request should look similar to the one you made against the PocketServer from your browser). **execute()** then returns immediately, not blocking while waiting for **load()** to return.

You may have noticed that there is actually no **load()** function defined in either SaveFile or PocketServiceRequest. The **load()** function we are actually calling belongs to the native Flash 5 XML object from which the PocketServiceRequest inherits. Although it is actually designed to load and parse XML files, we can still use it for its ability to make socket connections by overriding, or replacing, the XML specific methods with our own implementations. At the bottom of PocketServiceRequest, you'll find the following lines of code:

```
PocketServiceRequest.prototype.__proto__       = XML.prototype;
PocketServiceRequest.prototype.addParameter     = addParameter;
PocketServiceRequest.prototype.setService        = setService;
PocketServiceRequest.prototype.getQueryParameters = getQueryParameters;
```

```
PocketServiceRequest.prototype.clearParameters    = clearParameters;
PocketServiceRequest.prototype.execute            = execute;
PocketServiceRequest.prototype.onData             = pr_onData;
```

The first line is what establishes inheritance from the XML object. The second line through fifth lines are simply attaching various functions to the PocketServiceRequest. The last line, however, holds particular significance because **onData()** is not a function that I wrote. It is, rather, a function I inherited by extending XML. Because I'm primarily interested in using the XML object for its ability to make socket connections and therefore don't want it doing XML-specific processing on the response from the **load()** function, I replace **onData()** with my own custom implementation, which I call **pr_onData**.

 I prefer the method of overriding (or replacing) the XML object's onData method to simply using loadVariables() for two reasons: First, I like the call-back paradigm the XML object uses, and second, I like that the server response is handed back simply as an argument rather than being assigned to ActionScript variables in another movieclip. From a programming perspective, it is far more intuitive and makes for cleaner code.

Flash Player calls **onData()** when the response from the server is finished loading. The argument that is passed to **onData()** is a string containing the actual response from the server. We pass the response on to the listener through the **setResponse()** function, and SaveFile has finished its work. The **saveResponse()** method back in "control" completes the process:

```
function saveResponse(response) {
    if (response.indexOf("r200") == 0) {
        hideAll();
    } else if (!isValid(response)) {
        hideAll();
        error(No response from server.);
        return;
    } else {
        var msg = new String("There was an error saving your file. The server's ");
        msg = msg.concat("response was: \n");
        msg = msg.concat(response);
                hideAll();
                error(msg);
        }
}
```

saveResponse() will do one of three things depending on the response from server. If it finds the substring "r200" in the response (200 being the standard response for "everything went smoothly on the server"), **hideAll()** is called, which will obscure the Save prompt box and let the user get back to writing. If the response from the server is empty, **saveResponse()** can assume that the server was, for some reason, unable to respond, so an appropriate error message is passed to the **error()** method, which displays the message in a bright red alert box. If the response does not contain the substring "r200" and is not empty, **saveResponse()** assumes that an error occurred on the server, so again, an appropriate error message is formulated and passed to the **error()** method; however, this time the error message in the error alert box will actually contain a Java stack trace from the server, which will help you track down the difficulty.

 The r preceding the 200 (which stands for response) is there for no other reason than to compensate for an irksome bug I seem to have found in the beta version of PersonalJava. I found that if the first byte I tried to write to the socket output stream was a number (at least when wrapping the Output Stream in a PrintWriter), no data would end up getting written to the stream at all. Prepending a letter to the string ensures that all data gets written to the stream properly. Such are the joys of working with cutting-edge technologies.

Running the UI

The final step is to actually test the user interface. Running Flash on your Pocket PC device is fortunately far simpler than configuring and running Java. All you have to do is copy the appropriate files—the textTool.swf and textTool.html—over to your device and tap on textTool.html, which should look something like this:

```html
<html>
<head>
<title>textTool</title>
</head>
<body bgcolor="#ffffff">

<object classid="clsid:D27CDB6E-AE6D-11cf-96B8-444553540000"
    ID="PPC"

    width="220"
    height="140">
      <param name=movie value="textTool.swf">
      <param name=quality value=high>

    </object>
</body>
</html>
```

Pocket Internet Explorer will automatically start loading textTool.html, which will, in turn, load textTool.swf. For testing and debugging, you may want to run textTool.swf on your PC before moving it over to your device, in which case you can use the Flash Player or the Flash plug-in with any browser that supports it. Once again, we see the tremendous flexibility and convenience platform-independence lends both Flash and Java.

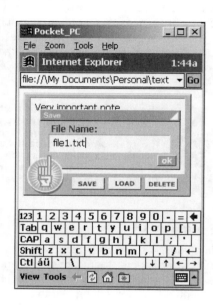

FIGURES 9.9 AND 9.10

TextTool's Flash user interface running in the Flash Player on Windows and running inside of Pocket Internet Explorer on my iPAQ. Notice how they are essentially indistinguishable.

SUMMARY

That's essentially all there is to TextTool. Twelve different Java objects, five Flash objects, and a multi-threaded client-server design may seem like a lot of work just to save, load, or delete a file; however, it's important to keep in mind that probably 90 percent of TextTool (including PocketServer and all three PocketServices) is actually generic, reusable services that can be extended quickly and easily to build a variety of applications, such as messaging clients, email utilities, even sophisticated systems with database back-ends. Admittedly, TextTool was a relatively simple example designed primarily for demonstration purposes. I'll leave it to you to take the technology to the next level.

10

SERVER-SIDE DYNAMIC CONTENT FOR FLASH-ENABLED DEVICES

by Mike Chambers

As has been discussed throughout the book, there are many techniques for creating dynamic Flash content for devices. However, up until now, all the techniques discussed have been client-side solutions that rely on ActionScript to create dynamic content. This chapter introduces Macromedia Generator and JGenerator, shows how they can be used to create dynamic content for devices, and examines two techniques for creating dynamic Flash content—the first completely server side, the second a combination of client and server.

With this information, you can dynamically author Flash movies that run on older Flash players (as far back as the Flash 3 Player). You also will be able to create complex Flash 4 or greater applications that contain all the data needed to dynamically create content. This allows you to create Flash applications that use dynamic data regardless of whether the device is connected to a network at the time the application is run.

Generator template authoring is no longer supported in Flash MX. Because of this, all the examples in the chapter require that the Flash 5 authoring environment be used.

For more information on Generator and other Macromedia server solutions, visit http://www.macromedia.com.

WHAT IS MACROMEDIA GENERATOR?

Generator is a server-side tool that dynamically creates data-driven graphics. Aside from Flash movies, Generator can also dynamically create GIFs (both animated and static), JPEGs, PNGs, QuickTime movies, and both Macintosh and PC Flash executables. It can be used for numerous tasks, but its main roles are to:

- Dynamically create data-driven Flash movies (or other media). Data can be retrieved from just about any source, including text files, URLs, middleware, and databases.
- Reduce file maintenance by enabling the automation of Flash dynamic content updates.
- Speed Flash content development through the use of reusable templates and objects that allow the creation of complex Flash elements such as charts, tickers, and tables.

For our purposes, we are primarily interested in the first point.

Generator consists of three main tools:

- **Online Mode.** Generator is accessed through a web server and dynamically creates data-driven media in real time (such as when the user requests the media).
- **Offline Mode.** Generator is executed from a command line interface. This can be used in conjunction with batch files and/or shell scripts to automate Flash maintenance tasks, such as updating dynamic content.
- **Authoring Extensions.** These come preinstalled with the Flash 5 authoring environment and allow the user to author Flash and Generator content using pre-built Generator objects that create complex Flash content. Even if the Generator server is not installed, the authoring extensions can be used to create static data-driven Flash files that include complex Flash elements, such as charts and tickers.

The authoring templates are available for all the platforms on which the Flash 5 authoring environment is available. They are not available for Flash MX.

WHAT IS JGENERATOR?

JGenerator was originally conceived as a Java–based open-source Generator clone and has quickly grown to encompass most of the functionality of Generator as well as adding quite a few features not available in Generator.

Besides being a dynamic graphics server, JGenerator is also a Java API for creating Flash movies from within Java. This allows developers to essentially create their own mini–server-side dynamic Flash solution in Java.

JGenerator's workflow and authoring are the same as Generator. Templates are authored within Flash and then processed and served from the JGenerator server. For the examples in this chapter, Generator and JGenerator are essentially interchangeable, and unless otherwise noted, when Generator is mentioned, you can assume the same applies to JGenerator.

You can find more information on JGenerator, as well as download it and its complete source code from http://www.flashgap.com.

ADVANTAGES AND DISADVANTAGES OF USING A SERVER-SIDE TOOL FOR DYNAMIC CONTENT FOR DEVICES

Now that you are more familiar with Generator and JGenerator, the following question arises: Why create dynamic content on the server side when you can create dynamic content on the client side by using Flash ActionScript?

The exact answer to that question depends on the specific goals of the project, as well as the features and limitations of the devices that are being targeted for deployment. However, there are a number of advantages to creating dynamic Flash-based content for devices on the server side:

- **Can store data within Flash movie when syncing.** Even if you use ActionScript to create your dynamic Flash movie, you can use Generator to place the data within the Flash movie before it is sent to or synced with the device. This allows you to use ActionScript to manipulate dynamic data and content even if the Flash movie is being run on a device without a network connection.

- **Dynamic content for older Flash players.** To create dynamic content with Flash alone, you must display that content on a Flash 4 or greater Player. The Flash 4 Player is the first version of Flash that included ActionScript that could load and manipulate data. However, by moving the dynamic content creation to the server side, you can create Flash 3–based dynamic content and thus make your content available to a wider range of devices.

- **CPU concerns.** Loading and manipulating dynamic content in Flash can be fairly CPU intensive. This is exacerbated by the relatively slow speed of CPUs found on some devices. This can lead to poor performing Flash movies, possible errors (both in the device and Flash Player), and an overall poor user experience. By moving the processing to the server side, you ensure that the process of creating the dynamic Flash content does not tax the user's CPU.

- **Template based.** Because Generator and JGenerator are template based, you can design/develop your content once, and then serve it to multiple devices. In fact, because Generator can create JPGs, GIFs, and QuickTime movies from the same template that it creates Flash movies, you can deliver content to almost any device, regardless of whether or not it has a Flash Player.

- **Easier development.** Depending on your project, creating dynamic Flash content with Generator can be easier than creating the same content using ActionScript. This is because Generator includes pre-built objects such as charts, lists, and tickers, which can greatly ease content creation.

There are also some disadvantages to using a server-side tool to create dynamic content for Flash enabled devices:

- **Requires server.** Server-side solutions require a server for deployment. This can mean higher development and maintenance complexity and costs. Furthermore, if you are not serving the content from your own server, this can also limit your options when trying to find a host to serve your content.

- **Cannot manipulate data when using Generator objects.** Although creating dynamic content with Generator objects can greatly ease the development, all the data remains on the server. Because of this, the data cannot be directly accessed and manipulated by ActionScript. To make the data available to ActionScript, you have to explicitly duplicate the data so that it can be manipulated on the client side.

CREATING GENERATOR TEMPLATES: THE AUTHORING WORKFLOW

All the files and examples discussed in this chapter are available for download from the book's web site (www.flashenabled.com).

Generator and JGenerator content begins with the use of the Generator authoring extensions that are included with the Flash 5 authoring environment. The extensions consist of Generator objects and commands that allow you to dynamically create and/or modify Flash movie elements on the server or desktop. This is an important point to remember. Generator templates are processed before they are sent to the Flash Player, unlike ActionScript, which is processed within the Flash Player.

Remember, Generator templates are processed on the server-side, before the movie is sent to the Flash Player.

ActionScript is processed on the client side in the Flash Player, after the movie has been loaded from the server.

To demonstrate how you can use Generator to place complex Flash elements into your movie and to present a better picture of the Generator content authoring process, we will walk through the process of creating a simple pie chart using the authoring extensions.

At the time that this was written, JGenerator did not have support for the Generator chart objects, including the Pie Chart object.

However, support for these objects is being worked on, and by the time you read this, JGenerator should have support for the chart objects.

1. Open Flash and create a new movie. Save the movie and name it **pie.fla**.

2. In the same directory that you saved pie.fla, create a text file called **pie_data.txt**. This file holds the data used to build the pie chart.

3. Open the Generator Objects Panel by selecting Window, Generator Objects. This window contains all the Generator objects (see Figure 10.1).

   Select the Pie Chart object, and drag it onto the movie stage. You will see a square, with Pie Chart in the top-left corner. This is the placeholder for the pie chart. The generated chart will be placed in the location of the placeholder, and will inherit all the properties of the placeholder, such as its x and y scale, alpha, and rotation.

FIGURE 10.1

The Generator Objects panel.

4. After you have placed the Pie Chart object in the movie, open the Generator Properties Panel (see Figure 10.2) by double-clicking on the Pie Chart object on the stage or selecting the object in the movie and going to Window, Panels, Generator.

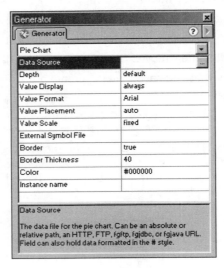

FIGURE 10.2

Generator Properties panel for the Pie Chart object.

This window contains the properties used to create the object, and allows you to customize how the generated element (in this case a pie chart) will look and behave. We are not going to worry about customizing the look of the pie chart right now. All we want to do is to specify the data source for the pie chart.

5. In the Data Source section of the Properties window enter **pie_data.txt**, and then save the Flash movie.

6. Open the pie_data.txt file with a text editor (such as Notepad or BBEdit), and enter the following data:

value, color, url
2, blue, "http://www.macromedia.com"
7, green, "http://www.newriders.com"
3, yellow, "http://www.markme.com"

At this point it is not important to understand the format of this file (we will discuss it in a little more detail later in the chapter), except to note that the first row contains the column names, and each subsequent row is a related set of data. It is very similar to a database record set.

7. Save the text file and switch back to the Flash application.

8. Be sure that the movie is set to be published as a Generator template by opening the Publish Settings window (File, Publish Settings) and checking the Generator Template (SWT) box.

9. You are now ready to test the movie. Select Control, Test Movie. You should see a pie chart similar to Figure 10.3.

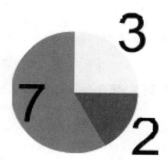

FIGURE 10.3

A simple pie chart created with Generator.

If you do not see a pie chart:

- Check the output window (Window, Output) for any error messages.
- Be sure that the pie.fla and pie_data.txt file are in the same directory.
- Check that the pie chart's data source property is set correctly.
- Make sure that the data source contains the correct data, with no missing commas, or line returns.
- Be sure that the movie is set to publish as a Generator template.

It is a pretty simple pie chart, but you can adjust the pie chart's settings in the Generator Inspector Properties window and further customize how the chart looks and works.

If you look in the directory that contains the FLA for the pie chart, you should find a file named pie.swt that was created when you tested the movie. SWT files are Generator templates and are used by the Generator server to dynamically create Flash or other graphic media. This is an important point. Once you have created a Generator template, a Generator server must process the template in order to create a Flash movie (or other media file).

Here is a summary of the Generator workflow:

1. Create content using the Generator authoring extensions within the Flash-authoring environment.
2. Publish the file and create a Flash movie (SWF), and a Generator template (SWT).
3. Use the Flash file (SWF) by itself, or copy the Generator template (SWT) to the Generator server to dynamically create the movie.

To dynamically process the templates, you would need to install the Generator server, and serve the templates from the server. However, that is beyond the scope of this chapter.

TWO TECHNIQUES FOR SERVER-SIDE DYNAMIC CONTENT CREATION

Now that you have examined the Generator workflow, you are ready to create some simple examples that demonstrate a couple of server-side techniques. For the first example we will use Generator to process some data and then use that data to dynamically create a Flash 3–based application that displays sports scores. The second example shows how to use Generator to place dynamic XML data within a Flash movie. ActionScript can then manipulate the data at runtime to create dynamic content.

Server-Side Dynamic Flash for Devices

The first technique we will examine revolves around creating dynamic Flash content entirely on the server. We will create a simple application that shows sports scores. The final file will be published as a Flash 3 movie and as an animated GIF. This ensures that the content will be able to be viewed on virtually any device regardless of the Flash Player version present, or whether there is even a player available.

1. Create a new Flash movie and name it **sportsa.fla**.
2. Open the Publish Settings windows (File, Publish Settings) and be sure that both Flash (SWF) and Generator Template (SWT) are checked. This tells Flash to create a Generator template in addition to a Flash movie.

Whenever you are creating a Generator template, make sure that both Flash (SWF) and Generator Template (SWT) are checked in File, Publish Settings.

3. Click the Flash tab in File, Publish Settings. Set the version number to Flash 3. You can publish your movie as a Flash 3 file because all the dynamic content generation is being done on the server, and thus does not rely on ActionScript. This is useful, as it ensures that you can display your movie on just about any device that has a Flash Player (for example, some versions of the Sega Dreamcast only support Flash 3).

4. Press the OK button and close the Publish Settings window. Open the Movie Properties window (Modify, Movie) and set the width to 230 and the height to 255. You can leave the frame rate at the default of 12.

Now that you have configured the basics of your movie, you need to step outside of Flash and create the data source that Generator will use to create the Flash movie.

Generator recognizes two data source formats. The first allows name/value pairs to be passed to Generator. The second, called a column data source, allows sets of related information to be passed to Generator, and is similar to a database result set. You will be using a column data source to pass the sports score data to Generator.

We will not spend a lot of time examining Generator data sources however, we will take a quick look at an example data source just so you can get a basic understanding of its format.

homeTeam, homeScore, visitorTeam, visitorScore, time, notes
"Washington", "78", "New York", "79", "final", "Johnson scores 23 on 8 of 9
➥shooting"
"Phoenix", "102", "Seattle", "98", "1:05 4th Quarter", "Phoenix has won 4 straight."

This data source contains three rows, two of which contain sports data. The first row contains the column names that the data in each subsequent row will be accessed by. The second and third rows contain sets of related sports data. Notice that the data is wrapped in double quotes, and a comma separates each section of data. Each piece of data corresponds to a column name in the first row, and each row is separated by a line return.

The data is wrapped in double quotes to prevent commas that are part of the data from confusing Generator. If you want to display double quotes within your data, you can escape them by placing a backslash (\) in front of the double quote you want to display. This tells Generator that the double quote is part of the data to be displayed.

You can also escape backslashes with another backslash.

For example:

"Mike Said, \"Isabel likes to eat\""

Notice that backslashes are placed before the inside double quotes, so that the quotes will remain part of the data.

5. Now that you have had a crash course in Generator column data sources, you can create one for our movie. In the same directory that contains the FLA for the movie, create a new text file and name it **sports_data.txt**.

6. Open the sports_data.txt file with a text editor and enter the following data:

    homeTeam, homeScore, visitorTeam, visitorScore, time, notes
    "Washington", "78", "New York", "79", "final", "Johnson scores 23 on 8 of 9
    ➡shooting"
    "Phoenix", "102", "Seattle", "98", "1:05 4th Quarter", "Phoenix has won 4 straight."
    "Dallas", "109", "Atlanta", "107", "Final", "Smith scores his 10,000th career point."
    "Toronto", "105", "Portland", "98", "Final", "Pearson has career high 19 rebounds."

This is a simple column data source that contains information about basketball games.

For this example we are using a simple text file to hold the data. However, as you have probably already realized, this is not very dynamic. In a production environment, you would probably have some middleware such as Java, ColdFusion, ASP, or PHP to dynamically create the data source. Instead of loading the text file, Generator would connect to the middleware, which would in turn send the up-to-date dynamic sports data directly to Generator.

7. Save the text file, and switch back to Flash.

8. Now that the data source has been created, you are finally ready to begin putting together your Flash movie. First you need to create the Movie Clip that actually displays the sports data. Create a new Movie Clip symbol and name it **scores tween**. This Movie Clip holds the Movie Clip that contains the actual sports data.

9. Create a second Movie Clip and name it **data**. This Movie Clip contains Generator variables that will be replaced with the data from your data source when the Flash movie is created.

10. The data source that you created contains the following variables: **homeTeam**, **homeScore**, **visitorTeam**, **visitorScore**, **time**, **notes**. These variables will be used to display data within your Flash movie. Using the Text tool, place each Generator variable on the stage within the **data** Movie Clip. This is done by surrounding the variable name with curly brackets (see Figure 10.4), like so: **{homeTeam}**.

The font properties and position that you use for the variables will be inherited by the data when it is displayed.

It is a good idea to place each variable on its own layer. This helps to organize the Movie Clip and can make it easier to work with, especially if the clip becomes complex.

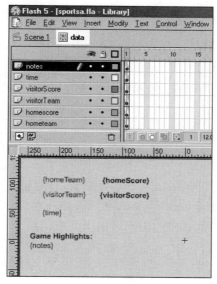

FIGURE 10.4

Data Movie Clip with Generator variables.

11. After you have placed all the variables inside of the data Movie Clip, open the scores tween Movie Clip, and place an instance of the data Movie Clip into it. You want the scores to automatically cycle through each set of scores by fading in and out. By placing the Movie Clip with the Generator variables inside of another Movie Clip, you can use an alpha/visibility tween to transition between scores.

12. Select the data Movie Clip on the timeline of the scores tween Movie Clip. We are going to set its alpha to 0%, tween it to 100% and then tween it back to 0%. Generator creates a Movie Clip instance for each set of data and places them back-to-back. When the movie plays, the scores will transition seamlessly from one to another.

13. With the data Movie Clip selected on the timeline open the Effects panel (Window, Panels, Effects) and set the alpha to 0% (see Figure 10.5).

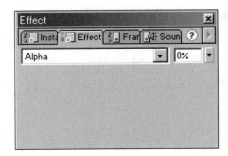

FIGURE 10.5

Effects panel with Alpha set to 0%.

14. On the timeline, select frame 5 and add a new keyframe (Insert, Keyframe). Select the Movie Clip instance on frame 5, and set the Alpha to 100% using the Effects panel.

15. Select frame 15 and add another keyframe. This is the point where the Movie Clip begins to fade out.

16. Select frame 20 and add another keyframe. Using the Effects panel, set the Alpha of the Movie Clip to 0%.

17. Now that you have added the keyframes and alpha changes, you need to add the tweens to the timeline. Select frames 1–5, and create a motion tween (Insert, Create Motion Tween).

18. Repeat step 17 for frames 15–20.

    At this point, if you scrub the timeline back and forth you should see the Generator variables fade in and out (see Figure 10.6).

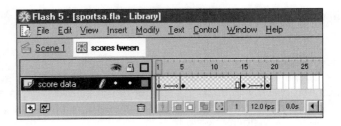

FIGURE 10.6

Scores tween Movie Clip timeline with tweens.

19. Switch to the main timeline and place an instance of the scores tween Movie Clip onto the stage.

20. With the scores tween Movie Clip instance selected open the Generator panel (Window, Panels, Generator) and select Replicate from the drop-down menu.

    Replicate is a Generator command that copies a Movie Clip for each row of data in a data source and then strings all the frames of the Movie Clips together, one after the other.

21. After replicate has been selected, its settings will appear in the Generator panel. For the Data Source setting, enter the name of the data source you created earlier (sports_data.txt). You can leave the Expand Frames setting to true.

When using a relative path, the path is relative to the location of the Generator template.

For a more thorough discussion of relative versus absolute paths, see the following resources at Macromedia.com:

- **For document-relative, site root-relative, and absolute paths, see http://www.macromedia.com/support/flash/ts/documents/ relative_urls.htm.**

- **For target paths, see http://www.macromedia.com/support/flash/ action_scripts/nesting_movies/nesting_movies05.html.**

22. That's all you need to do to create the movie. To view the movie select Control, Test Movie. You should see the sports scores fade in and out (see Figure 10.7).

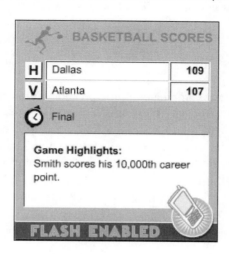

FIGURE 10.7

Final movie created by Generator.

If the scores transition too quickly, you can adjust the speed by adding or removing frames in the scores tween Movie Clip.

Generator took the scores tween Movie Clip and copied its frames for each row of data in the data source.

It is important to remember that our movie is a Flash 3 movie, which can be displayed on virtually any device with a Flash Player. Of course, you could have just as easily created a Flash 4 or 5 file using Generator, but if you do not need the added features and functionality provided by those players, there is really no need to publish at the higher version.

But what if you wanted to display the file on the widest range of devices, yet also desired some functionality and features provided by Flash 4 or 5 ActionScript? The solution is to create a stub movie with the added functionality that loads the Flash 3 movie. When displaying on devices with a Flash 4 or greater Player, the stub movie would load the Flash 3 movie (using loadMovie), and provide greater functionality. However, if displaying on a device with a Flash 3 Player, you could simply load the Flash 3 file directly.

Another advantage of using Generator is that you can create other graphic formats from the same template and data from which the Flash movie is created. Generator can automatically create an animated GIF file that displays all the scores. This makes it possible to serve your content to a device even if it does not have a Flash Player.

At the time that this was written, JGenerator could only output Flash movies, and could not dynamically create other graphic formats.

23. Using the same file that you created in the preceding example, open the Publish Settings window (File, Publish Settings) and check GIF Image (.gif).

24. Open the GIF settings by clicking on the GIF tab. This is where you can specify all the settings for the GIF file that Generator creates. For this example, you just need to be sure that Playback is set to animated. This tells Generator to create an animated GIF.

25. Click OK, and publish the movie (File, Publish). If you look in the directory that contains your FLA, you will find an animated GIF file named sportsa.gif that displays all the sports information.

If the template is served from a Generator server, you can dynamically choose whether to create a Flash movie or a GIF file on-the-fly by specifying the file type desired in the URL when the template is requested.

sportsa.swt?type=gif

Using this capability in combination with some simple detection scripts would ensure that your content could be viewed by virtually any device, regardless of whether it contained a Flash Player.

Advantages of server-side dynamic content for devices include the following:

- Works on Flash 3 Players and above.
- Allows dynamic content to be synced and then played on a non-network connected device.
- Can deliver non-Flash graphic content based on same template and data if Flash Player is not available.
- Modular development allows tiered functionality based on Flash Player present on device being targeted.

Disadvantages are

- Requires a server to deploy.
- Once raw data has been processed, it is not automatically available to ActionScript for further processing or manipulation on the client side.
- If you need to refresh the data, you will need to reload the SWF containing the dynamic content, which will almost certainly be larger than just loading the data.

A Client/Server Architecture for Dynamic Flash Content

In the previous section you used Generator to create dynamic content entirely on the server side. Not only did this allow you to create a Flash 3–based movie, but it also allowed you to create an animated GIF from the same template from which you created the Flash movie. However, this technique has the disadvantage that once the content has been created from the data, the data is no longer available to ActionScript. This prevents ActionScript from being able to manipulate the content and data at runtime. This leads us to our second technique, which uses Generator or JGenerator to embed the data into the Flash movie at the time that it is synced/transferred to the device, and then use ActionScript to manipulate that data at runtime.

There are a number of different ways you could structure the data in this approach:

- URL Encoded format to be loaded through loadVariables (this would not work with Generator).
- XML
- A custom format to be de-serialized by custom ActionScript.

Because you are transferring complex structured data, and you can use Flash 5, you will use XML to represent your data.

You will use Generator to dynamically place the XML into a Flash ActionScript XML object. When the Flash movie runs, it can then parse through the XML and use it to display the information. The benefit of this is that it allows you to use the advantages of Flash 5 ActionScript to manipulate dynamic data even if the Flash movie is viewed in a device that is not connected to a network.

1. Create a new Flash movie and name it **sportsb.fla**.

2. Open the Movie Proprieties window (Modify, Movie) and set the width to 230 and the height to 255.

3. Be sure that in File, Publish Settings, both the Generator (SWT) and Flash (SWF) tabs are checked. Open the Flash tab, and make sure that the movie is set to publish as a Flash 5 movie.

You can now create the data source that Generator will use to insert the XML into the Flash movie. First, let's look at what the sports data will look like represented as XML:

```xml
<xml>

    <game>
            <homeTeam>Washington</homeTeam>
            <homeScore>78</homeScore>
            <visitorTeam>New York</visitorTeam>
            <visitorScore>79</visitorScore>
            <time>Final</time>
            <note>Johnson scores 23 on 8 of 9 shooting</note>
    </game>
    <game>
            <homeTeam>Phoenix</homeTeam>
            <homeScore>102</homeScore>
            <visitorTeam>Seattle</visitorTeam>
            <visitorScore>98</visitorScore>
            <time>1:05 4th Quarter</time>
            <note>Phoenix has won 4 straight.</note>
    </game>
    <game>
            <homeTeam>Dallas</homeTeam>
            <homeScore>109</homeScore>
            <visitorTeam>Atlanta</visitorTeam>
            <visitorScore>107</visitorScore>
            <time>Final</time>
            <note>Smith scores his 10,000th career point.</note>
```

```
        </game>
        <game>
                <homeTeam>Toronto</homeTeam>
                <homeScore>105</homeScore>
                <visitorTeam>Portland</visitorTeam>
                <visitorScore>98</visitorScore>
                <time>Final</time>
                <note>Pearson has career high 19 rebounds.</note>
        </game>

</xml>
```

This is just a simple XML document that uses the same sports data used in the previous example.

You need to embed this XML into the Flash movie. You will do this on the server side with Generator by embedding the XML string into a Generator data source.

As we briefly discussed in the previous example, Generator has two data source formats, name/value, and column. You used the column format in the previous example. Because you only need to create one Generator variable that contains the XML, you will use the name/value format for this example.

Let's take a quick look at the name/value Generator data source format, which, as its name implies, is used to send name/value pairs to Generator. Here is an example:

```
name, value
firstName, "Squish"
occupation, "Kitty Cat"
```

The first line tells Generator that this is a name/value data source. The subsequent lines are name/value pairs. Each pair is separated by a line return, and the name is separated from the value by a comma. This example creates two Generator variables, *firstName* and *occupation*, that can be used to insert the data into the Flash movie created by Generator.

For this example, you need to store the entire XML data within a single Generator variable. This may sound complicated, but it is actually quite simple. Here is what your data source will look like:

```
name, value
sportsXML, "<xml><game><homeTeam>Washington</homeTeam><homeScore>
➡78</homeScore><visitorTeam>New York</visitorTeam><visitorScore>
➡79</visitorScore><time>Final</time><note>Johnson scores 23 on 8 of 9
➡shooting</note></game><game><homeTeam> Phoenix</homeTeam>
➡<homeScore>102</homeScore><visitorTeam>Seattle</visitorTeam><visitorScore
```

continues

➡>98</visitorScore><time>1:05 4th Quarter</time><note>Phoenix has won 4
➡straight.</note></game><game><homeTeam>Dallas</homeTeam><homeScore>
➡109</homeScore><visitorTeam>Atlanta</visitorTeam><visitorScore>107</visitor
➡Score><time>Final</time><note>Smith scores his 10,000th career point.</note>
➡</game><game><homeTeam>Toronto</homeTeam><homeScore>105</
➡homeScore><visitorTeam>Portland</visitorTeam><visitorScore>98</visitorScore>
➡<time>Final</time><note>Pearson has career high 19 rebounds.</note></
➡game></xml>"

The data source is actually just two lines (although the line is too long to fit on a single line in the book).

Basically, the data source looks like this:

name, value
sportsXML, XML Data Here

This stores your entire XML string into a single Generator variable named sportsXML.

First, all the formatting white space (extraneous tabs, spaces, and line returns not part of the actual data) has been removed from the XML. This makes the data easier to work with in Generator, and also makes the data easier to work with within Flash as we do not have to worry about white space being treated as an XML node. Second, the entire string of XML is wrapped within double quotes. Just as in the previous example, this is done to escape any line returns or commas within the XML data. If the XML contained double quotes, then you would have to escape those double quotes with a backslash.

Also keep in mind that you are using a text file to keep the example simple. In a production environment, the Generator data source and the XML it contains would most likely be dynamically created by some middleware such as Java or ColdFusion.

4. Create a new text document and name it **sports_xmldata.txt**. Place the data source shown previously into the text file and save it into the same directory as the Flash movie.

In the previous example you loaded the data source directly into a Generator command. However, for this example, you are not using an object, but rather dynamically inserting data that will be used by ActionScript. Because of this, you need to use the Generator environment variable button to load the Generator data and make it available on the main timeline, as well as all its children timelines (see Figure 10.8).

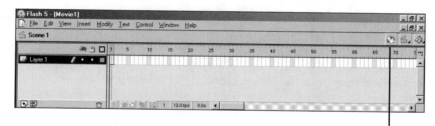

Generator Environment variable button

FIGURE 10.8

The Environment variable button.

5. Open the Set Environment window by pressing the Generator Environment variables button (see Figure 10.9). It is located at the top right of the Flash authoring environment.

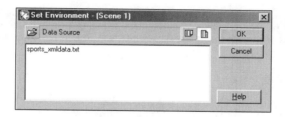

FIGURE 10.9

The Set Environment window with data source specified.

6. Type the name of the Generator data source that contains the XML, "sports_xmldata.txt" into the window. Make sure that the "Name/Value data layout" button is selected (see Figure 10.10).

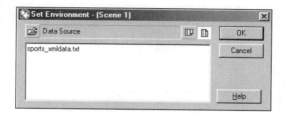

FIGURE 10.10

Set Environment window with Name/Value data layout button selected.

At this point when the movie is tested, any name/value pairs within the data source will be available to the entire Generator template. Using this data, you can now insert the XML from the Generator data source into an ActionScript XML object.

7. Select frame one on the main timeline and open the Frame Actions panel (Window, Actions). Remember that the XML is stored in a Generator variable called *sportsXML* (as defined in the data source). You need to transfer the XML into a Flash XML object by placing the Generator variable within an XML constructor.

scores = new XML("{sportsXML}");

Be sure that you add the double quotes around the Generator variable. This is necessary because all data inserted from a Generator variable are treated as strings by ActionScript.

This ActionScript code creates a new XML object called "scores" that contains all the XML sports score data. You can now access this data and do what ever you like with it using standard Flash 5 ActionScript. Best of all, this will work even if the Flash movie is run on a device that is not connected to a network.

The XML is not actually parsed into an ActionScript XML object until it is loaded into the player. Because of this, the same general guidelines discussed earlier in the book concerning performance and optimizations when using XML apply.

8. You can check to be sure that the XML was added to the XML document by tracing the contents of the XML object:

trace("The XML data is : \n" + scores);

This prints out the contents of the XML document to the output window.

9. Test the movie (Control, Test Movie). The output window should pop up and print the contents of the XML object (see Figure 10.11).

FIGURE 10.11

The Output window with trace of XML inserted by Generator.

Because the main emphasis of this example is using Generator to get the data into Flash, we will not look at how to actually use the data once it is within Flash. Utilizing the XML inserted by Generator simply involves parsing and manipulating the XML with standard ActionScript.

The advantages of this technique are as follows:

- Allows dynamic Flash content creation even when the movie is run on a non-connected device.
- Allows dynamic data and Flash content to be contained within one file.
- Data can be manipulated by ActionScript at runtime.

The disadvantages are as follow:

- Requires at least Flash 4 Player, and Flash 5 for use of XML.
- Depending on amount of data, and processing speed of device, can be CPU intensive.

SUMMARY

This chapter introduced Generator and JGenerator, and showed how these server-side tools can be used to create dynamic Flash content to be deployed on devices.

Because Generator and JGenerator use templates to author content, developers can develop in a more modular fashion serving different versions of files depending on the Flash Player available. In fact, if no Flash Player is available, alternative media, such as an animated GIF based on the same data, can be created and served. This virtually ensures that the content will be available to the user regardless of the capabilities of the device on which it is being viewed.

Finally, by embedding dynamic data into the Flash movie before it is sent to the device, developers can take advantage of the abilities of ActionScript to create Flash movies based on dynamic data even if it is being viewed on a device that does not have a connection to a network.

PART IV: FLASH FOR TELEVISION

11

FLASH CONTENT FOR TELEVISION

by Glenn Thomas and Markus Niedermeier

The television is the ultimate device. Everybody has one and each one works the same—turn it on and watch stuff. Content created for television in one country can, with minimal changes, be viewed in every other country in the world. The TV really is one of the most ubiquitous and powerful devices on the planet.

According to the Consumer Electronics Organization (**www.ce.org**) over 98% of American households contain at least one television, compared to around 50% of American households that have a computer. The average number of televisions is more like two and a half per American household. Americans have televisions in their living rooms, bedrooms, kitchens, and even bathrooms. It's a TV world.

Figures in the industrialized West are similar to those in the United States, while figures in the developing world are lower, but growing rapidly. If you really want to reach people on a massive, worldwide level, then use Macromedia Flash to create content that can be viewed on television.

Flash can be used to create programming for television in three ways. It can be used to create broadcast quality content that can play back directly on television. More and more creative professionals are using Flash to develop motion graphics and animation that can be played back on broadcast television, cable networks, VHS tapes, or DVD. Secondly, Flash can be used to create web-based content, such as navigational interfaces, home banking, chats, motion graphics, animation, and games that can be accessed by viewers through set top boxes equipped with TV browsers. The last way that Flash can be used is as part of enhanced TV broadcasts where the video broadcast triggers web-based content to appear. Viewers can enrich their television experience by exploring the enhanced material added to the broadcast.

There are both general television display issues and specific technical issues that have to be dealt with for each type of development. This chapter discusses these issues and uses examples to help smooth the transition to using Flash for television.

- General television display issues
- Flash for non-broadcast television
- Flash for broadcast television
- Flash for TV browsers
- Introduction to Flash for enhanced television

GENERAL TELEVISION DISPLAY ISSUES

There are different ways of using Flash for television. However, due to the nature of the television display, they all share a variety of common development issues. No matter how you produce Flash for television, you are certain to run into specific problems and limitations.

Many of these limitations today stem from the fact that standard TV technology generally needs to be backward compatible. In other words, today's consumer NTSC color television is still pretty much determined by the lowest common denominator—the 1950's black-and-white TV set, which still has to be able to generate a proper display from modern-day color TV transmissions.

Modern computer screens on the other hand aren't restricted to 525 or 625 horizontal lines or interlaced images. Monitors have a much higher definition and do generally better in displaying colors. Therefore, graphics created on a computer have to be adjusted for the poorer display quality of TV sets.

Fonts and Readability

Because television resolution is low and viewers are further from the screen, it's crucial to use easy-to-read fonts at a large point size. Fonts such as Helvetica, Arial, or other sans serif fonts are the most readable on televisions. Standard font sizes for readability are 18pt and above. Fonts inside of Flash should probably be set to 24pt and higher because Flash renders fonts a bit "fuzzier" than HTML and therefore are more difficult to read.

Graphics techniques such as drop shadows can be used to set off titles from a background. To distinguish text from background, the color contrast between them will have to bigger than on computer monitors. Larger fonts should be anti-aliased to avoid interlacing problems such as flicker.

Because text is difficult to read on television monitors it's important that text stays on the screen long enough for someone to read it. For the viewer's sake, err on the side of text being on the screen too long.

Safe Areas

Consumer TV sets do not display the full range of NTSC's 640×480 or PAL's 720×486 resolution formats. Due to an effect called overscanning, the average consumer TV loses a portion of the image. Therefore, crucial content should not be placed too close to the edges of your image. The safe area for action should be considered 10% smaller for action and 20% smaller for titles. If you are new to TV graphics, you should create safe area frames for your design in Flash (see Figure 11.1). They'll remind you to keep crucial content inside.

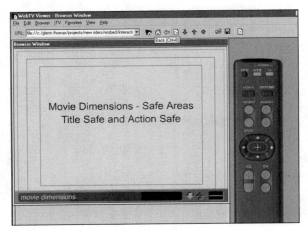

FIGURE 11.1

Creating title and action safe frames for your Flash movie allow content to be created that will be seen by viewers.

INTERLACING

One of the fundamental differences in how TV sets and computer monitors generate their images is the fact that standard TVs use interlaced images and computer monitors do not.

TVs generate an image by an electron beam that "draws" horizontal lines from left to right and top to bottom. However, these lines are not drawn one after another, but rather in two passes. In one pass the odd numbered lines 1, 3, 5, and so on are drawn; in the second pass, the even line numbers 2, 4, 6, and so on are drawn. This method, which divides the image into two separate "fields," is called interlacing. NTSC TVs display almost 30 frames per second, and thus have to create almost 60 fields per second.

Interlacing is one of these aspects in video technology resulting from TV's backward compatibility discussed earlier. Newer TVs could do perfectly without interlacing, but for old TV sets, it is the only way to refresh the screen 30 times a second without producing negative display effects such as strobing.

Computer-generated images are not made up of interlaced fields. Each frame is one solid image. When rendered by video editing software however, the formerly solid image will be broken up into two fields of alternating lines.

This has consequences especially for computer graphics with very fine horizontal lines or detailed structures. The result is often interlace flicker or moiré patterns. These display artifacts can be reduced or sometimes even eliminated in post production by applying blur filters in programs like After Effects, but it takes time to figure out the right balance and render everything frame by frame. It is better to plan ahead and experiment on single frames in preproduction. Use thick lines and make also sure to check the anti-aliasing option (smoothing) in the Export Settings when possible. This will take care of many interlacing problems right from the start.

Colors

More so than other television formats, like the European PAL or the new HDTV, NTSC has a specific problem in displaying colors. That's why many people refer to the NTSC acronym often as "Never Twice the Same Color."

In terms of technology solutions and workflow while preparing your Flash files, getting your colors TV-ready is probably one of the easier aspects of Flash to TV conversion. As with almost every other aspect in this list, it is better done in pre-production, so begin working with TV safe colors rather than changing them afterward.

Although color correction is fairly easily done with decent nonlinear editing systems (NLE) or the right plug-ins, the color palette should be developed and tested early on so that there won't be too many surprises at the end of the project. The quickest way to experiment with TV display is to buy an NTSC output card for your computer and connect an average consumer television as a monitor. That way you get instant feedback on your color choices.

If you don't have NTSC output, you can use several tools to create a NTSC-safe color palette. Microsoft's color picker (**http://developer.msntv.com/tools/colorpick/Default.htm**), for example, is an online tool that emulates how computer colors will look on a TV screen.

A variety of programs help render colors as NTSC safe colors. Photoshop provides such an option. It's possible to open a raster graphic with the Flash movie's color palette in Photoshop and then make it NTSC color safe. This graphic can then be imported back into Flash and vectorized to get a TV-safe color palette. This should be done prior to creating the entire Flash movie. It will not work for gradients or transparent colors.

Here are a few guidelines on how to achieve NTSC-friendly color schemes:

- A quick way to get close to color safe values is to avoid RGB component values above 240. Highly intense red, green, or blue displays poorly.
- Pure white doesn't display well on television for technical reasons. It may be the web's favorite background color, but TV viewers prefer darker colors anyway.
- Don't use heavily contrasting colors next to each other in a design. They "buzz" and overlap on display. Use transitional colors between contrasting colors to soften the effect.

Because colors are so immensely important for the aesthetic success of your content, it can be quite a challenge to find the right colors and color combinations, especially when your content needs to look good on both the web and on TV.

TV-Specific Viewing Habits and Aesthetics

To these objective technical issues, you have to add the human element of viewing habits and aesthetics that TV has developed in its over 50 years of existence as a mass medium. TV's success as the world's most important information and entertainment medium, relies very much on the fact that technologically speaking, everything is pretty much geared toward the lowest common denominator. So is the content, TV critics might add, but the fact remains that everyone can participate until the screen is busted. No upgrading of hardware, no downloading of plug-ins is necessary to view the latest episode of *The Simpsons*.

Designing for the lowest common denominator is not always obvious for Flash designers who very often disdainfully ignore users with low bandwidth and slow processors. It's possible to get away with that attitude on the web because in computer culture people are used to technical difficulties and slow downloads. Users are much more likely to blame themselves or their equipment than the creator of the poorly functioning content.

In TV it's fundamentally different. Viewers simply don't recalibrate their sets from show to show—even if you tell them to. So if the colors are off or type can't be read because it blurs, it's your fault. If you are creating content to be shown on TV sets, don't calibrate it for the high-quality studio monitors that you might be working with at the post-production facility. Many things will look great on high-definition equipment and will still be far from optimal on a regular consumer set.

Test your Flash-generated output thoroughly and make the cheap consumer TV your ultimate aesthetic benchmark. If everything displays well there, you're on the right track. As with a lot of things, common sense and design experience will get you far in transferring content to TV, even before video technicians apply their waveform monitors.

FLASH FOR NON-BROADCAST TV: VHS, MINIDV, DVD

Getting your web Flash animation on TV formats for presentation, testing, or just for fun is fairly easy and should yield great results, even if you have only consumer video equipment at your disposal.

All you need on your computer is a nonlinear video editing application such as Adobe Premiere or Final Cut Pro and a video card or firewire connection to output your movie. In case you want to put your movie on DVD, you will also need DVD authoring software. If you haven't done much video editing and are used to Flash file sizes, don't forget that video files require a lot of disk space. Another hardware consideration is that unlike with Flash, video rendering can take quite some time, and the faster the processor, the better.

On the video playback side, the consumer market offers three common options: analog output to VHS, digital output to MiniDV via firewire, or DVD authoring. Ideally, you should make up your mind when you set up your Flash movie, because analog NTSC and digital formats like MiniDV work with different resolution formats.

Preparing Your Flash File

Even when your Flash project is targeted mainly at an online audience, you can still improve its TV display quality by following our recommendations for testing, color correction, and general TV display issues, discussed earlier in the chapter.

If your Flash movie isn't in TV's 4:3 format, which is most likely, you should also apply the resizing techniques detailed later in this chapter. If you are close to 4:3 you might try and export your movie as it is and see whether you can live with the resulting distortion.

If your animation permits it, you can also try cropping the movie files to a 4:3 ratio and then fit them to the correct pixel frame size. You can do this in Photoshop or in good video or motion graphic software. By truncating the image you will definitely avoid distortions when resizing, but it might take quite some time to prepare each frame and render it.

Another good workaround is to create a frame or horizontal bars to surround your movie as it plays. In this way you maintain your movie's original dimensions on playback while adjusting the overall display ratio of the movie. TV Viewers are used to these "letterboxes" and it might be a more economic solution when you don't really need a full-screen display.

Because your web movie was probably originally created at somewhere between 10 to 15 frames per second, you also need to add frames to prevent your animation from running too fast when displayed on NTSC TVs. For desktop editing purposes, it will be enough to match your movie to NTSC's de facto frame rate of 30 fps.

Adjusting the movie's speed can be done either in Flash or after exporting the original lower-frame rate movie to the NLE. The NLE will definitely do the quicker job and you should give it a try before you get into the frame-by-frame work in Flash, because all the NLE really needs to do is to render a slow motion clip. Depending on how many frames your original Flash movie used, you have to figure out the percentage in relation to the standard 30 NTSC frame rate. So if your Flash file displayed 15 frames, for example, you have to tell your video editing software to create a 50% slow motion clip. This, however, might not produce the smoothest running animation, because the video software only duplicates frames—it does not create new and different in-betweens. In the end, your animation might look choppier than on the web.

If that's the case and you want perfect TV playback quality of your Internet animation, you will have to go into Flash, add frames manually, and create in-betweens where necessary. This might be more tedious, but working in Flash rather than in the NLE also gives you the chance to constantly review and edit the animation until you achieve the desired result.

When all manual adjustments are done in Flash, go to Publish Settings or Export Movie and choose an output format that is supported by your video editing software. Export Movie gives you a wider range of output options, especially for sequential files. It probably requires some testing in order to determine which one of the different export formats works best with your video editing software and produces the best video picture.

QuickTime is one of the major standards for non-linear video editing. Keep in mind though, that Flash for Windows doesn't let you export 'real' QuickTime videos; only Flash 5 for Macintosh allows you to do that. Flash for Windows exports only a separate Flash-layer inside a QuickTime movie and only few video software at this point, such as Final Cut Pro or Cleaner 5.1, support Flash-layers in QuickTime movies or are even able to import Flash's swf-files. In case your NLE doesn't know how to handle the 'flash-layered' QuickTime movie, you can import it into QuickTime Pro for example and then re-export it as a 'real' QuickTime movie. If you experience difficulties with QuickTime files, try using Windows avi-video or sequential image formats. Sequential Bitmaps should always be able to do the job and will provide your NLE with high quality images.

If you have sound in your animation and its quality and timing matters a lot, we recommend working on it in the NLE. Be sure your sound quality is as good as possible, because you don't need to fear file size and Flash player compression anymore. Also check the audio synching, especially when you use lip-synched voices or synched sound effects. If your sound is off, unsynch your video from your audio tracks or export them separately from Flash as a wav-file. Then go into the NLE's time line where you can easily manipulate either video or audio. When everything is fine-tuned, render your video and then record the output to one of the options that follow. As noted before, decide in the beginning which output format to use because it can make a difference in setting up the Flash file. The following sections tell you what to look out for.

VHS

For absolute video newcomers, VHS is the easiest of recording devices, because it requires the least expensive or complicated equipment and you don't really need to worry about compatibility issues because VHS is the only analog consumer video standard left on the planet.

Set the dimensions of your Flash movie to 640×480 and your frame rate to 30fps, which is the de facto desktop editing standard for analog NTSC and is sufficient for a lower-quality transfer. If necessary apply the resizing and correction methods discussed previously, export an avi (PC), a QuickTime movie (Mac), or sequential graphic files into your NLE, and edit the movie. Output your finished video via video card connections to the VHS, using S-VHS if possible.

MiniDV

If you are MiniDV-savvy or you need to composite your Flash-material with MiniDV-footage, you might want to use MiniDV as output-medium for your Flash material. In this case, keep in mind, that MiniDV uses a rectangular pixel aspect ratio of 720×480 to display an image. Computer graphics produced in Photoshop or Flash are generated in square pixels. (Refer to the "Broadcast TV" section for details about the different pixels.)

Here it should suffice to say that not all software or hardware you might be editing with lets you combine square and rectangular pixel sources or easily compensate the format difference. You might end up with the well-known distortion effects that appear when your source files aren't correctly interpreted by your NLE or compositing software (see Figure 11.2).

FIGURE 11.2

Piggidog on the left displays correctly. Piggidog on the right suffers from the distortion that a square pixel images displays on a rectangular pixel screen. Because Piggidog is a nonrealistic character it doesn't really seem to matter that much. The orange ball, however, clearly shows the degree of the distortion.

To avoid having your Flash content distort when recorded and played from a MiniDV device, post production pros recommend to simulate rectangular pixels in square pixel files by creating the graphics already in Flash at 720×534 and then distorting the aspect ratio to MiniDV's 720×480, either by using software that knows how to do this (such as After Effects) or manually by working with graphic file sequences in Photoshop. Don't get confused when your editing window on the computer screen still displays a squashed image. It will render nicely in your rectangular pixel video project and display fine when played from MiniDV.

DVD

The most elegant way to get your Flash on television these days is probably DVD authoring. With onboard DVD-burners and programs such as DVD Studio Pro and the consumer-friendly iDVD, Macintosh offers integrated solutions that make DVD authoring a question of "drag and drop." PC solutions are generally a little bit more "plug and play-around" before you get them to work, but then the results are just as good.

With DVD Studio Pro for Macintosh or Sonic DVDit! for PC, the three basic steps of encoding video and audio, creating DVD interfaces, and burning the DVDs are simple and self-explanatory. If you know little or nothing about desktop video and DVD authoring, let these programs take over once your Flash animation has been converted to QuickTime or avi. Preparing your Flash movie for DVD requires an aspect ratio of 720×480 and basically the same methods and precautions as described in the preceding "MiniDV" section.

If you are desktop video savvy and have one of the latest NLEs or plug-ins, you might favor other workflows though. Because there are new releases in this field on an almost daily basis, you might want to experiment a little. The overall trend in NLE development moves toward streamlining workflows. This means that the same application will usually support, that is, import and export, as many desktop video-relevant formats as possible, which of course include Flash and MPEG-2.

On the import side, Final Cut Pro already directly imports Flash's SWF files as does the highly recommended video encoding software Cleaner 5.1. On the export side, there's also a trend toward integrating stronger encoding tools into the core of video editing software. NLEs such as Avid Xpress, Ulead Media Studio Pro, and Premiere 6.0 now integrate encoding software, ship with plug-ins, or bundle video compression tools, making it possible to export a finished MPEG-2 directly from the timeline of these programs.

If you don't have to fine-tune your animation and your sound in a video editing software program there is also the possibility to bypass the NLE completely. Import your Flash file directly into Cleaner 5.1 and then export it as MPEG-2.

Workflows and end results vary greatly depending on which software and hardware setup you use, so be prepared to experiment. Not all onboard NLE encoding solutions provide satisfactory enough results to spare you time and trouble of importing and exporting your files through multiple, but better, encoding software. Find whichever workflow suits you best in getting Flash to MPEG and then move on to good DVD authoring software to actually make the DVD because no NLE at present will do that for you.

A note on the different DVD formats: The best to use for our purposes here are DVD-Rs. They hold 4.7GB of content and can be written to once, just like CD-Rs. They will play back fine on most set-top or computer DVD-players. The quality, due to consumer recording technology, is not as good as your professionally burnt Hollywood DVD-video, but will be sufficient for the project at hand.

Especially in the consumer market, there's an inflationary use of the term "broadcast quality." Consumers and most video equipment marketing people often seem to interpret the term as sharp and crisp-looking image quality. This is not the case. Blurred or noisy images can still be "broadcast quality" because that term only refers to strictly technical specifications that a commercial broadcast signal needs to comply with. So be careful when you buy desktop video editing equipment only because the package sports the label "broadcast quality." It might still be insufficient for commercial television.

FLASH FOR BROADCAST TELEVISION

Convergence, the unification of distribution channels, is a powerful concept in the entertainment industry and the goal that everyone is after. Cramming TV onto the web was for a long time the approach of choice and proved only mildly successful. With Flash, there is now an Internet tool, that sets out to make its way in the opposite direction, into TV.

Flash is an efficient software for the Internet and for animation on all sorts of computer appliances, no doubt about it. For all the well-known reasons, it has deservedly become the web entertainment's industry standard. But can it also become a viable tool for TV, video, or even film? Can it compete with established video motion graphics and animation technologies or find its niche?

Whenever a technology or an application from one media platform makes the quantum leap to another, there's a lot of buzz around it. If you filter the hype, though, the fact remains that broadcast TV now features music videos, trailers, commercials, and even entire cartoons, fully or partly produced in Flash.

Opportunities and Challenges for Flash as a Broadcast TV Tool

Even though there are companies that try to patent Flash-for-TV workflows, the application is still far from being a fully established or trusted broadcast animation or motion graphics tool. A lot of experimentation will have to be applied, before we can see all the possibilities that Flash might open up for broadcast media. In the commercial sector, it might need some strong arguments to win over clients who are used to spending big bucks for the most expensive video technology. When it comes to broadcast content or graphics for TV, Flash has four arguments going for it:

- **The Flash look.** This might be only a temporary argument, as styles change, but for image-conscious clients, this might be *the* argument to win them over. The Flash look with its bright uni color backgrounds, the placative typo, its geometrical shapes, and its ostentatiously simple 2D characters is very much en vogue these days, wherever you look (see Figure 11.3). Print design copies it and even TV ads and trailers emulate it using other standard video graphic tools. Very much like Graffiti at its height or more recently Digital Video, the Flash look enters the mainstream, combining sophistication with a certain street or even punk credibility. Whenever this look is called for, why not use Flash to create it?

FIGURE 11.3

The Piggidog character was created for an integrated German TV/web concept and clearly sports the Flash look.

- **The talent pool.** There is a very determined pool of Flash artists out there who massively pushes the boundaries—very much like digital video artists in the film industry in the '90s. The huge amount of talent and creativity, in the Flash community, both professional and amateur, has built up enough innovative steam, to pump creative energy back to the mainstream media. This is the new pool where the advertising and entertainment industry is fishing for ideas and talent.

- **Convergence.** "Create once, play everywhere" is a strong argument when advertising budgets, especially for the web, are scrutinized and cut down. Commercial content development increasingly focuses on simultaneous exploitation of distribution channels. But re-creating or reformatting of content for different distribution channels means additional and often unnecessary costs. Unlike video, Flash doesn't lose too much of its inherent quality when crossing the media boundary between TV and the web. Flash content comes closest to the ideal world of "creating once and playing everywhere." This is the niche where Flash might fit into video production, as more cost-conscious clients will be attracted to a technology that easily serves two media platforms at once.

- **Workflow and costs.** When it comes to creating animation, Flash is an incredible time and therefore money saver. Its drawing and designing functions are intuitive and easy to use when compared to many other motion graphics tools and due to the vector-based technology, incredibly efficient when it comes to CPU power, disk space, and render times. Also in contrast to many standard motion graphics or animation tools, changes can be made on-the-fly at almost any stage of the workflow. In the process of creation and reviewing, Flash can save a lot of time.

All the preceding arguments that speak so strongly for Flash as a broadcast tool were successfully tested in the production of Piggidog (see Figure 11.4), a cartoon character for a German TV show concept developed by Schwanstein Entertainment. The funny cartoon look, the great talent of Flash animators (Smashing Ideas' Matt Rodriguez in this case), the possibility to use Piggidog both on the web and on TV, and last but not least the incredibly quick and efficient production convinced the executive producer Stephan Reichenberger that Flash is indeed a viable broadcast tool, especially for creating cartoon characters.

FIGURE 11.4

Piggidog was a Flash-generated sidekick for show-host Erich Lejeune.

In the show's concept, Piggidog was designed to be keyed into footage of a virtual 3D set shoot to serve as a cartoon sidekick for human show host, Erich Lejeune. There had been earlier Piggidog designs by a traditional animator, but they had clashed too much with the look and feel of the computer-generated 3D set. Flash on the other hand offered the possibility to create a 2D character that combined tongue-in-cheek cartoon style with the sophisticated look of computer-generated images.

Producing the Flash animation took about a week, from first brainstorming to delivery of the finished files. After the client had selected the final design from a range of scanned and emailed pencil sketches, they sent an MP3 with Piggidogs's voice-over from Berlin to Seattle. With this soundtrack as a reference, the Flash animation was created: Piggidog talking, running, and jumping. In the end a whole set of mouths and body movements were uploaded as bitmaps onto the client's FTP-server. No recording to tape or burning CD-ROMs, no hassle with transatlantic overnight delivery. Back in Germany, the Piggidog files were keyed into the video, using After Effects and Media100 to composite, resize, move, and sync the animation's single frames with the video and the soundtrack of the virtual studio recording.

Planning Your Broadcast TV Project

Because Flash has not yet been fully integrated into professional TV workflows, such as other "prosumer" software like After Effects or Photoshop, there aren't many standardized Flash-for-TV procedures you can rely on at this point. Production methods, workflow, and workarounds will yet have to be invented, tested, improved, and standardized. For the time being, every new Flash-for-TV project is likely to pose new challenges.

Video production is a great deal more expensive than web production. You should therefore plan your Flash-for-TV project and its workflow carefully. Taking Flash-to-TV's specific challenges and limitations into early consideration can save a lot of frustration. Time and money for experimenting and testing is more wisely spent in Flash-preproduction than in expensive broadcast post. Be aware, that a "we fix it in the mix" attitude can prove increasingly dangerous the more technologies or formats are involved.

A lot of broadcast TV content and graphics are being produced on computers, and a lot is then played back on the Mac and PC via the Internet or local media such as DVD or CD-ROMs. Conversion procedures from TV to computer and vice versa are commonplace and, in theory, there's a technical solution for almost every transfer problem. If you've been on the wrong track, the good news is that thanks to all the different standards, formats, and technologies in video production, there's hardly anything that hasn't been converted, corrected, resized, or reformatted. The bad news is that the end product might not look like you wanted it to. Losses in quality, unforeseen problems in the conversion, and, most of all, the unexpected, and often considerable, costs that come with it can be frustrating.

And sometimes even the most sophisticated post production can't bail you out. Maybe the technology can't improve the look of your converted content or maybe it's just too expensive to fix. Your last resort could be to film your animation from a good computer screen. This had to be done for a well-known web cartoon, because no conversion process produced acceptable results for TV.

It does not take too much time to exclude the well-known problems from the beginning. So the most important advice when producing for broadcast TV is probably that you should consult with video professionals before you start to work in Flash and design *even* your Flash workflow accordingly. Test the *entire* production and conversion process with video engineers at your client network's facilities or consult independent post-production professionals *before* you sit down to your Flash animation.

Do consult the video pros, preferably at your client's network, and have them provide you with detailed technical specifications about what your Flash movie needs to have to do the following:

- To broadcast, in case you have to submit a finished master tape.
- To interface with the broadcast post-production workflow and its technologies, in case your Flash material needs to go into post to be formatted, corrected, or composited with other footage.

Don't underestimate the human element. There are very likely two camps here: the web-trained Flash artist, eager to prove that Flash can do anything, and the old video hand, that knows a million ways to do it just as well without Flash. If you deliver for a TV project, get in contact with the video post pros and have a talk about technical quality standards and the conversion process. Video techies very often despise anything that smacks of consumer market, like MiniDV or cheap software, especially when it enters their professional domain. Creating TV content or graphics with $300 software insults many video professionals. Because the conversion process from Flash to TV can pose challenges, it's good to have a technical contact at the network or the post-production facility, who won't immediately say "I told you so!" to you or your client. Video technicians are conservative for a good reason: they trust the proven methods before plunging headfirst into the unknown.

The different combinations of formats and technologies that you might encounter when working for TV, are probably too much for any non-video artist to keep up with. Your job as Flash producer should be to create great Flash content. You don't need to know everything that is happening on the video end of the production. But you should know, which issues are known troublemakers and what to ask from the video pros so that you can do your job of delivering high-quality Flash content that needs as little as possible correction.

The following section should give you an idea about what to keep in mind and what information to inquire about.

Resolution Formats

When outputting Flash to professional video, most careful pre-production planning should be applied to the question of which resolution format to use—that is, which aspect ratio your Flash movie should be created and delivered in—especially when it needs to be processed in a professional broadcast environment.

Beware, if all you know is that NTSC's "standard" format is 640×480. Even how-to articles for Flash often don't go further than that. But when working with commercial broadcast television and professional video post production, you will have to interface your computer workflow with professional videography and post-production technologies. In this case 640×480 might be the wrong choice.

Video technology has a long and successful track record of converting TV content back and forth between the different formats, and you won't be completely lost if you worked with the wrong format. But it is extra effort and extra cost, so for optimal results and smooth workflow, determine these things early with your TV client or your video pro consultant.

The following description of TV formats can serve as a checklist when planning your project.

NTSC (National Television Standards Committee)
NTSC is the American TV format used in North and Central America and also in Japan. It was developed in the 1950s and uses 525 horizontal lines to display an image. The frame rate for NTSC is 29.97fps.

When you work on an NTSC project, you have to watch out for the following resolution options in which you might have to deliver your files:

- **NTSC 640×480.** The format of 640×480 pixels is the de facto standard for NTSC desktop editing. It is certainly sufficient for noncommercial projects and in all-analog video environments.

- **NTSC 648×486.** This is the professional video industry's "preferred format" for analog NTSC and also supported by most NLE systems. The extra pixels here guarantee that your video's edges will under no circumstances be cut off in display. For consumer TV sets, this is an academic discussion because that area is already in an invisible range, but professional video workflows are often geared to the perfect 648×486. Many post production houses or networks prefer you to deliver this size.

- **D-1 NTSC 720×486.** Digital NTSC uses the same general 4:3 frame size as analog NTSC, so that it can be viewed on the same 4:3 TV set. But if you look more closely, you'll notice that although 640×480 has a perfect 4:3 ratio, 720×486 seemingly doesn't correspond to 4:3. The solution lies in the shape of the pixels. Digital NTSC achieves higher resolution by using rectangular instead of sqare pixels. That way the number of horizontal pixels in the 4:3 frame can be increased while the number of the vertical pixels remains the same.

Working with Square and Rectangular Pixels

Analog NTSC (like computer monitors) has square 1:1 pixels. Digital D-1 NTSC on the other hand, achieves higher definition by "cramming" more horizontal pixels (720) into the same 4:3 frame ratio, while keeping the vertical pixels at the same level (486). This can only be done by using rectangular pixels with a 0.88 pixel ratio instead of analog NTSC's 1.0 ratio.

Unfortunately, this division into a digital rectangular-pixel and an analog square-pixel geometry, can create problems when content from one world is transferred into another. Depending on the direction of the transfer, the frequent result is stretching or squashing of images.

This problem should be considered for your work in Flash. Because you create square-pixel art, you need to be conscious of the problem and take precautions so that your material won't be distorted or cropped, when it interfaces with digital rectangular-pixel content or equipment.

A lot of video hardware and software can interpret and convert rectangular versus square pixel sources correctly, if told to do so, especially when you are working with expensive high-end equipment and effects systems. But if you confuse square and rectangular sources or your video software can't handle this, you'll see distortions.

Simply, be sure to ask your post-production partner how to format your square pixel work for the digital workflow. An established method for video professionals to simulate rectangular pixel geometry in computer graphics, such as scans, Photoshop files, or Flash animations, is to set up and export the files with the bigger frame size of 720×540, import the artwork into an Adobe After Effects 720×486 composition and have the software do the conversion.

An alternative for shorter graphics file sequences, or if you don't have After Effects, is to create and export everything in 720×540, import it into Photoshop, and resize every file manually to 720×486.

PAL (Phase Alternating Line)

PAL is the most widely used television standard in the world, especially in Western Europe (except for France, which uses its own system, SECAM), in Australia, in much of Asia, except Japan and Korea, and in most South American countries. PAL was developed about a decade after NTSC and is generally considered to be the overall superior system. Images are better and sharper than NTSC's, because PAL uses 625 horizontal lines and a standard resolution of 720×486. A disadvantage of PAL is that it displays only 25 frames per second, which makes flicker worse. On the other hand, 25fps is not a fractional number, like NTSC's 29.97, and it's also close to film's frame rate of 24fps and therefore converts easily from and to film.

When you work on a PAL project, it never hurts to heed everything we suggested for NTSC projects. You won't have to be as concerned about colors, because PAL does better there, but the testing procedures should still be followed to avoid surprises.

Keep in mind that PAL, like NTSC, also uses different resolution formats: Analog PAL has 720×486, digital D-1 PAL has 720×576. Like D-1 NTSC, digital PAL also uses rectangular pixels, only with horizontal orientation as opposed to digital NTSC's vertical pixel orientation. To create rectangular pixel art from square pixel sources requires the same procedure as previously described for D-1 NTSC. The resolution to be used is 768×576.

HDTV

The best television format available today is HDTV, High-Definition Television. It still has only a niche existence but it is growing. HDTV's frame ratio is 16:9 and its resolution is either 1920×1080 pixels for interlaced images or 1280×720 pixels for progressive scanning system. Progressive scanning means that images are created in one pass and not two as with interlaced images.

Frame Rates and Timecodes

One of the first practical tasks when developing Flash animation for TV is to set the frame rate of your Flash movie. We have already discussed the methods of how to adjust frame rates of movies that have been created with less fps for the web. Here, the focus is on projects that are primarily or entirely aimed at TV. These projects of course should be produced from the beginning with TV frame rates. The following section should help to clear up some confusion about frame rates and timecodes, especially with NTSC. PAL's frame rate is 25fps, which for Flash projects is also handy, because all you need to do is set your movies frame rate to 25 and export to your NLE. No further considerations needed.

With NTSC on the other hand, it's once again not quite as simple. NTSC's frame rate is often given as 30 frames per second. This, however, is only an approximation, because the exact frame rate for NTSC is 29.97fps. The NTSC system departed from the previous perfect 30 fps for technical reasons when color TV was introduced.

For nonvideo professionals, the confusion often sets in when they are confronted with the fact that, NTSC timecodes obviously do use 30fps, as NLE's settings will often reveal. The answer lies in not confusing actual frame rate with timecode, which is simply a method of numbering your videos frames and synchronizing the numbers to time and duration of the video.

The timecode in 30fps is used for practical reasons, because nobody in video production can afford to figure out fractional 29.97fps with a stopwatch and pocket calculator to get exact duration and timing of video clips.

Having a real frame rate of 29.97 and a slightly "off" timecode, numbering 30fps, obviously generates an increasing discrepancy between a video's real duration and its stated duration on the timecode display. Therefore, standard NTSC timecode uses a trick to recalibrate its count to realtime. It doesn't drop or skip actual frames like the name "Drop-Frame Timecode" suggests, but only frame numbers. It simply skips displaying frame numbers in regular intervals to make exactly one hour of video appear as one hour in timecode.

Now where does that leave you as a Flash producer who has to deliver an animation for TV? The only thing to really remember and be aware of is that NTSC equipment always records and plays back at a precise frame rate of 29.97fps and not full 30 frames.

In other words, an exact hour's worth of programming will consist of 107,892 frames and not 108,000 as the 30fps might have suggested to you. If you deliver the latter, your animation is 108 frames or over 3 seconds too long.

Considering the practical workflow and the nature of Flash animations, this difference probably won't matter much in most productions. You may of course set your Flash movie to 29.97 as some video pros suggest, but the time and frame display in Flash is not as precise as in video equipment, so while creating your animation this might easily lead to additional confusion (see Figure 11.5).

FIGURE 11.5

For video purposes Flash's time display is too inaccurate and can lead to confusion.

Flash still displays a setting of 30fps in the field below the timeline, even when the actual frame rate is set to NTSC's exact 29.97 in the movie settings. However, Flash obviously calculates the correct duration of fractional frame rates. But this value is again given only in minutes, seconds, and rounded split seconds, not in minutes, seconds, and frames, as a TV time code would. To determine an exact timecode for a given frame in the timeline would require some calculation.

Longer Flash-generated programs, like cartoons, will almost certainly have to go into video post anyway, at least to mix and resync the sound to broadcast quality. In which case, it is always better to have a few frames too many.

If you have to deliver shorter motion graphics that need to fit an exact length, because they are used in a composition or because they are exactly timed for a programming window, then you should have your client give you the required length in precise frames and not only in minutes or seconds.

Once again, the frame rate issue, is something that should be mentioned and solved in preproduction planning. It is not a big deal for all practical reasons with most productions, but it's better to keep the terminology straight and not have to worry about the confusion it could create.

Interlacing Issues in Professional Post Production

Consult with your post-production partner not only on how to achieve best results for common interlacing problems, but also on how the process of interlacing or field rendering your computer graphics is handled. Depending on the nature of your animation or post-production's workflow, it might sometimes be better for you to provide a double 60fps instead of 30. (Make that 59.94 instead of 29.97, if your video techie is pedantic.) Interlacing fields from noninterlaced source material, the so-called "field rendering" process in programs like After Effects can yield better results when there is a full noninterlaced frame provided for each interlaced field to be created. Once again, considering that most Flash animations don't contain rapid motion, it probably won't make much of a difference. But ask the video pros, especially when your animation consists of fast-moving objects, shapes, or fills and you have made full use of your frame rate; that is, when every frame consists of a different in-between image.

If you don't have fast motion in your animation, your video pro will most likely tell you not to bother and simply to deliver 30 (29.97) fps for NTSC. For the "Piggidog" project in PAL, we submitted only 25fps and not the doubled 50. But because cartoon animation doesn't need fast motion to simulate movement, the composed video didn't confront us with any interlacing issues whatsoever (see Figure 11.6).

FIGURE 11.6

Piggidog's design didn't create any interlacing artifacts. His outlines are thick, anti-aliased, and there are hardly any thin horizontal lines.

Our conclusion on the Piggidog project was in every respect a successful test-run for Flash-for-TV production. Developing the character was easier and quicker than with any other animation method I have seen so far, and both the production workflow itself and the interfacing with the video post production was also smooth enough, that I don't see why Flash shouldn't make its way into broadcast TV. In the end, professionals and clients want an efficient technology that provides the best solution for the tasks at hand. Flash has its strengths and weaknesses when applied to video-oriented projects. One key to Flash's success in jumping the platform gap will be to take advantage of its strengths and to interface with other solutions and technologies wherever Flash can't do the job best. Thinking outside the box and designing innovative ways for workflow and technology interaction will be eminently important in planning and setting up Flash for TV projects.

FLASH FOR TV BROWSERS

Flash can be used to create interactive web-based content for television subscribers. Although terms in this industry vary widely, accessing web content through television is often called interactive television.

There's a large opportunity to create Flash programming to be deployed for television because Flash provides distinct advantages in this market. Compared to HTML, it's easy to create rich, high production value content for set top boxes using Flash. Games, shopping, tutorials, product demonstrations, digital greeting cards, chats, advertising, applications, and interfaces can be created quickly and with a minimal amount of layout problems. Flash provides a "what you see is what you get" application and design tool for TV browsers.

Designing for TV browsers presents a variety of challenges because the television does not display like a computer monitor and the set top box is definitely not a computer. Interactive television is such a new market that it's uncertain exactly what kind of programming consumers will respond to. As of yet there's still no "killer app" for the interactive television market. At this stage, what's definitely known is that the television is not a computer and people don't use it like one.

Web Access through the Television

Services such as MSN TV (**www.msntv.com**) allow viewers to access the web and proprietary online content through a special set top box that acts as a web browser. MSN TV provides a web access set top box that works with cable set top boxes, but needs to connect to the web through a standard 56K modem. In other services, the viewer's local cable company or a digital satellite provider supplies the web access set top box, the connection to the Internet (which can be broadband, narrowband, or both) and also controls access to proprietary content. Proprietary content runs the gamut from "walled gardens" containing entertainment, information, and useful applications to EPGs (electronic program guides), VOD (video on demand), and broadcast synchronization programs.

Web access through television tends to do well in parts of the world where home computer ownership is fairly low. A set top box is much cheaper than a computer, but still provides broadband or narrowband access to the parts of the Internet that people want to use—email, chat, information sites, search engines, music, and games.

As a service, web access through television has yet to be adopted in the United States by consumers or even deployed in a major way by cable companies. By contrast, the television has become a standard way to access the web in some countries, especially in Europe. In the United Kingdom, where 10–20% of people use interactive television, there's a viable market for web access television content.

What's a Set Top Box?

Anytime television viewers access the web or an enhanced TV program, they'll be using a set top box that contains a web browser. Sometimes called a receiver, set top boxes are made by large consumer electronics and technology companies such as Motorola (**www.motorola.com**),

Scientific Atlanta (**www.scientificatlanta.com**), PACE (**www.pacemicro.com**), and Philips (**www.philips.com**). Some set top boxes act as both the cable box and the web access box, while others only offer web access and must be used in tandem with a standard cable set top box.

The set top box severely limits the options of developers because it's not at all like a computer. Most set top boxes only contain enough computing power to get the most basic jobs done. They have slow processors and no hard drives. Set top boxes are designed to be as inexpensive as possible while still doing a decent job of displaying web and television content. Although they do this job admirably, designing for these devices is somewhat similar to designing for computers 8 to 10 years ago.

TV Browsers

Each set top box comes equipped with a TV browser. Because the browser is "built into" the set top box, plug-ins usually can't be upgraded. Some newer set top boxes allow the browser to be updated by putting the browser into Flash ROM, but the majority of boxes in consumer's homes currently do not.

This means that whatever plug-ins ship in the browser on the set top box will be what the viewer will always have. Because technology is evolutionary, many people with web access set top boxes will be stuck with old plug-ins. Early adopters of Web TV (currently MSN TV) still have set top boxes that can only display Flash 3. Those boxes still exist in homes around the United States. If those users never upgrade the set top box, then they'll never move beyond Flash 3. Developers need to be aware of the audience capabilities for viewing Flash content.

There are a variety of companies developing and deploying browser solutions for the web access, interactive, and enhanced television markets. Microsoft (**www.microsoft.com**), Liberate (**www.liberate.com**), Canal+ Technologies (**www.canalplus-technologies.com**), and OpenTV (**www.opentv.com**) are some of the best known of these companies.

The browsers these companies create allow content to be seen in web mode (web pages) or in TV mode (enhanced TV programming). It would be useful if all browsers adhered to the same standards and specifications (currently pushed by the Advanced Television Enhancement Forum at **www.atvef.com**), but sadly they do not. Instead, each company has developed specific browser technology that requires different development tools and practices to achieve similar results. The market is still too fractured with competing technologies to make creating standard web-based programming for television a straightforward exercise.

Luckily the browsers support various versions of Flash. This is why Flash is such a great solution for this difficult market—if the TV browser supports Flash, then it's possible to create one interactive television solution for playback on multiple set top boxes. Given that set top boxes might carry earlier versions of the player than is theoretically capable with the browser, it seems that Flash 4 is the most pragmatic choice for creating interactive television content at this time. The companies currently developing TV browsers support the following versions of Flash:

- Microsoft supports Flash 4
- OpenTV supports Flash 5

- Liberate supports Flash 5
- Canal+ does not support Flash

Challenges of Content Development for Television

Besides the basic Flash player version issue, there are a number of standard challenges in creating interactive content for television that developers must be aware of before they begin production. The following section sets out the main points that need to be understood and kept in mind throughout development.

Viewing Habits

With television, people are normally viewing the display from 8–12 feet rather than the 16–24 inches that is standard with a computer. There are also usually multiple people watching a television versus a single person at a computer. This means that graphics and text must be large to be readable and must stay on screen longer than when created for a computer monitor. Interface design should be simple and understandable from a distance. Multiple use for interactivity is more difficult, but it's useful to try to create interactive activities or content that allow more than one person to use in turn.

Simplicity

The television audience for web-based content may not have much exposure to computers or the Internet. Interfaces need to be kept extremely simple both for understanding and ease of navigation. The information architecture of a site or project needs to be extremely well-thought-out so that there are as few navigation categories as possible. Lots of choices will be hard to navigate on television and possibly confuse the audience.

Navigation

Most navigation of content on the television will occur with the tab button on an infrared keyboard or with the arrow keys on a remote. When navigating through interfaces on the television, it's standard for a yellow selector box or rectangle to surround the selected button or form element. This should be taken into account when designing interfaces so that important information is not obscured by the selector box.

Original set top boxes did not have a mouse with the keyboard. Although newer keyboards have a kind of mouse integrated into the keyboard, it's not nearly as responsive as a standard computer mouse so most users seem to still favor the tab key and arrow keys for quick movement around the screen.

To understand what this is like, set the mouse aside and attempt to navigate the web with only the tab key or the arrow keys. It can be extremely difficult at sites with complex navigation structures and becomes next to impossible if a site contains frames.

The biggest problem this presents to developers is that the tab and arrow control with buttons and form elements in Flash movies can be awkward. Flash reads elements for tabbing based on the horizontal and vertical positioning, the centerpoint, of the element. It's fairly easy to accidentally create symbols with centerpoints that cause Flash tabbing to move in an illogical manner through the interface, especially when form elements are added.

The other difficulty of navigation within most, if not all, TV browsers is that rollovers don't work. Buttons don't trigger the rollover action when tabbed onto with the keyboard or remote control, but instead trigger a press action. This creates real challenges for certain kinds of interface navigation that normally rely on rollovers such as drop-down menus.

Layout

Some TV browsers can't work with frames because the remote control won't move between them. It's best not to use frames in any layouts developed for TV.

HTML pages often have text layout problems on the TV browsers currently shipping with set top boxes. This is because many of the browsers, by default, increase the size of the fonts used in HTML pages for television readability.

Increasing the size of the font causes problems with text that wraps in columns or other well-defined areas of the page. Text that wraps in columns might end up with only one or two words per line. This quickly becomes unreadable. If there are fixed line breaks in the text, then the text can become hard to read because lines don't stay together properly when they break. Increasing the size of the font also often causes elements of the page such as graphics or Flash content to be pushed down or to the side in the layout.

This can definitely be a problem if Flash content is mixed with HTML content. It's important to carefully check the page layout on the television screen for text enlargement problems so that the Flash content doesn't get displayed in the wrong place.

Scrolling

Web users are used to scrolling down pages to access more content. Scrolling is still possible to do on televisions, but it's harder to do than with a computer mouse. The remote and the keyboard don't have the control over the interface that a mouse does on the computer. On some set top boxes and TV browser combinations, it's not even possible to scroll horizontally so content must fit the width of the television display.

The best solution to this problem is to make the content fit the screen size. Text and information can scroll automatically from right to left in the way it does now on news shows on television. In contrast, navigation can be provided to "flip" through pages of information more like a magazine.

Processors and Playback

Set top boxes are not computers with fast processors and good graphic cards. They are small, consumer devices primarily made to watch television. Their processors are slow and don't support intensive graphic redraw on the screen because that increases the cost of the box.

To optimize playback on these devices, stay away from the usual suspects in bad Flash playback, namely full-screen animation, animated transparencies, lots of symbols animating at the same time, animated gradients or transparencies, highly detailed animated drawings, and intensive ActionScript applications. With this in mind, keep the Flash movie as simple as possible while providing a rich experience.

Because creating content that plays back reasonably for TV browsers on set top boxes can be so difficult, it's important to develop for playback throughout the creative process. The most efficient way to do this is to plan the content and then begin creating it in a somewhat simplified format. At various stages of the production, test the playback on a TV browser and set top box in order to see if it works. If it does work, then it's possible to add more complexity to the design or animation. Keep testing the piece as complexity is added and then, at the point that it doesn't work well, it's possible to scale back slightly on the complexity to achieve proper playback.

The other way to develop content is to develop it as completely as possible. This will probably result in movies that are much too complex for reasonable playback on most set top boxes so it's then imperative to scale back the content until it plays properly. This is a reasonable way to work if the content must display well on computers (fast processors, good graphics cards) and on television (slow processors), but it's also very frustrating to have to cut back on the richness of content.

It's very difficult to create rich content that will play back well on both platforms so it's also possible to develop two separate projects in parallel, one for display on televisions and one for other devices such as computers. Although quite a lot of extra work in its own right, this may still be the most efficient way to develop content for these extremely disparate devices.

File Sizes

File sizes should be kept as small as possible because although many set top boxes are being delivered along with high-speed cable access, this is not always the case. It's important to know what the audience for content can handle because television viewers are not used to waiting for anything. If they've never been on the web and encountered download times for content, then it's likely that they won't wait for anything to load. Plan the file size of content according to what the audience can handle.

On the other hand, if the audience has broadband access, then take advantage of it and make content richer with higher-quality sound and images. These are the two main aspects of Flash production that add significantly to file size so don't compress the images too much and use stereo sound recorded at a high quality and export with little compression. This should result in higher production values in Flash content.

Hard Drives

Be extremely cautious about creating content that relies on the user having a hard drive. Although a few of the newer set top boxes have hard drives, most of them do not. This means that most content that requires client-side saving will not work properly. Cookies can no longer save user information and be retrieved by the Flash movie. It means that users will never have files cached on their hard drive and instead will have to get the files each time they visit a site. This represents a difficult situation because it makes preloading difficult and will normally extend loading times because every file in a site is loaded anew.

Connectivity

Set top boxes usually don't have great two way connectivity. The downstream rate (the speed of data coming into the device) is usually much higher than the upstream rate (the speed of data leaving the device). In many cases the downstream comes through a broadband connection, while the upstream goes through a regular modem connection over a phone line. Don't assume good upstream viewer connectivity when designing content. This seriously affects real-time content like chats, messaging, and games.

Multiple Windows

Most TV browsers don't allow multiple browser windows to be open at the same time. Avoid pop-up windows within a site because they will not show up properly. If there is a link to a pop-up window and the user selects it, then many TV browsers will show that window as a new full screen page on the television.

JavaScript and Other Programming Languages

JavaScript can be used with Flash movies to integrate more tightly into HTML pages and "talk" better with server-side applications. Unfortunately, JavaScript implementation is not standard across the different TV browsers so test against the target system early and often to ensure success. TV browsers are also mixed when it comes to adoption of Java or other controls such as ActiveX. Research the target platform before committing to developing content with these kinds of programming requirements.

Streaming Media

Flash can be used to combine with streaming media formats such as Windows Media Player. On systems where this is available, be aware that both Flash and video require significant processor resources. When the video plays, it's important that very little, if anything, is going on in the Flash movie.

Usually the video/audio will get the processor first so during playback the Flash movie will suffer dramatically. It's highly likely that frames will be dropped in the Flash movie when the audio/video is playing. If there's a lot of frame-based ActionScript, then the movie may not run properly because the ActionScript can be skipped.

Test, Test, Test

To review how web-based content will look in a set top box browser, it's possible to download the Web TV browser from Microsoft's web site. This is an incredibly useful tool for simulating playback of content on televisions and is available for both PCs and Macs. Currently the link is **http://developer.msntv.com/Tools/WebTVVwr.asp**. To work through the following examples, it's best to download and install this program.

Animation for TV Browsers

Let's look at a simple animation file to understand some of the issues surrounding Flash content for TV browsers and set top boxes. "The Prague Years" animation that was created for playback on Pocket PCs should provide a reasonable file to convert to television because the animation is fairly limited.

The first issue, and one that arises frequently with web-based content and television display, is that the cartoon is not at the correct dimensions. "The Prague Years" movie is sized at the vertical dimensions of 230×250, an incredibly awkward size for the horizontal dimensions of television (see Figure 11.7).

FIGURE 11.7

The cartoon doesn't look right on television at the size it was created.

The simple, but incomplete, way to deal with this is to surround the animation with a black "frame," set the background color to black (see Figure 11.8) and then resize the movie to 100% in the HTML (see Figure 11.9). This basically creates a letterbox style around the movie (in the case of "The Prague Years" this is vertical rather than horizontal, as you see in Figure 11.10). Unfortunately television viewers expect a full-screen experience so this quick and easy way to get simple content on the television is not that useful in the real world. Feature films are resized to fit television screens partly because viewers don't like letterboxing on their televisions.

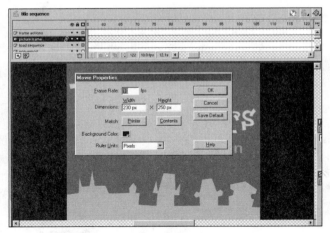

FIGURE 11.8

Change the background of the movie to black in case any of the movie bleeds outside the frame.

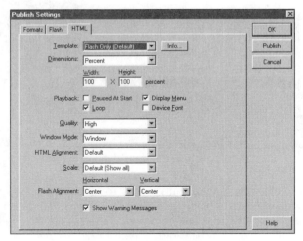

FIGURE 11.9

Resize the Flash movie in the HTML document.

FIGURE 11.10

"The Prague Years" letterbox is vertical.

 It's important to add vspace="0" hspace="0" in the BODY tag of the HTML page in order to make the Flash movie appear flush at the top and left sides of the television.

The difficult, but much better, way to get movies in the right dimensions is to resize the entire animation inside of Flash. Although time consuming, resizing does provide the best viewer experience.

1. The first step is to change the movie size to 640×480 in the Property Inspector (see Figure 11.11).

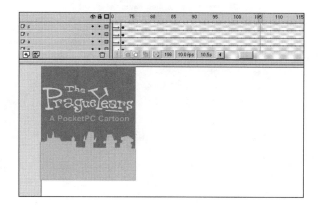

FIGURE 11.11

The movie stage area must be resized to 640×480.

2. Create a rectangular box that's exactly the same size as the new movie dimensions. An easy way to do this is to create the rectangle, select it, and use the align tool to resize it to the same size as the movie stage (see Figure 11.12). Make it a symbol and call it movie resize tool.

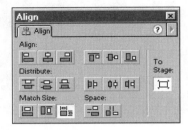

FIGURE 11.12

Create a movie dimension rectangle to help resize and place the graphics in the movie.

3. Now select this symbol and scale it down proportionally to the size of original cartoon. Place the symbol over the original cartoon so that it shows how the cartoon will "fit" into the larger movie dimensions (see Figure 11.13). When the cartoon is resized to fit the larger movie dimensions this will provide an easy visual cue to how the cartoon needs to be moved around the stage.

FIGURE 11.13

Proportionally resize the movie symbol to the size of the original cartoon.

4. Next, change the view of the graphical elements from solid to outlines. There are two ways to do this. The first is to select the small square box above the layers in the timeline (see Figure 11.14). This will Show All layers as Outlines. The second is to select View, Outlines. This turns the graphic objects into aliased outlines (see Figure 11.15). This can be useful when working with huge number of graphic symbols because it uses less computing power to render them. However, it can also make working with them difficult because the lines aren't graphically clean.

FIGURE 11.14

Select the small square box above the layer names to turn all the graphics on the layers into outlines.

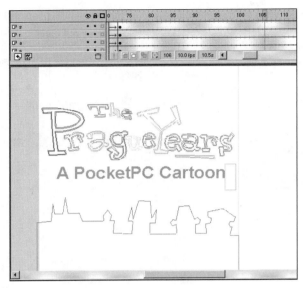

FIGURE 11.15

Turn graphics into aliased outlines to work more quickly and with less strain on the computer.

5. Unlock all the layers. Select the Edit multiple frames version of the onion skin and move the onion skin select heads to select all the frames in a scene (see Figure 11.16).

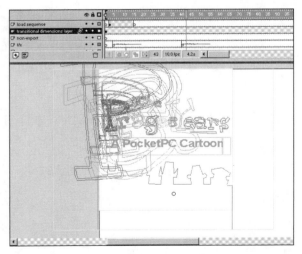

FIGURE 11.16

Use the Onion Skin tool to edit all the frames in a scene at the same time.

6. Be sure the stage is the active area by clicking on it with the arrow tool. Select all the objects on the stage with Edit, Select All (see Figure 11.17). In Flash 5, if the stage is not selected as the active area then Select All will select all the frames in the timeline instead of the graphics. This is an easy mistake to make.

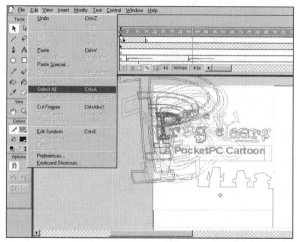

FIGURE 11.17

Use the onion skin and then the Select All command to select all the graphics.

7. Resize the graphics to the new movie dimensions using the Movie Resize tool symbol as a visual cue. When the Movie Resize tool symbol is the right size and matches the outline of the stage, then the resize has been successful (see Figure 11.18).

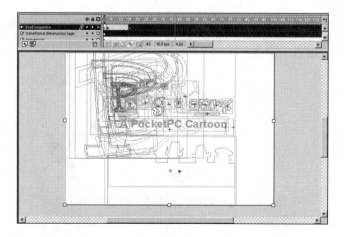

FIGURE 11.18

After the Movie Resize tool symbol is the same size as the movie stage area, the cartoon has been properly resized.

8. Turn off the onion skinning.

9. Change the view of the graphics back to normal by selecting View, Antialias Text or clicking the small square at the top of the layers (depending on how the graphics were turned into outlines).

10. Play back the scene to see if any objects were missed in resizing.

It's then possible to go through the movie scene by scene and quickly resize the entire animation and motion graphics sequence in this way. What quickly becomes apparent in transforming "The Prague Years" cartoon is that there is an enormous amount of detail missing from the sides of the cartoon. A lot of work will need to be done to fill in the background of the cartoon out to edges of the new movie dimensions.

PROBLEMS IN DEVELOPING ANIMATION FOR TV BROWSERS

Now that the cartoon is resized, it's crucial to check for any serious problems with viewing it through a TV browser. The main areas to check for in developing animation in Flash for TV browsers are playback, line, color, and bandwidth issues. The easiest way to do this is to review the animation on a TV browser emulator for the computer, such as the MSN TV browser. It's even better to view it directly on the target device, but this is often impossible.

Playback

"The Prague Years" was created for playback on handheld devices so all the action is shown as large as possible. Unfortunately, this means that a lot of the animation doesn't play back well on televisions when displayed full screen. In the Web TV browser even a simple walk cycle against a static background is very jerky and halts from moment to moment at full screen (see Figure 11.19).

FIGURE 11.19

Full-screen Flash animation through a set top box doesn't play back quickly enough.

To fix this the animation needs to be resized or the scene needs to be restaged. The easier of the two is to resize the animation (see Figure 11.20). Follow the steps described previously to make all graphic elements in the scene smaller. This may require that the background gets filled in around the edges, but this is generally preferable to completely reanimating a scene.

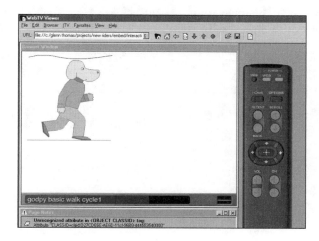

FIGURE 11.20

The walk cycle plays back at a faster speed when it's made smaller.

Lines

The lines around the characters in "The Prague Years" are hairlines (see Figure 11.21). Hairlines were originally used because of the reduced size of the handheld display and the way Flash resizes lines in symbols (line widths scale differently when symbols are resized). Unfortunately, using hairlines makes the lines fuzzy when playing back on television.

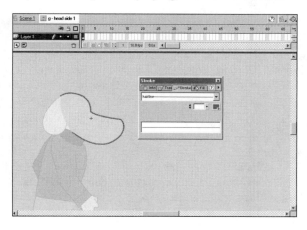

FIGURE 11.21

All the lines in "The Prague Years" are hairlines.

There are a number of solutions to this. The easiest is to live with a bit of flicker and say that television viewers are used to bad display. Although possible, it's unlikely the average viewer will enjoy poorly displayed animation.

The more time-consuming solution is to redo all the lines at a higher pixel width—over 2 pixels (see Figure 11.22). This line width resizing is an option that should be experimented with because it may or may not help the animation in question.

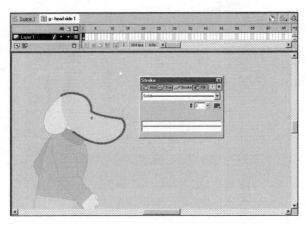

FIGURE 11.22

Lines larger than 2 pixels should look better on TV.

To get around the line-scaling problem, on resize it's possible to turn all the lines into paint fills. Select any line and then choose Modify, Shape, Convert Lines to Fills to make the line into a graphic fill. Unfortunately, this might significantly slow down the animation because using paint fills takes up more of the processor.

Color

After reviewing the cartoon in the MSN TV browser emulator, it's obvious that there are serious problems with colors in the cartoon. The color palette of the cartoon is, in general, much too bright for television. Using the television color safe palette discussed earlier in this chapter, it's important to go through the cartoon and tone down the colors to display properly on television.

There are a variety of solutions to this problem. It's possible to take all the RGB values of the colors in the Flash movie and create a color palette in Photoshop. Run the NTSC Colors filter on this palette and then transfer the new RGB values back to the colors in the Flash movie. It's quicker to take the RGB values and check the safety of the color in a tool like the one online at MSN TV (currently **http://developer.msntv.com/tools/colorpick/Default.htm**). This tool also contains a web-safe color palette that can be clicked on to determine the closest TV safe color. If the colors aren't TV safe, but still view reasonably on many different television screens, then it's possible to skip this step.

There can be problems with trying to get colors safe for television quickly. As an example, in certain instances throughout "The Prague Years," symbols with tint effects are shown as the wrong color on some television screens (see Figure 11.23). This is extremely distracting as symbols used to build the characters move between different shades throughout the cartoon. In this case it would have been better to develop the cartoon without using tint on symbols.

FIGURE 11.23

Symbols with tint effects might display with the wrong color values when shown with "TV safe" colors by the browser.

In "The Prague Years" this happens most often when the patch symbols are tinted using the Tint effect. The patches match other symbols when there is no Brightness change, but when the other symbols' color values have been changed with Brightness and the patch has the Tint effect to match this, the color values don't seem to match on a TV display. They match perfectly on a computer monitor, but the color shifting that occurs on a television display makes them a real problem.

The simplest solution to this problem is to create a new set of character patches for each main color in the cartoon's color palette (see Figure 11.24). These patches can then use the Brightness effect rather than the Tint effect to match color values (see Figure 11.25). Although this adds to file size in the Flash movie, it does fix the color problem.

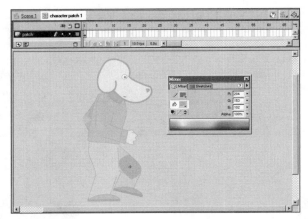

FIGURE 11.24

Create new color patches for the colors used in the cartoon's color palette.

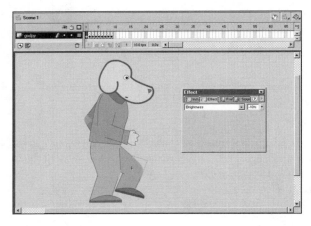

FIGURE 11.25

Use Brightness to match these color patches to the underlying symbol colors.

Bandwidth

"The Prague Years" was created for narrowband devices with small built-in memories, so file size is not an issue. If the target audience has broadband, then the cartoon could be significantly improved by outputting audio at a higher quality and adding more music or sound effects to the cartoon.

As can be seen, there's quite a bit of work that goes into redoing a simple file for proper display and playback on television. It's often much easier to create the simplified version for television first or create it in parallel to a more robust version for the web.

There are no hard-and-fast rules for creating great animation for playback on television displays through a TV browser. It takes a lot of trial and error to get the right combination of line, color, and animation that will play back well on these devices.

The optimal situation is to create a style of character and animation that is suited to display on TV browsers. Styles that work well are paper cut outs as in Blue's Clues, limited animation as in Japanese anime, and any other simple form of animation. There's certainly no chance to create feature film quality lifelike character animation in Flash for this platform.

Because it's fairly certain that the animation won't be the best part of the production because of all these playback issues, be sure that the story, writing, dialogue, and sound are fantastic. Great animation can't carry a bad story, but a great story can survive mediocre animation.

Interfaces for TV Browsers

Flash can easily create full rich media web sites for interactive television. Rather than clunky HTML page refreshes (page "blinks") when a user selects a navigation option, a more seamless, media-like experience can be created.

A hypothetical Flash site navigation will show tricks to developing for tab-based input devices such as remote controls or keyboards. In the example presented here, a company wants to create a web site about living on islands. The site needs to be accessible to TV viewers using a remote control. It's a straightforward site with only six main categories of navigation with several subcategories under some of them.

The standard way to create this navigation in a Flash web site would be to provide navigation at the left or along the top and then use drop-down menus or menus that pop out to the right of the main buttons. To investigate tab order, we'll place the navigation on the left.

The first step is to create a standard button that TV viewers will recognize as a button (see Figure 11.26). Standard TV browser navigation is not the place to win sophisticated art director design awards. Interface navigation design needs to be relatively large, cleanly designed, and easy to navigate. TV viewers are probably not used to highly designed navigation and will gravitate toward the simplest, easiest experience. In this case, a bevel edge signifies that the button is a button.

After the standard look and feel of the button is created, it's time to place the six buttons of the primary navigation on the left side of the screen. The first layout has the navigation bottom justified to the screen. This can be a problem in television displays because the TV browser might take up part of the screen and cut off the bottom button. Although it's possible to scroll down to what's cut off, it's better to design so that no scrolling is needed.

In testing with the MSN TV browser, the bottom button is cut off so the buttons need to be moved up the screen. It's important to begin designing a web site for TV browser display with an understanding of how much space the browser will take up in the screen.

After the buttons have been moved up so that they're all viewable (see Figure 11.27), it's time to test how easy it is to move around the buttons with the remote. In this case the buttons are so simple that the up and down remote buttons will move through the buttons properly as will the left and right remote buttons.

FIGURE 11.26

Viewers should recognize that a button is a button.

FIGURE 11.27

Main navigation should always be immediately viewable by the television audience.

The next step with the navigation is to add a rollover-type effect to open second tier navigation (see Figure 11.28). Unfortunately, the rollover action with buttons doesn't normally work for television because the remote doesn't work like a mouse.

To create a rollover effect, the button action must be changed to on press to make the second tier navigation pop out (see Figure 11.29). Rollout can't be used to close the second tier navigation so a more complex system of ActionScript must be created to track which button a user has activated and then provide an action depending on the next button a user moves to. Creating navigation for use by a remote control on a TV browser is definitely more difficult than creating navigation for a computer with a mouse.

FIGURE 11.28

Using rollover navigation is a standard interactive navigation practice.

Now the main problem with the navigation begins—the tab order is odd because of the second tier navigation. Flash moves around buttons and form elements based on the centerpoint of the symbol. Even though the centerpoints on all the buttons are the same so the order of the buttons is consistent and logical, it's still really easy to accidentally jump between the secondary navigation and the primary navigation by mistake (see Figure 11.29). It's not clear to the viewer when this will happen and why it happens because the viewer does not understand Flash tab order problems. To the viewer, it just doesn't work properly.

FIGURE 11.29

The viewer can easily jump from the second tier navigation to the main navigation by mistake, sometimes missing buttons in the process.

One solution would be to send all the primary navigation buttons, except the button with the open secondary navigation, to a non-button state in a movie clip. This would then mean that the viewer would have to go back to the original primary navigation button before moving on in the navigation. It would take some ActionScript to manage a complex navigation system, but it would work. It may not be the most intuitive navigation system for viewers so it's best to test this on any particular project.

After the secondary navigation is open, quite a lot of code needs to be written to track and then close the secondary navigation. Because there is no rollover state with most remote controls, it's impossible to know what specific parts of the navigation to close or not to close by simply using an invisible button (as would normally be the case in a Flash 4 movie). Instead, the whereabouts of the tab focus must be tracked at all times programmatically in Flash 4 syntax. This isn't a fun process to develop for in the more limited programming range of Flash 4.

There really isn't a great solution to the problems with this kind of standard interactive navigation design other than keeping navigation structures as simple as possible. Drop-down menus have fewer tab order problems than left side navigation so they might be a preferable starting point for layout.

The next part of the example file is the addition of a form element (see Figure 11.30). This form element messes up the left side navigation even worse. If the secondary navigation is open, it causes the remote to miss several of the main navigation buttons. It's then difficult to move around the interface to get to those buttons. This is because the centerpoint of the form element is at a different coordinate value than the buttons and takes over access to some of the buttons.

FIGURE 11.30

Form elements can quickly throw off tab navigation.

The easiest solution at this point is probably to redesign the entire site interface so that these tabbing issues don't exist, whether that means shifting to fewer navigation elements or reordering on the page. If that's not possible, then a good way to handle this is to go to a brand new page inside the Flash movie for form input. On the new page, the number of elements can be lowered so the tab order can be more easily controlled. When the user finishes the form or cancels the form input, the user is sent back to the main navigation. With television interfaces, less is much, much more.

Navigation keys don't use frames. However, they keep centerpoints for buttons in a consistent place, turn form elements into symbols and keep their centerpoints in a consistent place, and lay out the elements of the interface and test navigation before creating the whole site.

FLASH FOR ENHANCED TV

Enhanced TV offers content and data enhancements to traditional broadcast programming. In the standard scenario, a small visual icon appears during the programming that alerts the viewer to the fact that interactive content and information is available. When the viewer selects to see the enhanced experience, the interactive areas will either overlay the video or surround a smaller video feed.

In a news program, for example, the viewer could click the alert icon to access a news story in more depth. A popular show or movie could be surrounded by a chat application to allow geographically separate viewers to talk about what they're watching or just make new friends. A game show can allow viewers to play along in real time with the television show and even compete with all the other interactive players.

Given current viewing habits, it seems that news, sports, game shows, financial and educational programming, how to programming such as cooking shows, infomercials, music videos, and advertising offer the most robust areas to focus on creating enhanced television.

 Be sure that the interactive content adds to the TV show rather than distracts from it. Keep the interactive elements complementary to the show rather than the focus. Viewers will still primarily want to watch the television show.

Flash is beginning to be integrated into the synchronization tools that create these enhanced television experiences. The way enhanced television works is that triggers are created and sent over a portion of the broadcast signal with the television show. The trigger requests that the set top box load specific web-based content load and combine it with the television picture.

There are two types of triggers, both based on standards created by the ATVEF (Advanced Television Enhancement Forum, **www.atvef.com**). The ATVEF is a consortium of companies creating protocols for enhanced programming and its delivery to television.

Type A triggers deliver the information about the web URL over the broadcast signal and then require a modem connection to download the web-based content. Information delivery is in line 21 of the vertical blanking interval (VBI), the same line used for closed-captioning.

Type B triggers deliver both the URL and the content over the broadcast signal. Type B triggers can use lines 10 through 20 of the VBI, but can only use a certain number at a time. Broadcasts might be using these lines for other reasons as well.

Both types of triggers have advantages and disadvantages. Type A triggers deliver content more slowly, but never run into broadcast signal problems. Type B triggers can be faster, but require more of the broadcast signal to be free. Because interactive content creators don't always have control over this situation this can cause problems.

The exact technical nature of the ATVEF triggers is described in the documentation on its web site, but the main parts of the trigger defines the content that is requested, where it is requested from, and if there's an expiration date on the content.

Liberate operates a free partner program to gain access to its suite of tools, while both Microsoft and OpenTV offer a fee-based partner program. Liberate's program provides partner materials such as a television emulator that can play back enhanced TV programming on a PC if a TV card has been installed on the computer.

Over the next year, the enhanced TV market will begin to consolidate and provide opportunities in the United States to create programming. Until then, it's best to keep an eye on what's happening in the field and be ready for when opportunity arrives.

SUMMARY

Flash is an incredibly powerful tool for getting content quickly and cheaply onto one of the most powerful devices in the world, the television. People can watch TV in more ways these days, whether as regular programming, through recorded devices, as a web-access device, or in combination between the web and broadcast. Flash is the only tool that can create rich media content for people to watch in every way they might watch TV. With careful planning and execution, Flash can be used to create high-quality, engaging content for the device at the top of the media pyramid—the TV.

12

DEVELOPING FLASH CONTENT FOR THE SONY PLAYSTATION 2

by Fred Sharples

The doors that open with the idea of Macromedia Flash on Sony PlayStation 2 are dazzling: interfaces for games, media browsers and players, online game interfaces, Radar and HUD layers for 3D games, multi-user puzzle and board games, and cartoons.

However, Flash on the Sony PlayStation 2 isn't just a cool idea. It's already being used successfully in games out on the market.

The user interface systems on LucasArts *Star Wars Starfighter*™ and its sequel, LucasArts *Star Wars Jedi Starfighter*™, are created in Flash (see Figure 12.1). Our company, Orange Design, was hired to develop these projects.

You can find more information on LucasArts *Star Wars Starfighter*™ and its sequel, *Star Wars Jedi Starfighter*™ at

http://www.lucasarts.com/products/starwarsstarfighter/
and
http://www.lucasarts.com/products/jedistarfighter/

FIGURE 12.1

Main menu screen of *Star Wars Jedi Starfighter*™.

Orange Design is a small Flash studio based in San Francisco. We specialize in Flash applications, including games, business applications, and entertainment-related Flash web sites. We were fortunate to be asked to create the first publicly released Flash application for the Sony PlayStation 2. The Flash application was the graphical user interface for the LucasArts *Star Wars Starfighter*™ game. As with the other Flash-enabled devices, this one is changing rapidly.

In this chapter, we will take some educated guesses on the direction this change is going and provide some in-depth knowledge about how Flash can work on the PlayStation 2. Additionally, you'll find out about

- The advantages of developing game user interfaces in Flash
- Flash, game code logic, and their relationship
- Working with other programming languages
- The immediate future of Flash on PlayStation 2 and the Xbox

At press time, there are some licensing, technology, and timing issues that have yet to be worked out by Macromedia and its partners before a Flash Player for PlayStation 2 is released to the general public or Sony developers. The player that we will be discussing in this chapter is not available to the general public at this time. Please stay tuned to the http://www.macromedia.com web site for upcoming information and announcements about possible Flash products for the PlayStation 2. Also be sure to check out the book's website, http://www.flashenabled.com, and the New Riders' site, http://www.newriders.com, for up-to-date information.

THE THREE VERSIONS OF THE FLASH PLAYER

First, let's take a brief look at the three versions of the Flash Player available on the PlayStation 2 that have been shown or discussed by Macromedia, Sony, and Secret Level.

Secret Level is a development shop that develops tools, technology, and titles for the console game industry. Secret Level ported the Flash Player to Sony PlayStation 2 for LucasArts and Macromedia.

Generation 1: The Stock Scanline Flash Player (Flash 4)

The Stock Scanline Flash Player is a software port of the Flash Player that was completed in 2000 by Secret Level and was licensed to LucasArts for use in *Star Wars Starfighter*™. It does not take full advantage of the PlayStation 2 hardware and supports Flash 4 files only. It does not support the loadMovie command so we had to build the entire UI into one SWF file. Additionally, the performance of this player was an issue. We only had adequate frame rates when anti-aliasing was disabled and so we were only able to use very small and subtle animations in this interface. Although this player does support sound in Flash, we used the game code to play external sounds to keep the memory footprint low.

Generation 2: Strobe (Flash 5)

This is the code name for Secret Level's hardware-accelerated port of the Flash Player for Sony PlayStation 2. This is another port of the Flash Player for game developers, but is unique in that it utilizes a proprietary renderer developed by Secret Level. This renderer interprets Flash content into triangles that can be hardware accelerated by various 3D hardware. This version of Flash is capable of 60 frames per second and is the clear choice in further game related projects. It plays Flash 5 content and has also been ported to Xbox and DirectX 8x. It also supports loadMovie, allowing more bitmaps and larger files in general. Like its predecessor, the Strobe player supports sound embedded in the Flash movie, but we opted to use external sounds instead. This is the version of the player we used to develop the user interface for *Star Wars Jedi Starfighter*™.

Internet Version of the Flash Player

A precursor of the Internet version of the Flash Player was demonstrated at E3 (Electronic Entertainment Expo) in May 2001. Sony made several announcements at the Expo relating to the Sony PlayStation 2 and the Internet.

Sony will be releasing a Network Adapter and Hard Drive that will allow users to browse the Internet. The Network Adapter will use a DSL or cable modem and utilize a dual stack of Cisco's IPV6 and IPV4 protocols. This will let older systems with the current Internet protocol connect to the device, as well as the next generation Internet Protocol V6-enabled device. The main advantage of IPV6 is that it will be faster and expand immensely the existing set of IP addresses. It will also have improved auto-configure capabilities and better security.

Sony has also announced a partnership with AOL, who plans to deploy instant messaging, chat, email, and a version of Netscape on the Sony PlayStation 2.

Finally, Sony announced that Real Network's Real Player would be the basic streaming media player for the Internet platform on the PlayStation 2. Additionally, a software development kit will be made available to licensed game developers that will allow them to create Internet-enabled game titles.

Sony has announced five game titles that users can play over the Internet:

- *Tony Hawk's Pro Skater 3*
- *Twisted Metal Online*
- *Tribes II*
- *Frequency*
- *SOCOM*

At press time, there are a lot of unanswered questions for Flash developers who will use the Internet version of the Flash Player. These are some of the issues to be addressed:

- Will Sony PlayStation 2 users be allowed to browse the entire web?
- If not, how will Sony and AOL control the content?
- Will there be access to the Flash Player and tools to those who are not licensed Sony developers?
- How will the Flash Player perform in this environment?

Even with these questions unanswered, it seems clear that all the big players are behind this version and it seems to have the most potential and value for the majority of Flash developers.

FLASH DESIGN IN ACTION: OUR EXPERIENCE WITH LUCASARTS

This section relates our general experience gained as we built the first Flash application for the Sony PlayStation 2. We used the 1st Generation Flash Player and believe that a lot of what we learned will be useful to those of you who are reading this book to create Flash applications for the Internet or for game elements and interfaces.

When LucasArts first contacted us to discuss the user interface for their upcoming PlayStation 2 title *Star Wars Starfighter*™, we believed that we would be developing working design comps of the user interface in Flash before they committed their team to the task of building it out. We had a few meetings before it was revealed to us that we were actually going to be creating the interface itself, not simply designing it. We would be using a top-secret Flash Player that runs on the PlayStation 2.

A quote from the LucasArts Team from *Game Developer Magazine*:

> *"We had heard that a small San Francisco-based company named Secret Level was adapting Macromedia's Flash technology for us in Sony PlayStation 2 games...Macromedia content-authoring tools were far more elaborate than anything we could come up with in the same time frame. We also suspected that there was a wealth of Flash authoring expertise available from out-of-house contractors, which would help us smooth out the work load."*

LucasArts obviously needed a well-designed user interface for its game. The interface had to be easy to use, beautiful, and bring something new and fresh to the genre. It also had to be inexpensive to develop and easy to modify and localize. LucasArts wanted a team that didn't take away resources from its core technology and design group who were busy building out the game itself.

We suppose LucasArts chose Orange Design to build the interface because of our technology experience. Our web site and game style at the time was not very sci-fi and we think that there was some worry about us pulling it off design-wise. We found the challenge to be perfect for us. We got to play with a new style and genre and bring our experience into the mix. We were very surprised by the open-mindedness and flexibility we had from the LucasArts team. It was a great experience working with a team of their caliber.

Overall the project was a success and our design team, Mark Del Lima and Keiko Chaffee, received kudos for their great work from the press and from the LucasArts team. We built on that success with the subsequent release of *Star Wars Jedi Starfighter*™, where the team included Mark Del Lima, Keiko Chaffee, Pamela Miller, and Fearghal O'Dea. (See Figure 12.2.)

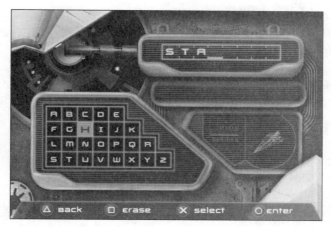

FIGURE 12.2

Code screen from *Star Wars Jedi Starfighter*™.

THE ADVANTAGES OF USING FLASH FOR SONY PLAYSTATION 2 GAME TITLES

In this section we will explain the differences between using Flash and using the traditional design process to build user interfaces for Sony PlayStation 2, and in doing so, illustrate the advantages to using Flash for console development.

Traditional Design for Console Games

Here is an overview of the traditional design process for console games. We will look into teams, software, and labor involved with this process.

Traditional Game User Interface Team

The traditional user interface team on 3D games consists of highly skilled 3D artists and programmers. Usually, the team is a subset of the team that created the game. Often times the user interface is left to the junior members of the team while the senior members stay on the game, working through bugs and polishing the art. Generally, the user interface is left until the end of the project when the team is tired, the money is tight, and the pressure to deliver is highest.

The user interface is usually not seen as glamorous and therefore it generally winds up not looking very sophisticated. There are many exceptions to this, but traditionally the user interface is left to the last second and therefore ends up being rushed.

Dedicated Software

In larger game development companies, the user interface is sometimes developed with a custom-created application that provides a rudimentary graphical user interface for the artists. The artist can lay out the elements and export a data set that includes the graphic bitmap, position, and sometimes behavior information that is saved and sent to the programmer. This dedicated software is custom made for each shop so artists must learn the proprietary tool. This knowledge is not transferable to other tools. A programmer must be available to maintain the application and make adjustments when necessary.

Procedural Layout and Animation

In most cases, the artists and programmers have to lay out the user interface using hand-coded coordinates. Adjustments are made pixel by pixel. Each iteration of changes requires a recompile that can take several minutes.

Sprite animation is even more difficult, requiring a programmer to calculate motion paths. If the path is erratic, straying from clean curves or straight lines, the artist has to give the path data on a frame-by-frame basis.

Impact of Late Changes to User Interface in Traditional Design

All this is further complicated by late changes to the user interface. A simple name change can require code changes and require an artist to go back to his image editing software to change it. In the procedural method, text is either presented by the game hardware or created by the artist as bitmaps. Using bitmaps looks better and gives flexibility over kerning and type effects. Device fonts can be changed more easily but there is no real way to preview how they will look until the game or user interface is compiled.

Designing User Interface for Console Games Using Flash

Flash provides several advantages over using the procedural method to create user interface elements. We'll compare this with the procedural process by looking at the typical team, tools, and labor.

Typical Flash User Interface Team

The typical Flash team is generally made up of a programmer and a Flash artist. In many cases this can be the same person.

Experience

The ubiquity of Flash gives a game development team a choice from a vast pool of talent. The wild, and sometimes unwieldy, experimentation of user interface on the web has resulted in a great number of innovative ideas. For every yearlong console game development cycle, a typical Flash team will have developed a dozen or more user interface projects for various applications and web sites.

Rapid Development

Flash is now a fairly mature product, having gone through several improvements to workflow and usability. These improvements make it much faster to develop a project than with a custom-made application that has had only a few revisions. Flash's maturity also means that many Flash artists have spent several years with it, making development extremely fast when compared to the procedural development process in the traditional method.

Impact of Late Changes to User Interface

The flexibility of Flash and the simple fact that web development is so fluid makes teams of Flash designers and programmers ready for last-minute changes. We learn to create projects that are modular. We keep all our text editable throughout the process. A project that is properly designed can be localized into other languages very quickly. On *Star Wars Starfighter*™, for instance, two people were able to localize the Flash user interface into Italian, German, Spanish, and French in about one week.

USER INTERFACE LOGIC FOR FLASH IN A GAME TITLE DEVELOPMENT ENVIRONMENT

By itself, Flash does not have the capability to handle all the duties required to interact with the PlayStation hardware and game code. In this section we'll discuss some of these requirements and look briefly into the custom protocols and logic needed for the project.

Communication Protocol between Flash and the PlayStation 2 Hardware

For the Flash interface to act and react it obviously needs to communicate to the PlayStation 2 game and PlayStation 2 hardware. For this communication to occur there will have to be some type of middleware that the user interface can talk to in its own language.

Middleware between the PlayStation 2 and Flash can be thought of as a type of interpreter between the actual C++ game code that controls the game and the Flash user interface and Flash. It can be as simple as some script functions in a text file.

There is a strong tendency to overlook the length of time it takes to build out the middleware layer for Flash. It is important that whoever takes on this task is highly skilled and has full knowledge and understanding of the underlying game code.

Who Drives, Flash or the Game Code?

There has been a lot of discussion with similar applications whether to create a "state machine" in C++ that basically drives Flash completely. A state machine is an application whose only job is to keep track of the state of the game and the user's actions. In this case, Flash would simply tell the state machine what buttons were pressed and the state machine would tell Flash which frame to go to or what info to display, and so on. There would be no logic inside Flash at all in this scenario. Because of various resource issues we decided that creating a state machine would be more time-consuming and be harder for us to test and debug.

So it seemed smarter for us to handle all questions and drive the UI on the Flash and ActionScript side. In other words, Flash asked all the questions. The middleware would never tell Flash what to do unless asked. When Flash got to a specific screen, we would ask the middleware layer from Flash what the state of things were and display based on the answer we got. For instance, we could ask the middleware layer if the user had unlocked certain missions in the game or what the current controller analog stick sensitivity setting was (see Figure 12.3). The middleware would simply respond to the current stick sensitivity query with something like "30". We would take that number and tell the display graphic to display the result (in this case a progress bar).

FIGURE 12.3

Controller settings from *Star Wars Starfighter*™.

Alternatively, if the user wanted to change the controller vibration setting, we would show them the settings as they pressed the arrow keys. In this case we would increase or decrease the progress bar using tell target commands. Once the user stopped and pressed the OK button, only then would we send back the corresponding number to the middleware layer that set the controller sensitivity setting.

Flash Commanding the PlayStation 2

In the Secret Level port of the Flash 5 Player, the procedure is to call a middleware function via the getURL Flash command in the format:

"callback://*function*."

For instance, to set the Sony PlayStation 2 to play in stereo sound mode, we would tell the middleware:

getURL ("callback://SetStereoStatus 2");

This calls the function in the middleware layer called **SetStereoStatus** and sets it to stereo (2). If we wanted to set the mode to mono, we would set this number to 1. This choice of digits is arbitrary and decided in the middleware layer. The middleware needs to actually be set up this way to communicate the information to the Sony PlayStation 2.

PlayStation 2 Code Commanding Flash

Of course, we have to ask questions of the middleware layer to get information about the Sony PlayStation 2 hardware settings or game settings.

For instance when we get to the sound screen, before displaying anything, we want to ask the middleware layer what the **stereoStatus** is.

getURL ("callback://GetStereoStatus stereoStatus");

One interesting thing here is that we set up the middleware to let Flash set the name of the return variable. So Flash is saying "tell me what the **stereoStatus** is and put that value into the variable named *stereoStatus*".

We built the UI and middleware as we went along and found that we needed to change variable names sometimes to keep them from sounding like they belonged to something else. For instance, the variable name *memorycardMessages* became *memoryCardAlerts* when we added alerts to the memory card screen.

So, getting back to the check for the StereoStatus value, the Sony PlayStation 2 would give us a value of 1 or 2 and then we would tell a movieclip to do something with it. Usually, we would go to a frame on a movieclip that would display Stereo or Mono.

The interesting thing is that when we query the middleware, we have to let the Flash movie go to another frame to actually receive the data, so all routines are at least two frames long. Now we will have the second part of the routine on the next frame:

```
play();
if (stereoStatus == 1) {
    // tell the stereo indicator movie clip to display mono
    mc_stereoStatus.gotoAndStop("mono");
} else if (stereoStatus == 2) {
    // tell the stereo indicator movie clip to display stereo
    mc_stereoStatus.gotoAndStop("stereo");
}
stop();
```

This two-frame routine can complicate things. Sometimes you are checking something on the PlayStation and then you can be "pulled" from that check mid-frame by a user action. The result is usually that you get stuck in a frame. Sounds weird and it is. You have to be ready for people to hit keys over and over again rapidly. Having a **play()** action at the beginning of the second frame seems to resolve these interruptions.

Other than these few issues, ActionScript behaves as expected on the Sony PlayStation 2 platform. We find no behavior differences between ActionScript in the web player and the Sony Playstation 2 player. There are only a few obvious things missing such as FSCommands and other external data calls such as loadVariables. In some ways it is easier than developing for the Internet in that file loading is not an issue and you don't need to account for latency to server-side applications.

FIGURE 12.4

Sound screen from *Star Wars Jedi Starfighter*™.

USER INTERFACE DESIGN ISSUES FOR SONY PLAYSTATION 2

There are several important issues to take into consideration when planning your first user interface for a game. The obvious ones are related to the game itself and are of course different for each game. There are a number of common variables that are important to understand when creating all PlayStation game interfaces.

Overview of Relevant Sony Requirements

One of the most important and somewhat daunting aspects of UI design for Sony PlayStation are the Sony Requirements. The Sony Requirements are a lengthy list of required behavior and messaging relating to the Sony hardware. Different regions can interpret these requirements differently so it's important to be conservative and to have a good understanding of them when beginning your design.

The Sony Controller and Key Mapping to Flash

Behind the computer and mouse, the Sony PlayStation Controller may be the most popular UI device in history. If you think about how many PlayStations there are on the planet and how many hours people spend holding the controller, it's sort of frightening because the controller is so incredibly simple. There is no keyboard and no mouse, yet you can drive such amazing experiences with it.

As a Flash designer, you constantly have to think of how to present complicated choices and decisions to a user holding the Sony controller.

For instance, what do you do when you have to spell a name? What if you have two things on the screen that are both controlled by the right and left arrows? How do you warn players who press the OK button quickly over and over in a series of alerts that doing so in certain cases will result in data loss?

Fortunately, Sony and its licensed developers have dealt with these problems. The trick for UI developers is to stretch the line between experimentation and the Sony Requirements. The Sony Requirements can be complicated and passing the test is tough. In *Star Wars Starfighter*™ we were dealing with a new machine that wasn't even released so we were all extra worried about these requirements.

So the Sony controller needs to be flexible, but familiar (see Figure 12.5). In some countries the OK button is the circle button. In other countries the OK button is the X button.

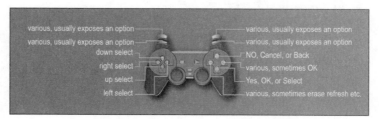

FIGURE 12.5

Sony controller with general mapping guide.

In some cases you have to break these rules. For instance in the alert that asks, "Are you sure you want to format the Memory Card?" we swapped the OK button functionality with the Cancel button functionality—a user wouldn't accidentally hit OK to delete every game he has been playing.

Translating all this to Flash is pretty simple. Each key has a corresponding ASCII letter key on a normal keyboard. The Flash developer simply makes some buttons that react to the key presses. The key mapping on the first generation player is done on a developer-by-developer basis. When or if the Internet version of the Flash Player comes out, we think that the key mapping would be part of the player. One of the shortcuts we made that helped with localization was that we made movieclips out of the buttons on the screen that we always reused.

The movieclip would always make a call like

parent.script.o_button_pressed();

In every screen where there was a layout of buttons, we always included this script that contained this call. So when we had to localize and swap the X button functionality for the O button functionality, we could swap out the code in the clips to change their behavior everywhere.

The Sony Memory Card

It is important to realize that dealing with memory cards is very difficult, very unglamorous, and can easily take up half your programming time. You have to deal with every thinkable issue when it comes to memory cards (see Figure 12.6).

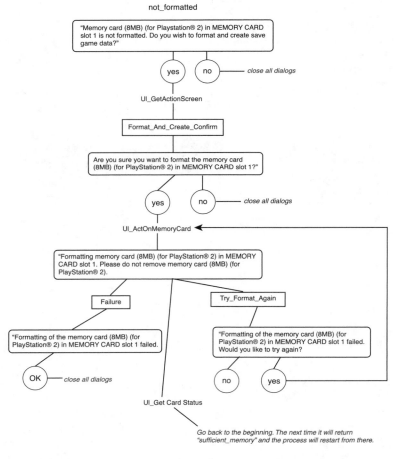

FIGURE 12.6

Example flow of the memory card format functionality.

For instance, here are just a few of the issues you need to deal with:

- Is the card full?
- Is the card formatted?
- Does the card have saved data on it?
- Is it a PlayStation 2 card?
- Is the card damaged?
- Are you formatting it?
- Is it done formatting?
- Are you reading from it?
- Did you tell the user how much space is on the card?
- Did you tell the user how big the game data is?
- Is the user sure he wants to format, create a game, or save one?
- Are you telling the user that the card is being read or written to?
- Did you warn the user not to pull out the card or swap the card?
- Did the user do that anyway?
- Did the user do that to both memory cards in both memory card slots?

So you get the idea. This is just a partial list we put together. It does not go into what happens after each Yes and No answer. Don't underestimate the time it takes to do this. There are no real shortcuts except perhaps having a knowledgeable person help you through the planning process.

Memory Footprint Issues

The memory footprint of the UI needs to be small enough to fit into RAM along with the player and parts of the game code. In our project, we did not run the actual game at the same time as the Flash UI and player.

Because of the frame rate issues and some minor renderer anomalies, we used bitmaps extensively. They took up more RAM than vector art but they always looked much better. It is surprising how much you can compress images and still have them look fine in NTSC mode. In most cases on *Star Wars Starfighter*™, we had to "butterfly" bitmaps. Because the designs were mostly symmetrical, we were able to split the bitmaps in two and remove one side (see Figure 12.7). Then we would use a symbol instance of the bitmap, duplicate it, flip it, and bring it together to show both sides.

You can "butterfly" graphics that are symmetrical in order to save memory.

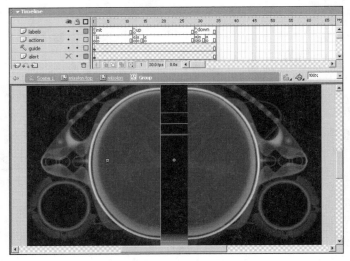

FIGURE 12.7

"Butterflying" a background image in _Star Wars Starfighter_™.

In _Star Wars Jedi Starfighter_™ we had the luxury of using the loadMovie command so we had much more flexibility when it came to memory issues. However, in both projects, we had to compress bitmaps extensively to fit.

Compressing bitmaps to save RAM memory is very different than compressing for the normal Flash web player. In RAM we are concerned with the "unpacked" size of an image. So compressing a big bitmap down to 30% using Flash export settings will not help much. The bitmap will still expand to close to its original size once it is used. Therefore, we needed to compress the image outside of Flash and then import it to save the optimal memory.

We used JPEG compression in both versions of _Star Wars Starfighter_™. Remember that you need to test on NTSC while compressing images. What looks bad on your monitor can be perfect on NTSC.

For more information on creating content for output on television, see Chapter 11, "Flash Content for Television."

Frame Rate Issues

The frame rate of the first generation player was frankly slow. Game developers shoot for 60 frames per second. On the web we are often satisfied to approach 24. By using more bitmaps and animating smaller areas of the screen, we were able to achieve something close to 24 frames per second. However, when using the Flash 4 version of the player, toward the end of the project, when everything was looking really nice, we begin to notice the poor quality of the fonts. The only way around this issue was the playback quality setting on the player. Basically, we set the player to "high" quality mode which anti-aliased the fonts, but brought performance down to a crawl.

So in the end, we threw out all our animation and transitions. It was a painful experience that we wouldn't want to repeat. Fortunately, there was some time at the end of the project to put in some new animations that were subtle and small enough to perform and give the UI some life. We used bitmaps when we could and minimized our use of alpha channels.

On the LucasArts *Star Wars Jedi Starfighter*™ project using the Strobe version of the Flash 5 Player, we ran into frame-rate issues when displaying large amounts of text. To get around this issue, Secret Level and LucasArts created a system to display the fonts as bitmaps rather than as triangles. We had to set all text fields as dynamic text—the player would read these and replace them with bitmapped system fonts. This was very effective but made the display of double-byte characters more difficult as you will read in the next section. To display double-byte characters, the only real solution is to use outlines laid out on a timeline.

The performance lessons learned here can be applied to all Flash players coming out on devices. Use small areas of the screen and don't use alpha or if necessary, only use it sparingly. The horsepower and screen drawing speed may not be there but there is only so much you can do despite it.

Localization Considerations

One of the ways that we saved money and time in the *Star Wars Starfighter*™ project was when we decided to localize into other languages. Imagine the labor involved in localization using traditional console UI design. In the Flash user interface for *Star Wars Starfighter*™, we created versions for French, German, Italian, and Spanish in just one week (see Figure 12.8).

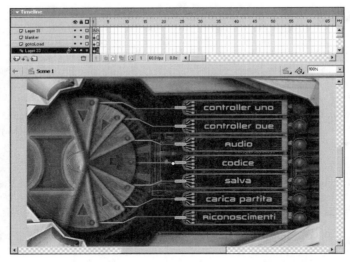

FIGURE 12.8

Localizing *Star Wars Jedi Starfighter*™ into Italian.

Text Length Issues

Our recommendation is to take all the text in your file and create an Excel doc with every word of text in it. Then, get a German translation early and apply the German text to your interface design before it is "locked in." (Of all the languages we were localizing to, German words usually take up the most space.) Place the new translated text into the Flash file early to be sure that your design is viable and flexible enough.

Double-Byte Character Support

If you will support Japanese or other languages that require double-byte characters, test early to make sure your C++ code and/or Flash Player is double-byte compatible. Make sure that dynamic fields display the characters correctly. In the current version of the Flash Player we use, dynamic text fields will not support double-byte text. Therefore, we needed to make sure that all the displayed text is made into outlines and laid out on a timeline.

Work with a native speaker if possible. It's too easy for English-speaking designers to mix things up if they don't understand the characters. It's a luxury to have someone right there with you.

Keep Everything Flexible

Keep ActionScript issues in mind, such as button functionality changes and text editing, as you build the project. Use text that can be edited in Flash whenever possible. Be sure to leave room around the edges of your text for unplanned changes. Even when you prepare, sometimes word lengths in other languages will surprise you.

Use an Experienced Designer

You need to have a Flash designer place all the text for every language. The Flash designer has to have a grasp of the structure of the file and where all the hidden alert movieclips are and so on. Also, the designer will have to make adjustments to the design; for instance, you want the balance of the buttons on the screen to be clean so you will have to adjust their locations to adapt to different button label lengths.

On LucasArt's *Star Wars Starfighter*™, we attempted to create a translation page in the Flash file so that a translator with no Flash experience would be able to simply paste the translated text into this page and the code would then display it throughout the file (see Figure 12.9). Technically, this is not difficult, but the end effect was visually inadequate. Because of the different word lengths in each language, we had a great number of alignment and word wrapping issues that could not be adjusted to work across all languages. Also, this method will not work for double-byte characters as we described earlier.

FIGURE 12.9

Star Wars Jedi Starfighter™. main menu screen development cycle.

THE FUTURE OF FLASH DEVELOPMENT ON CONSOLES

This section looks into the near future of Flash on Sony PlayStation 2, as well as the Xbox and PC. Before the players are released to the public, there are many variables and decisions to be made by Macromedia and Sony. Let's look into the best-case scenario and assume that these issues will be solved shortly.

Flash Player for the Internet

Currently, Sony only allows developers to use its tools and licenses after it approves of the game concept and the developers pay Sony a considerable sum. In return, Sony helps to distribute and market the games and provides developer support. Sony sees this approach as important to ensure that only high-quality games are available on the Sony PlayStation 2. Because Flash does not show off the Sony PlayStation 2 3D hardware, it does not seem likely that Sony will approve of normally distributed game titles created in Flash.

Having Sony support Internet Flash content could change the relationship between Sony and developers dramatically. It could open a large new market for Flash developers. There would be a large demand for online and multiplayer gaming, interfaces to existing web sites, and applications such as photo-viewing applications, media players, and financial software. Flash could easily become the de facto interface tool for the Sony PlayStation 2 applications.

Flash Player for Sony PlayStation 2 Game Developers

If the Strobe Flash 5 Player is released as a software development kit, the future for Flash in Sony PlayStation 2 games looks bright. The performance is much improved; we have proven that this approach, even when using the first generation player, is cost effective and viable. It was a success as a technology and the resulting design was a great accomplishment. Very few people realize that they are looking at Flash when they look at the *Star Wars Starfighter*™ UI or *Star Wars Jedi Starfighter*™. I think that's a good sign of technology and design integrating well.

What excites us in this space is the opportunity for using Flash as a layer above the game. This would allow us to use Flash for more of the overlay elements like HUD, Radar, and other real-time data.

What also excites us is the fact that the kit plays on Xbox and other devices using DirectX technology. This could open many new doors for Flash developers. The Xbox and PC version of LucasArt's *Star Wars Starfighter*™ have recently been released using the Strobe Flash Player. We expect that the release of *Star Wars Jedi Starfighter*™ will also use the Strobe player.

SUMMARY

In this chapter we explored the three different flavors of the Flash Player on the Sony PlayStation 2. We hope to see the public release or license of the Internet and Strobe version of the player soon and we anticipate that the Internet version of the player will be powerful as a user interface element to web applications.

We have shown that Flash on the PlayStation 2 is viable technically, aesthetically, and is financially advantageous over the traditional design process.

As more developers begin to use the Strobe player, we hope that they find the section on middleware and Sony hardware code requirements useful. In particular, we want to emphasize the need to brush up on these topics and to avoid underestimating the time it takes to handle Sony hardware, especially the memory card requirements.

We've found that although there are several issues with the Flash Player in regards to frame rate, we were able to surmount these with several design solutions, using bitmaps when possible, using bitmap rendered text, and avoiding the normal culprits like multiple alpha effects.

The memory issues we ran into were improved greatly with the Strobe player's loadMovie functionality; however, we still needed to reduce bitmap size on many screens using compression outside of Flash.

We want to re-emphasize the importance of planning for localization early and being cautious about double-byte character limitations in regards to dynamic text fields.

In the end, we hope you find this chapter useful, whether you are planning on using the Strobe player or the Internet player for Sony PlayStation 2. We are excited about the possibilities and we hope we have shed some light onto this new market for Flash developers.

PART V: THE FUTURE OF FLASH AND EMBEDDED DEVICES

CHAPTER 13 Afterword: Looking Forward

13

AFTERWORD: LOOKING FORWARD

by Troy Evans, Macromedia Flash Player Product Manager

How far we've come...

Since joining Macromedia in August 1999, I have watched Macromedia Flash Player develop from a player to a ubiquitous standard.

Upon my reflection I have witnessed the rapid evolvement of technology. In 1999, there was no concept of mainstream devices, such as personal digital assistants (PDAs) and smart phones.

One defining event occurred in 1998, when Flash Player was bundled with Netscape Navigator browsers and Microsoft Windows 95 and Windows 98. This prompted the creation of Flash content as well as Flash Player adoption.

Today Flash Player is the Standard Rich Client for Internet content and applications. It has the capability to create rich presentations, compelling user interfaces, interactive experiences, and applications (for example, online banks, reservation systems, digital dashboards). It is also extensively used for navigation control in hybrid Flash/HTML applications.

Some examples of the utilization of Flash Player can be found at the following:

- At Broadmoor (**www.broadmoor.com**), Flash is used for the interface to the reservation system, leveraging its rich media capabilities.
- General Motors (**www.gm.com**) uses Flash for its dynamic menu systems.
- USABancShares (**www.usabancshares.com**) has an online banking system completely created using Flash.

THE STATE OF DEVICES TODAY

Consumers and enterprises are migrating from desktop to devices, enabling the convergence of devices and data.

The delivery of compelling Flash content and applications on these devices excites consumers. For instance, for hardware manufacturers and service operators to become successful in the device space, they must convince consumers that they need to adopt new technology. This is why content plays a critical role in the creation of the value proposition for these new markets.

You, as Flash developers, already are delivering the content that motivates consumers to promote platform adoption.

Twenty percent of Flash developers plan to work on the development of devices such as PDAs and smart phones in the next year. Will you be next?

DEVICES IN THE FUTURE

"The web is about connecting people to computers through browsers to information. Two new waves will surpass the web: an executable Internet (applications) that greatly improves the online experience, and an extended Internet that connects the real world."
—*Forrestor Research*

Growth in devices (smart phones, PDAs, gaming consoles, and other mobile and embedded devices) is expected to outstrip desktop growth by 2004.

These devices will be connected to the Internet and sufficiently powerful for Flash Player. And in many cases, these devices will be marketed in contexts where Flash's strengths in design, media, and applications will inevitably make them powerful contenders.

The next wave on the Internet will feature rich applications with responsive user experiences. This wave will include both in-browser and out-of-browser applications.

As a Flash developer, these new challenges present you with the opportunity to bring the web to this next wave.

As Flash improves users' experiences and provides rich applications on the Internet and devices, the need for more Flash developers increases; as a developer, you can have a positive effect on the Internet and devices. You now have the information at hand to create content for Flash-enabled devices.

Troy Evans
February 2002

Troy Evans *is currently the Macromedia Flash Player Product Manager and has served as Product Manager since 1999.*

PART VI: APPENDIXES

APPENDIX

FLASH PLAYER FOR THE NOKIA 9200 COMMUNICATOR SERIES AUTHORING GUIDELINES

The authors would like to thank Macromedia for granting permission to use the material in these guidelines.

The Nokia 9200 Communicator series includes cellular mobile phones and devices that combine many key elements of third-generation technology. This technology includes a high-resolution color display, high-speed mobile email, a new user interface, and multimedia capabilities such as full-color video clips.

Macromedia Flash Player 5 is compatible with the Nokia 9200 Communicator series. Using Flash Player makes a wide range of applications and entertainment available to mobile users everywhere. Flash Player is also available on numerous platforms—including web browsers—and this ubiquity lets you author content once and deploy it to multiple devices and platforms.

Thanks to the individuals and organizations who provided content, examples and input for the Authoring Guidelines:

Mario Campion, Team SmartyPants
Troy Evans, Macromedia
Chris Gannon, GRAPHICO
Jim Hatlo, Cisco Systems
Chris Pelsor, Razorfish
Anna Marie Pises, Macromedia
James Rowley, Publicis Networks
Fred Sharples, Orange Design
Emile Swain, AKQA
Phillip M. Torrone, Flashenabled.com
Dan Webb, AKQA

SUPPORTED PLATFORMS

Flash Player is compatible with the Nokia 9200 Communicator series.

You can find more information on the Nokia 9200 Communicator by visiting: **http://www.nokia.com/phones/9210/index.html**.

LANGUAGES

Flash Player for Nokia 9200 Communicator series supports the following languages:

- Czech
- Danish
- Dutch

- English
- Finnish
- French
- German
- Hungarian
- Italian
- Norwegian
- Polish
- Portuguese
- Spanish
- Swedish
- Turkish

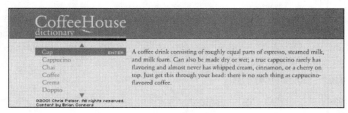

FIGURE A.1

Example Flash App for the Nokia Communicator: CoffeeHouse dictionary (created by Chris Pelsor).

Player Installation

Flash Player for the Nokia 9200 Communicator series is available on the Nokia software installation CD and from the Macromedia web site.

To install Flash Player on your Nokia 9200 Communicator from the Nokia 9200 Communicator software CD:

1. Connect the Nokia 9200 Communicator to your Windows computer.
2. Insert the Nokia software installation CD.
3. Follow the instructions on the screen, which will prompt you to install Flash Player.

You may also install Flash Player directly from the installation CD:

1. Connect the Nokia 9200 Communicator to your Windows computer.
2. Double-click the Flash_Player.SIS file found on the Nokia software installation CD.
3. Follow the instructions on your screen.

The player will also be available from the Macromedia web site: **http://www.macromedia.com/go/flashplayer_nokia_download**

To install Flash Player for the Nokia 9200 Communicator from the web site:

1. Download the Flash_Player.SIS file to your desktop computer.
2. Connect the Nokia 9200 Communicator to your Windows computer.
3. Run the Flash_Player.SIS by double-clicking on it.
4. Follow the instructions on your screen.

Once Flash Player has been installed on the Nokia 9200 Communicator, it can be accessed via the Extras menu on the Nokia 9200 Communicator.

DEVELOPING CONTENT

Developing Flash content for the Nokia Communicator is very similar to developing content for the Pocket PC. They both have slower processors and limited screen size. This section describes guidelines specific to developing content for the Nokia Communicator.

New Flash Player Functionality

Flash Player for the Nokia 9200 Communicator series has new platform-specific functionality:

- Pause button
- Volume control dialog

For more information on these features, see the "Controlling Playback" section.

Optimizing Flash Content for the Nokia 9200 Communicator

Because the processor on the Nokia 9200 Communicator is significantly slower than the processor for the Microsoft Pocket PC Player and desktop player, it is extremely important to take movie performance optimizations into consideration from the beginning of a project.

For tips and tricks on how to optimize Flash content for playback on the Nokia 9200 Communicator, see the individual sections that discuss specific optimizations.

By following some simple guidelines and carefully authoring your content, you can provide rich and compelling applications for the user.

Screen Size

One of the most important factors to keep in mind when developing Flash content for the Nokia 9200 Communicator is the screen size. The full screen resolution is 640×200, which is available when the Flash Player is running full-screen (see Figure A.2).

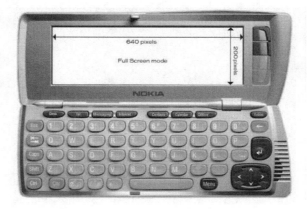

FIGURE A.2

Nokia Communicator with screen dimensions.

However, if the Flash Player is not running full-screen, the maximum space available to the Flash movie is 486×200. If the dimensions of the Flash movie are larger than the size that can be displayed fully on the screen, scroll bars will appear to indicate to the user that the entire movie is not visible. Figure A.3 shows an example of a Flash movie running in a player with the menus visible.

FIGURE A.3

Flash movie running within the Flash Player.

Sound

The Flash Player for Nokia Communicator has full support for sound output. However, due to the processor limitations, there are a number of caveats. Figure A.4 shows a sample sound game.

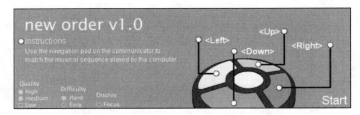

FIGURE A.4

new order sound memory game (created by Emile Swain, AKQA).

While mono MP3 is the only supported MP3 sound output, other MP3 settings may work. However, the quality of the playback depends primarily on the CPU utilization of your Flash movie at the time that the sound is played. Existing stereo MP3s may sound choppy at times due to their CPU processing requirements. We recommend that when using MP3 sounds, you only use mono sounds exported at 8kbs.

In addition, the Communicator will not play higher than 8KHz. Because of this we recommend that when using ADPCM and RAW sound formats, you sample it at 8KHz. This is because the device will resample anything over 8KHz, and thus sounds over 8KHz will only lead to higher processor utilization without any additional quality in sound.

The sound export settings for a Flash movie can be adjusted in the Flash Publish Settings window by choosing File, Publish Settings, Flash (see Figure A.5).

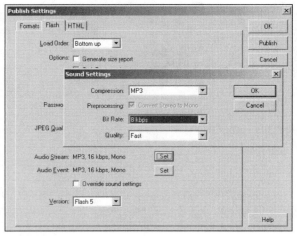

FIGURE A.5

Screenshot of setting sound output settings in Flash authoring device.

All other sound output formats available for export from the Flash 5 authoring environment are supported in Flash Player on the Nokia 9200 Communicator.

When processing a sound object in ActionScript, the Flash Player must take the following steps:

1. Create sound object in ActionScript.
2. Open audio device for playback (if it is not already open).
3. Play audio.

It is possible that all three steps will not be processed fast enough and the sound object will not play. This scenario is especially true if the sound is triggered at the beginning of a movie before it has completely initialized.

There are two solutions to this issue:

1. Make sure that the movie has fully loaded and initialized before allowing any sound events to be triggered.
2. Constantly play a silent sound object in the background of the movie. This step will ensure that the audio device is kept open and eliminates one of the preceding steps necessary to play a sound.

Fonts

Flash Player for Nokia 9200 Communicator Series includes two built-in device fonts:

- _sans (_serif is mapped to _sans)(proportionally-spaced font)
- _typewriter (standard-spaced font)

However, you are free to use any other font in your movie as long as it is embedded within the movie. Figure A.6 shows a sample application using fonts.

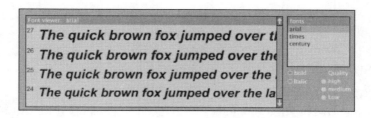

FIGURE A.6

Font Viewer showing font output on Flash Player 5 (created by Emile Swain, AKQA).

Input Methods/Keyboard

The Nokia 9200 Communicator contains a small, fully functional QWERTY keyboard, and it is the preferred method for text input (see Figure A.7).

FIGURE A.7

Nokia 9200 Communicator keyboard.

A number of hot keys exist in the Flash Player that have changed to conform to the Nokia 9200 Communicator Series standard:

- Exit has been changed from Ctrl+Q on the desktop projector to Ctrl+E on the Nokia 9200 Communicator.
- Full Screen has been changed from Ctrl+F on the desktop projector to Ctrl+T on the Nokia 9200 Communicator.

In addition, a number of new hot keys have been added to the Flash Player on the Nokia 9200 Communicator:

- **Cut**   Ctrl+X
- **Paste**   Ctrl+V
- **Copy**   Ctrl+C
- **Select All**   Ctrl+A
- **Toggle Cursor**   Ctrl+Q

Editable Text Fields

Flash Player for the Nokia 9200 Communicator Series has full support for text fields.

When the cursor is moved inside the editable text control, pressing and releasing the Enter key or double-clicking the space bar will cause the text control to take focus. When the editable text control is in focus, the virtual pointer will disappear and a beam cursor will appear inside the text control. All the keys (including space bar, Enter key, and arrow keys) will now work inside the context of the editable text. However, the user can select text using the Shift key and the arrows. Text selection is allowed only when the text control is *not* in focus. The user may use one of two techniques to select text:

- Move the virtual pointer to the beginning of the text string to be selected and then press down the spacebar to toggle from mouse-up to mouse-down state. At this point moving the arrow keys will cause the text string to be highlighted to the point of the position of the cursor. The user must press the spacebar once more to toggle from mouse-down to mouse-up state to complete the selection.

- While holding the Shift key, use the arrow key buttons to move the cursor and highlight the text you would like to select.

Once the text string is selected, you can use the Copy function under the Edit menu (or press Ctrl+C) to operate on the selected string. Cutting and pasting can only be done when the text field is in focus.

Navigation

The primary means of navigation within the Flash movie is through the use of the cursor, which is controlled by the Nokia 9200 Communicator arrow keypad located on the bottom right of the keyboard (see Figure A.8).

FIGURE A.8

Arrow keys on the Nokia 9200 Communicator control the cursor in Flash Player.

Tab Key Navigation

To be qualified as a Nokia-compliant application, an application has to be useful without using the pointer tool. This requirement also applies to Flash Player. However, when the pointer tool/cursor is turned off, the Tab key and directional arrows can navigate and change focus within a Flash movie.

The order of tab navigation is based on a left-to-right, top-to-bottom order. Tabbing is halted at the boundary (sides) of the Flash movie, which means that off-the-screen movie elements might not be directly accessible to the user. However, a user can tab to an off-screen element and Flash Player will bring focus to the element on screen.

The following rules apply when using the Tab key for navigation within a Flash movie:

- When each control is in focus, a yellow rectangular highlight will appear on the boundary of the control to indicate the focus.

- When a button is in focus, it will enter into the rollover state.

- Drag events are not possible (because there is no way to simulate a click-drag interface).

- When in Zoom-in view, the next "tab" selected item will always be partially visible in the viewing area, which means the page might be auto-scrolled to make the focus item visible.

- The Enter key will execute the onPress event of a button or enter into edit mode for an editable text field.

- Once an editable text field is in edit mode, the user may use the Esc key to leave edit mode, or use the Tab key to move focus to other control (thus reverting to focus navigation mode).

- Enter and Esc have no effect on the visibility of the cursor when in Tab key mode. Rather, the user has instant text-editing control in a highlighted text field.

Mouse Events/Buttons

The Flash Player was designed as a primarily mouse-based system, and a lot of Flash content relies on mouse-based events to drive the user interface. For example, developers may attach ActionScript to different states of a button that are triggered, depending on how the user interacts with it.

Although the Nokia 9200 Communicator provides a virtual pointer interface, it is not the equivalent of a mouse. Because of this, there are a number of limitations that the user and developer must be aware of.

As discussed previously, the four directional arrow keys control the movement of the virtual pointer. The Enter key is used as a left mouse button and there is no emulation of the right mouse button. The virtual pointer also uses the spacebar as a convenient way to momentarily toggle the mouse button up or down. (Note: After the user has momentarily changed to the mouse-down state by using the spacebar, the Enter key will act illogically and generate a button-up and -down key press sequence—instead of a down-up sequence).

Table A.1 shows the current behavior on the desktop and specifies new "Nokia friendly" behavior (please note that we also include the pen-based behavior for another point of reference).

Table A.1 Button Action Behavior Matrix

Desktop Behavior (Persistent Mouse)	Touchscreen Behavior (Stylus)	Nokia 9200 Behavior (Tab Key)	Nokia 9200 Behavior (Virtual Pointer)
Roll Over handler is triggered when the mouse is moved into a button without being pressed. Button left in **Over** state.	N/A	**Roll Over** handler is triggered when the control is in focus after user pressing the Tab key button [please check Tab key button.] left in **Over** state.	**Roll Over** handler is triggered when the cursor is moved into a button using the arrow keys while the mouse button state is up. Button left in **Over** state.
Press handler is triggered when the mouse is clicked inside of a button. Button left in **Down** state.	When the stylus is pressed inside of a button, it first triggers **Roll Over** handler, followed by **Press** handler. Button left in **Down** state.	When the control is already in focus and Enter key is pressed, **Press** handler is triggered. Button left in **Down** state.	When the cursor is already inside a button and the Enter key is pressed (or use spacebar to toggle from mouse-up to mouse-down state), **Press** handler is triggered. Button left in **Down** state.
Release handler is triggered when the mouse is released from a click while in the button. Button left in **Over** state.	When the stylus is released, **Release** handler is triggered followed by a **Roll Out** handler. Button left in **Up** state.	When the button is in focus and the Enter key is released, **Release** handler is triggered. Button left in **Over** state.	When the cursor is inside the button and the Enter key is released (or use spacebar to toggle from mouse-down to mouse-up state), **Release** handler is triggered. Button left in **Over** state.
Roll Out is triggered when mouse is dragged out of button with mouse up. Button left in **Up** state.	N/A	**Roll Out** is triggered when the button loses focus after the user presses the Tab key. Button left in **Up** state.	**Roll Out** is triggered when the cursor is moved out of button using the arrow keys while the mouse-state is up. Button left in **Up** state.

Table A.1 Button Action Behavior Matrix *continued*

Desktop Behavior (Persistent Mouse)	Touchscreen Behavior (Stylus)	Nokia 9200 Behavior (Tab Key)	Nokia 9200 Behavior (Virtual Pointer)
Drag Down is triggered when mouse is dragged out of button with mouse down. Button left in **Over** state.	**Drag Down** is triggered when stylus is dragged out of button with pressure. Button left in **Down** state.	N/A	**Drag Down** is triggered only after the spacebar is used to toggle from mouse-up to mouse-down state inside a button; subsequently, the cursor is moved outside of the button. Button left in **Over** state.
Release Outside is triggered when mouse is dragged out of button with mouse down and then released outside of the button.Button left in **Up** state.	**Release Outside** is triggered when mouse is dragged out of button with mouse down and then released outside of the button.Button left in **Up** state.	N/A	**Release Outside** is triggered when pointer is "dragged out" of button (see above) with mouse-down state and then the space bar is pressed to toggle from mouse-down to up state outside of the button. Button left in **Up** state.
Drag Over is triggered when the mouse is dragged back into a button after first being down in the button, then dragged out. Button left in **Down** state.	Triggers **Drag Over** when the mouse is dragged back into a button after first being down in the button, then dragged out. Button left in **Down** state.	N/A	Triggers **Drag Over** when the mouse is "dragged back" into a button by moving the cursor while in mouse down state after first being "dragged" outside the button. (see Drag Down) Button left in **Down** state.

To visually distinguish between the mouse-down and mouse-up toggle states, the appearance of the pointer changes from white (up state) to black (down state).

In addition, because virtual pointer navigation uses the spacebar, Enter key, and arrow keys, it is likely to interfere with some Flash content that relies heavily on processing such key events (for example, game contents). As a result, it is important to thoroughly test any existing content that you are porting to the Nokia 9200 Communicator series.

Animation

When animating content, keep in mind the CPU limitations of the device in order to prevent the movie from slowing down from frames being dropped. Here are some general guidelines to keep in mind when animating content:

- When determining the frame rate of your movie, keep in mind the processor limitation of the device. In general, we recommend a frame rate of 12 frames per second.
- If you need to provide intense or complex animation, experiment with dynamically changing the movie's quality settings. This change may noticeably affect the visual quality of the movie, so be sure to thoroughly test it.
- Limit the number of simultaneous tweens.
- Alpha effects on symbols are very CPU intensive, and they should be used judiciously. In particular, it is generally not a good idea to tween symbols that also have their alpha level adjusted.
- Avoid intensive visual effects. These effects include large masks, extensive motion, alpha blending, and complex vectors such as extensive gradients.

Figure A.9 shows a sample animation for the Nokia 9200 Communicator.

FIGURE A.9

Animation on the Nokia 9200 Communicator.

Used with permission of Team SmartyPants, Inc.

Game design and development: Team SmartyPants! Inc. and Gridbloc, Inc.

Lead illustrator: Miki Kohlyama for Team SmartyPants! Inc.

Gameplay patent pending

- In some cases, animating via ActionScript may produce more desirable results, however, you should avoid intense ActionScript. (See the "ActionScript" section later in this appendix for more information.)
- Experiment with combinations of tweens, key frame animations, and ActionScript-driven movement to produce the most desirable results.
- Most importantly, test frequently on your target devices under a number of configurations and situations (that is, Flash Player running at the same time as web browser).

USING BITMAPS

The Flash Player has a 12-bit display (thousands of colors) with no alpha support. Bitmaps higher than 16 bits within a Flash movie will be resampled by the Flash Player when deployed. Because of this, whenever possible you should optimize your bitmaps to 16 bits before they are imported into the Flash authoring environment. This guideline will give you more control over the final output as well as help ensure optimum performance.

Bitmap Versus Vector

Because Flash uses vectors to display content in the Flash Player, the processor of the device can be taxed when rendering graphics and animations. In general, the more vector curves being manipulated on stage, the more processing power is required. This fact also holds true for Flash content delivered on desktop machines. However, Nokia 9200 Communicator series devices are far less powerful than desktop machines, and even more care than normal should be given to avoid straining the processor.

When creating content for the Nokia 9200 Communicator series it is sometimes better to use bitmaps as opposed to vectors because vectors can be animated with less processor strain. For example, a vector-based road map of a large city would have too many complex shapes to scroll and animate well on a Nokia 9200 Communicator. A bitmap would work much better in this case.

Using bitmaps will produce larger files, however, so be sure to find the right balance of processor and memory requirements versus file size for the particular project. The current optimization caveats and limitations that exist for designing any Flash application also exist on the Nokia 9200 Communicator series. But on devices, the importance of dealing with these caveats becomes amplified. Because of the smaller screen, slower data transmission speeds, limited memory, and processing power, developers should take extra care in planning and testing.

Setting Bitmap Properties

Two important guidelines to consider when using bitmaps in Flash movies for display on the Nokia 9200 Communicator are as follows:

■ Apply anti-aliasing to a bitmap to smooth the edges in the image to help the display of images on smaller screens. This step improves the display of poorer quality images.

■ Select a compression option that reduces the bitmap file size and format the file for display on the device.

To select bitmap properties, use the Bitmap Properties dialog box by right-clicking on the image in the library and selecting Properties.

Select a bitmap in the Library window and in the Bitmap Properties dialog box (see Figure A.10), select Allow Smoothing to smooth the edges of the bitmap with anti-aliasing.

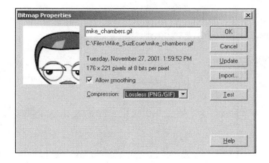

FIGURE A.10

Bitmap Properties window.

For Compression, choose one of the following options:

■ Choose Photo (JPEG) to compress the image in JPEG format. To use the default compression quality specified for the imported image, select Use Document Default Quality. To specify a new quality compression setting, deselect Use Document Default Quality and enter a value between 1 and 100 in the Quality text box. (A higher setting preserves greater image integrity but yields a smaller reduction in file size.) A balance and series of trade-offs exist between smaller file size and higher image quality; the same caveats with image quality for desktop system apply for devices, only amplified.

■ Choose Lossless (PNG/GIF) to compress the image with Lossless compression, in which no data is discarded from the image.

Use Photo compression for images with complex color or tonal variations, such as photographs or images with gradient fills. Use Lossless compression for images with simple shapes and relatively few colors.

Developers can also adjust the compression settings globally in the Publish Settings window (File, Publish Settings). To control bitmap compression in the Publish Settings, Flash tab, adjust the JPEG Quality slider or enter a value. As with the compression settings previously described, lower image quality produces smaller files; higher image quality produces larger files. Try different settings to determine the best trade-off between size and quality; 100 provides the highest quality and least compression.

ActionScript

The Flash Player for the Nokia 9200 Communicator Series contains complete support for Flash 5 ActionScript with the following exceptions:

- **getURL**   The getURL command is not supported.
- **FSCommand**   FSCommand is not supported with the exception of the FullScreen command and Quality setting.
- **Printing**   The Flash Player printing features are not supported on the Nokia 9200 Communicator.

Any nonsupported ActionScript commands encountered by the Flash Player when processing a movie will be ignored.

FIGURE A.11

L.E.D. Football for the Nokia 9200 Communicator series (created by Orange Design).

Because of processing speed limitations, complex ActionScript can severely tax the CPU. If an element of a movie is taking too long to process, a dialog box will appear to users informing them of the problem (see Figure A.12). Users will have the option to disable the processing of ActionScript in the movie. This step will effectively disable the entire movie.

Please confirm

A script in this movie is causing Flash Player to run slowly.
If it continues to run,
your computer may become unresponsive.
Do you want to abort the script?

FIGURE A.12

Error dialog appears when Flash movie takes too long to process.

Because of CPU limitations, developers should keep the following general guidelines in mind when developing ActionScript for Flash movies that will be deployed on the Nokia 9200 Communicator:

- Keep the ActionScript as simple as possible.
- Try to limit the number of loops. When running loops, try to limit the amount of actions taken within each loop.
- When using frame-based loops, make sure to stop the loop when it is no longer needed.
- String and Array processing can be extremely CPU intensive.

Using the following ActionScript library created by the Flash community can result in significant performance increases:

String.as is an ActionScript library that rewrites some of the built-in String functions, resulting in performance increases. In particular, the String.split() method has a significant performance increase. You can download the String.as library from: **http://chattyfig.figleaf.com/ ~bhall/code/string.as**.

The ActionScript XML object for Flash Player 5 has been optimized specifically for the Nokia 9200 Communicator. However, because of the memory and processor limitations of the device, thoroughly test any content that manipulates XML data. This step is particularly important when manipulating large or complex XML documents.

DEPLOYING CONTENT

This section describes issues to consider when deploying Flash content on the Nokia Communicator.

Standalone Player

The Flash Player for the Nokia 9200 Communicator series is a standalone player. Therefore, Flash movies embedded within HTML pages are not accessible to the Flash Player. Any Flash movies within an HTML page will be ignored by the browser and will not be displayed. No visual indication of the movie will be displayed within the HTML page.

Synching or Playing Content

Once the Flash Player has been installed on the Nokia 9200 Communicator, the player can be used to view local or network files. To view local files, the files must first be transferred to the Nokia 9200 Communicator before being viewed.

To sync Flash movies to the Nokia 9200 Communicator:

1. Download the SWF files to your Windows computer.
2. Connect the Nokia 9200 Communicator to your Windows computer.
3. Double-click the Nokia 9200 Communicator icon on your desktop.
4. Transfer the files to your Nokia 9200 Communicator by dragging them to the directory of your choice in the Nokia 9200 Communicator window.

Occasionally, you may need to transfer a Flash movie that requires other files, such as text files containing data for the movie, in order to function properly. However, the Nokia 9200 Communicator software automatically converts many types of files to a different format when copying them to the device. These files include TXT and XML, among others.

In order to prevent the Nokia 9200 Communicator software from altering the file extensions of files needed by a Flash movie, drag the files to the Nokia 9200 Communicator directory of your choice. When you release the right mouse button to place the files in the Nokia 9200 Communicator directory, choose Copy Here from the context menu that appears. Do not choose Copy and Convert. The files will be copied to the new directory without alteration.

Two ways exist to open local SWF files for viewing within the Flash Player:

- Using the Nokia File Manager, navigate to the Flash movie file that you want to display. Select the File button on the right of the screen and press Enter. The Flash Player automatically opens and begins to play the movie.
- With the Flash Player already running, press the Open File key, or the Menu key and then File, Open File. In the dialog box that opens, either enter the path to the Flash movie that you would like to run or press the Browse button and then browse to the location of the Flash movie (see Figure A.13).

You may also enter a file or URL path pointing to a Flash movie to play. If you enter a URL and the Nokia 9200 Communicator is not currently connected, a dialog box will appear asking if you want to connect to the Internet to retrieve the URL (user-defined).

Once you have entered the path to the Flash movie, press OK. If the Flash movie is local, it should play immediately. If it is from a URL, a status message will appear while the movie is loading. The movie will stream in the same manner that movies stream into web browsers on desktops.

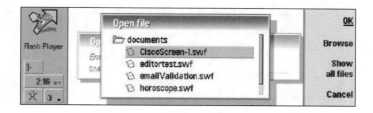

FIGURE A.13

Flash Player Open File browse dialogue.

Controlling Playback

The Flash Player allows you to control and adjust the playback of the Flash movie through a menu accessible via hardware keys to the right of the Flash Player (see Figure A.14).

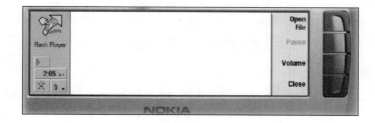

FIGURE A.14

Flash Player with hardware buttons.

The options in the menu are as follows:

- **Open File**   This allows you to open a Flash movie to play in the Flash Player. See the preceding section for information on how to use this function.
- **Pause/Play**   The Pause button pauses all elements of the current Flash movie, as well as prevents any user from inputting to it while it's paused. Once the pause button is pressed, it will change to a Resume button. To continue playing the movie, simply press the Resume button.
- **Volume**   The Volume button opens a dialog box that allows you to adjust the volume of the currently playing movie (it does not adjust the system volume for the entire device). Once the dialog box opens, you may raise and lower the volume level by using the plus (+) or (–) keys that appear on the right of the screen, as well as the up and down arrows on the keypad. Once you have set the volume to the desired level, press the OK button on the right of the screen or the Enter key on the keyboard (see Figure A.15).

  The Volume button will be unavailable if the current phone profile has Sound Notification set to Off.

FIGURE A.15

Flash Player volume dialogue.

- **Close**   This button closes the player as well as any movies that are currently running.

Adjusting the Flash Player Properties Through the Menu

No right-click menu exists on the Flash Player for Nokia 9200 Communicator. Most of the functions and information that would normally be contained on the right-click menu are available from the Flash menu, accessible by pressing the Menu key on the Nokia 9200 Communicator.

The following menu entries are not supported in the standalone Flash Player for the Nokia 9200 Communicator:

- Forward
- Backward
- Loop
- Print
- Close (the Close in Nokia is really Exit)
- Undo

By pressing the Menu key on the Nokia 9200 Communicator keyboard, you can access an additional set of menus that allow you to adjust the playback and settings of the Flash Player (see Figure A.16). When the menu is open, the Flash movie pauses. Once the menu is closed, the Flash movie automatically plays again.

The menu has the following options:

- **File, Open File**   This function allows you to open a Flash movie to deploy in the Flash Player. See earlier in this chapter for more information.
- **File, Disconnect**   This function disconnects any network connections that the Flash Player opens.
- **File, Close**   This function closes the Flash Player as well as any movies currently running.
- **Edit, Cut**   This function copies and removes the currently selected content. To retrieve the content once it has been cut, select Edit, Paste.

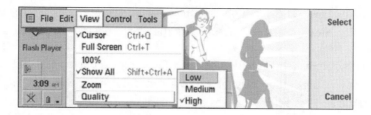

FIGURE A.16

Flash Player menu.

- **Edit, Copy** This setting copies the currently selected content to the Clipboard. You may paste the information into another area by selecting Edit, Paste.
- **Edit, Paste** This function pastes any content copied using Edit, Copy or Edit, Paste to the currently selected field.
- **Edit, Delete** This function deletes the currently selected text content.
- **Edit, Select All** This option selects and highlights all the content in the text field that has focus.
- **View, Cursor** This setting toggles to see if the cursor is available.
- **View, Full Screen** This function toggles the Full Screen mode for the Flash movie on and off.
- **View, 100%** When set to 100%, the Flash movie automatically scales to fit the entire available stage.
- **View, Show All** When selected, this function fits the current movie within the available player screen space while maintaining the original aspect ratio of the movie.
- **View, Zoom, Zoom In** This setting zooms in on the movie. To zoom out to the original size, select View, Show All.
- **View, Zoom, Zoom Out** This setting zooms out on the movie. To zoom in to the original size, select View, Show All.

  When zoomed into a movie, scroll bars may appear, indicating that the current Flash movie is zoomed in and some of it is not visible on the screen. However, the scroll bars cannot be used to actually scroll the movie to a different section. To scroll the movie, press Chr in combination with the arrow keypad that indicates the direction that you would like to scroll.

You may also zoom in and out of the current movie using the hardware Chr key in combination with the less than (<) and greater than (>) keys.

- **View, Quality, Low**   This function sets the Flash movie playback quality to low.
- **View, Quality, Medium**   This function sets the Flash movie playback quality to medium.
- **View, Quality, High**   This function sets the Flash movie playback quality to high.
- **Control, Play**   This setting plays the movie if it is currently paused or stopped.
- **Control, Pause**   This setting pauses all elements within the currently playing movie. When the device is shut or a phone call is received, Pause is automatically called on the Flash movie.
- **Control, Stop**   This setting stops the currently playing Flash movie.
- **Control, Rewind**   This function rewinds the Flash movie to the first frame, and then pauses the movie. To begin playing again, you must select Control, Play.
- **Control, Volume +**   This setting increases the volume of sound playback within the Flash Player. It does not affect system volume.
- **Control, Volume–**   This function decreases the volume of sound playback within the Flash Player. It does not affect the system volume.
- **Tools, About**   This setting displays information, including player version number, about the current Flash Player (see Figure A.17).
- **Tools, Receive via infrared**   This function toggles the infrared port on and off.

FIGURE A.17

Flash Player About dialogue box.

File Size and Memory Limitations

The actual RAM available for the operating systems and applications on the Nokia 9200 Communicator Series is only 8MB. Assuming that no other applications are running, there is approximately, 2.3MB of RAM available to the Flash Player. This amount is less if other applications are running. The limited amount of RAM available needs to be taken into consideration when creating content.

The largest file that the player can open is approximately 800K to 900K; however, this file size may vary slightly depending on the current state of the operating system. Again, it is very important to thoroughly test the movie.

If the Player runs out of memory, the user will be presented with an out or error message, and the Flash movie is stopped (including all scripts). The user will need to press any key to remove the message.

Due to the limited amount of RAM available, we recommend releasing resources within your Flash movie that are no longer in use. This step can be done in a variety of ways, including using ActionScript commands such as removeMovieClip, unloadMovie, or Delete.

You can check how much memory is currently available while the Flash Player is running by pressing Ctrl+Shift+M (see Figure A.18).

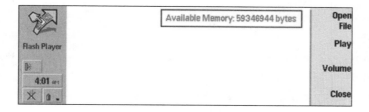

FIGURE A.18

Memory status window.

DYNAMIC CONTENT

Flash Player contains full support for all the ActionScript functions that allow the loading of dynamic data into the Flash movie at runtime. However, a few issues exist when developing dynamic Flash content for the Nokia 9200 Communicator Series.

FIGURE A.19

The Ringtone Generator allows the user to create custom ringtones and download them to the Nokia 9200 Communicator (created by James Rowley of ifdnrg.com).

Connected Versus Unconnected

If the Flash movie makes a request for data and the device is not currently connected, then the phone prompts the user to connect. While the dialog box is present and the phone connects, the ActionScript pauses until the data downloads. See the Network Connection Flow Diagram (see Figure A.20) for a chart on actions and events possible when using the Flash Player.

The connection dialog box may be disabled if the user chooses this Internet-settings option. If this occurs, the connection will proceed right away.

The user will be notified of the status of the connection via a small window. If the player is not able to connect, the user will also be notified.

Once the connection is made, the Flash Player keeps it open as long as necessary (see Figure A.20).

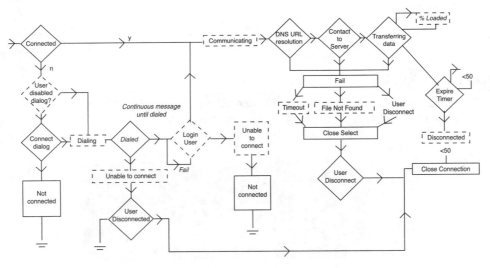

FIGURE A.20

Network connection flow diagram.

Domain Restrictions

When a Flash movie is loaded from the Internet to the player, all the usual data- and content-loading security and domain restrictions apply. However, if a movie is loaded from the file system, these restrictions do not apply.

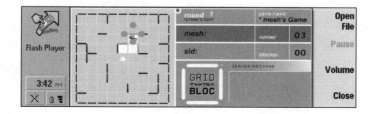

FIGURE A.21

GridBlock—Multiple player online game (created by Team SmartyPants.)

Bandwidth Considerations

Keep bandwidth considerations in mind when loading data from external locations. Only send data that is necessary for your movie. If you have to send large amounts of data, consider loading it in chunks so the movie appears to be more responsive to the user. Also consider using short variable names and XML tags.

For example, instead of:

<firstName>Mike</firstName>

try:

<fn>Mike</fn>

This shorter tag can help significantly reduce the amount of data that needs to be transferred.

Data Processing Considerations

After the data loads, the actual processing can be CPU-intensive and adversely affect the playback and performance of the Flash movie. If possible, try to process small chunks of data, as opposed to processing large amounts of data all at once.

Although the XML parsing in the Flash Player has been optimized for the Nokia 9200 Communicator series, parsing large amounts of XML data can still be processor-intensive. If all the data is not needed at once, consider making more frequent requests for smaller amounts of data. However, time spent loading the data from the network needs to balance against the added time required to load the data from an external source.

The Flash community has written an optimized ActionScript String object:

String.as This ActionScript library rewrites some of the built-in String functions, resulting in better performance. In particular, the String.split() method has a significant performance increase. You may download the String.as library from: **http://chattyfig.figleaf.com/~bhall/code/string.as**.

Device Detection

Client-side device detection through Flash is possible. It requires checking the Flash Player version number in ActionScript through the $version variable available on level0 of the movie.

For example:

```
var playerVersion = _level0.$version;
trace(playerVersion)
```

The player version for Flash Player on the Nokia 9200 Communicator is as follows:

NOK9200 5,0,95,0

The exact version may vary slightly. Check the Macromedia web site for any changes.

When detecting Flash Player on the Nokia 9200 Communicator, the first part of the version is the most important and reliable section. The second part is the specific version number of the player and could change depending on future releases.

This code detects the Flash Player for the Nokia 9200 Communicator series:

```
var playerVersion = _level0.$version;
if(playerVersion.beginsWith ("NOK9200"))
{
        //Player is on Nokia Communicator
}
else
{
        //Player is not on Nokia Communicator
}
/*
*       This is a simple function added to the built in String object that checks
*       if a String begins with the string passed into the function.
*/
String.prototype.beginsWith = function(s)
{
        return(s == this.substring(0, s.length));
}
```

You can use a stub movie that simply checks the Flash Player version and device that the movie is running on and then loads the appropriate movie.

Even though Flash movies can only be run through the Flash Player (and not a web browser on the Nokia 9200 Communicator) it is still possible to do server-side device detection. This step allows you to determine the type of device that the request is coming from, as well as which Flash movie to return.

When the Flash Player makes a request for a Flash movie, it sends the following HTTP_USER_AGENT value in the header of the request:

FlashPlayer/5.0 09/19/01

Retrieving this value on the server side, you can write middleware code that detects whether the request for a Flash movie is coming from a Nokia 9200 Communicator device. This detection basically lets the server send the appropriate content for the device. However, because new versions of the browser or operating system may be released in the future, the string above should only be used as a guide. Remember to always thoroughly test your detection scheme.

When the Flash Player makes a request for a movie, the middleware code that does the device detection must return a Flash movie to the player. The Flash Player for the Nokia 9200 Communicator series will not follow redirect requests.

TRADEMARKS

Flash Player 5® is a registered trademark of Macromedia, Inc.

Macromedia Flash® is a registered trademark of Macromedia, Inc.

Macromedia Flash Player® for the Nokia 9200 Communicator is a registered trademark of Macromedia, Inc.

Nokia Communicator® is a registered trademark of Nokia Corporation.

Nokia 9200 Communicator® is a registered trademark of Nokia Corporation.

B
APPENDIX

FLASH DEVICE MATRIX

by Mike Chambers

This appendix contains a matrix of devices that have some form of Flash support. Some of the devices are no longer produced, although you should be able to purchase them on ebay (**http://www.ebay.com**).

It seems as though there is a press release every other day announcing a new device that supports Flash. Be sure to check out this book's web site for the latest Flash device news and information.

Device	Flash Version	OS	Processor	Screen	Networking	Notes
Handheld Devices / PDAs						
Pocket PC 2002	5	Pocket PC 2002	206MHz Intel Strongarm	240x320	56k modem, wired and wireless Ethernet optional.	Only plays through Pocket Internet Explorer. No stand-alone player. FScommand not supported.
Nokia 9200 Communicator Series	5	Symbian platform, open for third-party developers	32-bit ARM9-based RISC CPU (52MHz)	640x200 full-screen. 486x200 available to Flash movie within player. Full-color screen with 4096 colors.	Data speed up to 43.2k (HSCSD)	XML parsing has been optimized. No browser plug-in, all playback is through Flash Standalone Player. Added functionality of Pause button, and Volume control. **http://www.nokia.com/phones/9210/index.html http://www.macromedia.com/go/flashplayer_nokia**

Device	Flash Version	OS	Processor	Screen	Networking	Notes
Set Top boxes						
Dreamcast	3/4	Custom Sega OS/ Win CE-based OS	Hitachi SH4 RISC CPU with an operating frequency of 200MHz at 360 MIPS/ 1.4FLOPS	Television/ VGA	Built-in 56k modem. Optional Ethernet broadband adapter.	Flash Player 4 supported provided through Planetweb browser version 3.0. Flash Player 3 support provided through Planetweb browser 2.6. **http://newbrowser. sega.com/ http://dreamcast. planetweb.com** The Dreamcast is no longer being produced, although it is still widely available.
Microsoft Ultimate TV	4		Depends on iTV implementation for company.	Television		**http://www. ultimatetv.com**
Web TV	3		150MHz R5230/ 167MHz R5231 (depending on model)	Television	56k modem	**http://www.webtv.com**
Sony eVilla	4	BeIA® 1.0	Geode GX1R® (266MHz) processor, Geode CS5530A	15" (14" viewable) Portrait FD Trinitron® CRT display (0.24-0.25mm AG pitch) 800 lines(H)x1024 pixels (V)	56k modem	Device has been discontinued. **http://www.evilla.com**

Device	Flash Version	OS	Processor	Screen	Networking	Notes

Internet Appliances

Device	Flash Version	OS	Processor	Screen	Networking	Notes
Microsoft/ Compaq Web Companion	5	Win CE 2.12	266MHz AMD K6-2	10.1" HPA flat panel color display 800×600 dpi resolution	56k modem. Optional USB Ethernet broadband connection.	Flash Player 5 within Internet Explorer 4. No standalone player. **http://www.linux-hacker.net/cgi-bin/ UltraBoard/UltraBoard. pl?Action=ShowBoard &Board= MSNCompanion http://athome. compaq.com/ showroom/static/ iPAQ/intappliance.asp**
Intel Dot. Station	4	Custom Linux* OS distribution	Intel® Celeron™ processor 300A (minimum)	14" CRT, 1024×768 resolution	56k modem	**http://www.intel.com/ internetappliances/ webappliance/ dotstation.htm**
3com Audrey	4	QNX 6.0 embedded, with Neutrino kernel and Photo GUI manager.	200MHz National Semiconductor Geode	Touchscreen: 7.8 in diagonal color screen Resolution: 640×480, 12-bit color	56k modem. Optional broadband/ Ethernet connection.	Device has been discontinued. Playback is through web browser. Streaming content is not supported. The entire Flash movie must load before it begins to play. **http://www.audrey-hacking.com http://www.linux-hacker.net/cgi-bin/ UltraBoard/UltraBoard. pl?Action=ShowBoard &Board=3Com_Audrey**

C

APPENDIX

FLASH DEVICE RESOURCES

Mike Chambers

This appendix contains a listing of useful sites and resources for finding information on Macromedia Flash, Flash on devices, and devices.

Of course, the device field is constantly changing, so be sure to check this book's web site (**www.flashenabled.com**) for the most up-to-date information and resources.

GENERAL FLASH DEVICE RESOURCES

The resources in this section apply to Flash devices in general.

Web Sites

Flash Enabled
http://www.flashenabled.com
The official web site for the book, as well as the top resource on Flash and device news and content.

Pocket PC Flash
http://www.pocketpcflash.net
This is the single best resource for Pocket PC Flash content and tutorials available.

Ultrashock.com Flash on Devices Resources
http://www.ultrashock.com/tutorials/devices/devices-resources.htm

Flash Player for Pocket PC
http://www.macromedia.com/software/flashplayer/pocketpc/
This is the official Macromedia/Pocket PC Flash Player site. It has links to the latest player downloads, authoring kits, resources, and content.

Pocket PC Flash Player FAQ
http://www.macromedia.com/software/flashplayer/pocketpc/faq

Forums/Mailing Lists

Flash Handhelds
http://webforums.macromedia.com/flash/categories.cfm?catid=195

Macromedia.flash.handhelds
The official Macromedia forum for Flash on devices. It can be accessed via a newsgroup or web forum.

Ultrashock.com: Flash & Devices forum
http://forums.ultrashock.com/forums203/forumdisplay.php?forumid=83

General Flash Resources

Flash Documentation

http://www.macromedia.com/support/flash/documentation.html

This includes the official documentation for Flash 3, 4, 5, and Flash MX.

Flash Support Area

http://www.macromedia.com/support/flash/

This is the first site you should visit when trying to find an answer to your Flash-related questions.

We're-here

http://www.were-here.com

One of the top Flash community sites and an excellent Flash resource.

Flashkit

http://www.flashkit.com

This is another great Flash community resource site with tons of downloadable examples and files.

ActionScript: The Definitive Guide

http://www.moock.org/asdg/

Colin Moock: O'Reilly Press

The single best resource on Flash ActionScript.

ActionScript.org

http://www.actionscript.org

This is a very good site for tutorials and resources on ActionScript.

Macromedia Designer and Developer Center

http://www.macromedia.com/desdev/

This site offers news, information, articles, tutorials, and all Macromedia products.

Mailing Lists

Flashcoders

http://chattyfig.figleaf.com

A great mailing list founded and run by Branden Hall focusing solely on ActionScript.

Flash Newbie

http://chattyfig.figleaf.com

A mailing list sponsored and run by FigLeaf software focusing on users new to Flash.

FlashMacromedia

http://groups.yahoo.com/group/flashmacromedia/

This is an active general Flash mailing list.

Chinwag Flashers

http://www.chinwag.com/flasher/

This is another very good general Flash mailing list.

Tools

Flash Assist
http://www.antmobile.com/

FlashAssist lets you open Flash content on your Pocket PC in three different window sizes:

240×268: Standard window with menu bar

240×295: Extended window, no menu bar

240×320: Full screen

Remote Display Control for Pocket PC
http://www.microsoft.com/mobile/pocketpc/downloads/powertoys.asp

This application allows a Pocket PC display to be displayed and controlled from a desktop/laptop computer. This is extremely useful when developing Flash applications for the Pocket PC, as well as for taking screenshots.

Pocket PC Developer PowerToys
http://www.microsoft.com/mobile/developer/downloads/powertoys.asp

These are useful apps for use on Pocket PC. Includes ActiveX plug-ins for Pocket IE, that give information about the device, as well as one that makes it easy to execute files from Pocket IE and also Flash.

TYPOGRAPHY/FONTS

miniml.com
http://www.miniml.com

This site contains fonts created specifically to use with Flash displayed on devices or small screens.

Fontographer
http://www.macromedia.com/software/fontographer/

This is a program published by Macromedia that allows you to create your own fonts.

dsg4 Bitmap fonts
http://www.dsg4.com/04/extra/bitmap/index.html

mini 7 Bitmap fonts
http://www.wpdfd.com/wpdtypo.htm#mini7

SERVER-SIDE DYNAMIC FLASH

Macromedia Generator
http://www.macromedia.com/software/generator/

JGenerator
http://www.flashgap.com
http://sourceforge.net/projects/jgen/

Generator and Flash Demystified
http://www.peachpit.com/books/catalog/72584.html
Mike Chambers, Phillip Torrone, and Chris Wiggins, Peachpit Press: 0201725843

Ming
http://www.opaque.net/ming/
Ming is a library that allows developers to programmatically create Flash movies from languages such as C and PHP.

FLASH AND JAVA

Sun Personal Java
http://java.sun.com/products/personaljava/

Sun Personal Java StrongArm Early Access
http://developer.java.sun.com/developer/earlyAccess/personaljava/
This site has an early access version of Sun Java JVM for StrongArm processors.

Chai VM
http://www.hp.com/emso/products/chaivm/
Java Runtime that comes with some Hewlett-Packard Pocket PC devices.

IBM Visual Age Micro Edition
http://www.embedded.oti.com/
This is a Java JVM for embedded devices.

Waba
http://wabasoft.com/
A Java-like programming environment.

Jeode Runtime
http://www.insignia.com/products/default.asp
This is a Sun Authorized Java compatible JVM.

DEVICE RESOURCES

This section lists resources that can help you find out more about devices.

Microsoft Pocket PC

Resources in this section focus on the Microsoft Pocket PC.

Developer Information

Microsoft Pocket PC
http://www.pocketpc.com/
This is the official site for the Microsoft Pocket PC operating system. It contains Pocket PC and device news, information, and downloads.

Microsoft Developer Area for the Pocket PC
http://www.microsoft.com/mobile/developer/

Community, News, and Information Sites

Pocket PC Thoughts
http://www.pocketpcthoughts.com
News and information on Pocket PC and devices.

Pocket PC Passion
http://www.pocketpcpassion.com/

BrightHand
http://www.brighthand.com

PDABuzz
http://www.pdabuzz.com

CeWindows
http://www.cewindows.net

InfoSync
http://www.infosync.no

LudiPocket
http://www.ludipocket.com/e

PocketNow
http://www.pocketnow.com

The gadgeteer
http://www.the-gadgeteer.com

Forums

Microsoft Pocket PC Newsgroups
microsoft.public.pocketpc
microsoft.public.pocketpc.developer
Official Microsoft newsgroups on Pocket PC

cewindows.net Forums
http://discuss.cewindows.net/cgi-bin/ubb/Ultimate.cgi

Pocket Internet Explorer/JScript

Internet Explorer for Pocket PC—HTML and Object Model Reference
http://www.microsoft.com/mobile/developer/technicalarticles/html.doc

Pocket Internet Explorer Resources at Pocket PC Developers Network
http://www.pocketpcdn.com/sections/pie.html

HTML Tags, MIME Types, Security Types, and URL Types Supported in Pocket Internet Explorer
http://support.microsoft.com/default.aspx?scid=kb;EN-US;q158479

Database Access Using JavaScript
http://www.pocketpcskins.com/jsadoce.html

Designing Pages for Pocket IE
http://www.microsoft.com/mobile/developer/technicalarticles/pie_dev.asp

Microsoft XML Support with the Internet Explorer for Pocket PC
http://www.microsoft.com/mobile/developer/technicalarticles/pie_xml.asp

Scripting with Flash Player and ActiveX
http://www.macromedia.com/support/flash/ts/documents/activex_script.htm

An Example of Communication Between JavaScript and Flash
http://www.macromedia.com/support/flash/ts/documents/java_script_comm.htm

Using JavaScript with the Flash Player
http://www.macromedia.com/support/flash/ts/documents/tn4160.html

Calling Methods from JavaScript
http://www.macromedia.com/support/flash/publishexport/scriptingwithflash/scriptingwithflash_06.html

Different Approaches to Setting Variables in a Flash Movie
http://www.macromedia.com/support/flash/ts/documents/set_variables.htm

Moock.org
http://www.moock.org/webdesign/flash/
This is probably the single best resource for information on Flash/JavaScript integration.

Pocket PC Web Servers

Web servers that can run on the Pocket PC platform and can be used with Flash to create nearly full-featured applications.

ASP for Pocket PC
http://www.microsoft.com/downloads/release.asp?ReleaseID=29414

Windows CE Web Server
http://msdn.microsoft.com/library/default.asp?URL=/library/wcedoc/wceinet/webserv.htm

ApacheCE
http://www.rainer-keuchel.de/wince/apache-ce.html

The Apache web server ported to Windows CE with support for CGI.

GoAhead Web Server
http://www.goahead.com/webserver/webserver.htm

Embedded web server that supports dynamic content through the use of embedded JavaScript, Active Server Pages, and CGI.

Pico Web Server
http://homies.dyndns.org/~rotonde/picowebserver/

Creating Video for Pocket PC

WildForm Flix
http://www.wildform.com/

Tool that encodes video for use within the Flash Player.

Windows Media Encoder
http://www.microsoft.com/windows/windowsmedia/wm7/encoder.asp

Pocket PC profiles for the Pocket PC Windows Media Player
http://www.microsoft.com/windows/windowsmedia/software/pocket/create.asp

Encoding Audio and Video for the Pocket PC
http://msdn.microsoft.com/library/default.asp?URL=/library/en-us/dnwmt/html/encodppc.asp

Windows Media Free Bonus Pack (Lots of cool stuff)
http://www.microsoft.com/windows/windowsmedia/download/bonuspack.asp

Putting Home Movies on the Pocket PC
http://www.microsoft.com/mobile/pocketpc/stepbystep/homevideos.asp
http://articles.pocketnow.com/content.cgi?db=articles&id=55

Useful Third-Party Pocket PC Applications

Create eBooks for the Pocket PC
http://www.ebookexpress.com/

Microsoft Reader Add-In
http://www.microsoft.com/reader/download_rmr.asp

Mycasio
http://www.mycasio.com

Mazingo
http://www.mazingo.net

Adobe PDF Viewer
http://www.adobe.com/products/acrobat/readerforppc.html

Pocket Mac
http://www.pocketmac.net/
This allows you to connect and sync a Pocket PC device with an Apple-based computer.

Pocket PC-Related Hardware

Compaq iPAQ
http://www.compaq.com/products/handhelds/

URThere @migo
http://www.urthere.com/

Toshiba GENIO e570
http://www.csd.toshiba.com/pda/pda_home.html

Casio E-200
http://www.casio.com/personalpcs/section.cfm?section=19

Hewlett-Packard Jornada
http://www.hp.com/jornada/

Audiovox Maestro
https://www.audiovoxonline.com/webapp/commerce/command/ExecMacro/
Audiovox_Online_Store/macros/avox_PPC.d2w/report

NEC
http://www.nec.com

mmo2
http://www.mmo2.com

Symbol
http://www.symbol.com

Intermec
http://www.intermec.com

3Com Audrey

AudreyHacking.com
http://www.audreyhacking.com
This is an excellent resource site on hacking and developing for the 3Com Audrey.

Sowbugs Audrey Page
http://www.sowbug.com/audrey/
This is another excellent resource on Audrey information.

I-Appliance BBS: Audrey Hacking Forum
http://www.linux-hacker.net/cgi-bin/UltraBoard/UltraBoard.pl?Action=ShowBoard&
Board=3Com_Audrey&Idle

slinger webserver Documentation
http://qdn.qnx.com/support/docs/tcpip50/user_guide/utils/slinger_util.html
slinger is the web server that comes installed with the Audrey.

Microsoft Ultimate TV

Ultimate TV web site:
http://www.ultimatetv.com

Microsoft/Compaq Web Companion

Compaq Home Internet Appliances
http://athome.compaq.com/showroom/static/ipaq/i ntappliance.asp

MSN Companion
http://msnc.msn.com/v2/companion/

I-Appliance BBS: MSN Companion Hacking Forum
http://www.linux-hacker.net/cgi-bin/UltraBoard/UltraBoard.pl?Action=ShowBoard&
Board=MSNCompanion

Sega Dreamcast

PlanetWeb Web Browser
http://newbrowser.sega.com/

DC Emulation
http://www.dcemulation.com/

Flash for Video/Television

Microsoft TV Design Guidelines
http://www.microsoft.com/tv/working/content/desguide.asp

Flash to Video FAQ by FlickerLab
http://www.flickerlab.com/flashtovideo/

Microsoft TV Color Picker
http://developer.msntv.com/tools/colorpick/Default.htm
An online tool that emulates how computer colors will look on a TV screen.

WebTV Browser
http://developer.msntv.com/Tools/WebTVVwr.asp
Useful tool for simulating playback of content on televisions.

ATVEF
http://www.atvef.com
Advanced Television Enhancement Forum

Adobe Premiere
http://www.adobe.com/products/premiere/main.html
This is a tool for editing digital video.

Adobe After Effects
http://www.adobe.com/products/aftereffects/main.html
This is a tool for editing and creating effects for digital video.

Apple Final Cut Pro
http://www.apple.com/finalcutpro/
This is a tool for editing digital video.

General Device News and Information

Slashdot.org
http://www.slashdot.org

IapplianceWeb
http://www.iapplianceweb.com/

Linux Devices
http://www.linuxdevices.com

AUTHOR WEB SITES

Mike Chambers

http://radio.weblogs.com/0106797/

Robert M. Hall

http://www.impossibilities.com

Steve Leone

http://www.unplug.tv

Bill Perry

Pocket PC Flash
http://www.pocketpcflash.net

Fred Sharples

Orange Design
http://www.orangedesign.com

Glenn Thomas/Andreas Heim

Smashing Ideas
http://www.smashingideas.com
http://www.smashingideasmobile.com

Phillip Torrone

Flashenabled.com
http://www.flashenabled.com

Fallon
http://www.fallon.com

D

APPENDIX

POCKET PC DEVICE DETECTION

by Mike Chambers

This appendix contains various scripts and code examples for detecting the Pocket PC 2002 operating system and Macromedia Flash Player 5 for Pocket PC.

SERVER-SIDE DETECTION

This section contains server-side examples that detect the Pocket PC operating system. The code snippets check to see whether the request comes from a browser on the Pocket PC operating system. If so, the code snippet redirects to a success.html page; if the request does not come from a Pocket PC device, the code will display that the request does not come from a Pocket PC device.

The code detects the Pocket PC by searching for the string "PPC" in the HTTP_USER_AGENT field sent by the browser along with the request. This technique can be used to redirect the user to different versions of a Flash movie depending on what device or browser the request is made from.

Note that only the first code example is documented, but all the code examples follow the exact same steps.

Macromedia ColdFusion

This ColdFusion code detects whether a request came from Pocket Internet Explorer running on a Pocket PC device.

```
<!--
        Get the user agent from the request sent by the browser.
-->
<cfset userAgent="#CGI.HTTP_USER_AGENT#">

<cfset isPocketPc = false>

<!--
        Check to see that the user agent is not blank, and if it contains the string
        ➥"PPC".

If it does, that means the request came from a Pocket PC, otherwise, the request
➥did not come from a Pocket PC.
```

```
—->
<cfif (userAgent IS NOT "") AND (find("PPC", #userAgent#) GT 0)>
        <cfset isPocketPc = true>
</cfif>

<cfif isPocketPc>
        <cflocation url="success.html">
<cfelse>
        You are <b>not</b> connecting with a Pocket PC device.  </cfif>
```

PHP

This PHP code detects whether a request came from Pocket Internet Explorer running on a Pocket PC device.

```php
<?php

        $headers = getallheaders();

        $userAgent = $headers["User-Agent"];

        $isPocketPc = false;

        if($userAgent != null && strpos($userAgent, "PPC"))
        {
                $isPocketPc = true;
        }

        if($isPocketPc)
        {
                header ("Location: success.html");
                exit;
        }
        else
        {
                out.print("You are <b>not</b> connecting with a Pocket PC device.");
        }

?>
```

JSP

This JSP code detects whether a request came from Pocket Internet Explorer running on a Pocket PC device.

```
<%

        String userAgent = request.getHeader("User-Agent");

        boolean isPocketPc = false;

        if(userAgent != null && userAgent.indexOf("PPC" , 0) > 0)
        {
                isPocketPc = true;
        }

        if(isPocketPc)
        {
                response.sendRedirect("success.html");
                return;
        }
        else
        {
                out.print("You are <b>not</b> connecting with a Pocket PC device.");
        }

%>
```

ASP

This ASP code detects whether a request came from Pocket Internet Explorer running on a Pocket PC device.

```
<%

        userAgent = Request.ServerVariables("HTTP_USER_AGENT")

        isPocketPc = false

        if(userAgent <> "" AND (InStr(userAgent, "PPC") > 0)) then
                isPocketPc = true
        end if
```

```
        if isPocketPc then
                response.redirect("success.html")
        else
                response.write("You are <b>not</b> connecting with a Pocket PC
                ➥device.")
        end if
%>
```

CLIENT-SIDE DETECTION

The code snippets in this section check on the client side to determine whether the Flash player is running on a Pocket PC 2002 device.

Flash

This ActionScript detects whether a Flash movie is running on the Flash Player 5 on a Pocket PC device.

```
/*
*       This is a simple function added to the built in String object that checks
*       whether a String begins with the string passed into the function.
*/
String.prototype.beginsWith = function(s)
{
        return(s == this.substring(0, s.length));
}

var playerVersion = getVersion();

if(playerVersion.beginsWith("WINCE"))
{
        //Pocket PC 2002 <u><b>Detected;
}
else
{
        //Pocket PC 2002 NOT detected;
}
```

Pocket Jscript

This Jscript code detects whether the HTML page/Jscript is being run in a browser on the Pocket PC operating system.

```
*var strNav = navigator.userAgent;
// Check for Windows CE (Pocket PC, Palm-size PC, Handheld PC, Handheld PC Pro)

        var isCE = strNav.indexOf("Windows CE");

        if(isCE > -1)
{
//add Windows CE specific code
        }
        else
{
//add code for other platforms
        }

// Check for Pocket PC
        var isPPC = strNav.indexOf("240x320");

if(isPPC > -1)
{
// add Pocket PC specific code
}
else
{
// add code for other platforms
}
```

E

MICROSOFT POCKET INTERNET EXPLORER ON POCKET PC 2002

by Mike Chambers

Microsoft Pocket Internet Explorer on Pocket PC 2002 has the following features and capabilities:

HTML

3.2

Tables, forms, frames, and MSXML supported.

Floating frames not supported.

VRML not supported.

(New HTML tags: **DIV/SPAN**, **CAPTION ALIGN**, **DIV ALIGN**, **TABLE ALIGN**, **IMG HSPACE**, **IMG ALIGN**, **BODY VLINK**, **BODY ALINK**, **BR CLEAR**, **BASEFONT COLOR**, **TH COLSPAN**.)

WAP

WML, WBXML, WBMP, WSP, WMLSCRIPT.

DHTML

Only InnerHTML/InnerText. No DHTML DOM.

Protocols

HTTP1.1 (http, https), HTTP 1.1 compression, FTP, FTPIR, NNTP, file://, AvantGo, and OEM and user can supply others via URLMon interface.

Scripting

Windows CE JScript 3.0 (ECMA-262 compliant).

No support for Regular Expressions. No support for Vbscript.

ActiveX Controls

Supported. ActiveX Controls cannot be automatically downloaded but can be called if previously registered on the device. An ActiveX Control can now "fire" an "event," which can have JScript code attached to it (via a web page).

Downloading controls

Supported. Download location, determine file size, and monitor the progress of the download. Users can also cancel large or slow downloads.

XML support

MSXML 2.5 Data islands supported. For more details, view **http://www.microsoft.com/mobile/developer/pie_xml.asp** and **http://www.microsoft.com/mobile/developer/techncalarticles/iexml.asp**.

Cascading style sheets
Not supported.

Font downloading
Not supported.

Data binding
Not supported.

Java
Supported. Via third-party applications.

Native file formats
GIF, JPEG, BMP, XBM, PNG, HTML, TXT, SWF*

GIF89a format is displayed but without animation.

*Other formats such as Flash SWF require ActiveX Control.

Recording file formats
WAV, WML, and others via MIME type handlers.

User-Agent string
Mozilla/2.0 (compatible; MSIE 3.02; Windows CE; PPC; 240x320).

Cache
Supported.

Subscriptions, offline browsing
Supported through mobile favorites and third-party applications.

Colors /resolution
No limits (devices currently support 64k colors).

Auto-complete URL
Supported.

Link highlighting
Underlined.

View HTML source
Not supported. Third-party applications.

Favorites
Supported through mobile favorites.

Input devices
Touch, keyboard, third-party hardware.

Cookies

Max number elements (4KB max each) set by Registry, persistent to HDD (users WININET).

User authentication

Anonymous, Basic, NTLM. No support for Digest.

Security

SSL2, SSL3, Private Communication Technology (PCT) 1.0, SGC.

Newsgroups

Supported through third-party applications.

CDF

Not supported.

MIME type helpers

Supports application and pluggable MIME Helpers and Filters.

Printing

Supported through third-party applications.

Web server

Supported. Included in Pocket PC 2002 SDK and supported through third-party applications.

F

APPENDIX

USING FLASH FOR DEVELOPING TOUCH-SCREEN KIOSKS

by Robert M. Hall, **www.impossibilities.com**

By now you are aware that there are many alternative areas in which you can apply your skills as a Macromedia Flash MX developer. There is one more area that may be of interest to you and that is the interactive touch-screen kiosk market. This is a variation on the standard desktop PC or web deployment of Flash MX movies, in that it combines aspects of the desktop environment along with total control over the method in which your work is presented, accessed, and manipulated. The types of touch-screen kiosks you might already be familiar with are: bridal registry stations in your local shopping mall or specialty boutique, information touch screens in hotel lobbies, airports, train, and bus stations, and in-store virtual catalogs and price-scanning stations. If you look closely you will find kiosks just about wherever you go. The touch-sensitive ATM machine is becoming more and more popular as well. Thanks to the advances in Flash 5 and now Flash MX with its advanced scripting capabilities ala ActionScript, you as a developer have a full-fledged application development environment. A world of opportunities has opened up for you in which you can use your existing skills to tap potential revenue resources and explore new ways to deploy content.

The appendix examines working with Flash MX in a touch-screen kiosk environment. Specifically, it focuses on the issues that arise when working with touch-sensitive screens as the primary input device. Many of the principles are similar to that of working with Flash 5 on a Pocket PC device, so this will not be totally unfamiliar territory if you have read all the way through the book to this point or have familiarized yourself with the Pocket PC 2002 Flash 5 Authoring guidelines.

PLANNING DEPLOYMENT OF FLASH MX ON A TOUCH-SCREEN KIOSK

The first question you need to ask yourself when laying the groundwork for a Flash MX based kiosk on a touch-screen system is: "Will I be able to make the kiosk do what I need it to do with Flash alone, or will I have to use additional software to complement Flash MX?" Perhaps you may need to control hardware devices or peripherals attached to the kiosk. For example: Your kiosk project may need to receive input from a bar code scanner that is attached to the kiosk, or receive input from some other specialty input device.

Obviously, these extra devices may dictate the platform or operating system that is the core of your kiosk, but one avenue to consider if you are deploying on a Microsoft-based platform, such as Windows 95/98/ME/NT/2000/XP, would be to use an ActiveX control to handle talking to the hardware. FScommands or geturls issued from within your Flash MX application to a hidden frame in a browser-based design could trigger commands that contain embedded ActiveX objects. These ActiveX objects could be programmed to talk (at a lower level than Flash is currently capable of) to the actual system drivers, such as a bar code scanner serial driver, or even the operating system itself.

Another solution would be to run a web server directly on the kiosk and use a back-end scripting language or middleware to handle the communication to your hardware. Writing a custom Apache module or an ISAPI or DLL for Microsoft IIS to talk to your hardware is certainly an option you may pursue. Although those are not necessarily skills that every Flash MX programmer has in his personal toolbox, these are the types of challenges you may come up against in developing a kiosk system with Flash MX as the primary user interface and application. Thus, you should keep an open mind to additional expenses or development costs associated with using Flash MX in this manner should the situation call for it.

If you have a large-scale deployment that requires customized control over the environment, then you might also explore the option of licensing the Flash Player Source Code SDK directly from Macromedia. Macromedia has an online application form at:

www.macromedia.com/software/flashplayer/licensing/sourcecode/

There are very stringent requirements set forth by Macromedia for this program, and not everyone who applies will be able to participate. Macromedia has geared this program to third parties who can meet certain financial and business criteria. These criterion, along with others at Macromedia's discretion, are used to determine if a company can participate in this program. So this option might not be for the individual Flash MX developer, but it is a good thing to know about and have as an option to consider if the project you are working on would merit a license. If Macromedia approves you, you have full access to the Flash Player source code, whereby you could customize it directly from the original C++ source code to talk directly to the device you are deploying on. Imagine the possibilities of being able to add functionality to the Flash Player at that level. Currently, this program covers the Flash 5 Player. Nothing has been announced as of the writing of this book in regards to the Flash 6 Player.

These are just a few examples of a variety of hurdles you may need to overcome. The best way to identify these obstacles or challenges in a project is to begin with a detailed road map of what exactly your kiosk needs to do, and what specialty hardware will need to be used. This should be as detailed as possible so that you may lay out your plan of attack. The main items listed next should definitely be considered when creating such a road map because they are crucial to designing and deploying a Flash-based kiosk. This is in addition, of course, to the road map or functionality outline of the Flash application itself.

- Will the Flash Player be all that is required for full application functionality?
- Will the kiosk be browser-based, standalone, or a custom Flash container?
- What types of input devices will the kiosk require other than the touch screen?
- Will the kiosk require custom hardware or software to complement the Flash Player?
- Will the kiosk require a live network connection?
- Will the kiosk be using dynamically generated data?
- On what platform will the kiosk be deployed?
- How much screen real estate will the kiosk require?
- What type of touch screen will the kiosk need?
- In what type of environment will the kiosk live?

- What is the demographic of the user of the kiosk?
- What special needs of the user should be taken into consideration?

GENERAL TOUCH-SCREEN HARDWARE INFORMATION

Before we delve into tips on using Flash with touch screens, you need some background on the types of touch screens available. After you know what is available, you will be able to take into consideration the following items:

- Where will my kiosk be deployed?
- What type of traffic will the kiosk receive?
- What type of person will be using the kiosk?

Because there are many types and manufacturers of touch screens, you need to determine these items to make the right decision on the type of touch screen you will be using. The types available cover quite a range: standard indoor models, to outdoor models that can withstand precipitation and the elements, to heavy-duty models with security glass for limiting the viewable range to only a few degrees directly in front of the screen, thus preventing shoulder surfing of secure information. This appendix covers two basic types of kiosk that are within the reach of a developer on a budget who wants to experiment or delve into this market without too much capital outlay. There are many manufacturers of touch screens; the following list is not exhaustive, but covers many popular providers of touch-screen technology.

Elo TouchSystems, Inc
6500 Kaiser Drive
Fremont, CA 94555
800-356-8682
http://www.elotouch.com/
eloinfo@elotouch.com

Troll Touch
25510 Avenue Stanford, Suite 106
Valencia, CA 91355-1131
661-257-1160
http://www.trolltouch.com
info@trolltouch.com

3M Touch Systems
300 Griffin Brook Park Drive
Methuen, MA 01844
978-659-9000
http://www.3m.com/us/electronics_mfg/
touch_systems/index.jhtml
touch@mmm.com

DMC Co., Ltd.
508 Kamisakunobe
Takatsu-ku, Kawasaki 213-0034, Japan
+81-(0)44-866-2111 (Japanese)
+81-(0)44-866-2118 (English)
http://www.dmccoltd.com/
sales-e@dmccoltd.com

Viewmagic Inc.
2917 Bayview Drive
Fremont, CA 94538
510-226-6250
http://www.viewmagic.com/
info@viewmagic.com

KDS Pixel Touch, Inc.
1957 Cedar Street
Ontario, CA 91761
909-923-6124
http://www.pixeltouch.com/
sale@pixeltouch.com

Touch Controls, Inc.
520 Industrial Way
Fallbrook, CA 92028
800-848-4385
http://www.touchcontrols.com/
sales@touchcontrols.com

Preh Electronics Inc.
590 Telser Road, Unit B
Lake Zurich, Illinois 60047
847-438-4000
http://www.preh.com/
prehsales@preh.com

KEYTEC, Inc.
1293 North Plano Road
Richardson, TX 75081
800-624-4289
http://www.magictouch.com/
sales@magictouch.com

Jayco mmi
1351 Pico Street
Corona, CA 91719-3373
877-529-2648
http://www.jaycommi.com/clearswitch.html
danstead@jaycopanels.com

Intech Bearing, Inc.
1999 Tellepsen Street
Houston, TX 77023
888-868-2439
http://www.ezscreen.com/
sales@ezscreen.com

Touch Dynamic, Inc.
107 Trumbull Street, Ste B6
Elizabeth, NJ 07206
888-508-6824
http://www.touchdynamic.com/
support@touchdynamic.com

The companies listed above offer a variety of touch-screen systems, typically based on four different types of screen technologies: capacitive, resistive, infrared, and SAW (surface acoustic wave). You would be wise to investigate each company to see what each offers and how their solutions can benefit your specific application. Depending on the model and whether it is used or new, the prices range as low as a few hundred dollars to several thousand. The approximate price range for a single desktop 15-inch LCD touch screen is $750 to $1,200. A CRT-based touch screen, depending on size, can be as low as a few hundred dollars for a 14-inch model with 15-inch models in the $600 range and up. 17-inch models start around $750 and go up from that price to nearly $1,400 for 21-inch models. You might be able to save on costs by considering a retro fit touch-screen kit for your existing monitor. All these prices are approximate and each manufacturer has its own specific models and features that can add or subtract from the base price of a touch screen. An example of this would be a desktop model versus a model specifically designed for installation into a kiosk enclosure, or mounted in or on a wall. Also many of the resellers provide discounts on quantity pricing; this can come into play as most kiosk applications are deployed in more than one location.

ALTERNATIVE TOUCH-SCREEN TECHNOLOGY

Before we go further, it is worth mentioning a few other items that are similar to touch screens.

The now discontinued 3Com Audrey Web Appliance is a self-contained unit with a touch-sensitive 640×480 screen that utilizes a stylus for input. The nice thing about the Audrey is that it has built-in support for displaying and interacting with Flash 4-based content. You might be able to pick up one of these on eBay for less than $100.

You can find more links and information on using the Audrey in Appendix C, "Flash Device Resources."

There are also touch-sensitive web tablets, such as Fujitsu's Pen Tablets:

www.fujitsupc.com/www/products_pentablets.shtml?products/pentablets/stylistic_3500

as well as Transmeta Crusoe Processor–based web tablets. Most tablets capable of running a variant of the Microsoft Windows 95/98/ME/NT/2000/XP operating system should support the Flash Player plug-in. The recently announced Mira by Microsoft doesn't have too many public details about its capabilities, but you can imagine that if it's based on a version of XP, then there is a good chance that there will be a Flash Player available.

Finally, if you would like to use a touch screen during the development process for creation of Flash projects, then you can use the Wacom Cintiq. This is a 15-inch LCD that is not only touch sensitive but has 512 levels of pressure sensitivity, and can even detect the tilt of the stylus, allowing you to make unique brushstrokes. It also supports the newer DVI standard for connecting to your graphics card for better detail instead of going through a standard VGA connector. Since Flash 4, the Flash authoring environment has built-in support for taking advantage of the pressure and tilt sensitivity of Wacom devices. The Cintiq product is designed to either stand or be held for use.

See Wacom's site **www.wacom.com** for more information about the unique Cintiq product.

SPECIFIC TOUCH-SCREEN HARDWARE NUANCES AND TECHNOLOGIES

Now that we have covered the hardware and manufacturers that are out there, let's cover some specific models to get a better idea about the details of the technologies. This appendix focuses on a few models from Elo TouchSystems (**www.elotouch.com**) as this company covers each type of technology available and all its models work well on all the platforms on which the Flash authoring tools are available, with the notable exception of driver availability for Mac OS X. (See the information earlier in the chapter about Troll Touch for a touch-screen vendor who caters to Mac users and has announced a tentative release of OS X–compatible drivers for its products.) The Elo TouchSystems screens plug directly into any standard VGA monitor port on a PC or Macintosh. Older Macs with built-in video cards that do not utilize the DB-15 VGA connector standard can use an inexpensive adapter to allow the connection of the touch-screen monitor cable. The touch-screen input is sent to the computer via a serial or USB connection (depending on your need and model you purchase) that plugs into your computer and with the help of a driver becomes your new mouse. Yes, you can still use your existing mouse or input device right along side of it as long as you have enough ports to connect them at the same time. This is ideal for testing your Flash application throughout the entire development process. The USB versions are also ideal for this in that you can typically have more USB devices connected to a computer than serial devices. (Another note about Troll Touch is that its products have native support for older ADB-based Macintosh computers. What better way to utilize that old Mac IIci sitting in your closet than as a touch-screen controller for your home appliances).

The installation process of the drivers is simple, and the drivers are available on the web at any time from the Elo TouchSystems web site at **www.elotouch.com**. Once installed, it only requires a simple restart before you calibrate and use the touch screen for input. The two types of models mentioned are differentiated in several ways. Elo offers standard CRT tubes and also flat panel LCD models. The flat LCDs are great for embedding into kiosk enclosures due to their lower heat output and smaller size. Both of those can be crucial in the design of the physical presence of your kiosk. The CRT and LCD versions are available from Elo in the four different technologies mentioned previously plus a fifth specialized version of the SAW type. Elo has a brand name associated with each type of technology to differentiate itself.

The first version we will cover in this appendix is the AccuTouch variety. The AccuTouch responds to the pressure of an object on the screen. Elo also has an infrared-based solution that stands up well to outdoor and rough use based on a technology developed by CarrollTouch. Elo acquired CarrollTouch in 1999. The CarrollTouch systems have an invisible grid of infrared light that your finger disrupts and registers as input with the monitor. These devices stand up well to heavy abuse because there is no calibration needed because the grid is always aligned with the screen. Elo's other main variety is its IntelliTouch technology, which uses surface acoustic waves (SAW) that traverse across the glass surface above the screen. In order to register a touch, your input device disrupts the waves; in this case our device is a human finger. There is also a SecureTouch, which is a variation on the IntelliTouch that adds tempered glass to resist breaking, and iTouch, which is a version of the surface acoustic wave-based screen, except that there is no glass overlay. The sound travels directly on the surface of the CRT glass, allowing the full dynamic range and viewable area of the CRT to be utilized. Each of these three technologies has their pros and cons. The author of this appendix prefers the IntelliTouch and its glass screen that can be wiped clean, its extremely long warranty, its resistance to wear and its high density of registration points. However, if you were to try and navigate or "press" with a pencil point on an IntelliTouch screen, it would not work. The point on a pencil is not large enough to disrupt the surface waves and register a touch. If you reversed the pencil and navigated with the eraser instead, the touch screen would be able to register a touch. On the flipside, the AccuTouch can be pressed with anything since it responds directly to pressure. In theory you could use any part of your anatomy to trigger the display. The AccuTouch system might be better if you determined that you would like a person to be able to use a stylus attached to your kiosk by a cable, to register his input instead of a finger. It should be noted that vendors like Troll touch and Elotouch Systems could retrofit an Apple iMac to have a built-in touch screen. These all-in-one units are ideal for educational kiosks, similar to ones you might find in a museum exhibit for children.

GENERAL TIPS FOR WORKING WITH TOUCH SCREENS

Now that we have examined the hardware and its manufacturers, we are ready to cover some of the tips and techniques that are useful when working with touch screens.

- **Keep an eye on your angle of attack.** Certain touch screens are actually sensitive to the angle at which they are touched. This is not a physical item, but actually an optical illusion. SAW (Surface Acoustic Wave)-based screens with their extra glass layer, depending on its thickness, can fool the eye slightly during calibration. Typically, targets are presented during calibration for you to press with your finger or stylus. Even the tiny difference a small sheet of glass over the screen makes can sometimes throw off a person visually as they go to click on the targets and calibrate the screen, depending upon the angle at which you are viewing the screen. So standardize the viewing height at which your screen will be calibrated and presented. An extraordinarily tall person will see the screen at a different angle than a person of average height and this may be just enough to throw her finger aim off by one-quarter of an inch and thus make navigation with small buttons more difficult. Even a left-handed person may have a slightly different touch angle to her finger than a right-handed person. Try your input, as both a left-handed and right-handed individual. It wouldn't hurt to try using your knuckles and thumbs as well if your application is geared toward children.

- **Don't forget the environment.** If your application might be deployed in an area where the temperature can get very chilly, consider that your users may be gloved when they attempt to use the touch screen. In this case, you should also allow extra room between the buttons. The type of screen you use is also a factor here as some of the technologies mentioned here are better suited for gloved operations. Resistive technology–based screens and SAW screens are ideal for this, whereas capacitive-based screens are not.

- **Determine the screen real estate you need.** Do some tests and see at what resolution you need to run your application. Will 640×480 be enough? Is 800×600 enough real estate for all your content or will you need to go higher? This may dictate the type of display you purchase or deploy on. If you are using a standalone player or projector you should build your application at a size that will allow scaling to fill the entire screen, so be sure your document can scale proportionally to fill the screen. Because the resolution you need will affect your purchasing decisions, it is a good idea to tackle this question early in the planning stages of your project.

TIPS FOR DEVELOPING FLASH APPLICATIONS ON TOUCH SCREENS

Now that you are aware of the manufacturers of touch screens, the technologies behind the screens, and the questions you need to answer to decide on which one to use, what are the things you should keep in mind when developing a Flash application for a touch screen?

- **Stay away from rollovers.** Most touch screens only register either on or off pressure and not distinct levels of pressure. Thus, a rollover button would not function correctly. This is similar to the functionality of a Pocket PC and the authoring guidelines for that platform. Use press, press/release, or a combination of these to trigger your actions.

  If you previously used the rollover to draw attention to the areas a user might interact with, you should rethink the flow and direction of your application and use other hints to guide the user through your navigation. Clear and concise navigation is key to making an effective Flash–based touch-screen application. Limiting the choices available at any one time, if possible, will help guide the user through your application in a logical fashion.

- **Turn off the cursor.** Because you can jump directly to any point on the screen simply by touching, turn off the cursor with the **mouse.hide()** function. The cursor will only get in the way and detract from the interface. On a Pocket PC the cursor is not visible regardless of a setting, but because your touch-screen kiosk may be based around the standard version of the Flash Player or plug-in, you will need to do this in the Flash document.

- **Determine your container.** If you are using a browser-based environment to contain and display your Flash content, keep in mind invisible frame borders or other OS-specific items that may limit the amount of screen real estate you have to play with. A good trick on the PC side is to modify a shortcut to Internet Explorer that will prompt it to go into kiosk mode and take over the whole screen. You can simulate this manually by pressing F11 and disabling the menu bar, address bar, and so on. To hardcode a shortcut to do this automatically on the launch of Internet Explorer 4 and up, navigate on your computer to where Internet Explorer is installed (typically c:\Program Files\Internet Explorer\) and make a shortcut to Internet Explorer. Then modify the properties for that shortcut to add a –K so that it looks like the screen shown in Figure F.1.

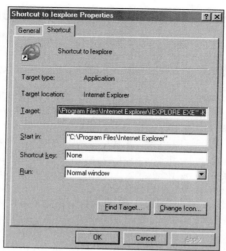

FIGURE F.1

Setting the properties for a custom Internet Explorer kiosk shortcut.

Now when you launch Internet Explorer with this shortcut, you are placed automatically in kiosk mode. Menu bars, address bars, status bars, and so on, are not available, and the only way to quit is Alt+F4. You can, however, still switch between applications with Alt+Tab. So if your application is browser-based, you might have to investigate third-party applications to help further lock down the environment, unless you do away with the keyboard completely and only allow touch-screen input.

If you are using the standalone player or a projector-based application, use the FScommand or new Stage object to control the scaling or full-screen mode of your application.

■ **Use a virtual keyboard.** If you do decide to remove the keyboard from the equation, yet your application requires keyboard input, consider including a virtual keyboard in your Flash application. Plan your application to allow room in your design to have an onscreen virtual keyboard. An example of this is the ATM interface in Figure F.2 and is similar to the virtual keyboard included with the Authoring Guidelines released by Macromedia for the initial developer version of the Flash 4 Player for Pocket PC platform.

FIGURE F.2

A virtual keyboard being used for text input in a touch-screen ATM interface.

- **Allow for variations on the "pointer factor."** Keep in mind the size and shape of your stylus and constantly test to be sure the layout of the Flash buttons or interactions are not so close together that they cause the user to have to attempt his input more than once. Having as many people as you can test this with actual fingers is helpful as well. Don't assume that your finger or the way you point at the screen will be the same as every other person. If you have the room, make your buttons larger and spaced further apart than you normally would.

- **Consider invisible frames.** If you have to talk to many different ActiveX objects to allow your Flash application to interact with hardware, consider using an invisible 1-pixel-high frame in your layout to which you can direct **getURLs**. Using the **onload** method in the body tag, you can have "trigger" HTML files that are designed to talk to and load individual ActiveX objects, instead of using the FScommand to invoke or call particular subroutine of one large ActiveX object. You could also build an ActiveX container to hold the Flash OCX and talk to it directly with ActiveX methods.

  For more information on this last technique, see:
  www.macromedia.com/support/flash/ts/documents/activex_script.htm.

  JavaScript is also another method to communicate with the Flash plug-in, but there are limitations when using this method from browser to browser and from platform to platform.

  See Appendix C, "Flash Device Resources," for links to resources on using Flash with JavaScript.

- **Combining technologies.** You can combine JavaScript, ActiveX, and VBScript. For example, JavaScript can retrieve information from a VBScript and pass it back into a Flash movie.

- **Consider LocalConnection.** A brand-new feature of Flash MX and the Flash 6 Player is the capability for two or more open and active Flash content areas or applications running on the same machine to talk and pass information back and forth to each other. This is done without the need for JavaScript or ActiveX and is done totally in Flash using the new LocalConnection object.

See the example on the web site (www.flashenabled.com) covering the LocalConnection Object.

- **Consider your content and purpose when deciding on the actual touch-screen size.** A 20" touch screen might be good for a medical application where a doctor is reviewing images and making choices, and might not be good for a touch-screen application where someone is entering credit card information. A clever idea for PIN entry is to have the keys appear on screen in a different order each time the screen is presented. This can be an effective method to prevent shoulder surfing of PINs in a touch screen environment. For example, a virtual keypad will have digits 0–9. Make an array object containing the values 0–9. Then using the following example code, build an array shuffle method:

```
Array.prototype.shuffle = function() {
    var len = this.length;
    var i = len;
    while (i—) {
        var p = random(len);
        var t = this[i];
        this[i] = this[p];
        this[p] = t;
    }
};
pins = new Array();
for (x=0; x<=9; x++) {
    pins[x] = x;
}
function doit() {
pins.shuffle();
trace(pins[0]+" "+pins[1]+" "+pins[2]+" "+pins[3]+" "+pins[4]+"
Â"+pins[5]+" "+pins[6]+" "+pins[7]+" "+pins[8]+" "+pins[9]+" ");
}
setInterval(doit, 1000);
```

Shuffle the array and use the shuffled results to order the way the PIN input items are placed on the screen. Thus, every time the PIN entry screen is presented, it is in a different order, preventing the casual onlooker from knowing which buttons the user is pressing. Of course, be sure that the users know that the numbers will be shuffled for security reasons; otherwise they may get confused and press the wrong numbers.

- **Constant testing and retesting.** The most important part of the process is to constantly test how the interface works on your touch screen as you develop. If at all possible, use the same make or model of touch screen during development as the one that will be used in the deployment.

If you don't have access to the touch screen while developing the application, you can still test for the live area on a demo. The live area is the area of the screen that will be viewable and that accepts users' input. Get access to the targeted device for an hour or so and test for the live area on the touch screen. A good rule of thumb is to allow a 1/4- to 1/2-inch margin on all edges of your application where no button activity will be placed. This prevents users from having difficulty selecting items with their fingers near the border of the screen, and prevents problems if the screen becomes misaligned.

Finally, if using the Flash Player 6, you can also use the System.capabilities object in conjunction with the new Stage object to automatically determine or configure the size of your Flash-based application, depending on the screen resolution. See the example file touch_stage.fla on the web site that accompanies this book. Launch the published .swf from this document in a standalone Flash Player on your target machine with the targeted screen connected. Change the document to full-screen mode. This Flash document uses the stage object to show you how a full-screen Flash document will scale and fill the screen. Use the up-, down-, left-, and right-arrow keys to cycle between the various scaling modes. Wherever a press from a stylus or finger is registered in this document, a virtual fingerprint is left with the x and y coordinates of the location where the press was registered. This can be helpful in determining your layout. Drop a mockup of your layout into a background layer of this movie to see how well your planned button spacing might work. This file also iterates through the System.capabilities object, displaying the value of each.

- **Use high-contrast interfaces if possible.** This is especially important if you are using resistive- or capacitive-based touch screens, as their technology requires several layers of material in the touch screen to work and these layers can sometimes degrade the saturation or intensity of the screen. SAW screens are better suited for applications that demand color fidelity and intensity of your Flash application.

Also consider the visually impaired. Some users may be color blind and unable to distinguish between certain colors. This renders your interface difficult or impossible to use. You should also be aware of federally mandated guidelines for meeting the Americans with Disabilities Act and how they might apply to your project. There is a new accessibility feature of Flash MX and the Flash 6 Player that works in concert with screen reader technology, allowing the user to hear the interface and prompts. For more information about the official ADA Standards For Accessible Design covering topics ranging from wheelchair entrance ramps all the way to ATM interface design and specifications, see the following government web site: **www.usdoj.gov/crt/ada/stdspdf.htm**.

Macromedia additionally has an excellent resource section on its site devoted specifically toward accessible design methodologies for its products including Flash. It is available at: **www.macromedia.com/macromedia/accessibility/**.

Use sounds to complement visual clues. If the environment allows for it, add narrative sound to help instruct a user, either as feedback to input or as a guide to navigation. Also be aware that, by default, some touch-screen drivers, such as Elo TouchSystems, automatically provide sound-based feedback to screen touches. Typically they can be disabled in the control panel or settings for the particular driver you are using so they don't conflict with sound in your Flash application. Visiting the accessibility resource on Macromedia's site you will also find information about sound as well.

■ **Utilize the new Flash MX video features.** The Flash 6 Player is now a perfect delivery vehicle for streaming video. Don't forget this when bidding on a job. Now your touch screen interface can deliver video, as well as Flash–based content. You may require other tools during production, but having one main technology to deliver it on your touch-screen interface will simplify deployment. An excellent idea for a Flash-based touch-screen kiosk would be a glorified instant snapshot kiosk. Hook up a web cam to a standalone projector on a web-enabled touch-screen kiosk and within minutes you could build a kiosk that allows users to take a snapshot and have it delivered to a friend via email. A perfect vacation spot kiosk to replace the standard postcard.

EXPLORING THE POSSIBILITIES

Armed with the knowledge this appendix has presented, you should have a good frame of reference for exploring the possibilities and opportunities that using the Flash product line in combination with touch screens can provide to your clients. By now you have also realized that Flash isn't just for web sites any longer. It can also be used to build engaging, dynamic, interactive kiosks. Flash provides developers with a consistent environment for creation and presentation of user interfaces across a broad spectrum of devices. Flash can and should be everywhere.

G

APPENDIX

WHAT'S ON THE WEB SITE

Additional resource material for this book is located at **www.flashenabled.com/book**. You will also find a link to this site from the book's title page on **www.newriders.com**.

flashenabled.com will give you everything you need to complete each of the projects in the book. Just access the files on the web site and follow the instructions in the book. For your convenience, you will also find all the source code on the web site in each set of files.

The site contains the following sections:

Updates

This section lists any updates and corrections to the chapters and files.

Source Files

This section of the site includes all the source files that are used in the book, listed by chapter.

Resources

This list includes anything extra you might find useful, links to other sites, technical documents, fonts, design inspiration, content, as well as some surprises.

Feedback

We really want to know what you think about the book, so send us some comments, good or bad! You can reach us at **authors@flashenabled.com**.

Index

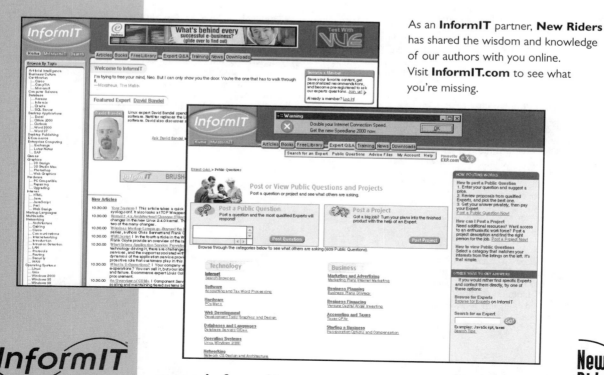

FLASH MX

**Flash Deconstruction:
The Process, Design, and
ActionScript of Juxt
Interactive**
Todd Purgason, Phil Scott
Bonnie Blake, Brian Drake
$45.00, 0735711496

**Flash ActionScript for
Designers: Drag, Slide, Fade**
Brendan Dawes
$45.00, 0735710473

Flash MX Magic
Matthew David, et al.
$45.00, 0735711607

Inside Flash MX
Jody Keating,
Fig Leaf Software
$49.99, 0735712549

**Object-Oriented
Programming
with ActionScript**
Branden Hall, Samuel Wan
$39.99, 0735711834

**Flash Enabled: Flash Design
and Development for Devices**
Phillip Torrone, Branden Hall,
Glenn Thomas, Mike Chambers,
et al.
$49.99, 0735711771

**Flash to the Core:
An Interactive Sketchbook
by Joshua Davis**
Joshua Davis
$45.00, 0735712883

**Skip Intro: Flash Usability &
Interface Design**
Duncan McAlester,
Michelangelo Capraro
$45.00, 073571178X

Flash Audio Magic
Brad Kozak, Eric Dolecki,
Craig Swann, Manuel Clement
$39.99, 0735711941

ActionScripting in Flash MX
Phillip Kerman
$39.99, 0735712956

**Flash MX Application Design
and Development**
Jessica Speigel
$45.00, 0735712425

The Flash Animator
Sandro Corsaro
$49.99, 0735712824

The Flash MX Project
Cheryl Brumbaugh-Duncan
$35.00, 0735712832

New
Riders

VOICES
THAT MATTER

VOICES THAT MATTER

HOW TO CONTACT US

VISIT OUR WEB SITE

WWW.NEWRIDERS.COM

On our Web site you'll find information about our other books, authors, tables of contents, indexes, and book errata. You will also find information about book registration and how to purchase our books.

EMAIL US

Contact us at this address: **nrfeedback@newriders.com**

- If you have comments or questions about this book
- To report errors that you have found in this book
- If you have a book proposal to submit or are interested in writing for New Riders
- If you would like to have an author kit sent to you
- If you are an expert in a computer topic or technology and are interested in being a technical editor who reviews manuscripts for technical accuracy
- To find a distributor in your area, please contact our international department at this address. **nrmedia@newriders.com**

- For instructors from educational institutions who want to preview New Riders books for classroom use. Email should include your name, title, school, department, address, phone number, office days/hours, text in use, and enrollment, along with your request for desk/examination copies and/or additional information.
- For members of the media who are interested in reviewing copies of New Riders books. Send your name, mailing address, and email address, along with the name of the publication or Web site you work for.

BULK PURCHASES/CORPORATE SALES

The publisher offers discounts on this book when ordered in quantity for bulk purchases and special sales. For sales within the U.S., please contact: Corporate and Government Sales (800) 382-3419 or **corpsales@pearsontechgroup.com**. Outside of the U.S., please contact: International Sales (317) 581-3793 or **international@pearsontechgroup.com**.

WRITE TO US

New Riders Publishing
201 W. 103rd St.
Indianapolis, IN 46290-1097

CALL US

Toll-free (800) 571-5840 + 9 + 7477
If outside U.S. (317) 581-3500. Ask for New Riders.

FAX US

(317) 581-4663

GO ONLINE FOR MORE FLASH ENABLED

This book is just the tip of the iceberg—there's lots more information online at **www.flashenabled.com**.

Check out all the latest news about Macromedia Flash development, including upcoming conferences and author appearances, eBook content we didn't have room for in the book, special updates on devices, and new applications in the works.